# The Predictive Postcode

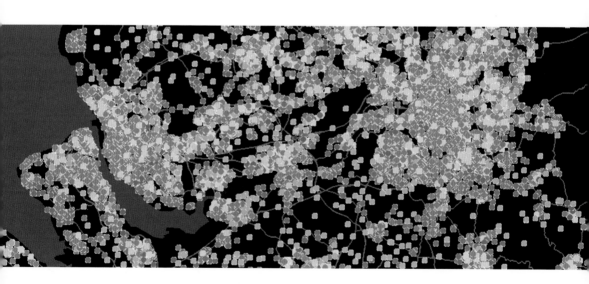

Sara Miller McCune founded SAGE Publishing in 1965 to support the dissemination of usable knowledge and educate a global community. SAGE publishes more than 1000 journals and over 800 new books each year, spanning a wide range of subject areas. Our growing selection of library products includes archives, data, case studies and video. SAGE remains majority owned by our founder and after her lifetime will become owned by a charitable trust that secures the company's continued independence.

Los Angeles | London | New Delhi | Singapore | Washington DC | Melbourne

# The Predictive Postcode

## The Geodemographic Classification of British Society

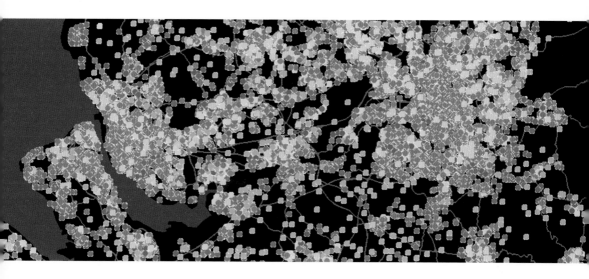

# Richard Webber & Roger Burrows

Los Angeles | London | New Delhi
Singapore | Washington DC | Melbourne

Los Angeles | London | New Delhi
Singapore | Washington DC | Melbourne

SAGE Publications Ltd
1 Oliver's Yard
55 City Road
London EC1Y 1SP

SAGE Publications Inc.
2455 Teller Road
Thousand Oaks, California 91320

SAGE Publications India Pvt Ltd
B 1/I 1 Mohan Cooperative Industrial Area
Mathura Road
New Delhi 110 044

SAGE Publications Asia-Pacific Pte Ltd
3 Church Street
#10-04 Samsung Hub
Singapore 049483

Editor: Robert Rojek
Editorial assistant: Catriona McMullen
Production editor: Katherine Haw
Copyeditor: Kate Campbell
Proofreader: Camille Bramall
Indexer: Richard Webber
Marketing manager: Susheel Gokarakonda
Cover design: Stephanie Guyaz
Typeset by: C&M Digitals (P) Ltd, Chennai, India
Printed in the UK by Bell & Bain Ltd, Glasgow

**Library of Congress Control Number: 2017954859**

**British Library Cataloguing in Publication data**

A catalogue record for this book is available from
the British Library

ISBN 978-1-5264-0233-2
ISBN 978-1-5264-0234-9 (pbk)

At SAGE we take sustainability seriously. Most of our products are printed in the UK using responsibly sourced
papers and boards. When we print overseas we ensure sustainable papers are used as measured by the PREPS
grading system. We undertake an annual audit to monitor our sustainability.

'It's not your genetic code, bank account, ethnicity or social class designation that best reveals your secrets, but your zip- or post-code. Richard Webber and Roger Burrows uncover how your micro-geography reveals who you are in spatially divided nations.'

**Danny Dorling, Halford Mackinder Professor of Geography, University of Oxford**

'We've all heard the saying, "you are what you eat", but most of us are incognisant of the "you are where you live" adage which has come to prominence in contemporary marketing practices. In this superb new book by Richard Webber and Roger Burrows, sociological and geodemographic frameworks are brought together to demonstrate how physical address, and geolocative data, come to define a person's life chances and trajectory in important, if unseen, ways. The innovative approach developed by the authors has resonance for how social research and public policy is enacted, but it also attests the ways in which political and economic power progressively flows through the material environment and its virtual overlay. This wonderfully written and thought-provoking text is sure to become a classic in the urban studies and marketing fields, but also in public and policy debates about data-driven social stratification.'

**Gavin J.D. Smith, Deputy Head, School of Sociology, Australian National University**

'Recent political and cultural upheavals have created a growing sense of how geography and identity reinforce one another. In this fascinating study, Webber and Burrows track the pre-history of geodemographic analysis, weaving between the history of sociology with more recent commercial research methods. At a time of rising public awareness of gentrification and "left behind" populations, and growing anxiety surrounding the power of data analytics, this book provides crucial context for a number of our most pressing contemporary concerns.'

**Will Davies, Reader in Political Economy, Goldsmiths University of London**

'Trump's success in the US and that of populist campaigns in Europe are a wake-up call to opinion leaders everywhere. Differences in values and attitudes are displacing traditional classifiers such as age and income as the principal points of fracture in Western societies. The lack of mutual understanding between communities is both the result of these divisions and a major contributor to them.

Classifying consumers according to the types of neighbours among whom they live is routine practice among our US and Canadian clients, revealing as it does the closeness with which these new cultural divisions align with very specific aspects of their customers' behaviour. The type of neighbourhood their customers live in adds extra predictive power to models dependent on person-level data sourced from social media and customer data.

The book is remarkable in its ability to integrate insights from different spheres of knowledge: academic theory with commercial practice; marketing with geography and sociology; statistical methods with fresh insights into everyday behaviour. If you're not already familiar with geodemographics then this book will change the way you think about, understand and connect with your fellow citizens.'

**Jan Kestle, President and CEO, Environics Analytics, Toronto, Canada and the USA**

'In the last two decades, geodemographic segmentations have transformed the way political parties, in the UK and around the world, understand the electorate and how they target and segment the channels, content and framing of their voter contact and messaging, from doorstep canvassing through leaflets and direct mail to Facebook. This book explores the fascinating detail of the spatial structure of our society and social change, and why the fine-grained scale of those patterns is so important to everyone seeking to win elections today.'

**Tim Waters, Head of Contact Creator, Targeting and Analysis, The Labour Party**

'A compelling account of how geodemographics can challenge dated survey methods and simplistic measures of deprivation and of class to enhance our understanding of society through the effective application of "commercial sociology".'

**Richard Harris, Professor of Quantitative Social Geography, University of Bristol**

'When I introduced geodemographics to the Automobile Association thirty years ago, it generated many novel and valuable insights into customer behaviour. As a result our communications came to be targeted far more precisely. This remains a vitally important application for geodemographics today. However, the scope of geodemographic analysis is much wider than just marketing. *The Predictive Postcode* uses geodemographics to provide a fresh understanding of social change during a highly dynamic period in the UK's history and in a way which is accessible to the general reader.'

**Peter Mouncey, Editor in Chief, International Journal of Market Research; former Group Marketing Services Manager, Automobile Association**

'Drawing on examples from across the social sciences, such as school catchment areas, cities and neighbourhoods, crime and voting patterns, the book is full of wonderful stories about *how* and *why* the intersection between people and places matters so much in understanding contemporary societies.

*The Predictive Postcode* is both a political and methodological exegesis. At its heart, the authors throw a powerful punch at traditional statistical analysis. By revealing how qualitative and quantitative classifications are now routinely used, reinforced and morphed by the socio-technical infrastructures that are now part and parcel of our digital everyday lives, Webber and Burrows pave the way for an alternative kind of social science.

This is a beautifully accessible book, relevant to anyone interested in finding new ways of resisting and intervening the deeply unjust socio-cultural divisions that now mark so many societies worldwide.'

**Emma Uprichard, Reader, Centre for Interdisciplinary Methodologies, University of Warwick**

'A unique and fascinating book that distils a lifetime of experience building geodemographic classifications and makes a robust case for their use as a framework to explore a wide range of socio-economic problems.'

**Alex Singleton, Professor of Geographic Information Science, University of Liverpool**

'This book is historical, methodological, and personal. It situates and traces the development of geodemographic practice. Webber and Burrows show how this powerful method can yield insight into the evolution of neighbourhoods, cities, and countries. This book clearly outlines the past, present, and potential future of geodemographics and in so doing will be of acute interest to leaders in the academy, industry, and government looking to better understand their customers, constituents, and/or research subjects.'

**Seth Spielman, Associate Professor of Geography, University of Colorado, Boulder**

# CONTENTS

# LIST OF FIGURES

# LIST OF TABLES

# ABOUT THE AUTHORS

Richard Webber is the originator of the geodemographic classifications, *Acorn* and *Mosaic*, and for many years managed the micromarketing divisions of first CACI and then Experian. He has held Visiting Professorships at UCL, Kings College and, since 2016, the University of Newcastle. He has worked with academic colleagues from across the social sciences to apply geodemographic forms of analysis to a wide range of research topics, many of which pertain to on-going debates in demography, geography, politics, sociology and urban studies.

Roger Burrows is Professor of Cities at Newcastle University and Visiting Professor of Sociology at Goldsmiths, University of London. He was previously Pro-Warden for Interdisciplinary Development at Goldsmiths. He has also worked at the University of York, the University of Teesside, the University of Surrey and the University of East London. He has published mainly on: housing and urban studies; the sociology of digital technologies; health, illness and the body; methods; and the metricization of higher education.

# ACKNOWLEDGEMENTS

We would like to thank Robert Rojek at SAGE for commissioning this book. A number of colleagues, both within and without the academy, have made useful contributions, either by making direct comments on various parts of the book or by engaging us in debates about the topics covered. Some have also previously contributed to jointly authored pieces that we draw upon here. Although they may not agree with some of what follows, thanks are due to: Rowland Atkinson; Tim Butler; David Davidson; Will Davies; Mike Featherstone; Nick Gane; Giles Goyder; Guyonne James; Aidan Kelly; Caroline Knowles; Simon Parker; Trevor Phillips; Ruth Raynor; Louise Ridley, Mike Savage; and Emma Uprichard. Thanks are also due to Joseph Nettleton Burrows and Cathryn Britton for help with the proofreading of the final manuscript. We would also like to thank the referees of the original proposal and the two anonymous readers of the draft manuscript, all of whom made very useful comments and suggestions, which we have done our best to respond to. Thanks are also due to Experian for permission to publish data linked to *Mosaic*. Finally, thanks are due to the ESRC for funding the various projects we have been involved in that we have drawn upon here.

London, Newcastle and York
July 2017

# PUBLISHER'S ACKNOWLEDGEMENTS

Chapter 2, excerpt from *Geodemographics, GIS and Neighbourhood Targeting*, by Harris, R., Sleight, P. and Webber R., 2005. Republished with permission of John Wiley & Sons Inc. and permission conveyed through Copyright Clearance Center, Inc.

Figure 2.1 from Park R.E., Burgess, E. and McKenzie, R. (1925) *The City: Suggestions for Investigation of Human Behaviour in the Urban Environment,* Chicago: Chicago University Press. Reproduced with permission of University of Chicago Press.

Chapter 9, excerpt from Furbank, P. N., *Introduction* in Hardy, T., *Tess of the d'Urbervilles: A Pure Woman* (1974) Pan Macmillan: London. Reproduced with permission of the Licensor through PLS Clear.

# PREFACE

## An unlikely collaboration

This book is the fruit of what may seem to many readers an unlikely collaboration. It is between specialists in two fields which would not normally be expected to engage with each other, let alone find a common language through which to communicate insights about urban structure or even write a book. One is the founder and former manager of the micromarketing division of a major global information services company, the other an urban sociologist with an interest in methodological debates in the social sciences.

Such a dialogue would have been unlikely were it not for there being a little-known connection between these fields, a connection that this book aims to make more apparent. In Chicago, in the 1920s and 1930s, a group of sociologists developed a framework for analysing urban structure that continues to influence the academic study of cities today. What is less well known is how this framework also came to influence the way consumer marketers analyse and target prospects for their products.

In this book, we trace the influence of the Chicago School, as it came to be known, on both academic social science and the marketing industry. We show how, from the early 1980s onwards, ideas that had their origins in the Chicago School of Sociology began to be transformed as commercial organizations started to incorporate them into the computer algorithms they embedded in some of their decision support systems. These systems, which have developed apace over the past four decades, have come to drive the business strategies of many hundreds of well-known organizations.

However, very few academic social scientists are aware of the knowledge produced by these systems. When discussed at all, it tends to be in relation to topics such as surveillance, privacy, and the role of profiling in social life (Goss, 1995a; 1995b; Lyon, 2003; Phillips and Curry, 2002). These are all important issues, but the narrow focus on them has tended to divert attention from the broader, often methodological implications of such systems. It has only been in the last decade or so that the implications of these forms of commercial knowledge have come to be recognized by the academic social sciences (Burrows and Gane, 2006). The reasons for this will be a major focus of this book. Suffice to say for now that what has come to be termed 'commercial sociology' is now seen as constituting a major challenge to the jurisdiction of academic social science over the study of the 'social' (Savage and Burrows, 2007). A prime driver of 'commercial sociology' is a form of data analysis that has come to be known as geodemographics.

Put simply, geodemographics is a branch of social analysis that recognizes that where you live matters to any understanding of your values, behaviour and choices as a consumer. It uses data from various sources to place each citizen into a category according to the type of neighbourhood in which he or she lives. Marketers have long known that such classifications are extremely useful for understanding variations in purchasing habits, tastes, values and so on. We argue that policy-makers, academic social scientists and market researchers are among a number of groups who could similarly benefit from a more extensive engagement with geodemographic modes of analysis.

## What is the purpose of writing this book?

Our overarching contention is quite straightforward. It is that contemporary debate on many matters of social, cultural and political importance would be hugely more productive were the social groups whose welfare is the subject of these debates to be described in terms of the type of neighbourhood they live in. Such a proposition may seem strange to many social scientists and members of the policy-forming classes. If so this belies the fact that this method of classification has a long history of successful operational use in marketing and communications, and not just in the commercial sector. It is extensively used in policing, health, local administration, arts marketing and not-for-profit fund-raising, and not least in the databases that political parties use to drive the targeting of their general election campaigns.

This contention follows from our experience that today a geodemographic envisioning of society often provides an analytically more productive framework for understanding social behaviour than do many other more mainstream approaches. There is no doubt that in its heyday the concept of social class provided a powerful concept for explaining differences in social behaviour. However, there are now many sociologists, geographers, political commentators and 'lay' contributors to public debate who are troubled by its seeming inability, and indeed that of other traditional classifications, to capture the tectonic socio-spatial and cultural differences manifested in the Brexit vote in the UK, the election of Donald Trump as US president in 2016 and the UK general election of 2017. This inability is emblematic of a crisis in the social sciences that is even more fundamental than that forewarned over a decade ago (Savage and Burrows, 2007).

Our overall contention, that where a person lives is often a more reliable basis for understanding them than their class or other individual attributes, carries with it a series of other methodological contentions, for example relating to the appropriateness of different forms of data, statistical methods, methodologies, descriptive language, visualization and so on – themes which recur throughout the book. These contentions have led us to conclude that though there continues to be analytic value in many of the criteria such as class, race and ethnicity, gender and sexuality, stage of the life-course and so on by which we group people and which are so embedded in the measures used to describe social behaviour, they need to be operationalized in a very different manner to that which currently pertains within much research practice. Too easily we slide into the assumption that these groups have a degree of internal homogeneity which research evidence suggests they clearly do not have. Almost all the evidence we put forward in this book suggests that members of each category of these criteria behave very differently according to precisely where they live.

These issues, we believe, are relevant to a very diverse audience, not just policy- and opinion-formers, social scientists and consumer marketers, but to a series of other professions involved in delivering services to 'lay' people and, not least, to the intelligent lay-person curious about how his or her personal data is used by business and the state.

To this end, following this preface, the book is split into two main parts and a brief coda. The five chapters of Part I deal with the historical and methodological development of how neighbourhoods are described, culminating with descriptions of the types of neighbourhood identified by various versions of *Mosaic*, the classification that consumer marketers have deployed more extensively than any other over the past 40 years. In Part II each of the five chapters takes a more detailed look at well-known types of residential neighbourhood defined by *Mosaic* and uses research data linked to *Mosaic* to contribute fresh insights into a series of substantive topics of current social and political interest. The book concludes with Part III, a brief coda, offering two very brief chapters, one a summative geodemographic 'travelogue' around the sites of major sociological studies across Britain, and the other a final methodological reflection on the book and some concluding thoughts.

Chapter 1 begins with a detailed exposition of a common form of geodemographic analysis. Although not every reader will necessarily follow its every feature, most should get a strong initial sense of the form and functioning of the method of social research that is the subject of this book. The rest of the chapter introduces debates about the nature of neighbourhoods, how they might be classified and to what ends. The chapter concludes by introducing, in general terms, the nature of geodemographic perspectives on social life.

Chapter 2 forms a historical examination of a range of antecedents to the emergence of geodemographic analysis. It charts an arc through the work of Charles Booth in London, the Chicago School of Sociology, the work of rural sociologists in Wisconsin, the emergence of the theory and practice of human ecology, factorial ecology and, finally, statistical cluster analysis, ending with a description of the very first geodemographic system – *PRIZM* – built in the US by sociologist-cum-entrepreneur Jonathan Robbin.

Chapter 3 describes the emergence of geodemographics in the UK within the context of a study of poverty in Liverpool carried out in the early 1970s. It is described in detail because many of its conceptualizations, innovations and modes of presentation were to set important standards for the later development of geodemographic classification. The chapter then describes how the Liverpool study evolved into a national classification, how this in turn came to the attention of commercial users, and how, against initial expectations, a research framework designed to identify different manifestations of deprivation became a serviceable tool for distinguishing different types of wealthy people.

Chapter 4 describes the development of geodemographics proper in the UK; first the development of the *Acorn* system, and then the development of *Mosaic*. It describes various methodological innovations, perhaps the most important of which was to supplement census statistics with transactional data of various sorts, prefiguring what has since become referred to as 'big data'. The chapter concludes with an account of the international spread of systems for neighbourhood classification.

The final chapter of the first part of the book, Chapter 5, considers how well the various versions of the *Mosaic* classification capture the historic evolution of new forms of residential neighbourhood within British cities, towns and villages. As such it also provides a description of how geodemographic classifications have come to envision change in British society. The chapter concludes with some critical reflections on methodology.

Opening Part II of the book, Chapter 6 marks the first of a series of studies of how a socio-spatial approach can contribute to the understanding of particular social and political issues. These chapters, whilst each tackling a specific substantive topic, also draw upon a range of methodological innovations specific to geodemographic forms of analysis in a manner not necessarily possible with other forms of research. The specific focus of this chapter is the Liberal Metropolitan Elite and, in particular, the seeming inability of measures of social class to account for its distinctive values, party political alignment and multicultural sympathies.

It is in such neighbourhoods that geodemographic classification is particularly effective in demonstrating the existence and power of 'neighbourhood effects' (van Ham et al., 2012).

If Chapter 6 is focused on the behaviour of what Goodhart (2017) has termed 'anywhere' people, then Chapter 7 focuses on their supposed antithesis: 'somewhere' people. These are neighbourhoods where 'dwelling', belonging and having a strong sense of attachment to place play a key role in the formation of personal identity. We examine how geodemographics can identify the location of a particular subset of this group of people – families, often in employment, living in socially isolated social housing estates in large provincial cities – and advance reasons why levels of educational attainment in such places should be so low and forms of petty anti-social behaviour so high. By linking data on pupil performance to type of neighbourhood and to measures of multiple deprivation we show that the assumed association between levels of neighbourhood deprivation and levels of educational attainment tend to break down in this and certain other types of neighbourhood.

Chapter 8 tackles issues of race, ethnicity, migration and the complex patterns of ethno-cultural settlement that vary so significantly across contemporary Britain. In this chapter we adduce changes that have occurred since 2011, the date of the last census, by drawing upon a form of big data, people's names, and develop metrics capable of demonstrating how minority communities vary in terms of housing preferences, geographical movement, segregation and social mobility.

Chapters 9 and 10 shift the emphasis from issues of class and ethnicity within places towards analyses of different types of place per se. In the first of these two chapters we examine the changing character of the British countryside. The methodological innovation here is to compare the population characteristics of UK rural neighbourhoods at different points in time and hence identify long-term changes in their character. Of all the different types of neighbourhood we examine in the book we believe that those pertaining to rural Britain are the ones that have changed the most over the past 40 years and yet have perhaps been researched the least.

Just as Chapter 9 accounts for the very different types of neighbourhood which co-exist in rural communities, Chapter 10 explains the reasons for the emergence of a number of very different types of residential neighbourhood found in coastal communities. It argues that the decline, which reflects changing tastes in holiday destinations, accommodation and activities, has impacted different coastal communities in very different ways. It uses maps to show that within any individual coastal resort there is likely to be a high degree of segregation between those neighbourhoods which were developed to serve the needs of summer visitors and those designed to meet the needs of better-off retirees.

The book ends with Part III, a brief coda: two short chapters offering some concluding substantive and methodological reflections.

## Challenges to established methods arising from 'commercial sociology'

Although we believe any account of geodemographics is of interest in its own right, there are many features of the way in which geodemographic classifications are built and their categories described that divide opinion among public servants and social scientists. Indeed, any consideration of the methods used in geodemographics offers the opportunity to engage in a number of wider debates, many of them very important, about the efficacy of research methods in general. Today many of these methods are so well established that the assumptions on which they are based are no longer made explicit in the existing social research methods literature, or not to the extent that perhaps they should be. The remoteness of these practices from lay understandings of society may well be one of the reasons for the decline in the level of respect in which 'experts' are today held by some lay people.

Here are some of the everyday social scientific concepts with which geodemographic methods allow us to re-engage in discussion: the validity of 'ideal types' as analytic summaries of otherwise complex social phenomena; the role of taxonomies, typologies and classifications in facilitating cross-disciplinary dialogue; the extent to which different forms of political correctness should constrain the terminology used to label different categories; the relationship between quantitative and qualitative research methods; the relationship between descriptive, predictive, theoretical and prescriptive forms of analysis; the relationship between theory and evidence; and so on.

Discussion of geodemographic classification also allows us to engage in a number of new debates: the manner in which lay understandings of neighbourhoods differ from those of professionals; the use of visualization tools; the value of methods of data reduction; and, crucially, the rhetoric and the realities of analysing what has come to be known as big data. We are excited by how a description of geodemographics can be used as a conduit for methodological debates of this sort.

For example, although a quantitative technique, geodemographic forms of analysis paradoxically result in highly nuanced qualitative descriptions of neighbourhoods. When compared with the lived realities of specific places, these often show a remarkably strong alignment with ethnographic descriptions based upon detailed qualitative observations (Butler with Robson, 2003; Parker et al., 2007).

More qualitative, ethnographic forms of social research tend to be more accessible to non-specialists and lay-people than quantitative forms based typically on survey methods and statistical modelling. With an analytic focus on attempting to describe and explain the meanings, understandings, motivations and actions of people within particular contexts it regularly delivers vivid accounts of the life and times of particular places.

Qualitative researchers tend to be less troubled by the desire to isolate the impact on social processes of individual variables; inherent in their practice is the recognition that social processes are the result of complex interactions between all manner of cultural, economic, political, technological and social phenomena, that nonetheless result in the production of the particular 'structures of feeling' – to use the language of Raymond Williams (1977) – or variations in habitus and cultural field – to use the language of Bourdieu (1984) – that come to mark out particular neighbourhoods.

A distinctive feature of geodemographics, which can be disturbing, is that it does not give any *a priori* analytic foregrounding to any particular single variable or combination of variables, or to any single source of social identity; rather the particular combination of socio-spatial attributes that are used to classify a particular neighbourhood and then to describe it can be contingent upon variations in all kinds of phenomena, even those that have not been used to build the classification. For one type of neighbourhood it may well be a particular combination of occupational class, population density and ethnicity that best defines its fundamental character; for another socio-cultural grouping it might be a particular combination of data on donations to charities, party political support and dietary preferences that gives the clearest characterization.

This contrasts with the traditional template commonly used for the analysis of social behaviour. This tends to involve the construction of complex causative models based on an explicit series of additive individual causations each represented by individual variables derived from a questionnaire-based survey. Although these sometimes include interaction effects between variables, the overall aim is usually to quantify the separate effects of 'class', 'gender', 'race' or whatever on variations in some dependent variables of interest, maybe 'voting', 'health' or 'attitudes'. As we have already indicated, it is our view that such practices lie at the very heart of the failure of the social sciences to provide credible interpretations of the tectonic socio-cultural divisions that now mark post-Brexit Britain and Trump's America.

The solution involves more than just replacing information from questionnaires with a corresponding array of data fields from big data, although that may well help in some respects, and it is not just about being able to account more adequately for 'neighbourhood effects', although this is crucial too; rather, what is at stake is the need for a fundamental shift in how we both conceptualize and operationalize socio-spatial processes.

Part of the problem no doubt results from a methodological segregation between academic social science, central government and the market research industry on the one hand and consumer marketing and local government on the other. Until the last decade, mainstream academia seemed to have displayed a collective intellectual amnesia about geodemographic forms of analysis (Burrows and Gane, 2006). It is no accident that during the debates (McKie and Ryan, 2016) that accompanied the belief that there was a 'coming crisis of empirical sociology' (Savage and Burrows, 2007) it was geodemographics that was foregrounded as the exemplar form of a parallel (or shadow) 'commercial' social science that could be considered as challenging the jurisdiction of academic social science over the study of the 'social'.

The argument was that whereas in the 1950s through to the early 1990s sociologists could claim a series of distinctive methodological tools – the survey method, sampling, face-to-face interviewing, observational methods and so on – that allowed them clear points of access to social relations, in the subsequent period social data of various sorts have become so routinely gathered, analysed and disseminated, that it was no longer clear precisely what constituted the distinctive role of academic sociologists.

If 50 years ago, the argument goes, academic social scientists could be viewed as occupying the apex of a social science research apparatus – albeit a rather limited one – in the contemporary period their position has become somewhat marginal, as a huge research infrastructure has developed, largely outside of the academy, as an integral feature of what Thrift (2005) characterizes as knowing capitalism. For Thrift this is an era where capitalism has begun to 'consider its own practices on a continuous basis…to use its fear of uncertainty as a resource…to circulate new ideas of the world as if they were its own…to… make business out of, thinking the everyday' (Thrift, 2005: 1). Geodemographic forms of analysis are part of this infrastructure; an infrastructure where circuits of information proliferate, become ubiquitous and embedded in numerous kinds of information technologies (Kitchin, 2014).

## A contribution to the literature on the 'social life of methods'

A secondary theme that recurs throughout the book is about how best to position geodemographics within the history and development of social research methods. Although we begin by formally locating the method within the history of social research – the work of Booth, the Chicago School, human ecology and so on – we also offer a more narrative and reflexive account of how it developed from the early 1970s to the present day. We tell the story of its institutional development and how changes in access to data, new technologies, political and commercial shifts and other factors, have all contributed to the refinement of the technique.

Although one can easily find formal technical introductions to this method of analysis (Harris et al., 2005) until now this has been a largely untold history, much of it located outside of the academy. One of our intentions is to provide an informal behind-the-scenes account of the development of geodemographic research of the sort beloved by those interested in the history of social research such as in the collections of Bell and Newby (1977), Bell and Roberts (1984) and, more recently, Crow and Ellis (2017).

Statistical methods, impersonal though they may seem, are never just neutral technologies of data collection and analysis. Conflicting attitudes towards the validity or otherwise of individual methodologies often reflect more deep-seated differences regarding the acceptability of the social realities which they are complicit in co-constructing (Osborne and Rose, 1999; Saetnan et al., 2011); indeed, they also reflect conflicting attitudes towards the legitimacy of different modes of knowing, theoretical and observational, rational and empathetic. So it is the case with geodemographics, perhaps even more so than other methods, given the manner in which such classifications are created by commercial organizations and used by powerful actors whose uses of these classifications are not necessarily transparent.

So, this account can also be read as a contribution to work on what has become known as the 'social life of methods' (Savage, 2010; 2013). This approach has various aspects to it, but at its heart is a concern to understand methodological developments not just as a series of abstract techniques but, rather, as crucial technologies in the development of the infrastructures of knowing capitalism and without an understanding of which their dynamics cannot be fully understood; our account of the history of geodemographics can thus be read alongside others concerned with methods, techniques and technologies as – to use the language of the approach – social and cultural 'inscription devices' (Osborne et al., 2008): survey methods, sampling theory, qualitative interviewing (Savage, 2010); SPSS and other statistical software packages (Uprichard et al., 2008); social network analysis and depth interviews (Savage, 2008); population statistics (Osborne and Rose, 2008); new digital technologies (Ruppert et al., 2013); and even the humble tape recorder (Back, 2016).

Though geodemographic classifications appear to be based on highly nuanced, statistically robust clusters of self-similar postcodes that provide a useful basis for describing how one type of neighbourhood differs from another, and which are able to account for socio-spatial variation on any number of different dimensions of interest to social scientists, market researchers and consumer marketers, it has been the labelling and sometimes the narrative characterization of these clusters that have been frequently cited as reasons for the reluctance of public servants and social scientists to adopt them. This is a great pity because, as we hope to demonstrate in the second half of the book, geodemographic classifications, on their own or in combination with other data sources, can contribute fresh and important analytic insights relevant to current political issues and to debates about the health and future direction of British society.

There is no doubt that the manner in which such ideal typical clusters have been labelled in order to make them intelligible to users in commercial organizations has deflected potential academic users from data resources which might otherwise have provided an analytic early warning system – one better able to alert us to the economic, socio-cultural and demographic underpinnings that have unleashed the political conditions that we now have to confront (Davies, 2016; 2017).

## Our selection of illustrative material

In the UK, a number of different geodemographic classifications compete for use. Commercial vendors own most of them. One, the Output Area Classification (OAC), is built and maintained in the academy. Rather than confuse the reader by using categories from different classification systems and built at different points of time we have decided wherever possible to standardize on the use of the version of *Mosaic* released in 2003. Occasionally, and we make clear when we do so, we use the version released in 2009. This does not necessarily imply that we restrict the data we then analyse to data sources in 2003 or 2009.

There are several reasons why we decided to undertake most of our illustrative analyses using the 2003 version, rather than a more recent vintage of *Mosaic*. It is our opinion that this is the schema that is most aligned with a social scientific sensibility; it is also the schema with which the builder – Webber – was the most satisfied; it is the one which has been most extensively used to analyse social behaviour; it is the one for which we have access to the most behavioural data for analysis. It is also the version of *Mosaic* that Experian, its owners, have given us permission to use. The implications of the proprietary nature of such data will also be a topic we discuss later in the book.

# Part I
Neighbourhood Classification and
the Analysis of Social Behaviour

# 1

# NEIGHBOURHOODS AND THEIR CLASSIFICATION

byrdes of on kynde and color flok and flye allwayes together

William Turner in his *The Rescuing of the Romish Fox*,
first published in 1545 (Swami, 2016: 162)

## What sorts of people are passionately concerned about human rights?

A few years ago, a human rights charity commissioned an analysis of the 235,000 adults on its supporter file. Had a civil servant and not a human rights charity commissioned the analysis, or had it been a social scientist attached to a university who delivered it, the most likely output would have been a series of tables in a format similar to Tables 1.1 and 1.2.

**Table 1.1**  Age of Human Rights Charity Supporters

| Age | % of supporters |
| --- | --- |
| Aged 15–24 | 29 |
| Aged 25–44 | 43 |
| Aged 45–64 | 17 |
| Aged 65+ | 11 |
| Total | 235,358 |

**Table 1.2**  Social Class of Human Rights Charity Supporters

| Social class | % of supporters |
| --- | --- |
| Professionals and managers | 48 |
| Non-manual | 29 |
| Skilled manual | 10 |
| Semi-skilled | 9 |
| Unskilled | 4 |
| Total | 235,358 |

But this was not how the analysis was conducted; instead a very different mode of analysis was used, one that has come to be known as *geodemographic profiling*. Instead it was a table in a format similar to Table 1.3 that appeared at the heart of the analysis.

So, what do the various columns of Table 1.3 indicate? Let us start with the categories listed in column A. These are known as *Mosaic* Types.[1] They do not describe supporters in terms of any personal characteristics, but rather according to the types of people most likely to live in the same streets as they do. Each has a code which is organized sequentially, 01–61, within a hierarchic structure, A–K.

Next to these *Mosaic* Types and their associated codes in column B we see the numbers of UK adults living in each Type at the time of the analysis – in total some 46,336,087. So, for example, 366,079 adults live in the geodemographic Type E31, labelled *Caring Professionals*.[2] This happens to be 0.79 per cent of UK adults. Column C reveals how the 235,358 supporters of the human rights charity are distributed across these same categories. So, we see that 9,858 of their supporters, which happens to be 4.19 per cent of the total, are classified as living among neighbours characterized as *Caring Professionals*. Figure 1.1 shows a street typical of that Type.

Column D is a simple index comparing the percentage of supporters who live in each *Mosaic* Type with the percentage of the national adult population; so, in the case of *Caring Professionals*, the index of 530 is obtained when the 4.19 per cent of supporters is divided by the 0.79 per cent of adults and multiplied by 100. The higher this index value, the greater is the likelihood that a resident living in this geodemographic type will be a supporter of the charity. In this example, the figure of 530 indicates that *Caring Professionals* are some 5.3 times more likely to be supporters of the charity than the national average. That is a substantial difference. It is the highest of any of the 61 Types.

*Mosaic* is an example of what is known as a geodemographic or neighbourhood classification system. There are three features of this form of analysis which warrant particular attention at this point. In terms of operational efficiency, the

**Table 1.3** Distribution of Human Rights Charity Supporters and Far-Right Political Party Members by Geodemographic Type

| Mosaic UK Types | No. of UK adults | No. human rights charity | Human rights charity index | No. far-right political party | Far-right political party index | Liberal/ far-right index |
|---|---|---|---|---|---|---|
| Total | 46,336,087 | 235,358 | 100 | 10,652 | 100 | 100 |
| A01: Global Connections | 297,628 | 6,696 | 443 | 13 | 19 | 2,332 |
| A02: Cultural Leadership | 410,972 | 10,784 | 517 | 40 | 42 | 1,231 |
| A03: Corporate Chieftains | 756,157 | 5,763 | 150 | 90 | 52 | 288 |
| A04: Golden Empty Nesters | 571,636 | 5,598 | 193 | 100 | 76 | 254 |
| A05: Provincial Privilege | 856,529 | 7,037 | 162 | 142 | 72 | 225 |
| A06: High Technologists | 1,086,198 | 5,326 | 97 | 190 | 76 | 128 |
| A07: Semi-Rural Seclusion | 743,582 | 7,474 | 198 | 138 | 81 | 244 |
| B08: Just Moving In | 92,664 | 1,118 | 238 | 6 | 29 | 821 |
| B09: Fledgling Nurseries | 552,702 | 1,298 | 46 | 125 | 98 | 47 |
| B10: Upscale New Owners | 746,614 | 1,983 | 52 | 156 | 91 | 57 |
| B11: Families Making Good | 1,268,856 | 3,521 | 55 | 327 | 112 | 49 |
| B12: Middle Rung Families | 1,474,251 | 4,250 | 57 | 400 | 118 | 48 |
| B13: Burdened Optimists | 1,043,034 | 2,075 | 39 | 283 | 118 | 33 |
| B14: In Military Quarters | 69,287 | 85 | 24 | 15 | 97 | 25 |
| C15: Close to Retirement | 1,761,619 | 6,459 | 72 | 413 | 102 | 71 |
| C16: Conservative Values | 1,549,347 | 3,845 | 49 | 367 | 103 | 48 |
| C17: Small Time Business | 1,075,281 | 5,914 | 108 | 307 | 124 | 87 |
| C18: Sprawling Subtopia | 1,410,391 | 4,981 | 70 | 350 | 108 | 65 |
| C19: Original Suburbs | 1,142,253 | 11,517 | 199 | 213 | 81 | 246 |

*(Continued)*

**Table 1.3** Distribution of Human Rights Charity Supporters and Far-Right Political Party Members by Geodemographic Type

| A | B | C | D | E | F | G |
|---|---|---|---|---|---|---|
| Mosaic UK Types | No. of UK adults | No. human rights charity | Human rights charity index | No. far-right political party | Far-right political party index | Liberal/ far-right index |
| C20: Asian Enterprise | 538,821 | 1,888 | 69 | 52 | 42 | 164 |
| D21: Respectable Rows | 781,005 | 6,949 | 175 | 221 | 123 | 142 |
| D22: Affluent Blue Collar | 1,656,092 | 3,439 | 41 | 579 | 152 | 27 |
| D23: Industrial Grit | 1,137,408 | 3,926 | 68 | 439 | 168 | 40 |
| D24: Coronation Street | 1,465,309 | 3,196 | 43 | 502 | 149 | 29 |
| D25: Town Centre Refuge | 432,647 | 2,292 | 104 | 111 | 112 | 93 |
| D26: South Asian Industry | 411,740 | 823 | 39 | 44 | 46 | 85 |
| D27: Settled Minorities | 651,232 | 5,804 | 176 | 93 | 62 | 284 |
| E28: Counter Cultural Mix | 492,497 | 9,419 | 377 | 54 | 48 | 785 |
| E29: City Adventurers | 472,430 | 10,112 | 421 | 33 | 30 | 1,403 |
| E30: New Urban Colonists | 506,395 | 13,118 | 510 | 54 | 46 | 1,109 |
| E31: Caring Professionals | 366,079 | 9,858 | 530 | 51 | 61 | 869 |
| E32: Dinky Developments | 336,829 | 2,083 | 122 | 61 | 79 | 154 |
| E33: Town Gown Transition | 287,707 | 5,826 | 399 | 24 | 37 | 1,078 |
| E34: University Challenge | 128,021 | 1,501 | 231 | 14 | 49 | 471 |
| F35: Bedsit Beneficiaries | 237,811 | 2,634 | 218 | 32 | 58 | 376 |
| F36: Metro Multiculture | 566,924 | 2,891 | 100 | 55 | 42 | 238 |
| F37: Upper Floor Families | 558,468 | 1,168 | 41 | 123 | 96 | 43 |
| F38: Tower Block Living | 152,026 | 256 | 33 | 25 | 72 | 46 |
| F39: Dignified Dependency | 318,786 | 831 | 51 | 73 | 99 | 52 |
| F40: Sharing a Staircase | 194,737 | 277 | 28 | 13 | 29 | 97 |

**Table 1.3** (Continued)

| A | B | C | D | E | F | G |
|---|---|---|---|---|---|---|
| Mosaic UK Types | No. of UK adults | No. human rights charity | Human rights charity index | No. far-right political party | Far-right political party index | Liberal/ far-right index |
| G41: Families on Benefits | 607,928 | 510 | 17 | 143 | 102 | 17 |
| G42: Low Horizons | 1,082,371 | 1,379 | 25 | 266 | 107 | 23 |
| G43: Ex-Industrial Legacy | 1,205,826 | 1,541 | 25 | 333 | 120 | 21 |
| H44: Rustbelt Resilience | 1,185,753 | 1,829 | 30 | 338 | 124 | 24 |
| H45: Older Right to Buy | 1,141,315 | 1,836 | 32 | 286 | 109 | 29 |
| H46: White Van Culture | 1,304,765 | 3,518 | 53 | 429 | 143 | 37 |
| H47: New Town Materialism | 1,012,699 | 1,328 | 26 | 324 | 139 | 19 |
| I48: Old People in Flats | 259,363 | 308 | 23 | 51 | 85 | 27 |
| I49: Low Income Elderly | 553,768 | 1,950 | 69 | 150 | 118 | 58 |
| I50: Cared for Pensioners | 550,815 | 488 | 17 | 90 | 71 | 24 |
| J51: Sepia Memories | 304,527 | 1,117 | 72 | 41 | 59 | 122 |
| J52: Childfree Serenity | 376,338 | 5,862 | 307 | 70 | 81 | 379 |
| J53: High Spending Elders | 538,744 | 4,249 | 155 | 93 | 75 | 207 |
| J54: Bungalow Retirement | 550,903 | 1,045 | 37 | 139 | 110 | 34 |
| J55: Small Town Seniors | 900,733 | 4,933 | 108 | 203 | 98 | 110 |
| J56: Tourist Attendants | 83,593 | 865 | 204 | 19 | 98 | 208 |
| K57: Summer Playgrounds | 171,447 | 1,027 | 118 | 35 | 88 | 134 |
| K58: Greenbelt Guardians | 1,276,747 | 6,138 | 95 | 311 | 106 | 90 |
| K59: Parochial Villagers | 1,081,238 | 3,619 | 66 | 236 | 95 | 69 |
| K60: Pastoral Symphony | 485,001 | 4,173 | 169 | 110 | 99 | 171 |
| K61: Upland Hill Farmers | 166,263 | 1,484 | 176 | 28 | 74 | 238 |

**Figure 1.1** *Mosaic E31 Caring Professionals*, Park Avenue, Hull, HU5 3ER

feature which most distinguishes a geodemographic profile is how easy it to produce tables such as Table 1.3. All that it requires is for the charity to know the *postcodes* of their supporters. No survey questions need to be asked, no responses processed (Savage and Burrows, 2007; 2009).

In terms of social theory, the feature which most distinguishes a geodemographic profile is that it categorizes people not on the basis of their own personal characteristics, such as age, gender, ethnicity and so on, but on their geographical location, that is, according to the characteristics of their immediate neighbours.[3] Notwithstanding the variety of age groups, genders, ethnic groups and, in particular, *social classes*,[4] who live next door to each other in the same type of postcode, this form of classification often proves just as predictive of people's behaviour as does information held at the person level. This gives powerful support to the belief that personal behaviour continues to be hugely influenced by social norms at the local level, even in the era of social media.

In terms of statistical methods, the feature that distinguishes a geodemographic profile is that it uses what are referred to as *multivariate* categories. Geodemographic categories are multivariate in that the set of variables used to construct them typically represents different dimensions of social character. This is by contrast with social surveys where customer or client behaviour is typically cross-tabulated against a series of separate *univariate* categories such as age, as in the case of Table 1.1, or the measure of social class used in Table 1.2. Clearly the definition of a multivariate category such as K57 *Summer Playgrounds*, is more complex than the definition of a univariate category such as persons aged over 65. But it does not necessary follow that multivariate categories are any more difficult to interpret than ones built using data representing a single dimension.

When they see a table such as Table 1.3 for the first time, some readers may question how appropriate it is to use a label such as G41 *Families on Benefits* to describe a particular geodemographic type. Others ask on the basis of what evidence can it be possible to justify a label such as B13 *Burdened Optimists*. How literally can a concept such as D24 *Coronation Street* be taken, some may ask?[5] And where can they find the information they need to understand the meaning of *Caring Professionals*?

Other people question whether it is appropriate for public servants to be making use of categories that have been developed for use by commercial organizations. Others fear that if such classifications are the intellectual property of commercial organizations this may limit their use in social scientific research. All these critical questions are ones we address in the chapters that follow.

Moving from the *format* of Table 1.3 to its *substantive implications*, perhaps the most striking is how strongly the level of support for the charity varies between one geodemographic type and another. It may be intellectually reassuring to learn that the most fertile neighbourhood type for the charity is labelled *Caring Professionals*. But is the scale of these geographical differences greater or less than the differences in the degree to which the charity appeals to different social classes? How far is this concentration the result of social pressures, 'peer' or 'neighbourhood' effects in the language of the social sciences? Is it the distinctive social values of its residents that cause the charity to pick up so many supporters among *Caring Professionals*; perhaps this is the reason why residents in these types of postcode are so especially receptive to the campaign for human rights? Or are supporters clustered geographically because *Caring Professionals* are disproportionately found in university towns where there is likely to be a thriving local group?

At a more fundamental level we could ask what are the social and political dynamics that have caused the issue of human rights to resonate so deeply with residents in the neighbourhoods characterized by *Symbols of Success* (the term that is given to the Types in Group A), see Table 5.4 on pp. 114–15 for more details, and to those in *Urban Intelligence* (the term that is given to Group E)? Maybe the emotions of residents in categories in Group B, *Happy Families*, are so invested in the care of their young children that they can't be persuaded to focus on the wider issue of human rights. If Labour-leaning categories in Groups G and H show so little concern for human rights, whereas Labour-leaning categories belonging to *Urban Intelligence* are so exercised by them, what does this contribute to our understanding of the tensions that divide different groups within the Labour Party for example? There are so many questions of this sort that can arise from a detailed examination of the variations in the index values of the different *Mosaic* Types.

At about the same time as this analysis was being carried out, someone leaked the names and addresses of members of a far-right political party. Columns E and F of Table 1.3 chart the distribution of the party's 10,652 members across the same geodemographic types. It is not surprising that the geodemographic types the party draws its support from are very different to those of the human rights charity. Its most fertile recruiting areas are neighbourhoods classified as D24 *Coronation Street*, D22 *Affluent Blue Collar*, D23 *Industrial Grit* and H46 *White Van Culture*.[6] The likelihood of a person being a party member exceeds the national average by more than 40 per cent in each of these categories.

Tables 1.4 and 1.5 illustrate another commonly used form of geodemographic analysis. The object of an analysis of this sort is to provide broader insight into the lifestyles of particular groups of people, in this case the supporters of the far-right party. Table 1.4 is produced by comparing the geodemographic profile of party members with the profiles of a large number of other behaviours held in what is referred to as a *profile library*, a concept which is explained in greater detail in Chapter 6. From the many hundreds of demographics and behaviours that have been profiled by *Mosaic* this table reveals the ones which are the most *positively* associated with the types of neighbourhood in which support for this far-right party is especially concentrated.[7]

It would interest few readers to learn that employment in lower supervisory occupations and readership of mid-market newspapers were the most distinctive characteristics of the types of neighbourhood where the party finds it easiest to recruit supporters. More interesting but less obvious is that its members tend to

**Table 1.4**  *Characteristics and Behaviours Most *Positively* Correlated with Membership of Far-Right Political Party*

| Domain | Category | Correlation |
| --- | --- | --- |
| Occupation | Lower supervisory | 0.790 |
| Newspapers | Popular or mid-market daily newspaper | 0.735 |
| Interests | Camping and caravanning | 0.701 |
| Employment status | Part time | 0.695 |
| Industry | Manufacturing and mining | 0.671 |
| Travel to work | Car or van | 0.628 |
| Shops visited | Morrisons | 0.625 |
| Religion | Christian | 0.599 |
| Number of rooms | 5–6 rooms | 0.593 |
| Interests | Pets | 0.591 |

live in the types of neighbourhood where people like going camping and cara-vanning. What might we learn from this? Is it that this form of holiday and the far-right party both appeal to a similar group of people, characterized by a strong sense of self-reliance and a dislike of externally imposed controls? Or do they both appeal to patriotic people with little enthusiasm for exploring foreign cultures? Maybe both explanations for the association are valid.

Much more revealing are those behaviours that are most *negatively* associated with people living in the types of neighbourhood where supporters of the far-right party are most numerous. Table 1.5 reveals that the two strongest negative associ-ations are with making international phone calls once per week or more and with households containing adults from two or more ethnic groups. Party supporters, or their neighbours, are also among the least willing to support third world, disaster relief or human rights charities. Maybe such relationships are too predictable to be of any real value, but at least they confirm the ability of geodemographics to iden-tify behaviours which 'go together' even where these data are held on databases which have never been physically linked.

We decided to introduce this chapter with these two practical examples in order to demonstrate the key proposition of this book. It is that the value of geography as a framework for analysing social behaviour is not limited to its ability to reveal the physical location of citizens or customers. It also has

**Table 1.5**  *Characteristics and Behaviours Most Negatively Correlated with Membership of Far-Right Political Party*

| Domain | Category | Correlation |
|---|---|---|
| Telephones | International phone calls at least once per week | −0.772 |
| Ethnicity | 2+ ethnic groups in household | −0.695 |
| Newspapers | The *Times* | −0.693 |
| Charities | Third world charities | −0.684 |
| Born | Far East | −0.677 |
| Born | Middle East + western central Asia | −0.675 |
| Newspapers | The *Independent* | −0.675 |
| Charities | Medical research charities | −0.669 |
| Interests | Art | −0.660 |
| Newspapers | The *Guardian* | −0.658 |
| Charities | Disaster relief charities | −0.643 |
| Charities | Human rights charities | −0.639 |
| Charities | Deaf charities | −0.636 |
| Charities | Blind charities | −0.628 |
| Qualifications | Degree | −0.626 |
| Charities | Homeless charities | −0.601 |

the capacity to deliver a deep sociological understanding of the social groups that engage in particular behaviours. Indeed, by virtue of their multivariate nature, some might claim that this is because the social character of the categories that are encoded within a geodemographic classification, such as *Caring Professionals*, are so much more nuanced than the relatively crude constructs that feature in the stub section of a survey questionnaire.

For example, the profile of the charity's supporters is the first of many in this book which will demonstrate the ability of geodemographics to illuminate not just the growing divide between the core values of the metropolitan liberal elite and the conservative working class, but also the cities and parts of cities where these contrasting groups tend to live. A good indication of the depth of this divide can be seen in the 'Liberal/far-right index' contained in column G of Table 1.3. Here the index of support for the human rights charity has been expressed as a ratio of the index for support of the far-right party. At one extreme, in A01 *Global Connections*, this ratio is well over 100 times greater than at the other end of the spectrum, G41 *Families on Benefits*.

## How lay people conceive of neighbourhoods

So far we have alluded to some of the integrative capabilities of geodemographics – for example, how it can integrate the social with the geographical, the quantitative with the qualitative, age with class and housing type, the theoretical with the operational. In this section we consider some of the other integrative possibilities of geodemographics as a form of classification. Can it be used to bridge the different ways in which expert and lay (non-expert) groups conceptualize different types of neighbourhood within the city? Or indeed to provide a common language which might stimulate greater cross-fertilization of insights between different professional disciplines?

In the *natural* sciences, academics and professionals typically converse using a commonly agreed set of terms which are consistently defined and applied and which provide a broadly agreed representation of the objects of their study: Linnaeus established conventions for the classification of plants and animals; Arthur Holmes codified absolute dates for classifying geological time scales; the Dewey Decimal classification system is the most widely used method for classifying books in the library; and so on. Where would their respective sciences be without these taxonomic infrastructures?

In the *social* sciences, such sets of terms – classification systems or taxonomies – are less precise and more contested. In contrast to those of the natural sciences they are also less stable over time (Bowker and Star, 1999).

In respect of urban studies the social scientific community is just one among a large number of different groups, some professional, others lay, whose expertise requires at least some understanding of the behaviour of different social groups and the types of neighbourhood in which they tend to live.

Most lay people build up an extensive repertoire of languages with which to describe social groups that have distinctive sets of values and patterns of behaviour. The everyday or *vernacular* language they use for this purpose often draws upon popular and highly mediated personality and behavioural assumptions. It is striking how often their judgements relating to these social groups are articulated using geographic references based on *where* these groups are believed to live: 'Hampstead Intellectuals', 'the Notting Hill Set', 'Sloane Rangers', 'East End Hipsters', 'the man on the Clapham omnibus' and so on. Most judgements of this sort are made instantaneously, without any conscious reflection and with no more thought than people use when inferring the social group a person belongs to from their physical features, gait, accent or the clothes that they wear.

Physical appearance carries hugely more weight in all these forms of judgement than it does in 'expert' modes of knowledge. But this reliance on appearances and the lack of any formal evidence-based or codified knowledge base does not inhibit lay people from making stereotypical judgements. These judgements function more adequately than many experts might have imagined for navigating pathways through an otherwise complex and nuanced urban realm.

Lacking an understanding of abstract and generalized concepts, one might suppose that lay people's confidence in their ability to characterize others by where they live would be limited to the towns, suburbs and individual streets of which they had first-hand experience. In practice, and no doubt aided by the stereotyping and lampooning of which the media is so fond, it is very much down to their ability to interpret visual images that lay people are able to form judgements about the character of places geographically far removed from those of which they have personal, lived experience. For example, few people would have any difficulty recognizing what types of people lived in the streets illustrated in Figure 1.2 or those illustrated in Figures 5.1, 5.2 and 10.1, which appear in later chapters.

Within popular discourses such judgements are the product of an understanding that is mostly tacit, acquired without deliberate intent, expanded incrementally over many years, its depth and detail seldom recognized even by its owners. Most would recoil from any request to communicate their knowledge in an organized, systematic form, finding it easier to associate categories of neighbourhood with visual images rather than the written word. As a result, it is not by accident that the homes displayed in estate agents' windows – and increasingly on their websites (Botterill, 2013) – typically feature photographs of the *exteriors* of vendors' houses and that these photographs are taken from the street.[8] It is a testament to their tacit knowledge that many potential home-buyers can instantly translate a

Church Street, Staverton, Daventry, Northants, NN11 6JJ

Lower Stoke, Limpley Stoke, Bath, BA2 7FR

West View, Minskip, York, YO51 9HZ

Back Lane, Souldern, Bicester, Oxon, OX27 7JG

**Figure 1.2** *K58 Greenbelt Guardians*

property's appearance into a judgement of how easily they, or not infrequently their children, would 'fit in' socially with other residents in the street.

Nor is it by accident that when newspapers report the fraud, corruption or other anti-social activities of apparently comfortably-off miscreants, their accounts are invariably embellished by photographs of the homes (invariably described as 'mansions', 'stuccoed' or 'detached') in which the subjects of these stories live. Once again it is visual images that make it possible for readers to locate the social space in which the subjects of these reports have been living, an aspect that is usually more interesting to them than the precise geographic location of their homes. Tacit though the 'common knowledge' of lay people normally[9] is, this seldom precludes them from articulating their observations and sharing them with other people. Indeed, for many people, making sense of fine residential distinctions is an enjoyable subject for social intercourse. Nor is such gossip necessarily idle since, when people search for somewhere new to live, their ability to 'read' the social character of a street from its physical appearance is critically important in helping them find the right kind of neighbourhood to move to.

But how much of the language of these conversations is used by academic, public sector and commercial groups? After all, most neighbourhoods owe their physical form to previous decisions of planners, local authority housing departments, private developers and volume house-builders, as well as the advice of social researchers and social policy analysts. In order to research these needs it would be surprising, if indeed it were the case, if these agents did not share at least some common language with the sorts of people for whom this housing was intended, what their preferences for different locations and styles might be and whom they would wish to have as neighbours.

## How professionals conceive of neighbourhoods

Compared to lay people, most of whom share a broadly common language for describing types of neighbourhood, any discussion about neighbourhoods which involves communications between different professional groups often has to navigate a veritable Babel of languages, each seemingly as unintelligible to each other as they are to lay people. To illustrate this complexity, Table 1.6 lists just some of the groups for whom an understanding of the residential composition of different neighbourhoods is of critical professional importance. In it we examine differences between sociologists and geographers from the world of academia, planners and public servants from the government sector, and marketers and land economists from the world of business. Each differs in terms of: their possible roles; interests; mechanisms for bringing about change; the means by which they might measure the 'success' of interventions; the means by which they attempt to manage conflict; and, particularly important, the sources of data upon which they draw to describe a neighbourhood.

In addition to these professional groups it is pertinent to consider the perspectives of lay groups, residents and citizens, because they too have an interest in what makes a neighbourhood successful. We use the term 'citizens' to refer to residents who involve themselves in voluntary organizations that represent residents' opinions and interests to professionals in the government and business sectors.

Not only do different categories of 'expert' acquire their professional knowledge from different academic disciplines; their claims to expertise also involve distinctive approaches to *descriptive*, *predictive*, *theoretical* and *prescriptive* modes of engagement with neighbourhoods. What differentiates these professionals from others with similar training is the frequency with which they have to test their interpretations of neighbourhood structure against those that are held by lay actors, particularly citizens. It would be much to everyone's benefit if

**Table 1.6**  Schematic Representation of Different Actors' Approaches to Understanding Neighbourhood Differences

| Domain | Residents | Citizens | Sociology | Geography | Planning | Business | Government | Land economy |
|---|---|---|---|---|---|---|---|---|
| Job function | Householders | Volunteers | Community development officers, social workers | Transport planners, retail modellers | Planners | Marketers, Market Researchers | Civil servants, police officers, local government officers | Developers, estate agents |
| Feature of interest | Order, no anti-social behaviour | Active community organizations | Cohesion | Proximity and accessibility | Aesthetics, vibrancy | Consumption of products and media | Client groups, configuration of services | Land ownership |
| Agents of change | Police | Consultation | Community activism | Infrastructure | Statutory policies | Advertising campaigns | Programmes | Deals |
| Measure of success | Being recognized in the street, house price appreciation | Size of membership, Victory on planning applications and appeals | Social capital | Network utilization | Approval of policies | Market share | Satisfaction rating, attainment of targets | Yield |
| Source of data | Neighbours, corner shop, local newspaper | Local authority, FOI | Qualitative studies | Census, official statistics | Registries and gazetteers | Marketing databases, surveys | Commissioned research, Index of Multiple Deprivation | Contacts |
| Management of conflict | Social pressure | Petitions, judicial review | Public pressure | Migration | Consultation and planning appeals | Budgets | Elections | Market forces |

the communication of these differences in understanding of residential structure could be expressed in a common language, both in situations of conflict and when there is a need for the different actors listed in Table 1.6 to collaborate.

Why should different professional groups use different theoretical and conceptual frameworks for describing neighbourhoods and their character? We believe the answer is largely to do with history. That is to say that the particular sources of data on which they have to rely often reflect the methods of data collection that prevailed at the time when their occupational roles were first professionalized and when the theories that govern their professional practice were first formulated. For different professions, these methods can be qualitative fieldwork, statistical surveys, customer records, health and education performance statistics or even what is now described as 'big data' (Burrows and Savage, 2014).

In addition to the different methods and sources of data that professional groups rely on, it is obvious that there are specific concerns that dominate the perspectives from which different professional groups approach their subject. For example, for a geographer or sociologist working in a university *research environment*, urban structure represents a very significant field of research, some of whose long-established and highly respected body of theoretical thinking will be summarized in Chapter 2. An aspect of neighbourhoods which is of particular interest to many of them is the impact on communities of unequal levels of economic resource, political influence and what has come to be termed social and cultural capital (Kennett and Forrest, 2006). Academic researchers also claim distinction from other groups for the critical importance they attach to the understanding of social and economic *processes*, and in particular how they contribute to social change at a local level, and to the different levels of status that are attached to living in particular types of neighbourhood.

Allocating public funds on a geographical basis is central to the activities of many *civil servants*. Virtually any publicly funded programme designed to channel additional resources into areas of greatest need now requires justification based on a conception of the area's level of *multiple deprivation* (see, for example, Shiels et al., 2013). Understanding *why* particular neighbourhoods may be 'deprived', or in what particular respects they are deprived, is not necessarily as relevant to the formal process of allocating programme funds to local schools, hospitals or other public facilities as lay people might suppose. What matters is *how* deprived their populations are.

In recent years, public sector professionals employed by *local councils, health authorities* and the *emergency services*, have been exhorted to take more account of local needs and preferences by tailoring the mix of services, the manner in which they are delivered and the channels by which information is communicated to clients belonging to particular population groups. The consequent reconfiguration of service provision requires an ability to assess relative levels of demand not just in individual neighbourhoods but also in the categories of neighbourhood that are represented in their authority's area. Ideally this categorization should be done at a finer level of granularity than the electoral divisions into which local authorities are divided. Nevertheless, to ensure they receive a fair share of central government funding, they are also obliged to communicate with civil servants using the language of *indices of multiple deprivation* (IMD) (Smith et al., 2015), which ranks areas on a complex but essentially ordinal scale ('league table') of need.[10]

Had space permitted we could also have included in Table 1.6 criminologists, market researchers and a small group for whom an understanding of neighbourhoods is of critical importance, the *managers of the election campaigns* of political parties. As party affiliation weakens and old-established measures of social class become less predictive of voter alignment, these campaign organizers increasingly try to target electors with value sets likely to be aligned with the broad policy positions adopted by their party's leader. The work of these specialists is invariably more effective if, as they do, they categorize the neighbourhoods that voters live in in a way which is consistent with those used by their pollsters when tabulating how respondents intend to vote. These categories need to be intelligible to their media-buying teams and, most of all, to those who advise party leaders on political strategy (Webber, 2006).

Many of the *business analysts* employed in the site location and market planning departments of multiple retailers have degrees in geography. A clear understanding of residential distinctions and patterns of segregation is crucial for this group (Leventhal, 2016) if they are to generate the information needed to ensure that new branches are opened in potentially profitable locations. These analysts' responsibilities often include providing their merchandising department with information on the products and brands that are likely to appeal to the types of consumer living in the catchment areas of existing and new stores. Given the length of time over which investment in a new branch needs to be amortized, analysts often assist retailers' property departments by alerting them to social processes which might result in changes in the future social make-up of the relatively localized catchments served by each new store. For example, a pub group might want to be assured that a potential new property is not in an area increasingly being populated by people with a Muslim background, an immigrant group who generally refrain from the consumption of alcohol. The focus of the retail analyst will therefore be less on social status and power relationships than on the *behavioural* differences that characterize different neighbourhoods.

*Estate agents* clearly view neighbourhoods in terms of average property prices and their year-on-year movements. But the more successful estate agent is likely to have a 'feel' for homes of different sizes and architectural styles that different social groups prefer – a matter which often involves a highly nuanced sense of people's tastes. To increase the likelihood of sales, the successful estate agent will also assure potential purchasers of social changes that are likely to have a favourable impact on future property values.

With so many different actors, each with their focus on very specific aspects of urban structure, is it any wonder that they share so little common language?

Is it for historical or cultural reasons that these different groups should have developed different terminologies for describing the same types of residential neighbourhood? Perhaps. Or is it that the overall pattern of urban differentiation is just too complex for any one of these groups to grasp, with different groups using different conceptual frameworks to describe different aspects of the same overall pattern? Maybe. Do conflicting social and career interests explain why different groups develop modes of speaking which deliberately exclude outsiders? Almost certainly. Perhaps, as in other fields of study, the problem is a more philosophical one. Rather than it just being an issue of differential social constructions of reality, perhaps the assumption of an ontological unity in what constitutes a neighbourhood is not sustainable?[11] With this we disagree.

Our explanation is rather different. It is that for each group of actors, the concepts by which neighbourhoods are *described* have, over time, become too heavily enmeshed with the metrics whereby the impact of policy changes are *predicted* and performance *evaluated*. For example, it is hypothesized that high levels of deprivation contribute to low educational attainment. Tests confirm the hypothesis. Data are collected regarding the level of deprivation in the postcodes in which pupils live. Specific schools are then awarded additional funding on the basis of a postcode premium. Levels of deprivation, which require to be collected for technical reasons, then dominate the language by which school catchments are then described. Yet no parents, when asked in everyday conversation to characterize either themselves or their neighbourhoods, describe themselves in terms of a score on a national index of multiple deprivation. The reliance on deprivation data to determine funding has the effect of preventing parents from accessing other forms of information which might help them better understand what makes the pupil intake of their children's school different from any other, or indeed how the pupil intake differs from the demographics of the catchment area that it serves.

No one would doubt the need for professionals to employ prescriptive, evaluative and predictive language which is specific to their professions. But it is difficult to see any logical reason why different professional understandings need be based on profession-specific systems for describing the demographics of the population of any residential area. Were a common language to be adopted, if only for description, it would at least be more likely for insights gained in a particular field of knowledge to cross-fertilize others to mutual advantage.

# Understanding how neighbourhoods change

Whilst each of these different professional groups[12] might appear to have its own perspectives on the aspects of neighbourhoods which have particular relevance to its professional decisions, there are important respects in which the objects of their interest will have changed in recent years, as indeed have their needs for conceptual systems. Perhaps the most significant of these is the growing role played by notions of *taste* in various explanatory schemas. The growing importance social scientists now place on this concept as a basis for understanding *social distinction* and *social stratification* – and in particular at the expense of income differences and occupational status – is often attributed to the influence of the French sociologist Pierre Bourdieu (Bridge, 2006; Savage, 2011), especially his book *Distinction* (Bourdieu, 1984).

It is his work in particular that has underpinned the emergence of an approach called *cultural class analysis* in which differences in supposedly autonomous or freely chosen cultural practices and preferences are given at least as much weight as are more deterministic explanations grounded in more economically based notions of what traditionally have been described as socio-economic classes (Savage, 2016; Savage et al., 2015). This perspective has informed a number of neighbourhood studies predominantly in middle class areas (Bacqué et al., 2015; Butler with Robson, 2003; Savage et al., 2005).

It has not just been academic research that has been affected by the apparent weakening of associations between social status, occupational status and household income: marketers and their advertisers increasingly find it more productive to target consumer communications on the basis of their values and tastes – which for example are more aligned with attitudes towards climate change, animal welfare, fair trade and cultural diversity than traditional 'structural' variables such as age and class. Divisions of the city based on values, attitudes and tastes create distinct neighbourhood clusters which are very different to those based on traditional measures of social class, income and wealth.[13]

These are just two of the changes that are beginning to impact upon professional understandings of neighbourhoods. Others include the growing levels of spatial inequality that are of particular interest to geographers and sociologists, whose recent research increasingly focuses on the growing concentration of the 'super-rich' in London at the expense of peripheral regions (Atkinson et al., 2016a; 2016b; Burrows et al., 2017). Likewise, the escalation of property prices, the rapid increase in rents and the growing financial obstacles young families face when wanting to buy their own homes (Filandri and Bertolini, 2016) have just as significant implications for estate agents, developers and consumer marketers as they do for university researchers.

The growth in the size and *diversity* of Britain's ethnic communities – both established and more recent – and the tendency for many of them to cluster together in very specific parts of British cities, also calls for adjustment to the frameworks traditionally used for describing different parts of the city, and further diminishes the appropriateness of divisions based exclusively on income, wealth or occupational status (Catney, 2016).

One effect of the growth of the internet has been to make consumers more aware of the value of information. Fostered initially by the emergence of price comparison sites and subsequently by portals which provide information about properties for sale and movements in average local prices, an increasingly confident citizenry routinely searches for comparative local information on topics such as school rankings, hospital performance and air pollution levels (Burrows et al., 2005). Thus, at the margins, tacit knowledge is beginning to be displaced by measurements based on more formal conceptual systems for comparing areas.

This, we suspect, will lead to competition between purely quantitative descriptions, such as the rankings used by civil servants, which have the benefit of being easy to understand but which tend to be somewhat shallow in descriptive resonance, and the qualitative descriptions, often accompanied by *visualizations*, that are more commonly used by marketers, which we believe correspond more closely with citizens' own tacit knowledge, even if the data derive from unfamiliar sources.

It is these formal measurements and conceptual systems for understanding neighbourhoods that are the primary concern of this book. As we have shown, debates relating to urban structure, social change and the relationship between neighbourhood and social status are rarely conducted according to vocabularies, classifications or taxonomies that have universal acceptance. More often than not, academics, public servants, the commercial sector and members of the public use their own distinct vocabularies to conceptualize neighbourhoods. As we have already indicated, this book chronicles the historical development and contemporary application of one particular mode of understanding neighbourhoods, *geodemographic classification*; it is an approach that can offer some degree of rapprochement between these various vocabularies. Although occasional references are made to it in academic literature, it is an analytic approach that has been developed by, and is most commonly used by, market researchers, business analysts in the commercial sector, political parties, the police and local government.

# Geodemographics as a means of categorizing different types of neighbourhood

Geodemographic classifications, an example of which we used to open this chapter, were developed simultaneously in the United States and the UK in the early 1970s and are now widely used both in commerce and local government. They are used to a lesser extent within the academy.[14] The form they now take might be somewhat different to that which pertained when they were originally developed, but the essential insight that underpins their construction remains the same: that if a set of areas are similar to each other across all widely used measures of demographic structure, they are also likely to be very similar across almost any manifestation of social values, behaviour and consumption.

This observation – 'that knowing where someone lives provides useful information about *how* that person lives' (Harris et al., 2005: 2) – is, however, clearly not one just restricted to the producers of such classifications. Over time it has become a deeply culturally embedded idiom popularized, of course, as 'birds of a feather flock together';[15] this referring to the manner in which people with similar characteristics, interests, tastes, values and so on tend – through various complex mechanisms – to cluster together in close socio-spatial proximity to each other (Cheshire, 2012).[16] We will discuss some of these mechanisms throughout the book, largely through empirical examples. However, it is worth pointing out at the outset that though homophily – love of the same – is manifest in many facets of social life (McPherson et al., 2001), it is perhaps nowhere more noticeable than in where people end up living (Bishop with Cushing, 2009; Savage et al., 2005).

We will return later in the book to examine some of the mechanisms through which social space comes to be 'segmented', 'clustered' or, as Batty and Longley (1994) prefer, 'fractal'[17] in its form. However, it has long been known that there exists a strong mathematical basis for accepting that a range of locally orientated neighbourhood behaviours by individuals and households can lead to the emergence of 'segregated' socio-structural spatial forms at an urban scale that were not necessarily the intended outcomes of the actors engaging in the original behaviours. The classic statement of this is Schelling (1971), who demonstrates that even small individual preferences for living close to others 'similar' to oneself – on whatever dimensions – can lead to hugely disproportionate aggregate residential 'segregation' effects.[18] Of course, a whole set of other socio-economic, cultural, political and, increasingly, technological forces now also contribute to the emergence of complex fractal geographies (Ellison and Burrows, 2007) – increasingly recognized as occurring not just across *lateral* space, as traditionally mapped, but increasingly in terms of *verticality* as different socio-economic and cultural groups find themselves segregated at different levels in multi-storey residential buildings (Graham, 2016).

In the next two chapters, we will detail the antecedents of the geodemographic classifications that are widely used today. It is a complex tale that will take us to the London of Charles Booth at the turn of the twentieth century, to rural Wisconsin in 1915, to the Chicago School of Sociology in the 1920s and 1930s, to the work of sociologists, geographers and planners in New York, London and, crucially, Liverpool, to the commercial corporate world of multinational marketing organizations from the 1980s through to the police and local government in the 1990s; a major theme will be that, although the practice of geodemographic classification originated in the world of the academy and urban policy, it has been equally relevant to the worlds of commerce and local administration (Burrows and Gane, 2006).

Geodemographic classifications in the UK mostly operate at the level of the *unit postcode*,[19] such as PL19 9JL, and describe in the region of 60 or more different types of neighbourhood. Their purpose is not just to describe the character of different forms of neighbourhood (Parker et al., 2007): their unique role is to facilitate the linkage of information from different sources. For example, in an election campaign a political party is likely to commission pollsters to track the salience of different issues among different groups within the electorate. For the results of these polls to drive the selection of streets that should be canvassed or the scripts of telephone callers, the categories used to report the poll findings need to be consistent with the categories used by letter-box distribution companies and with at least one of the fields held on the database from which electors are selected for telephone canvassing and for selecting the most appropriate telephone script to use.

Likewise, the manufacturer of packaged goods, having used research surveys to identify the social groups to which a particular product can be most profitably sold, will want to know the television programmes which this *target group* is most likely to watch; the leaflet distribution sectors with the highest proportions of letter boxes belonging to households in this category and the retail outlets whose catchments cover the largest proportion of consumers of this type. To co-ordinate these activities it is critical that, when they communicate with the packaged goods manufacturer, market research companies, television stations, door-to-door distribution companies and national supermarket chains employ a consistent set of categories within a commonly agreed taxonomy.

As we have already seen, though, the reason why geodemographic classifications of neighbourhoods operationalized at unit postcode level are so widely used is because they are able to predict all manner of behavioural outcomes of interest to their users. When the UK census office first published statistical information at the neighbourhood level in 1971, it was reasonable to assume that what caused behaviour to differ from neighbourhood to neighbourhood was the relative mix of people or households based on categories such as age, education, housing tenure and occupational status. Since then countless research projects have shown that, whilst differences in the population mix are clearly important, the neighbourhood in which a person lives also plays a significant incremental role in influencing that person's likely behaviour (Webber, 2004). For example, two groups of individuals, precisely matched on every single demographic such as age, gender and social class, are likely to vote in different ways if the neighbourhoods in which they live have different population mixes. The performances of their children in Key Stage educational tests are also likely to differ. So too will the food they eat and the destinations they choose for their annual holidays. In other words, a neighbourhood exerts an independent and autonomous effect in its own right. The results of this process are, as already mentioned, often described as *neighbourhood effects* and this is a subject we examine in greater detail in Chapters 6 and 7.

The phenomenon of neighbourhood effects is recognized by many different groups of experts involved in the research and delivery of services at a neighbourhood level. What geographers describe as neighbourhood effects are similar but not wholly synonymous with what sociologists understand as peer effects, transmitted via social networks and cultural norms.[20] Public servants now subscribe to the belief that living in a disadvantaged neighbourhood confers incremental disadvantage to all residents irrespective of their personal circumstances. As we have discussed, it is on the basis of this belief that central government devised and applies the IMD to the prioritization of neighbourhoods for area-based programmes. Notwithstanding the growth in online shopping, marketers are keenly aware of the influence of neighbourhood on the brands that people purchase and the channels they use to undertake transactions.

What is less clearly understood is just how these 'neighbourhood effects' come into play. Is it that the consumer searches out a neighbourhood where he or she expects to find people with like-minded values, tastes and consumer preferences? Is it that groups of people whom we assume to be similar when we categorize them on the basis of age, gender or social class, happen in practice to be less uniform than we imagine, these traditional forms of categorization being inadequate in capturing important differences in attitude and lifestyle? Is it that over time the mix of products and services that can be bought from local shops affects the norms and expectations of local residents? Or is it that the prevailing ethos of a neighbourhood has a direct impact on what are considered normal forms of behaviour?

We would argue that it is the last of these explanations, albeit in tacit form, that motivates parents seeking to live within the catchment area of what, on frequently used measures, is considered a 'good' school. Consciously or unconsciously parents understand that notwithstanding differences in teaching standards and facilities, their children's personal development and educational attainment will almost certainly be affected by the social backgrounds of the other children in their class (Webber and Butler, 2007).

To many people it appears intuitively self-evident that a multivariate taxonomy of neighbourhoods will be less effective in predicting differences in personal behaviour than a statistical model that uses multiple regression – or something similar – to add together the explanatory power of a series of separate single-dimensional classification systems such as age or class when applied to individual people (think back to Tables 1.1 and 1.2). After all, by aggregating individuals of different genders, ages, ethnicities and social classes to create area averages and then classifying neighbourhoods on the basis of many different

characteristics at once, it would seem inevitable that much of the original variability in individual behaviour would be lost. Though this may appear intuitively
self-evident, statistical studies consistently find that the type of neighbourhood a
person lives in is seldom a less good predictor of individual behaviour than any
single demographic variable.

There are also a number of technical reasons why a taxonomy based on
neighbourhood proves particularly useful for certain categories of user. One
relates to the homogeneity of the cases being classified, in the case of a
neighbourhood classification, individual postcodes, in the case of individuals
specific age bands, social classes, levels of educational attainment and so on.
As a general rule, the individual postcodes that fall within the same taxonomic
category tend to be more uniform in terms of their behaviours and consumption than are the citizens, consumers or residents that are grouped together on
the basis of a one-dimensional measurement system such as age, gender or
occupational status.

This has great significance for marketers, retailers and those who deliver public
services, such as policing, health and education, all of whom need to be able to
form a judgement about the relative demand for services in specific geographical areas. When predicting levels of demand, whether for products or services, a
mathematical model based on multivariate taxonomy at the neighbourhood level
is likely to be much more reliable than a model based on individual characteristics
whether at the person or household level.

Table 1.7 illustrates how *Mosaic* can be used to build a simple model for
estimating the relative level of demand for a grocery product within a localized

**Table 1.7** Simple Model to Predict Consumption of a Grocery Product in
a Local Catchment Area

| A | B | C | D |
|---|---|---|---|
| *Mosaic* Type | % households in catchment area | National propensity to purchase ketchup (UK mean = 100) | Column C × Column B / 100 |
| D26: *South Asian Industry* | 10.0 | 84 | 8.4 |
| G42: *Low Horizons* | 32.7 | 142 | 46.4 |
| G43: *Ex-Industrial Legacy* | 31.3 | 141 | 44.1 |
| G45: *Older Right to Buy* | 26.0 | 116 | 30.2 |
| Overall index on ketchup for catchment area | | | 129.1 |

catchment area (Sleight, 2004: 380). In this example, the catchment area contains four *Mosaic* categories only, and the grocery product for which demand is to be estimated is ketchup. Essentially the model weights the proportion of the catchment area in each *Mosaic* type by the national average propensity of consumers of that type to purchase the product. In this example catchment area per household consumption is estimated at 29 per cent above the national average. Such a model is likely to be most reliable for a product whose pattern of consumption has no regional bias and whose variations in consumption are captured by the different social dimensions that are used to build the classification. It will almost certainly be more reliable than one based solely on social class, or on age, or on ethnicity.

In summary, there are a number of different qualities that may render a taxonomy of neighbourhoods effective, not just its ability to capture observable economic and socio-cultural differences. To be effective it needs to be widely adopted by different professional groups who participate in the market place for identifying and reaching target groups more efficiently. It also needs to define neighbourhoods at a level of scale which matches the scale at which neighbourhood effects really do make a difference to people's behaviour. The neighbourhoods that fall within each category also need to be sufficiently similar in terms of all significant dimensions of social differentiation that are known to influence variations in consumer demand or social need on a geographical basis.

The nature – if not the detail – of geodemographic classifications should now be apparent. There is much about their history, construction and use that is of interest, and we will detail this in the chapters that follow.

## Notes

[1] The classification used here, by way of an introductory example, is the *Mosaic* classification originally released in 2003 by Experian. It is the most widely used of a number of different geodemographic classifications.

[2] As we will discuss in later chapters, this is the 'commercial' label attached to this particular neighbourhood type. Such labels appear in italics. A more discursive 'public-sector' describes the type as: 'Well-educated singles and childless couples colonizing inner areas of provincial cities'.

[3] This is perhaps one of the main reasons why so many people, when invited to comment on the validity of the *Mosaic* code they are classified under, respond that it is a more accurate classification of their neighbours than it is of them!

[4] The analysis of social class has recently seen something of a revival, perhaps because of the success of the *BBC Great British Class Survey* (Savage et al., 2015). We hope to show in this book how a geodemographic mode of analysis – although not directly designed with academic social science in mind – can offer

major new analytic and substantive insights, not just in relation to social class but also into the manner in which social class intersects with age, gender, geography, ethnicity and other univariate categorizations.

[5] These neighbourhood types are described in the public-sector version of the classification, in turn, as: 'Families, many single parent, in deprived social housing on the edge of regional centres' (*Families on Benefits*); 'First generation owner occupiers, many with large amounts of consumer debt' (*Burdened Optimists*); and 'Low income families living in cramped Victorian terraced housing in inner city locations' (*Coronation Street*).

[6] The last three of these types, in order, are described in the argot of the public-sector version of the classification as: 'Comfortably off manual workers living in spacious but inexpensive private houses' (*Affluent Blue Collar*); 'Owners of affordable terraces built to house nineteenth-century heavy industrial workers' (*Industrial Grit*); and 'Residents in 1930s and 1950s London council estates, now mostly owner-occupiers' (*White Van Culture*).

[7] To be clear, it is not possible to attach such profile data to the *actual* cases, only to the postcode types within which such people live. Thus, what follows might best be described as a very simple form of spatial micro-simulation, which needs to be mindful of the potential for ecological fallacy.

[8] Although we must note that in recent years there might be some evidence that the availability of exterior shots of flats and houses is no longer such a strong norm. Especially in 'new build' developments and upmarket renovations on 'brown-field sites' it seems to be the case that visualizations of interior design aesthetics are prioritized over external views of the buildings.

[9] We say 'normally' here because, as we discuss later, there is some evidence that with the on-going 'informatization' of neighbourhoods (Burrows and Ellison, 2004) *some* members of the public (normally the more affluent and/or better educated) do appear to be developing a more codified, data-driven sense of neighbourhood differences; a process likely to accelerate with the increasing usage of 'geoweb' resources (Smith et al., 2016) able to popularize a wide range of different envisionings of local areas (including some of those used by different professional groups, to be discussed in what follows).

[10] The IMD is going to reoccur as a backdrop throughout this book so it is worth a brief excurse here, at the outset. The IMD has been through various iterations since 2000. In its most recent iteration, 2015, it takes data from various official sources at the census Lower-layer Super Output Area (LSOA) across seven different domains – (1) income, (2) employment, (3) health and disability, (4) education, skills and training, (5) barriers to housing and services, (6) living environment,

and (7) crime – and, through a complex set of statistical procedures (Smith et al., 2015), ranks each of the 32,844 LSOAs in England from the most to the least deprived. However, this does mean that two LSOAs that are ranked at the same point on the scale might be very different *types* of places, their equivalent location on this particular measure of multiple deprivation deriving from a very different combination of attributes.

[11] Perhaps, as in fields such a medical anthropology (Mol, 2002), we have to accept the cognitive discomfort which results from the possibility that we are working with multiple ontologies that only rarely cohere into a unified object of study.

[12] All of which, to a greater or lesser extent, were once conceptualized by Pahl (1970) as 'urban managers' – unified only to the extent that they were able to influence the allocation of urban resources and thus mediate recursive relations between what on some occasions he termed 'spatial patterns and social processes' and, on others, 'urban processes and social structure'. However, Forrest and Wissink (2017) are of the view that, under contemporary circumstances, such a conceptualization now appears hopelessly dated.

[13] A stark demonstration of this was recently published in the New York Times – www.nytimes.com/interactive/2016/12/26/upshot/duck-dynasty-vs-modern-family-television-maps.html. The article examines 50 different maps to demonstrate very strong associations between preferences for various TV shows and a range of cultural and political attitudes. Neighbourhoods in which the TV show *Duck Dynasty* was popular were amongst the most likely to have voted for Donald Trump.

[14] A number of competing commercial geodemographic classifications have been developed over the years: *Acorn*; *Cameo*; *Censation*; *Likewise*; *Locale*; *Mosaic* (on which we will focus, for reasons that will soon become apparent); $P^2$ *People and Places*; *PRIZM*; *Sonar*; and others. A number of non-commercial classifications have also been produced, the most commonly used of which is the OAC: www.opengeodemographics.com. Details are included in the Appendix to this book.

[15] The earliest reference to this is noted at the head of this chapter.

[16] It is worth noting how Claritas, the owner of *PRIZM*, a geodemographic classification widely used in the United States and discussed in the next chapter, asserts in its promotional literature that it is a 'fundamental sociological truism that "birds of a feather flock together"…[and that]…"You are where you live"' (quoted in Goss, 1995a: 134).

[17] The term 'fractal' is used to describe a pattern which results from a series of discrete and independent decisions which, without there being an overall plan, nevertheless result in the creation of a seemingly organic and self-organizing pattern.

[18] A simple computer simulation of this is available here: http://projects.indi catrix.org/segregation.js/. For a discussion about the broader influence of this model on analytic and political thinking about the urban form, see Fuller and Harwood (2016).

[19] Postcodes are structured hierarchically, supporting four levels of geographic unit: *Areas* (e.g. PL) of which there are currently 124; *Districts* (e.g. PL19) of which there are currently 3,114; *Sectors* (e.g. PL19 9) of which there are currently 12,381; and *Unit Postcodes* (e.g. PL19 9JL) of which there are currently approximately 1.8 million that are 'live'.

[20] For example, neighbourhood effects can operate through common exposure within a local area to the values and behaviours of groups of people very different from oneself, such as members of diverse immigrant communities, as well as people with a similar outlook. Peer-group effects only operate through exposure to local others whom one perceives to share a common set of values and aspirations. In a sense, therefore, peer-group effects can be considered as constituting a subset within the larger set of neighbourhood effects.

# 2

# THE PRECURSORS TO GEODEMOGRAPHIC CLASSIFICATION

## Charles Booth's *Descriptive Map of London Poverty*

The previous chapter highlighted how discussion of the city is often hampered by the absence of any consistent taxonomy for describing different types of residential neighbourhood. It introduced a concept which might be capable of addressing this deficiency, that of geodemographic classification. This chapter explores the key methodological and conceptual innovations that prefigured the emergence of such classifications in the 1970s. The most celebrated of these are the maps of London poverty created by Charles Booth in the final decades of the nineteenth century and the models of urban structure developed by the Chicago School of Sociology in the 1920s and 1930s.

From the 1940s onwards general theories of urban structure have benefitted from numerous advances in how data are collected, in how they are represented in map form, in how what have been termed 'natural areas' of the city have been identified and in techniques for revealing intelligible patterns implicit in complex data sets. Consideration of these advances paves the way for a discussion, in Chapter 3, of the practice of geodemographic classification itself and then, in Chapter 4, of the development of this form of classification from the mid-1970s until the present day.

Although, of course, he does not use that term to describe the product of his and his co-workers' considerable labours, Charles Booth's *Descriptive Map of London Poverty*,[1] first published in 1889, is commonly cited as the earliest research exercise to prefigure geodemographic classification (Burrows and Gane, 2006; Dalton and Thatcher, 2015; Harris et al., 2005: 30–7). Though 'descriptive' Booth's map was just one part of his broader lifetime mission to foster a deeper understanding of the origins of poverty in urban Britain. Booth constantly sought to gain political support for a more systematic approach to the elimination of poverty than was being provided by the sporadic and untargeted efforts of the charitable classes. That he was a member of the official committee in charge of the 1891 census is indicative of the value he placed on the systematic collection of data. His response was typical of the Benthamite approach to social problems advocated by a cadre of non-conformist, philanthropic business owners of whom Booth was an archetypical and active member. It was also to become a hallmark of the Fabian approach and it is no accident that Beatrice Webb was at one time a member of Booth's survey team.

In order to collect data for each household across London, Booth used the reports of school board visitors (SBVs). Their establishment was a consequence of the Compulsory Education Act of 1877, which attempted to track the children of the poor in order to ensure that they were receiving an adequate education. As Selvin and Benert (1985: 73) explain, this involved each SBV 'keeping a detailed record of every poor family in his [sic] district, noting such details as the occupation of the father, his income, the number, ages, and sexes of the children, the parents' habits of sobriety, the cleanliness of the household' and so on.

Selvin and Bernert go on to record that Booth preferred to interview SBVs rather than household members on the grounds that a direct interview would have been considered an 'invasion of privacy'.

In more common parlance SBVs were truant officers. As Bales (1992) points out, although Booth's analysis is sometimes considered to be one of the first social surveys, this is, in reality, a misrepresentation. As Bales (1992: 83) explains: 'It is actually a detailed and personalised collection of data from middle class informants…[the SBVs].' Each SBV was interviewed for 20–30 hours based upon the contents of their notes and record books.

After careful checking of their returns, Booth personally inspected each neighbourhood covered by the SBV and, as we might describe the process today, 'triangulated' his findings with data from the census, whose collection he also oversaw. It is significant that people living and working in an area were asked for their opinions about the *neighbourhood* they lived in, not their own *personal circumstances*.

These data were then used to place each household into one of eight mutually exclusive and exhaustive categories of 'class', rank ordered from A to H in ascending order of status. The eight were then grouped into five higher order categories (Pfautz, 1967),[2] again ordered by social status. These are summarized by Harris et al. (2005: 32) as follows:

| A | The lowest class – occasional labourers, loafers and semi-criminals |
|---|---|
| B | The very poor – casual labour, hand to mouth existence, chronic want |
| C and D | The poor – including alike those whose earnings are small, because of irregularity of employment, and those whose work, though regular, is ill paid |
| E and F | The regularly employed and fairly paid working class of all grades |
| G and H | Lower and upper middle class and all above this level |

Significantly for developments which were to follow, Booth recognized that the spatial distribution of these different classes of household was anything but random. Although the pattern was not entirely uniform, for the most part households in similar classes tended to be 'clustered' in close spatial proximity to each other. Booth was the first, but as we shall see in later chapters by no means the last, to use colour to indicate the locations where distinct categories of household lived. Following Harris et al. (2005: 32) these were as follows:

| Black | The lowest grade (corresponding to Class A) |
|---|---|
| Dark blue | Very poor (corresponding to Class B) |
| Light blue | Standard poverty (corresponding to Classes C and D) |
| Purple | Street mixed with poverty (usually C and D with E and F, but including Class B in many cases) |
| Pink | Working class comfort (corresponding to Classes E and F, but containing also a large proportion of the lower middle class of small tradesmen and Class G) |
| Red | Well-to-do; inhabited by middle class families who keep one or two servants |
| Yellow | Wealthy |

Although Booth was alert to the fact that there was a far-from-perfect correspondence between the distinct categories into which he classified households and the locations in which such classes of household clustered together in spatial propinquity,[3] knowing where in the city a household lived usually proved a reliable predictor of its social class or status (Pfautz, 1967: 193). For many commentators, it is this explicit association between geography and social class, 'the analysis of people by where they live' (Harris et al., 2005: 35), that makes Booth's work the foundational text in a tradition that, after many other developments, was to result in the development of geodemographic classifications.

# The Chicago model of urban structure

The next approach frequently cited as contributing to the emergence of geodemographic classification is that of the Chicago School of Sociology (Abbott, 1999; Bulmer, 1984; Platt, 1998; Smith, 1988). How far the work of Booth influenced its innovative approach to urban mapping (Burrows and Gane, 2006; Curry, 1998: 164; Harris et al., 2005: 37–42) is not as unambiguous as is often assumed. For example, the synopsis contained in the definitive four-volume collection of critical assessments of the Chicago School edited by Plummer (1997) contains a clear articulation of the widely held view that:

> Drawing upon the nineteenth century British social survey methods of Charles Booth and others, and influenced by continental European social theorists, the Chicago School moved in an ethnographic direction as they studied immigrant communities, neighbourhood zones and leisure life.

It might be supposed then that it was the conceptual and methodological work of Booth that influenced the construction of what Davis (1998: 363–4), following the lead of Smith (1988: 28), characterizes as '[t]he most famous diagram in social science'. This was the 'combination of half-moon and dartboard depicting the five concentric urban zones which appear during the rapid expansion of a modern American city such as Chicago'. This diagram, reproduced in Figure 2.1, was the work of Ernest Burgess.[4]

Davis (1998: 363), in his usual pithy style, summarizes the function of what Park et al. (1925: 55) call the 'chart', as follows:

> For those unfamiliar with the Chicago School of Sociology's canonical study of the 'North American city' (actually, 1920s Chicago generalized archetype), Burgess's dartboard represents the spatial hierarchy into which the struggle for the survival of the urban fittest supposedly sorts social class and their respective housing types. As imagined by academic social Darwinism, it portrays a 'human ecology' organized by...such 'ecological' determinants as income, land values, class and race...

If, as Parker (2015: 33–6) suggests, the primary contribution of Booth had been to *describe* the spatial distribution of social classes in the contemporary city, the contribution of Park, Burgess and McKenzie (1925) and their Chicago colleagues was to combine many of the conceptual ideas[5] circulating at that time so as to *explain* the processes which caused these patterns. But what was the relationship between the work of Booth and that of the Chicago School?

There is no doubt that many members of the Chicago School were acquainted with the work of Booth (Harris et al., 2005: 37; Pfautz, 1967: 5–6; Thrasher, 1927).

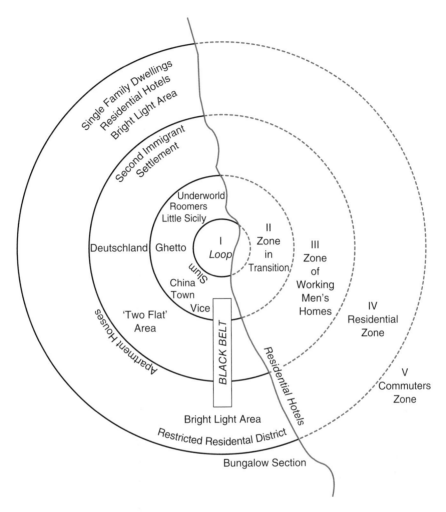

**Figure 2.1** Burgess's Chart of Urban Areas of Chicago, 1920
*Source:* Park *et al.* (1925: 55).

Indeed, the *Life and Labour of the People in London* is included in the annotated bibliography of Park et al. (1925: 188), where it is described as the 'most comprehensive study of London in existence' and is praised for 'its description of the natural areas of that city'. It is suggested that the descriptions of city life it offered 'should be cross-referenced with most of the categories suggested in this [*The City*] outline'. However, it was for Booth's capacity for *qualitative description* rather than his statistical or cartographic expertise for which they held him in highest esteem. Parker (2015: 40) makes this point when he quotes Park (1952 [1929]: 77) reflecting that it was not:

Booth's statistics, but his realistic descriptions of the actual life of the occupational classes – the conditions under which they lived and labored, their passions, pastimes, domestic tragedies, and life philosophies with which each class met the crises peculiar to it…which made the studies a memorable and permanent contribution to our knowledge of human nature and society…

What was distinctive about the Chicago School was that its members 'instituted a paradigmatic and enduring interest among urban sociologists and geographers in establishing general principles about the internal spatial and social structure of cities' (Harris et al., 2005: 37). Departing from the practice of topographers, who had traditionally recorded the features that were *specific* to particular places, the Chicago School sought from the outset to develop methods which could map *generic* components of the city's structure, particularly those represented in Burgess' 'half-moon and dartboard' diagrams. Though Chicago was the laboratory for their research, it was assumed that examples of such *functional* areas would be present in almost every North American city of any size.

These components formed elements of what proponents increasingly described as the overall 'ecology' of the city. First, it was conceived that struggles over land value resulted in broad concentric rings of different housing classes radiating out from the central business district (CBD), in the case of Chicago the area inside the 'loop' (the railway that encircled the city's centre). These rings included a zone of transition, a zone of working men's homes, a residential zone and a commuter zone.

Second, embedded within and occasionally cutting across these broad zones, can be deciphered what Featherstone (1974: 53)[6] identifies as three different categories describing a more granular set of 'natural areas' within Burgess' 'human ecology' framework. These comprised 'culturally homogeneous areas', 'areas in which the population members possess some common characteristic' and 'geographically well-defined areas of the city'. These came to form a number of distinctive types of ecological niche that one would expect to find in any city of Chicago's sort. Neighbourhoods of each type shared broadly similar economic, socio-demographic, cultural, physical and/or ethnic characteristics.

As can be seen from Figure 2.1, examples were 'China Town', 'Little Sicily', the 'Ghetto', 'Deutschland', a distinct 'Black Belt' traversing a number of concentric zones, a 'slum', an area of 'vice', a 'bright light area', an area of 'second immigrant settlement', 'single family dwellings', a 'two flat area', a 'bungalow section' and so on. Implicit in the model is the proposition that, as one moves further out from the urban core towards the suburbs and commuter zones, neighbourhoods become ever more 'middle class'.

Using this approach, Chicago was divided into 75 'local communities' or 'natural areas', 'which represented a particular combination of the 600 or so census tracts' (Featherstone, 1974: 55).[7] Although many of the labels applied to these natural areas of the city may appear pejorative to modern researchers,[8] the aspiration to uncover the fundamental socio-spatial structure of the city was both laudable and unambiguous. Harris et al. (2005: 39) summarize what is involved in this analytic process:

> The idea…provides one conceptual definition of what we mean when we talk of neighbourhood analysis – the analysis of areal…units within which we hope the characteristics of the population are sufficiently similar to each other and also sufficiently different from the population of other areas that we can reasonably describe each area, and its population, as being and belonging to a neighbourhood; as being a distinct geographical feature.

Most commentaries on the Chicago School stress how critical such analyses were in providing a *backdrop* to the ethnographic work which was undertaken throughout the city during the 1920s and 1930s. Quantitative and mapping[9] techniques might have provided the means by which the underlying socio-spatial structure of the city was revealed, but urban ethnography, the field interview and participant observation in particular, were the techniques which made it possible to describe the lived realities and the dynamic ebb and flow of these urban communities. In the work of Charles Booth, they found inspiration for the 'realistic descriptions of the actual life' of the city which affirmed for them the value of an ethnographic stance. His work was *not* the inspiration for advancing their quantitative and cartographic practices. How this was done was, in practice, highly pragmatic but was certainly *not* influenced by his approach.

Compared to the extensive literature that records the ethnographic practices of the Chicago School, relatively little has been written about their use of mapping and statistical techniques.[10] It was these techniques which underpinned the development of what in the 1920s and 1930s was to become known as Social Area Analysis and, from the 1940s onwards, factorial ecology (Singleton and Spielman, 2014: 559). As we shall see, both these developments were important precursors of contemporary forms of geodemographic analysis. So, we might ask, if the work of Charles Booth in London was not a significant influence on the *methods* deployed by the Chicago School to identify 'natural areas' of the city as part of a broader urban ecology, what were the methodological antecedents that it did draw upon?

# The cartographic imagination of the Chicago School

In the opinion of Featherstone (1974: 65–102) these antecedents are not easy to identify. Although it is possible to reconstruct a relatively coherent 'general statement of…the central principles of the Chicago sociologists' theory of human ecology' (Featherstone, 1974: 16), how this was *concretely operationalized* is more difficult to decipher. However, the use of *maps* and the *accumulation of mapped data* of various sorts over periods of time do appear to have been fundamental contributors, albeit not always explicitly articulated, to the identification of 'natural areas'.

A culture of mapping had long been established at Chicago and, from 1916, lectures on mapping were included in sociology courses. Featherstone (1974: 70) quotes Burgess (1964: 5) as remembering how: 'In every course I gave…there were one or two students who made maps…maps of any data we could find in the city that could be plotted'. Featherstone (1974: 70) also describes the plethora of styles of map used in the study of urban delinquency, *spot maps* – 'in which a dot on the map is used to represent the home address of a delinquent boy who had appeared in court during a particular period of time'; *rate maps* 'that show the ratio between the number of offenders and a total population of the same age and sex group'; and *zone maps* in which:

> five concentric zones are set up which mark off the city territory into zones of from one to two miles in width…[and]…zone rates…represent a combination of square-mile area rates [which] exhibit a regular gradient falling from the highest rate in Zone 1 to the lowest rate in Zone 5.

There is also strong evidence to suggest that, in addition to simple spot, rate and zone mapping of the city, Park, Burgess and their colleagues were strongly influenced by methodological innovations in rural sociology, particularly those involving the creation of *isotropic* maps (Mowrer, 1938). This is logical given that the purpose of an isotropic map is to identify the existence of natural communities and the boundaries which separate their spheres of influence. The most obvious sources of information for creating these maps were journey patterns. These made it possible to delineate the 'catchment' area of a commercial hub for each of the different kinds of service it provided to its residential or agricultural hinterland.

In this context it is understandable that both Featherstone (1974: 116–17) and, more recently, Porter and Howell (2012: 25–33) should make compelling assertions that one of the strongest influences on the early methodological development of the Chicago School was the work of the now little-known Charles Galpin's (1915) *The Social Anatomy of an Agricultural Community*.[11] Galpin[12] was the first to hold a professorship in rural sociology in the USA. Although there is no mention of his work in *The City* (Park et al., 1925), Porter and Howell (2012: 29) point to a later paper by Park (1929: 60–1)[13] in which he makes explicit reference to the impact on his thinking of Galpin's work. The paper opens as follows:

> Some thirteen years ago, Dr. C.J. Galpin published…a stimulating little paper called *The Social Anatomy of an Agricultural Community*… The purpose of the paper was eminently practical… Its method was to plot, on a series of maps, the actual relations – economic, political, and social – of the farm populations… These observations have given rise to the natural area… Since 1915, further studies of the kind that Galpin initiated have been made of urban communities…the same methods have been extended…to the city, its suburbs, and to the work regions in which the city dominates.

For Porter and Howell (2012: 29) the conclusions are clear:

> This direct attribution of Galpin's work as an influence on one of the most prominent schools of thought in American Sociology, the Chicago School, is rarely recognized…the importance and influence of Galpin's introduction of the isotropic map as a method for understanding social organization is largely understated in the history of the discipline and urban sociology… [However] it remains clear…that the innovative approaches developed by Galpin provided a framework from which some of the most influential work of the Chicago School was put forth.

Galpin had carried out a social survey in 12 villages, towns and cities in Walworth County in the state of Wisconsin. His respondents were all people with deep knowledge of the local community and of the social networks embedded in its trade patterns: teachers; bankers; the clergy; librarians; and so on. He also collected information on the boundaries of school districts, on patterns of newspaper circulation and a raft of other social and commercial activities. It was collected with the aim of understanding patterns of spatial connectivity within these different communities and more specifically the distances farmers would travel in order to undertake different types of activity, such as banking, purchasing supplies or having their hair cut. All these data were then 'mapped' with the aim of establishing the extent of the sphere of influence of each settlement for different forms of activity.

Galpin's maps showed how the shape and extent of various overlapping spatial 'communities' varied as between: 'trade'; 'banking'; 'newspapers'; 'milk'; 'church'; 'high school'; 'libraries'; and so on. These various representations of the sphere of influence of different communities were then overlaid in order to reveal the social anatomy of overlapping 'communities'. In this way, it was possible to ascertain the 'natural areas' within a rural environment and to define the boundaries of each one (Porter and Howell, 2012: 28).

Featherstone (1974: 118) also points to a further set of mapping techniques that may have been a 'further possible influence' on the empirical operationalization of human ecology within the Chicago School. These were associated with land economy. Their significance was perhaps most clearly articulated by Hurd (1903: 25) in his *Principles of City Land Values*. This study was an early

> attempt to establish…methods for predicting the distribution and change of urban land values. To this end he collected maps, local histories and information on mortgages and rentals for various cities in an attempt to work out principles of urban growth.

## Human ecology: a metaphor for understanding urban segregation

Taken together these mapping techniques, combined with the detailed ethnographic work for which the Chicago School is so renowned, provided much of the basis for a distinctive empirical human ecology approach to the study of the city which evolved during the years following the zenith of the Chicago School.[14] As Featherstone (1974: 118) expresses it:

> As well as the background influence of plant ecology, land economics, and rural sociology in providing a basis from which Park arrived at his first tentative formulation of human ecology, it is evident that further impetus for the subject's development resulted from the programme of research into the city of Chicago. It is of course very difficult to assess how far the empirical studies proved to be a stimulus to the development of human ecology or conversely how far human ecology provided a frame of reference which was conducive to the research which resulted in the empirical studies of the city. What seems to be of importance is that there is strong evidence of the parallel development and reciprocal interplay of human ecology and the empirical studies of the city, and it is possible to speculate that neither human ecology nor the empirical studies would have been developed to such an extent without some mutual interchange.

The origins of urban human ecology in the Chicago School and its subsequent institutionalization within so much sociological teaching, especially in America, is relevant to our review because it is claimed that contemporary forms of geo-demographic analysis have their 'origins in the work of human ecologists' (Singleton and Spielman, 2014: 559). Certainly it was the case that the Chicago School's influence on the development of human ecological approaches was immense. Featherstone (1974: 122) points to a bibliography provided by Quinn (1940), who lists a total of 347 books and articles on human ecology published during the period 1925–39, all of which in varying degrees claim to have been influenced by the theoretical and empirical work of the Chicago sociologists in the 1920s. However, compared to the voluminous output of the Chicago School,[15] the work of human ecologists claiming such an influence is now little read.

Although it is primarily in the work of the likes of Hawley (1950) that the human ecology approach is most clearly codified conceptually (Porter and Howell, 2012: 35–51) it is the work of researchers engaged in more technical aspects of empirical social research on socio-spatial structures within the human ecology tradition that forms the clearest link between the work of the Chicago School and the construction of the first geodemographic classifications in the 1970s. As already noted, Singleton and Spielman (2014: 559) point to the large body of technical work dealing with 'representations created by factorial ecology and social area analysis [that] attempted to reduce the complexities of human settlements into simplified typologies' in this regard.

Much of this work could not have been done were it not for the increased willingness of the US Census Bureau to publish statistics at the level of the census tract. For area blocks, containing on average 4,000 people, researchers could access an ever-increasing range of counts describing the economic, family and ethnic status of their residents. The work of Shevky (Shevky and Bell, 1955; Shevky and Williams, 1949) was important since it demonstrated how the seemingly infinite number of possible variables that could be created from these counts could be summarized into a limited and hence more manageable number of critical *dimensions* of urban differentiation. This process, by its very nature, also led to discussion about how accurately these new statistical metrics captured existing theoretical concepts such as urbanization, social rank and segregation, and about how best to conceptualize the additional dimensions whose existence the statistical metrics implied. The process of *data reduction* inherent in these methods hugely simplified the task of associating neighbourhoods with specific categories of 'social area'.

*Data reduction* is a data management process which is by no means specific to the study of urban structure. The principle underlying the process of data reduction is that the progressive expansion in the volume of data available for analysis sooner or later causes its analysis to become unmanageable unless the data set can be stripped of at least some of its redundancy. For the study of urban structure this requirement was caused by the ever-finer level of geography for which census statistics were made available.

Redundancy is particularly likely to arise when a theoretical concept is associated with two or more different census variables, as in, for example, the simultaneous availability of 'average number of rooms per dwelling' and the 'proportion of dwellings with five or more rooms'. Clearly the two variables are measuring more or less the same thing. Another example would be the use of census statistics of five different zones within the accommodation block of a single military base. The variables constructed for each of these zones are likely to have such similar values that, in this instance, no real benefit is achieved from accessing census statistics at such a fine level of geographic detail.

One objective of data reduction is to reduce a plethora of variables into a smaller and more manageable set of key dimensions. Another is to organize what would otherwise be an unmanageable and seemingly formless mass of statistical evidence about areas by grouping them into a typology of human settlements simple enough for a non-specialist to understand (Harris et al., 2005: 39; Singleton, 2016: 215; Singleton and Spielman, 2014: 559).

Social Area Analysis therefore gave way to the use of forms of statistical analysis now beginning to draw upon developments in statistical software and increases in computational power (Uprichard et al., 2008) – factor analysis in particular – which allowed measurements of a much larger number of demographic characteristics to inform the understanding of urban structure. The general term used to describe these techniques is 'multivariate' – since the techniques examine the interconnectedness of different variables. The term used to describe the practice of identifying key dimensions from within a set of variables became known as factorial ecology (Harris et al., 2005: 39).[16]

It is not the intention of this book to provide more than a passing description of the statistical techniques used in geodemographic classification. A more detailed account of these methods can be found in Harris et al. (2005: 147–84). However, some of what differentiates factorial ecology from more contemporary forms of geodemographic analysis does require a basic understanding of the features which distinguish one form of multivariate analysis from another.

In simple terms, and as we have indicated, post-Shevky work in human ecology developed into factorial ecology, which relied upon the statistical technique of *factor analysis*. The geodemographic classifications that emerged in the early 1970s relied on the application of a quite different form of data reduction, *cluster analysis*. The difference between these two techniques can be illustrated as follows. Imagine the typical contents of a database containing a number of different demographic attributes for a set of neighbourhoods within a large region. It is arranged as a two-dimensional grid in which each row represents data pertaining to a neighbourhood, and each column pertaining to a variable derived from responses to a different survey question, for example the proportion of residents aged over 65 or the proportion owning their own home. Cluster analysis groups together an otherwise unmanageable number of separate *neighbourhoods* (each a separate row) into a manageable number of *clusters*, each containing zones which are as similar to each other as possible with respect to their value on the different variables contained in the columns of the grid.

By contrast *factor analysis* groups the unmanageably large number of *variables* (each a separate column) into a smaller and more manageable number of underlying *factors* in such a way that these new dimensions are in as strong an alignment with their component variables as it is possible for them to be. Both techniques are examples of data reduction but one, factor analysis, reduces the number of variables into underlying *latent factors*, the other, cluster analysis, groups geographical areas together into *emergent clusters*.

# Geodemographic classification engages with the commercial world

*PRIZM* and *Acorn* are the names which were given to the first widely used systems of geodemographic classifications, *PRIZM* in the United States, *Acorn* in the UK. Both classifications applied cluster analysis to statistics for local areas published by the US and UK census agencies. Although both classifications were built using data for administrative areas, they both owed their success to their ability to link their results to customer or citizen records using postal geography as the bridge. Notwithstanding their similarities, the two systems were built quite independently and were brought to market almost simultaneously.

The originator of the *PRIZM* system in the United States was Jonathan Robbin,[17] a graduate in sociology, demography and statistics, who studied at Harvard, Columbia and New York universities in the 1950s. Whilst a member of the faculty of Sociology at New York University, Robbin developed one of the earliest computer packages for large-scale cluster analysis (Goss, 1995a: 133; Weiss, 2000: 24). In 1961 he left the academy to apply his sociological and statistical expertise to social and business problems. In 1971 the company he founded, Claritas,[18] was commissioned by the US Department of Housing and Urban Development to develop a system for targeting housing grants to cities with a history of rioting (Weiss, 2000: 142). This project resulted in the construction of what subsequently became branded as *PRIZM* – the *Potential Rating Index for ZIP Markets* – a classification using census tract statistics. Developed from 1974, and launched on the commercial market in 1978, it linked census to postal geographies in such a way as to associate each of the 36,000 US five-digit zip codes with one of 40 mutually exclusive and exhaustive 'lifestyle clusters'.

According to the critical cartographer Mark Monmonier (2002: 146) there were three features of *PRIZM* that were essential to its success. First, Robbin transformed the geography of the data; he saw the value of converting census statistics from the 'tracts' used to manage the collection of the census responses into ZIP codes (which function in much the same way as postcodes in the UK). Not only was this a level of geography that people understood, it also constituted a field on the address element of each customer record. This enabled commercial users to evaluate each cluster not just in terms of the census variables used to build it, but also in terms of the numbers and purchasing habits of customers who lived in it.

Second, and crucially, he combined well-worn techniques of factor analysis, so beloved of the factorial ecologists, with the use of cluster analysis: 'To make the results useable, he reduced the hundreds of census variables…to a mere thirty-four principal factors…[a]fter scoring every ZIP on each of the thirty-four factors, a computer partitioned ZIP codes into forty clusters' (Monmonier, 2002: 146).

Third, by persuading market research companies to add a *PRIZM* code to each record on their respondent databases, he made it possible to compare *PRIZM* categories according to survey, consumer and media data as well as customer data. This linkage with behavioural and lifestyle databases provided users with far more comprehensive and compelling characterizations of each *PRIZM* cluster than would otherwise have been possible. Even clients who had no databases from which they could examine the purchasing behaviour of previous customers could now use survey databases to infer from the cluster of any ZIP code which of their products to promote to which customers, which proposition local residents would be most likely to respond to, and what language and imagery would be most effective in persuading them to do so. What's more, they could use market research survey data to establish which *PRIZM* clusters their competitors were most successful in selling to.

Table 2.1 lists the original 40 clusters, the thumbnail descriptions that were developed for each and, based on 1987 census block groups, an estimate of the proportion of US households in each cluster.[19] It is a summary version developed from data presented in Weiss (1988: 45; 2000: 12–13). The clusters are ranked in descending order of affluence, using a weighted average of median incomes, median house values and the percentage of the population who are college graduates.

In Chapters 4 and 5 we will encounter similar classifications – albeit often far more nuanced – that have been developed over time and for a number of different national markets. The importance of the *PRIZM* classification is that it represents the very first instance of Social Area Analysis being promoted as a tool for business and marketing decision-making.

Whilst Robbin was promoting *PRIZM* in the USA, Richard Webber was applying virtually identical methods in a not dissimilar context. After graduating in economics at Cambridge he moved to Liverpool to study transport planning. Required to learn to code and program, he there developed a cluster analysis software program to classify parliamentary constituencies. After joining the Centre for Environmental Studies (CES)[20] in London, in 1973 he was commissioned by Liverpool City Council to provide a basis for identifying the parts of the city for which various programmes to combat urban deprivation would be most appropriate.

**Table 2.1** *PRIZM* Neighbourhood Types: the Original 40 Clusters

| Cluster name | 'Thumbnail' description | Median income $ k | Median home values $ k | College graduates % | US households % |
|---|---|---|---|---|---|
| *Blue Blood Estates* | America's wealthiest neighbourhoods | 70.4 | 200 | 50.7 | 1.1 |
| *Money & Brains* | Posh big-city enclaves of townhouses, condos and apartments | 45.8 | 150.8 | 45.5 | 0.9 |
| *Furs & Station Wagons* | New money in metropolitan bedroom suburbs | 50.1 | 132.8 | 38.1 | 3.2 |
| *Urban Gold Coast* | Upscale urban high-rise districts | 36.9 | 200 | 50.5 | 0.5 |
| *Pools & Patios* | Older, upper-middle-class, suburban communities | 35.9 | 99.8 | 28.2 | 3.4 |
| *Two More Rungs* | Comfortable multi-ethnic suburbs | 31.3 | 117.1 | 28.3 | 0.7 |
| *Young Influentials* | Yuppie, fringe-city condo and apartment development | 30.4 | 106.4 | 36.0 | 2.9 |
| *Young Suburbia* | Child-rearing, outlying suburbs | 38.6 | 93.3 | 23.8 | 5.3 |
| *God's Country* | Upscale frontier boomtowns | 36.8 | 99.5 | 25.8 | 2.7 |
| *Blue-Chip Blues* | The wealthiest blue-collar suburbs | 32.3 | 72.6 | 13.1 | 6.0 |
| *Bohemian Mix* | Inner-city bohemian enclaves à la Greenwich Village | 22 | 110.7 | 38.8 | 1.1 |
| *Levittown, USA* | Aging, post-World War II tract sub-divisions | 28.8 | 70.8 | 15.7 | 3.1 |
| *Gray Power* | Upper-middle-class retirement communities | 25.3 | 83.4 | 18.3 | 2.9 |
| *Black Enterprise* | Predominately black, middle- and upper-middle-class neighbourhoods | 33.2 | 68.8 | 16.0 | 0.8 |

*(Continued)*

**Table 2.1** *PRIZM* Neighbourhood Types: the Original 40 Clusters

| Cluster name | 'Thumbnail' description | Median income $ k | Median home values $ k | College graduates % | US households % |
|---|---|---|---|---|---|
| *New Beginnings* | Fringe-city areas of singles complexes, garden apartments and bungalows | 24.8 | 75.4 | 19.3 | 4.3 |
| *Blue-Collar Nursery* | Middle-class, child-rearing towns | 30.1 | 67.3 | 10.2 | 2.2 |
| *New Homesteaders* | Ex-urban boomtowns of young mid-scale families | 26 | 67.3 | 15.9 | 4.2 |
| *New Melting Pot* | New immigrant neighbourhoods, primarily in the nation's port cities | 22.2 | 113.7 | 19.1 | 0.9 |
| *Towns & Gowns* | America's college towns | 17.9 | 60.9 | 27.5 | 1.2 |
| *Rank & File* | Older, blue-collar, industrial suburbs | 26.3 | 59.4 | 9.2 | 1.4 |
| *Middle America* | Mid-scale, mid-size towns | 24.4 | 55.7 | 10.7 | 3.2 |
| *Old Yankee Rows* | Working-class rowhouse districts | 24.8 | 76.5 | 11.0 | 1.6 |
| *Coalburg & Corntown* | Small towns based on light industry and farming | 24 | 51.7 | 10.4 | 2.0 |
| *Shotguns and Pickups* | Crossroad villages serving the nation's lumber and breadbasket needs | 24.3 | 53.3 | 9.1 | 1.9 |
| *Golden Ponds* | Rustic cottage communities located near the coasts, mountains or lakes | 20.2 | 51.6 | 12.8 | 5.2 |
| *Agri-Business* | Small towns surrounded by large-scale farms and ranches | 21.4 | 49.1 | 11.5 | 2.1 |
| *Emergent Minorities* | Predominately black, working class, city neighbourhoods | 22.1 | 45.2 | 10.7 | 1.7 |
| *Single City Blues* | Downscale, urban, singles districts | 18 | 62.4 | 18.6 | 3.3 |

Table 2.1 *(Continued)*

| Cluster name | 'Thumbnail' description | Median income $k | Median home values $k | College graduates % | US households % |
|---|---|---|---|---|---|
| Mines & Mills | Struggling steel towns and mining villages | 21.6 | 46.4 | 8.7 | 2.8 |
| Back-Country Folks | Remote, downscale, farm towns | 19.7 | 41.1 | 8.1 | 3.4 |
| Norma Rae-Ville | Lower-middle-class mill towns and industrial suburbs | 18.6 | 36.6 | 9.6 | 2.3 |
| Smalltown Downtown | Inner-city districts of small industrial cities | 17.3 | 42.3 | 10.0 | 2.5 |
| Grain Belt | The nation's most sparsely populated rural communities | 21.7 | 45.9 | 8.4 | 1.3 |
| Heavy Industry | Lower-working-class districts in nation's older industrial cities | 18.4 | 39.6 | 6.5 | 2.8 |
| Share Croppers | Primarily southern hamlets devoted to farming and light industry | 16.9 | 34 | 7.1 | 4.0 |
| Downtown Dixie Style | Aging, predominately black neighbourhoods, typically in southern cities | 15.3 | 35.4 | 10.7 | 3.4 |
| Hispanic Mix | America's Hispanic barrios | 16.3 | 49.6 | 6.8 | 1.9 |
| Tobacco Roads | Predominately black farm communities throughout the South | 13.3 | 27.2 | 7.3 | 1.2 |
| Hard Scrabble | The nation's poorest rural settlements | 12.9 | 27.7 | 6.5 | 1.5 |
| Public Assistance | America's inner-city ghettos | 10.9 | 28.4 | 6.3 | 3.1 |
| Total | | | | | 100.0 |
| National Median | | 24.3 | 64.2 | 16.2 | – |

This project resulted in further refinements of his cluster analysis software, including the ability to evaluate clusters on the basis of records containing the home locations of the Council's various service departments' clients (Webber, 1975).[21] This work contained a number of significant innovations – both methodological and conceptual – that established the initial conditions for the development of the first geodemographic classifications to cover the entire UK at small area level (Webber and Craig, 1976; 1978) – the 'Classification of Residential Neighbourhoods' (CRN).

Like Robbin in the USA, Webber in due course forsook the world of academia and urban policy to apply his algorithms to business applications. At the information systems company CACI he built and commercialized *Acorn*, a system that became increasingly accepted by both public and private sector organizations as a means of profiling customers on the basis of their postcodes. In 1985 he left CACI to join CCN Systems (CCN),[22] where he developed a rival geodemographic classification, Mosaic, the subject of Chapter 4.

## Notes

[1] The 1898–9 revised version of which is available online in a searchable format at http://booth.lse.ac.uk. This is probably a more useful source than the definitive 17-volume third edition of his *Life and Labour of the People in London* (Booth, 1902–3). Also worth tracking down is the excellent BBC2 TV series *The Secret History of Our Streets*, first broadcast in 2012, which compares the contemporary circumstances of a number of streets in London – Deptford High Street, Camberwell Grove, Caledonian Road, Portland Road, Reverdy Road and Arnold Circus – with their classification by Booth.

[2] However, as Parker (2015: 33) points out, although 'Booth's social categories have been considered a forerunner of modern methods of sociological analysis' they were, in fact, 'based on the classification used in the 1891 census'. As we have already noted, Booth was also a member of the official committee for that census charged with making recommendations for its improvement (Harris et al., 2005: 35).

[3] Some neighbourhoods or streets, those colour-coded purple and pink especially, were of a more socially mixed character but even some with an otherwise more uniform class character could in Booth's terminology contain a 'sprinkling' of households from other classes.

[4] There are various versions of this famous diagram available – the published version can be found in Park et al. (1925: 55) and this can be found reproduced in Harris et al. (2005: 38), Parker (2015: 43) and many other places. Davis (1998: 364) produces a more stylized version in order to compare and contrast it with his radically

updated version – the ecology of fear – inspired by the work of William Gibson (Davis, 1998: 365); see the discussion in Burrows (1997) based upon an earlier pamphlet published by Davis in 1992 – *Beyond Blade Runner* – an updated version of which is published as chapter 7 of Davis (1998). However, perhaps one of the most interesting versions is the undated hand-drawn version found in the papers of Ernest Burgess, which is believed to be the earliest version of the diagram. It was displayed, alongside many other maps and diagrams, as part of the *Mapping the Young Metropolis: The Chicago School of Sociology, 1915–1940* exhibition held between 22 June and 11 September 2015 at the University of Chicago Library. The image can be found at: http://goo.gl/1IAdmC.

[5] As Wyly (2015: 2520–6) points out in his discussion of what he terms the 'urbanisation of evolutionary consciousness', these conceptual ideas were a complex amalgam of Darwinism refracted through emerging neoclassical economic thinking, eugenics, innovations in multivariate statistics and much else besides.

[6] This unpublished Durham University MA thesis, accessible online at http://etheses.dur.ac.uk/10049/, is one of the first outputs produced by our friend and colleague Mike Featherstone, the founding editor of the journal *Theory, Culture & Society*. Although Martin Bulmer supervised the thesis he does not cite it in his own account of the Chicago School (Bulmer, 1984) produced a decade later, although Featherstone is thanked in the acknowledgements. It provides a compelling and incredibly detailed account of the relationship between theories of human ecology and the rise of empirical sociological research methods in Chicago, and has been drawn upon extensively here.

[7] Until this time such tracts were used only for the *collection* of statistics and not, as would happen later, for their publication.

[8] Although, as we have already hinted in Chapter 1, the labelling of contemporary geodemographic types is sometime subject to similar accusations.

[9] It is important to remember however that, prior to the development of contemporary technologies, the production and dissemination of maps was very much less common than it is now. For instance, newspapers and even books and academic articles would be very hard pressed to print maps of a usable quality.

[10] Although see the coverage given in Bulmer (1984: 151–89).

[11] A shortened version of this important text can be found as part of Chapter XVII, pp. 490–7, in an archived set of readings in rural sociology, originally collated and edited by John Phelan from the Massachusetts Agricultural College, Amherst, Massachusetts, and published in 1920 by Macmillan: http://goo.gl/dJU0Qz.

[12] For more on the background and thoughts of this now rarely recognized figure in the history of sociology, see Galpin (1937).

[13] Featherstone (1974: 116) locates an earlier, but less gushing, source. He quotes Park and Burgess (1921: 212) referring to Galpin (1915) as 'an important study'. However, they continue – making their commitments to 'ecological' approaches to the city very clear – 'With due regard of these auspicious beginnings, it must be confessed that there is no volume upon human communities comparable with the several works on plant and animal communities'.

[14] It is worth noting – and it is a theme to which we will return in relation to contemporary technological developments – that while in the approach of Booth it is the aggregate characteristics of the resident population that comes to define particular localities, within the Chicago School approach it is often the *mobility of populations* and the boundary limits of their movements, some self-defining and others set by institutions, that come to define particular 'natural areas'.

[15] Featherstone (1974: 5) notes that there were some 44 books and monographs published in the years 1923–9 alone.

[16] Abler et al. (1971), Berry and Kasarda (1977), Rees (1972) and Timms (1971) all provide useful overviews of the huge amount of work produced in this area of investigation.

[17] Full details of his career can be found at: www.ricercar.com.

[18] Which was in due course acquired by AC Nielson.

[19] *PRIZM* continues to be produced and updated; its most recent manifestation can be found here: www.claritas.com.

[20] The Centre for Environmental Studies was an environmental think-tank established in 1967 by the Wilson Labour government. It was an independent charitable trust set up for the purpose of carrying out research in the planning and design of the physical environment. It began with a large Ford Foundation award and grants from the British government.

[21] Although copies of this report are available in some university libraries it is not widely accessible. Readers wishing to consult a scanned copy should email a request to rogerjburrows@gmail.com.

[22] It changed its name to Experian in 1996. For a detailed history of the company, see: www.experianplc.com/about-experian/history.aspx.

# 3

# THE EMERGENCE OF CONTEMPORARY GEODEMOGRAPHICS

## The post-war discovery of inner city deprivation

The emergence of contemporary geodemographics owes much to the techniques and thinking described in Chapter 2. However, it is unlikely that it would have developed in the form it did were it not for various analytical advances pioneered during what was known as the Liverpool Inner Area Study (what, in short form, we refer to as the Liverpool study). This chapter describes how, in the early 1970s, the city's planners decided to adopt a form of Social Area Analysis as a framework by which to address the problems of poverty and inequality which were so extensive in their city at that time.[1] To understand the reason for the funding of this study and the methods that it used, it may be useful first to consider some of the developments in town planning practice that occurred during the years immediately following World War II.

When Beveridge drew up his blueprint for Britain's post-war welfare state, poverty was to be relieved by a series of grants to citizens rendered financially vulnerable through events and conditions such as unemployment, retirement, disability and maternity.[2] This strategy was a radical departure from that which had been used to tackle poverty during the 1930s. Then, following the collapse of heavy industry, it was through regional policy that the state sought to ameliorate the worst manifestations of social inequality. The benefit of these interventions – the construction of new industrial estates and improvements to the transportation network – were felt throughout local communities.

Beneficiaries might live disproportionately in small towns such as Wrexham or Jarrow which had been reliant on a single industry but did include members of all social classes and all income groups.

It was not the intention of these policies to address forms of disadvantage which occurred at a neighbourhood level. Nor did they. Indeed, among the neighbourhoods on which they had the least impact were the very inner suburbs of large provincial cities which were to become the prime focus of neighbourhood-based policies in the 1960s.

In the opinion of Savage (2010) the organizational controls that were developed in order to fight World War II contributed to the emergence of a new cadre of technocratic managers with a greater willingness and confidence to undertake significant physical and social interventions in the public interest. If the creation of the National Health Service and the nationalization of the economy's 'commanding heights' were the prime achievements of this group, so too was a programme that resulted in a major physical reconstruction of the nation's housing stock. In addition to New Town Development Corporations, new 'planned' residential neighbourhoods were conceived on the outskirts of every large provincial city to replace the legacy of outworn, insanitary and over-crowded accommodation inherited from the pre-war period.

In these cities, the clearest manifestation of this policy was the practice of what was described as 'slum clearance'. The systematic demolition of terraced housing dating from the Victorian era and the 'decanting' of their residents to newly built 'council estates' on the urban periphery has had a lasting effect on the physical and social structure of Britain. Its legacy is discussed in Chapter 7.

However, intrusive schemes such as the proposed redevelopment of Covent Garden (Christie, 1974)[3] and the elevated motorways that were to form part of the London Motorway Box attracted increasingly well-organized opposition. Meanwhile social workers and community development officers made their planning colleagues aware of the increasing levels of estrangement felt by residents decanted to distant council estates, notwithstanding the improvement of their household amenities. As the deleterious impact of housing policy on community structure became more apparent during the 1960s, the dirigiste ethos of the planning profession found itself subjected to serious challenge.

In a progressively less deferential era, voluntary organizations and a rash of newly formed local amenity associations mounted increasingly assertive campaigns against municipal practices. They did so directly, bypassing the elected representatives who until then it was assumed would be the conduits for the disaffections of local residents. Particular sources of agitation were the disruption caused by the construction of new arterial roads (Barker and Aldous, 2009) and the unanticipated and unintended impact of re-housing schemes. Both contributed to the decline of what later became referred to as 'Social Capital'.

It was not just residents in the newly built estates, with their shallow sense of belonging to a local community, who suffered from the disruption of traditional kinship and social networks.[4] The falling population of inner city neighbourhoods discouraged meaningful investment whether in public or in private infrastructure. The traditional focal points for these communities appeared to be entering a period of terminal decline.

The wider impact on housing policy, on planning and on planning education was described by David Eversley (1973: 162) – at the time, the Chief Planner (Strategy) for the Greater London Council – in the following words:

> The needs of the people on whose behalf planning and building took place, became more explicitly the concern of the planning profession and most syllabuses of planning schools in the 1960s began to give increasing attention to something one can call, charitably, 'social aspects of development plans'... There was still no recognition at all that planning (and design) were an integral part of the whole process of government, that good or bad plans would materially alter the distribution of wealth and real incomes, make or mar community life, and, in short, become the most important expression of a prevailing social ethic ruling the relationship between government and people.

Immediately after 1945 the public had trusted planners to arbitrate between competing interests and to pay due regard to the wider public interest, not just that of sectional groups. By the time Eversley was writing in 1973 the force of popular campaigning and the arguments advanced in evidence from sociological studies resulted in planners and planning consultants investing greater resources in the mathematical simulation of alternative options. This helped them to demonstrate that the recommendations they made were at least rational and at best optimal.

Discussing the results of the large number of sociological studies that filled the bookshelves of his office, Eversley (1973: 240) comments not just on the difficulty of reconciling the competing findings of different social-scientific studies but also in establishing the contexts in which particular findings are relevant and the locations to which particular recommendations are appropriate. 'Each honest author warns' he notes, 'that this is not exportable, and though we have found this outcome here in Bethnal Green, or that in Shotts, it does not follow that if you did the same things again, the same consequences would follow'. We return to some of the implications of this observation in the final chapters of the book.

The preceding pages help to explain the circumstances which led to a realization that poverty and disadvantage were not just the result of personal circumstances but of neighbourhood disadvantages too. This recognition was the reasoning behind the decision of the Labour government led by Harold Wilson to commission a major research study into how best to revitalize what, in the language of that time, were referred to as 'inner city areas'. The study was to be undertaken in conjunction with three local authorities, Birmingham, Lambeth and Liverpool. Teams of researchers and local planners would identify programmes which would most effectively combat residents' sense of being caught up in a negative spiral of population decline and disinvestment.

The study provided sufficient funding to set up a series of pilot projects, the purpose of which was to assess the effectiveness of different forms of investment in community facilities. There was no explicit requirement to restrict these programmes to the inner city. But it would have been difficult for this not to have been the outcome given the statistical and on-the-ground evidence gathering that preceded the selection of the pilot projects.

## Liverpool adopts a schema based on Social Area Analysis

A distinctive feature of the Liverpool study was the decision by the city's planning department to commission CES to build a taxonomy of the city's residential neighbourhoods. The intention behind this decision was to provide a rational basis for taking decisions concerning the relative level of disadvantage experienced by different types of social area within the city.[5] More critically it would help planners to identify the social areas in which particular new programmes would have greatest impact.

The taxonomy used cluster analysis to group together census enumerations districts (EDs) which were broadly similar across a wide range of demographic indicators. These indicators were selected from the *Small Area Statistics* tables published by the (then) Office of Population Censuses and Surveys (OPCS). They were derived from responses from the 1971 census. Contrary to received wisdom and subsequent practice it was thought that better results would be produced if they were not subjected to factor analysis.

Prior to 1975 it was the practice of the city planning department to rank neighbourhoods on the basis of results of what, in the technocratic language of the day, was described as the 'Liverpool Social Malaise Study'. The intention of that study was to provide an objective method of directing funds for neighbourhood development to what were considered the 'worst' areas of the city. The study followed the practice of the factorial ecologists by examining the statistical relationship between the various measures of deprivation. Using these relationships, it ranked each area of the city according to the strength of its claim for priority area resources. The method was to prefigure the creation of the Index of Multiple Deprivation (IMD), discussed in Chapter 1, the criterion which is the technique now most commonly used by public servants when arbitrating on the competing claims of different neighbourhoods for special funding.

The city planners laboured under a number of limitations of this approach. If there was any correspondence between 'natural areas', as would have been understood by the Chicago sociologists, and the boundaries of electoral wards, the units of geography used by the Social Malaise Study to measure disadvantage, this would be by accident rather than by design. These units were, in any case, much larger than Liverpool's 'natural areas' and far from homogenous in terms of either character or social need.

For the purpose of the Liverpool study, a very practical problem was that an ordinal ranking necessarily resulted in the same small number of wards being put forward as candidates for virtually every single area-based programme. This posed a serious political problem in a city where poverty was endemic across a very high proportion of its local communities. It also negated an implicit assumption of the overall research project, that *different communities* suffered *different manifestations of disadvantage* for which *different prescriptions* were appropriate. It was decided that rather than use a statistical proxy for the overall level of each area's disadvantage it would be more useful to make a *qualitative differentiation*, in the tradition of the Chicago School, which would distinguish neighbourhoods according to their type of deprivation, not just their level, and which would throw light on the structures and processes that contributed to their particular disadvantages.

## The classification of Liverpool neighbourhoods

The decision by OPCS to publish 'Small Area Statistics' was a response to two emerging trends. One was the advances in the volume of census statistics that it had become possible for computer systems to store and analyse. The other was the ease with which statistical analysis techniques could manipulate geographically referenced data.

The clustering of Liverpool's census enumeration districts (EDs)[6] resulted in the identification of 25 recognizably different types of neighbourhood. These were arranged within a hierarchical framework with five higher order groupings, as shown in Table 3.1.

A key development which contributed to the success of the project was the decision by the city planning department to build a gazetteer which associated the home addresses of users of the city's various public services with the census EDs in which they lived. By measuring how many of the clients of the city's different service departments lived in each of the 25 types of *social area*, the project team could now evaluate the clusters generated by the clustering algorithm in terms of residents' use of specific public services not just in respect of

**Table 3.1** The Five Principal Geodemographic Groups Identified by the Liverpool Social Area Analysis Study

| Cluster name | % population | Description |
| --- | --- | --- |
| Areas of High Status | 22 | A high status owner-occupied area with stable families |
| Rooming House Areas | 9 | An area of subdivided housing with young people and furnished privately rented accommodation in small units |
| Inner City Council Estates | 9 | Flats in dockside areas replacing former slums |
| Outer Council Estates | 33 | Mostly low rise estates on what previously had been green-field sites |
| Areas of Older Terraces | 27 | An area of Victorian terraced housing, mostly privately rented unfurnished and much of it lacking an inside toilet |

**Table 3.2** Variations in Per Capita Demand for Services Provided by Liverpool City Council by the Five Principal Types of Neighbourhood Identified by the Liverpool Social Area Analysis Study

| Measure | Areas of High Status | Rooming House Areas | Inner City Council Estates | Outer Council Estates | Areas of Older Terraces |
|---|---|---|---|---|---|
| Infant mortality | 75 | 157 | 158 | 69 | 118 |
| Illegitimacy | 35 | 247 | 185 | 83 | 96 |
| Infectious diseases | 68 | 167 | 143 | 82 | 110 |
| Children in short-term care | 22 | 199 | 154 | 113 | 95 |
| Children in long-term care | 15 | 272 | 212 | 74 | 104 |
| Delinquency | 21 | 91 | 397 | 93 | 75 |
| Supervision orders | 22 | 108 | 313 | 111 | 75 |
| Disinfestation | 52 | 82 | 265 | 84 | 104 |
| Possession orders | 27 | 124 | 189 | 136 | 77 |

*Note:* Rates are normalized so that a value of 100 constitutes the average for the city.

the census variables used to build the classification. It was this information that provided the researchers with an understanding of the different manifestations of disadvantage that were experienced by residents in the different clusters. It is not difficult to imagine how statistics of the type shown in Table 3.2 provided a sound basis for deciding the forms of community provision that should be prioritized in different parts of the city.

Not surprisingly it showed that services associated with the poor physical condition of housing and with an outworn environment were the most pressing priorities in the clusters characterized by 'Older Terraces'. The problems most likely to be experienced by residents in the 'Rooming House'[7] clusters were rooted in weak community organization, unstable household relationships, substance abuse and what the dominant discourses of the time considered a social problem, single parenthood (Bradshaw and Miller, 1991).

The 'Inner City Council Estates' were characterized by low wages, a disproportionate reliance on benefits and households possessing insufficient savings to tide them over in times of need. 'Peripheral Council Estates' were characterized by large child populations, inadequate leisure facilitiess for young adults and by neighbours whose help could not always be relied upon in time of need. Residents in 'Middle Class Owner Occupiers' made relatively few demands on council services other than grants for their children to attend university.[8]

The manner in which service delivery data were organized in the Liverpool study differed from conventional practice in one key respect. Clearly the ED[9] is too granular a unit to analyse service data. With an average of 151 households, EDs have too few residents using particular services for statistics at that level to be used with any degree of statistical confidence. The standard response to this problem is to group neighbourhoods for which data exist into larger geographical pieces on the basis of their *proximity*. In Liverpool, these larger pieces would be electoral wards.

It was agreed that a more efficient alternative would be to group areas on the basis of their *similarity*. This involved consolidating statistics for each census ED with those for other similar EDs rather than with those which were merely geographically contiguous. Though the number of clusters in the Liverpool study was smaller than the number of electoral wards in the city, the clusters were far more different from each other in terms of level of service demand. Summarizing information on demographic or service demand for geographical units on the basis of *similarity* proved statistically far more 'efficient' than the previous practice of grouping EDs on the basis of *proximity*. Much less of the variance in the original data was lost.

This conceptual difference, grouping neighbourhoods on the basis of similarity rather than proximity, though seeming simple at the time and a practice which has subsequently found many more adherents in business, marketing and local administration, has achieved less traction in academia and central government. People continue to find it difficult to break out from the cultural habit of drawing bounded lines around units of administrative geography and referring to them as 'areas' or 'zones'.

It would be misleading to suggest that the city planners were surprised by the sharpness of the patterns that emerged from the cluster analysis. However, the quantitative evidence generated by the taxonomy did help them to justify the locations in the city where they had proposed that particular pilot projects should be trialled. Likewise, at a more detailed level, the pattern of the clusters suggested the existence of many other relationships which until then had gone unnoticed. For example, whilst there are copious references in academic literature to the social stratification of neighbourhoods dominated by owner occupation (Burrows, 2003; Forrest et al., 1990) and, to a lesser extent, private renting (Kemp, 2015; Rugg and Rhodes, 2008), academics, public servants and marketers often overlook the degree of social stratification that occurs within the social housing sector (Burrows, 1999; Watt, 2009). In Liverpool at this time there was clear evidence of 'better' tenants being rewarded with transfers to 'better' estates, while accommodation in estates that had the poorest reputations was offered to those in most urgent need. In future years, these differences were to be exacerbated as residents in the 'better' estates increasingly opted to take advantage of 'right-to-buy' legislation (Dunn et al., 1987).

Organized in the way the clustering algorithm presented it, the data showed big variations in the average size of a typical family in different types of neighbourhood. On average, tenants of Liverpool's social housing tended to have many more children than did private tenants or owner occupiers in neighbourhoods of older terraced housing. It became evident that the practice of using the number of rooms per household member as one of the criteria for allocating public housing led indirectly to the tendency of council estates to contain disproportionately large child populations. As we shall see in Chapter 7 this appeared to result in higher levels of vandalism and in what later became referred to as anti-social behaviour.

By giving preferential access to large families, the council's housing allocation system inadvertently resulted in a much larger proportion of Liverpool's Roman Catholic population living in council estates than in neighbourhoods of equivalent status in the private sector. A Catholic family, at that time, tended to contain more children than a Protestant one. By the 1960s political divisions had started to mirror this sectarian divide. Wards dominated by social housing returned Labour candidates whilst wards of older terraced housing proved the most fertile areas for candidates of the (protestant) Orange Party, still active in Liverpool as late as the 1970s, and subsequently of the Liberals and later Liberal Democrats.

A convention was adopted whereby red was used to denote the clusters of social housing, yellow the clusters of older terraces and blue the clusters of suburban high status. The choice of these colours was by no means accidental. They matched the political parties that these neighbourhoods returned in Council elections, they corresponded to the colours of the football clubs residents supported and, according to data from the Driver and Vehicle Licensing Agency, they matched the colours of the cars that residents in these neighbourhoods were most likely to drive.[10]

The results of the cluster analysis provided one especially clear demonstration of the 'neighbourhood effects' we discussed in the opening chapter; of how location affected the life-chances of people who in other respects would appear to be similar. The 1971 census revealed that, across Liverpool as a whole, unemployment rates varied very considerably by social class.[11] Adults belonging to the lowest occupational stratum, the 'unskilled', experienced an unemployment rate of 18.4 per cent compared with a rate of only 2.8 per cent amongst the highest occupational stratum, 'professional occupations'. But these city-wide averages concealed considerable variations between different types of social area. In the inner city council estates, an unskilled worker was at a far greater risk of unemployment, 27.6 per cent, than his or her counterpart in a leafy suburb, where the corresponding rate was just 6.1 per cent.

Why should such stark differences exist? Should we infer that an unskilled worker in an inner city council estate is more at risk of unemployment because he or she faces greater competition for a local unskilled job? Or is it that the category 'unskilled worker' comprises a group that is less homogeneous than it is assumed to be, the unskilled worker living in a leafy suburb maybe being a very different type of person than one living in an inner city council estate? Both explanations are almost certainly valid. This example supported the contention that the place where a person lives has an incremental effect on their life chances which is quite independent of any category of personal characteristics. Examples such as this gave strong theoretical justification for the decision to combat poverty on a neighbourhood basis.

Most taxonomies are hierarchical. In other words, they first divide a population into two or more categories on the basis of one or more attributes. They then sub-divide these initial categories in more detailed sub-groups, sometimes on the basis of categories used in the primary classification, sometimes on other ones.

A good, if not always uncontested (Simon, 2012) example, might be taxonomy of different ethnic groups, such as that used in the 2011 census in England and Wales.[12] In this operationalization of the concept, the population is first divided into five broad groups:[13] White; Mixed/multiple ethnic groups; Asian/Asian British; Black/African/Caribbean/Black British; and Other ethnic group. Within each of these five groupings between two and five further sub-categories are then introduced. So, by way of illustration, the White category is further divided into: English/Welsh/Scottish/Northern Irish/British; Irish; Gypsy or Irish Traveller; and Any other White background (which the respondent can declare). The Asian/Asian

British category is further divided into: Indian; Pakistani; Bangladeshi; Chinese; and Any other Asian background (which the respondent can again declare). Various other nested categories divide the three other broad headings.[14]

Neighbourhood classification works in a quite different way. In this case an algorithm finds the detailed set of categories which most efficiently describe the variations in the character of a series of geographical units, whether post-codes, EDs or whatever. Only at a later stage does the algorithm search for similarities between these categories and organize them into a smaller number of higher level groupings. In the Liverpool study, the higher level groupings are not imposed on the basis of pre-existing theories of urban structure, but emerge from the algorithm's own attempts to find an optimal higher order classification. Developers can, of course, override which higher order grouping a lower level category is placed in. Sometimes they do. But such overrides are infrequent and tend to occur only at the margins. In most instances the higher order groupings suggested by the computer algorithm are adopted as being the ones most likely to resonate with users.

In the Liverpool study, it is evident that the attribute which most strongly sep-arated the five higher order groupings was house tenure. Of the five higher level neighbourhood groups there are: one dominated by owner-occupiers; two charac-terized by streets containing a mixture of private renting and owner occupation; and two consisting almost exclusively of council tenants. A clear distinction is also made in terms of the age of the housing stock: two of the groups consist predom-inantly of pre-1914 housing stock; one group consists of local authority housing replacing existing stock; and two groups represent development since 1914 on what at that time were green-field locations.

It is not just in Liverpool that housing type is the criterion that the cluster algo-rithm identifies as the one which distinguishes the higher order categories most efficiently. Nor is the primacy of housing, or more particularly of tenure, a direct result of the number of different housing variables contained in the OPCS Small Area Statistics, which, at that time, contained no information on type of house (flat, terraced, semi-detached, detached and so on) or a house's age. It reflects the fact that the type of housing one finds in a neighbourhood is crucial to explaining the types of people who live in it.

The reason for housing having primacy, both in the Liverpool classification and subsequent geodemographic classifications, is that most streets in a British city will have been built at a single point in time and usually with houses of a similar size and style. They are much easier to describe in terms of their housing characteristics than they are in terms of the diverse ages, household compo-sitions and occupational standings of their inhabitants because housing is the respect in which they are most uniform. In addition, when we drive or walk down a street, the physical characteristics of the houses are much more visually evident than are the appearance of the people who live in them, and it is their house type that is the feature of a street that we are most likely to remember not least because so much of memory is visual.[15]

In the 1970s, when cluster analysis was used to build a taxonomy for the Liverpool study, it was a technique much less commonly used than multiple regression and principal component analysis, especially among academics. Multiple regression and principal components analysis tend to be most effective when the object of a research project is to explore the statistical validity of a particular proposition or theory. In such instances, analysis follows theory. By contrast the use of cluster analysis implies no *a priori* set of theoretical assumptions. It allows data to form itself into patterns relatively[16] independently of the analyst.

Results of the Liverpool study and later classifications received a mixed reaction. Some academic researchers criticized the absence of any substantial theoretic basis to the taxonomy and were uncomfortable with what they felt to be subjective, qualitative descriptions of the categories that emerged.[17] On the other hand, the planners found it easy to recognize the various categories that had been created and found their elected representatives receptive to the output since they too could accept the validity of the categories that the cluster analysis had produced.

# Building a taxonomy of UK neighbourhoods

Once Liverpool's various EDs had been assigned to their 25 clusters and had become used as the basis for neighbourhood planning, the four other Merseyside local authorities, Knowsley, Sefton, St Helens and Wirral, commissioned the extension of the Liverpool typology to their own neighbourhoods. Most of their EDs could be relatively well described by one or other of the 25 Liverpool clusters. However, two additional types of neighbourhood were required to adequately describe EDs in parts of Southport and New Brighton. One new cluster described neighbourhoods containing many former seaside boarding houses, at that time not infrequently in multiple occupation, the other developments of bungalows which attracted retired owner-occupiers. Both these types feature in Chapter 10.

CES, the organization which had performed the statistical analysis on behalf of Liverpool and the other Merseyside districts, now found itself being commissioned to build neighbourhood classifications for other local authorities. Cumbria County Council[18] used the results to develop strategies for different types of neighbourhood in its structure plan and two London boroughs, Camden and Haringey, used them to identify neighbourhoods suffering different forms of deprivation. Unlike the extension of the Liverpool project to the other Merseyside districts, these projects required the development of entirely new taxonomies.

Aware of this new use for its Small Area Statistics, OPCS then approached CES with a view to creating a series of national typologies, each one classifying units in different layers in Britain's administrative hierarchy. The first ones were developed for use by central government and involved the classification of local authority districts (Webber and Craig, 1976; 1978) and of parliamentary constituencies (Webber, 1978a). These studies were followed by further classifications more relevant to local government, that of the 16,700 wards and parishes and the 120,000 EDs for which OPCS publish Small Area Statistics (Webber, 1977; 1978b).

The national classification of EDs now provided local authorities with a choice, either to commission a bespoke classification for their area or to use the results of a standard classification optimized at the national level. Most opted for the latter. Although the national classification gave them a less detailed description of the patterns of residential segregation within their area than a bespoke classification would have done, it enabled them to set their own neighbourhoods within the context of a national picture.[19] This proved particularly useful when bidding for central government funding.

# Evidence of the limitations of social class as a predictor of consumer behaviour

The CRN ('*C*lassification of *R*esidential *N*eighbourhoods') was the name given to the CES classification of wards and parishes. Until 1978 the use of the CRN was restricted to the various departments of local government. However, in that year, Ken Baker, the statistician responsible for sample design at the market research firm British Market Research Bureau (BMRB), attended a presentation of the taxonomy to local authority planners. The reason for his attendance was that the Bureau had unsettled some subscribers to its flagship Target Group Index (TGI) survey when it changed the process it used to select the sample of wards and parishes in which its interviews were held. It was feared that this change might have been responsible for apparent year-on-year changes in the proportions of respondents reported to have purchased the various consumer products or to have consumed the various national media covered in the survey.

The consequence of Baker's attendance at the CES seminar was the purchase by BMRB for £160 of a copy of the directory containing the cluster codes of each of Britain's 16,000 wards and parishes. Baker used this directory to append a neighbourhood type code to the records of respondents to the most recent TGI survey. This, Baker hoped, would dispel anxiety among clients that interviewers had somehow avoided interviewing respondents in poor neighbourhoods where their safety might have been compromised or indeed in wards where they might have found it difficult to obtain interviews from the very rich.

Baker matched these codes to his research database and established the degree to which the distribution of his survey respondents replicated the distribution of the UK population as a whole. The comparison was not unfavourable. Baker then, out of curiosity, thought that it might be interesting to find out which were the types of neighbourhood where particular products sold best. It soon became evident that the type of neighbourhood a person lived in proved just as predictive of consumer behaviour as did traditional demographic classifications such as age, household composition and, most importantly, social class (Baker, 1991).

By the 1970s the TGI had become the principal supplier of 'single source' information to advertising agencies and media buyers. The concept behind the TGI was that if media owners could obtain from a 'single source' information about the media preferences of purchasers of different products and brands, then they could show potential advertisers how well their product profile matched that of the medium, thereby improving their attractiveness to advertisers.

Baker used the CRN taxonomy to demonstrate differences in the profile of consumer behaviour and media consumption among different fragments within what had previously been assumed to be an undifferentiated middle class.[20] In particular, the classification distinguished what might be described as 'suburban' middle class neighbourhoods – places such as Harrow or Bromley as they then were – from high status inner city neighbourhoods – places such as Edgbaston in Birmingham, Withington in Manchester or Dulwich or Blackheath in London.

As tabulating behaviour by type of neighbourhood became increasingly popular among TGI subscribers, advertisers began to apply pressure on other survey contractors to enrich their survey databases with the CRN or other neighbourhood taxonomies. Many did.[21]

The distinction between two types of middle class community, one suburban, the other located in more central urban environments, was the finding that most intrigued Baker, his colleagues (Bermingham et al., 1979) and TGI subscribers. It is one of considerable significance to marketers as well as to sociologists and to political scientists. In suburban environments, the middle classes tended to read The *Daily Telegraph* and The *Sunday Times*. Middle class respondents living in places such as Blackheath or Edgbaston were more likely to read The *Guardian* and The *Observer*. This distinction was equally evident in respect of sport. Middle class respondents in suburban communities tended to play golf. Tennis was more popular in places such as Islington or Clifton, in Bristol. The two fragments of the middle classes avoided each other on holiday, the former preferring a Mediterranean cruise, the latter a gîte in the Dordogne, and in choice of wine, white for the former and red for the latter. Today, such distinctions may appear obvious but at the time their discovery was a revelation.

Judged in terms of behaviour and taste there was clear evidence, even at this time, of an emerging bifurcation within the middle classes, one which has since become much sharper. A metropolitan elite, liberal, inclusive and internationalist, contrasted with a more conservative middle class, more restrained, cautious and provincial, which preferred to surround itself, both socially and geographically, with people with similar tastes to its own and which was lukewarm – at best – in its celebration of diversity.[22]

What Baker had done at BMRB, quite without intention, was to facilitate access to a wealth of evidence of the relationship between neighbourhood characteristics and consumer behaviour. Product by product, brand by brand, it became possible for consumer marketers to reconsider whether target audiences, which they had previously described in terms of occupational classifications, were, in practice, better described in terms of the types of neighbourhood they lived in (Baker, 1991). This realization – quite independent of the thinking of Bourdieu[23] – gave support to emerging theories which conceived of social groupings in terms of taste and the distinctions that arose from highly nuanced forms of consumption.

Evidence of tastes associated with particular types of neighbourhood included holidays, newspaper and magazine readership, TV programmes watched, cars, wines and spirits – indeed virtually all luxury goods. But these differences also applied at a very mundane level. For example, the market for frozen goods, which had previously been considered as a classic middle classes phenomenon, was found to be particularly well developed among people living in rural areas. Not only did these people have the space for a separate freezer cabinet but they had further to travel to reach a supermarket and therefore tended to shop less frequently.

Few vendors of sports goods had ever identified what the CRN showed them as being a prime market for the sale of golf clubs. That was people living in military accommodation. These people, as it turned out, were also excellent prospects for cameras and video equipment. Both vodka and brown sauce were consumed disproportionately by tenants in Scotland's most disadvantaged social housing. People in pre-1914 terraced houses kept cats – perhaps to deter mice? – people in better-off council estates kept dogs – perhaps to deter burglars?

A huge volume of evidence of behavioural differentiation tumbled out pell-mell. Explanatory theories just could not keep up with the number of hypotheses. Whereas increasingly sophisticated statistical techniques had improved researchers' ability to support or discredit *pre-existing* hypotheses, here was a tool with the ability to generate *new* hypotheses. It did not necessarily negate established explanations of differences in consumer behaviours but it did, on occasion, challenge their salience.

Evidence of such a systematic relationship between neighbourhood and consumption was particularly compelling at a time when the efficacy of traditional measures of social class began to be undermined by deep-seated changes in society. As a result of growing occupational specialization, a larger number of people became employed in occupational roles of which even close family members had little understanding.[24] When other people do not understand what your job entails, how can your occupation be an effective signifier of your social status? Your career promotion and financial success can only be displayed using other means of which consumption, taste and where you live are among the most visible markers.

The growth of the public sector in general and of the caring professions in particular also contributed to a progressive weakening of the relationship between class and political party affiliation, whilst the entrance of women into these and other new professions made it increasingly problematic to establish the overall social status of households in which two or more people went out to work.[25]

Where once families tended to pass on their social class and political affiliation to subsequent generations, the widening of access to university education in the late 1960s following on from the Robbins Report in 1963, complicated the ascription of status. Does the new graduate identify with social groups whose behaviours, as evidenced in tastes, experiences and political affiliations, echo those he or she will have grown used to during childhood or youth?[26] Or do graduates identify with the social class of the new occupational groupings which a degree now allows them to become members of?

Notwithstanding upward mobility, or perhaps because of it, the occupation of a graduate's parents may become a better indicator of class than their own occupation. The democratization of popular culture and of clothing fashions made it far more easy for people not to identify with any class at all, or to identify with that of their upbringing, without causing social friction with partners, colleagues or with neighbours. In practice this new egalitarianism, rather than causing class to wither away, resulted in the increased emergence of different, more highly nuanced forms of social distinction.[27]

Since then, privileged access to select social groupings, invitations to dinner parties, weekend parties or sporting events, was increasingly conferred on people who were able to demonstrate a finely nuanced understanding of manners, protocols and tastes. How you earned your money has not become unimportant but less important than it used to be. The characters of Thackeray's *Vanity Fair* clearly shared the same understanding of rank – with the monarch at the pinnacle of a social pyramid, surrounded by the court, the aristocracy, industrialists and professionals and so on. By contrast, the basis for ascribing status in late twentieth-century British society was much more contested. For some, the highest status lies with celebrities, whether from the fields of fashion, the media or sport, most of whom would earn far more than a cabinet minister. Others judge status in terms of public prominence or in terms of recognition within their own profession. To others status is conferred by the possession of creative talent or impact on the wider world. The last dimension of these is a common determinant of status in universities, publishing houses and the arts.

One consequence of this fragmentation is a parallel fragmentation in the different forms of behaviour that confer distinction, increasingly resulting in the formation of different elites and in their preference for different types of housing, different residential locations and different types of neighbourhood. Many picture the home of a successful footballer, whether correctly or not, as a vulgar, unnecessarily large residence, over-fortified with gates and railings as in television series such as *Footballers' Wives*. In the popular imagination, top-flight lawyers are pictured living in Georgian houses in super-gentrified Islington whose undecorated external appearance belies evidence of professional success. Successful stockbrokers commute from period farmhouses, surrounded by manicured lawns, orchards, stables and staff accommodation. Their gardens overlook areas of outstanding natural beauty and they live within easy reach of country villages unspoiled by the accretions of modern developer estates.

Celebrities cluster in Notting Hill, the French in Kensington and the internationally footloose increasingly in serviced apartments overlooking the Thames. As we will see later on, there is little evidence to suggest that this popular notion of where different elites tend to live is terribly wide of the mark.

At the other end of the spectrum, what had in Victorian times been considered as the 'deserving' and the 'feckless' sections of the working class are increasingly fragmented, particularly in terms of social attitudes and social values. Traditional social values have been retained, or at least remain highly respected, in areas that we will later describe as conforming to *Ex-Industrial Legacy*[28] where risk-averse communities still retain collective memories of how to cope with economic collapse. The population of inner London estates acclimatizes to large increases in ethnic diversity and alternative forms of household structure. Englishness still stirs the emotions of tattooed new town residents whose white vans parade England flags as they deliver plumbing or maintenance services to affluent suburbanites in not-too-distant locations.[29]

The link between status and neighbourhood is in a continuous state of flux as neighbourhoods accommodate themselves to deep-seated changes. In Chapter 10 we will see how rootless beneficiaries of social security payments, many of whom had been persuaded to forsake cities for cheaper accommodation in former boarding houses in declining seaside resorts, create their own distinctive forms of non-conforming neighbourhood.

In Chapter 9 we see how stable middle class families, who were once the mainstay of the better areas of small market towns, have migrated to the countryside where they imagine, sometimes correctly, that they and their families will thrive in a close-knit rural community. Meanwhile those who in previous generations would have been employed as agricultural labourers now find jobs and more affordable accommodation in the small market towns from which new rural migrants had themselves emigrated, some in flats over shops others in cheap new developer estates. Whether by choice or necessity, social groups with a common past, common circumstances and common aspirations do seem to find themselves clustering together into distinct forms of community.

## Notes

[1] The earlier studies of Lupton and Mitchell (1954) and, more generally, Mitchell et al. (1954) give a good sense of the social problems afflicting post-war Liverpool.

[2] Of the many excellent accounts of the development of the welfare state up to the mid-1970s – the period we discuss here – perhaps the most compelling is Timmins (2001).

[3] See also the discussion by Anne Bransford – 'The Development Battle: The Community's struggle to save Covent Garden' – which is available at: www.covent gardenmemories.org.uk/page_id__37.aspx.

[4] See, in particular, the classic sociological account by Young and Willmott (1957).

[5] An excellent analysis of the history of Liverpool and the economic and social challenges it has faced through the twentieth century can be found in the various essays contained in Munck (2003).

[6] Strictly it was groups of EDs that were clustered, the grouping using a contiguity-constrained hierarchical clustering algorithm in which EDs were constrained from grouping across ward boundaries.

[7] This term may appear, on reflection, a rather odd one in this context given its American usage. The history of such accommodation in a US context is discussed in Groth (1994: 90–130) in a chapter on 'Rooming Houses and the Margins of Respectability'; a better term might have been 'Boarding House' or 'Lodging House'. Its use is explained by the coverage given to the Chicago School on the Liverpool Planning course attended by the person responsible for the labelling of the Liverpool categories.

[8] As Le Grand (1989) demonstrated, in the era before student fees, the allocation of grants by local authorities to local students in order that they may study at university was – along with some forms of expenditure on the NHS – a major reason why, unexpectedly, the middle classes often did disproportionately better out of the welfare state than the working class.

[9] These were the smallest areal units in the 1971 census geography hierarchy. These areas were each the responsibility of a single census enumerator. The 103,129 English 1971 EDs contained an average of 446 persons and 151 households.

[10] Neighbourhoods of the very highest status have the highest proportion of black cars. Silver and blue are found in wealthy suburbs, white in retirement enclaves, red in municipal estates, and green in rural areas and small towns.

[11] The 'Registrar-General's Social Classes' were first introduced in 1913 and were only renamed in 1990 as 'Social Class based on Occupation'. The classes are formally described as follows: I Professional occupations; II Managerial and technical occupations; III N Skilled non-manual occupations; III M Skilled manual occupations; IV Partly-skilled occupations; and V Unskilled occupations.

[12] The details are available here: www.ons.gov.uk/peoplepopulationandcommunity/culturalidentity/ethnicity/articles/2011censusanalysisethnicityandreligionof thenonukbornpopulationinenglandandwales/2015-06-18.

[13] In what follows we have left the capitalization and description of the categories exactly as they appear in the census questions.

[14] Geological series likewise may initially be divided into igneous and sedimentary and then further on the basis of the period in geological time when they were formed: Palaeolithic Neolithic; and so on.

[15] As we will see later, this has proved to be convenient when visualizing geodemographic categories.

[16] Of course, the analyst may use his or her theoretical knowledge to interpret the character of the clusters – but not to create them. Clearly the analyst also has to make decisions about the variables used to build the classification and to calculate similarities between areal units, the relative weights that should be given to them and the number of categories. There are also decisions that have to be made about the nature of the form of cluster analysis used – algorithms can of course differ somewhat depending on the software used (Uprichard et al., 2008; 2009).

[17] See in particular the exchange between Openshaw et al. (1980) and Webber (1980): an early manifestation perhaps of later cleavages in the statistical imagination between multivariate causal and more descriptive modes of analysis (Uprichard et al., 2008; Savage and Burrows, 2007; 2009).

[18] Exponents of geodemographic classification can be criticized for a tendency towards architectural over-determination based on the proposition that all instances of a cluster will necessarily conform to a single building style. The Cumbria structure plan included a telling example to the contrary. In Barrow-in-Furness, a single cluster was found to include both mid rise nineteenth-century tenement blocks of a design more typical on Clydeside and a permanent caravan site. On investigation it transpired that what these census areas had in common was a large number of young, recently arrived, single residents, many of them male. Both housing types

were ideally suited to the needs of trainees recruited to work in the Vickers ship-yard. Despite their differences in physical form the two types of accommodation provided a similar function within the urban system.

[19] A good example of the use of the national taxonomy occurred when Wirral Borough Council, which had tried unsuccessfully to argue the case for its inclusion in priority area programmes, a case which had been rejected by the (then) Department of the Environment on the grounds that overall the authority did not have an outstandingly high proportion of very deprived groups, now submitted evidence of the distribution of its population by type of neighbourhood in comparison with the national average. Using a national taxonomy, it could now demonstrate that statistics for Wirral as a whole concealed the fact that a very high proportion of its population lived in particularly disadvantaged neighbourhoods, this concentration previously having been obscured by the presence within the borough boundary of many exceptionally wealthy neighbourhoods, many along the Dee estuary. The bid was successful.

[20] It is worth noting that in some of the earlier work of Mike Savage (Savage et al., 1995: 99–131) the TGI is used in order to demonstrate this. This was one of the first instances in which social scientists used detailed market research data to underpin what is essentially a piece of academic social research. In this analysis, they examine associations between income and patterns of consumption in order to differentiate between three fractions of the middle class that they label as: *ascetic*; *post-modern*; and *undistinctive*.

[21] The only interest BMRB took in the CRN classification was as a tool for generating more representative sample points for survey interviews and as a field for survey cross-tabulation. In retrospect it might seem strange that senior executives at BMRB did not recognize the opportunity that 'ownership' of the geodemographics business line might expand the services they delivered to their clients. Otherwise the history we are narrating here could thus have been a very different one.

[22] Now might be a good time to revisit column G of Table 1.3 showing as it does the relative distribution of membership of a human rights charity as compared to a far-right political party across different neighbourhood types.

[23] One cannot but be struck by the similarity of some of these findings with those emerging out of the far more theoretical concerns of Bourdieu (1984) in his monumental treatise on *Distinction*, which at about the same time begun to identify the major cultural cleavages amongst the French middle and upper classes.

[24] One is reminded of the scene in Tom Wolfe's *The Bonfire of the Vanities* in which Sherman, the main character, tries to explain to his daughter what he does for a

living – he is a 'bond salesman' working in Wall Street. He finds it hard to explain and she begins to look confused and then bursts into tears. Her friend's father had already explained to her in very clear terms what work he did as a carpenter.

[25] There was a huge sociological literature responding to this question in the 1980s (see Dale et al., 1985 for a useful overview).

[26] The Bridge Group, a charitable policy association researching and promoting socio-economic diversity and equality in the UK, has promoted the use of such a question on employment application forms in order to track equality in recruitment.

[27] Explained at the time to lay audiences in popular books such as *Class* by Jilly Cooper, published in 1979.

[28] This is a type of postcode identified in the 2003 version of the *Mosaic* and already displayed in Table 1.3. It refers to neighbourhood types in which older people, many in poor health, having worked in heavy industry and living in mainly low rise social housing, predominate. The full details of the schema are documented in Chapter 5.

[29] As so chillingly rendered in J.G. Ballard's final novel *Kingdom Come* published in 2006. It opens with these lines: 'The suburbs dream of violence. Asleep in their drowsy villas, sheltered by benevolent shopping malls, they wait patiently for the nightmares that will wake them into a more passionate world…'.

# 4

# THE WIDER ADOPTION OF 'COMMERCIAL SOCIOLOGY'

## Marketers' use of data on different neighbourhood types

In the early 1970s CACI, a US consulting organization, obtained a licence from the US Census Bureau to act as a census agency. This permitted it to hold statistics for census tracts and to resupply these in formats which met the needs of US retail chains. Within minutes a fast food chain could use an online system to access demographic data for the catchment area of any potential new outlet. Being able to evaluate a potential new location with such speed, the chain could now home in more quickly on available sites which had the greatest chance of commercial success.

In 1978 a similar agreement reached with the OPCS enabled CACI to launch a similar service in the UK. It is not difficult to understand the potential value of the CRN to CACI, especially given its link to the TGI, since this now made it possible to provide retailers not just with information on the demographics of a catchment area but also on the types of products most likely to appeal to local residents. It was for this reason that in 1979 CACI recruited Webber to transform what was then a ward-based CRN into one based on census enumeration districts (EDs). CACI rebranded the CRN as *Acorn* (*A Classification of Residential Neighbourhoods*). It was to this year that we might date the birth of geodemographic classifications proper in the UK.[1]

*Acorn* still relied on cluster analysis and census statistics. Its categories were the same as the CRN's – after all it was necessary that these should be consistent with the categories used by the TGI. But it possessed two innovative features. First, its level of geographic resolution was increased from 17,000 wards and parishes to some 120,000 census EDs. Second, it incorporated a cross reference between postcode and census ED. This enabled a user to submit a list of customer postcodes and, from a report such as Table 1.3, identify the types of neighbourhood in which customers were most likely to live.

The principal applications it was expected that geodemographics would be used for are evident from the presentations of a seminar held at the Café Royale on 9 October 1980, a year after the launch of *Acorn*. The seminar was sponsored jointly by CACI and the BMRB. It was organized by Admap, a specialist media events organization and chaired by John Billett, at that time the media director of the advertising agency Allen Brady Marsh. It attracted 300 attendees.

In the context of discussion of the relative discriminatory power of geodemographics and social class it is noteworthy that one of the presentations was entitled '*Acorn* as an alternative to Social Class in identifying The *Observer* reader'. The speaker was an executive of a media-buying group. Her employer optimized advertisers' spend by selecting media whose demographic profiles best matched the known profiles of their target customers.

BMRB explained how it had used geodemographics to improve the representativeness of the sample areas it selected for interviewing survey respondents. Another speaker revealed that his advertising agency used geodemographics to brief members of its creative team since it enabled them to better visualize the target audience for their television advertising campaigns.

'Branch development and product mix' was the title of a speaker who explained how geodemographics could be used to optimize the location of new branches and the assortment of products they sold.

The financial services organization Western Trust and Savings shared with the audience how they used geodemographics first to profile their customers, so that they could know what types of neighbourhood yielded both the most responsive and creditworthy borrowers, then to identify shopping centres whose catchment areas contained high proportions of the best performing types and finally to mail households that belonged to these geodemographic categories that lay within the catchment area of each branch. They revealed that *Military Bases* was their most responsive segment.

Other speakers explained how geodemographics was now enabling advertisers to select the most effective local newspapers in which to advertise, the most productive door-to-door distribution areas for the delivery of promotional leaflets and the optimal outdoor poster sites to buy for national advertising campaigns. A paper covering both personalization of copy and list selection was presented by the head of the direct marketing consultancy used by Great Universal Stores to advise on its catalogue mailing strategy.

As is evident from the topics covered at the Café Royale seminar, many of the organizations that were first to recognize the potential value of neighbourhood typologies were large companies such as Readers Digest and Great Universal Stores who had developed successful business models for selling products to their customers directly through the post, rather than through high street stores. In their day these were recognized as the most sophisticated practitioners of what had become known as 'direct marketing'.

The practice of direct marketing originated in the United States. It addressed the problem, particularly acute in the sort of rural communities Galpin researched in the Midwest (see Chapter 2), where recently settled farmers lived inconveniently far from high streets of what in the 'old world' might have been described as market towns. Many of these people had a good command of English and a high level of literacy. When the US Mail introduced a special tariff for printed matter, a new breed of 'catalogue' companies found it profitable to trade directly with these farmers via direct mail. Companies, of which Sears Roebuck was the most successful, made bulk purchases of merchandise relevant to the needs of rural customers, displayed them in a catalogue, mailed the catalogue to clients and fulfilled orders using the postal service. Because of its location, Chicago[2] proved a particularly convenient city from which to operate businesses of this sort.

Having access to information about their customers, how often they responded, how much they spent and what lines they bought placed these catalogue companies at a considerable advantage over manufacturers who sold to customers via retail outlets. They hired statisticians to create the advanced models which could optimize their communications with their clients.

Despite being able to build up a detailed profile of *existing* customers, many of these companies struggled to apply targeting techniques of equivalent sophistication to the recruitment of *new* customers. Many resorted to selecting names from the 'mailing lists' that they were increasingly able to rent from specialist list brokers. These lists contained the names and addresses of people who had subscribed to newspapers or magazines or who had a history of buying other products by direct mail.

In Britain, at least at that time, the names of their readers were less likely to be known to publishers due to the practice of newsagents delivering papers to people's homes. This made it harder for UK catalogue companies, such as market leaders Great Universal Stores and Littlewoods, to source a sufficient number of mailable names and addresses from rentable lists to meet their increasingly voracious needs. In due course, both companies overcame this constraint on new customer recruitment by investing in the data capture of the electoral rolls compiled and distributed by the electoral registration departments of local authorities. Whilst this investment generated the much larger number of mailable names and addresses these companies needed, both found it a challenge to decide which were the best names and addresses to select for a catalogue mailing.

By overlaying consumer credit information, they were able to avoid mailing households with a proven record of non-payment. Recording the number of times an address had failed to respond to a mailing enabled them to remove serial non-responders from their prospect mailings. The advantage of the post-code system and of neighbourhood taxonomies such as *Acorn* was that it now became possible to identity *positive prospects* rather than merely to rely on rejecting negative ones. Neighbourhood targeting was particularly effective for identifying social groups for which agency-based mail order systems were appropriate – a key component of the proposition being the offer of consumer credit. This feature of the proposition was particularly valued before the arrival of the now ubiquitous credit card provided a more convenient source of short term credit.

It turned out that the best targets for this business were women looking after a family home and not in formal employment – 'housewives' in the parlance of the time – living in settled neighbourhoods in predominantly industrial towns, in *Mosaic* neighbourhood types such as G44 *Rustbelt Resilience* and D21 *Respectable Rows*.[3] They tended to live either in the more stable council estates or in streets of 'respectable' pre-1945 terraced housing with modest front gardens and a back yard. Their husbands tended to work in skilled craft jobs and to drive to work in inexpensive cars. Typically, these women had school age or older children; others had children in employment but still living at home and often contributing to the household's income. They were likely to be on good terms with neighbours and to have extended family living nearby, both attributes of a good mail order agent. They received little direct mail and often felt privileged to receive special and personalized offers. So specific a target audience would clearly have been impossible to reach on the basis of person-level characteristics. For them *Acorn* avoided the Scylla of inner city inability to pay, and the Charybdis of suburban financial self-sufficiency and disdain for products purchased from the pages of a catalogue.[4]

In addition to the large catalogue companies, this form of targeted mailing proved attractive to organizations, such as American Express and Readers Digest, whose products appealed to a very specific type of consumer. Other marketers cleverly combined this information with the data they held on their existing customers to drive the selection of products that should be promoted to existing rather than new customers. Previously a high-street bank would find it difficult to distinguish between customers who make little use of an account because their income was low from those who made little use of it because they undertook most of their financial transactions using the products of their competitors. Appending geo-demographic codes to customer records separated these two groups. If an inactive customer lives in the *Mosaic* Type A01 *Global Connections*, then it is likely that inactivity will be the result of them using a competitor's service. If they were in

G42 *Low Horizons*, then it is questionable whether the relationship could be made to generate significantly higher income by the customer being sold other products.

As a general rule, the less information a business holds about its customers and the fewer products it sells to them, the greater the value to the business of geodemographic classification as a basis for differentiating customer communications.

## The postcode system and big data begin to enhance the relevance of geography to marketing

It is not difficult to understand why such typologies of neighbourhoods might prove to be so useful to these catalogue companies, and why CCN, a subsidiary of Great Universal Stores, should have recruited Webber in 1985 to develop *Mosaic*. However, the ease with which geodemographic categories could be matched to the electoral roll and used in prospect mailing was greatly enhanced as a result of the launch by the Royal Mail in 1974 of the UK postcode system. The objective of the system was to reduce the cost incurred in sorting mail. Today, of course, the postcode system lies at the heart of a plethora of operational systems. But when it was introduced, the Post Office feared that the process of appending postcodes to the addresses of existing customers would be seen by the direct marketing industry as an unwelcome burden.

In 1982 the Royal Mail commissioned John Billett, who had chaired the Café Royale seminar, to address this problem. He then proposed a system which would incentivize volume mailers to adopt their new postcode system. Branded the *Consumer Location System*, it put a proposition to heavy users of direct mail. Submit the addresses of your customers to the Royal Mail and, in addition to postcoding this list, it will create an analysis of the Types of social area in which your customers are particularly likely to live. Supported by this evidence, the Royal Mail then invited users of the system to rent from a national version of the electoral roll the names and addresses of consumers falling within these social areas.

Using this service, an importer distributing a prestige brand of car through local dealers might discover that people living in postcodes classified as, for example, A06 *High Technologists* were the best buyers of their marque. They could then purchase a mailing list of all electors living in *High Technologists* postcodes within half an hour's drive of a local dealer and mail them with an invitation to a test drive at their local dealership.

In the early years of geodemographics there was no reason to suppose that data other than census statistics would ever be used to build neighbourhood taxonomies. This assumption was first challenged in the Netherlands, where, as a result of the misuse of personal information by occupying forces during World War II, there has been a presumption against publishing census statistics at a small area level. It was in the Netherlands that, with the assistance of CCN, the country's largest catalogue company, Wehkamp, a subsidiary of Great Universal Stores, launched *MAP*. *MAP* was the first neighbourhood taxonomy based exclusively on data derived as a by-product of the purchasing habits of households, in this case Dutch ones; a source of data that prefigures what – with ubiquitous digitization processes – has more recently come to be described as big data (Burrows and Savage, 2014).

Encouraged by the success of the Dutch system, in 1987 CCN developed *Mosaic*, a hybrid UK system, relying on a mix of census statistics and 'transactional data'. By way of illustration, Table 4.1 lists some of the sources of 'transactional data' used in the construction of the 2003 version of *Mosaic*.

**Table 4.1**  Some Transactional Data Sources Used to Construct *Mosaic* 2003

| Topic | Indicator |
| --- | --- |
| Financial behaviour | Shareholdings |
| | Directorships |
| | County Court Judgements |
| | Poor payment records |
| Property characteristics | Council tax bands |
| | Property values |
| | Property sales |
| | Year of introduction of the postcode |
| Demographic | Average years at address on electoral register |
| | Electors with names from different ethno-cultural backgrounds |
| Proximity | Generalized measure of proximity to population |

How, when added to census statistics, could data from non-census sources improve the effectiveness of a neighbourhood taxonomy? In the UK, there were three justifications. The first is that the addition of non-census sources increased the number of different aspects of social structure which the cluster algorithm could use to distinguish meaningful clusters. This was particularly the case in relation to affluence for which the census contains relatively few measures. For example, incorporating statistics at postcode level on the proportions of adults who were company directors or large shareholders sharpened the delineation of high status clusters.

The second improvement was the greater geographic granularity of the places being classified. On average, there are around 15 postcodes in a census ED. In previous classifications these would all have been given the same classification. By adding transactional data, summarized at postcode level, the clustering algorithm was now able to identify instances where different postcodes within the same census ED might be more accurately assigned different classification codes.

The third benefit of combining non-census data sources with census statistics was that the cluster codes given to social areas could be updated on a regular basis to take account of local changes in demographic structure. Though it was not in the interest of users for the categories of the classification systems to be changed more often than every ten years, non-census data sources could now be used to update the social area which best described each individual postcode. Non-census sources also made it possible to assign classifications to postcodes that had been introduced by the Post Office since the date of the previous census, which, over the span of an intercensal period, can amount to as many as one in ten of all postcodes.

# Neighbourhood classification gains adherents among new user groups

Although an important aim of this book is to open up an engagement between geodemographics and analytic, methodological and substantive debates in the social sciences, it is well worth recording the manner in which geodemographic classifications have advanced in the years following the Café Royale seminar.

One of the most important advances that took place during the 1980s was the embedding of geodemographic data and concepts within Geographical Information Systems (GIS) and the integration of these tools within the decision support tools used by retailers and by direct marketers. Unlike at the time of the Café Royale seminar, when all geodemographic applications had to be commissioned via a bureau, these were increasingly undertaken running specialist software in-house on desktop computers, often by analysts with backgrounds in a social scientific discipline. It was this feature which tended to give *Mosaic* a competitive advantage over *Acorn* in these early years.

Table 4.2 illustrates one typical output of such systems: an 'area profile'. This particular report compares the population mix of Tavistock's retail catchment area with that of the UK as a whole using the 2009 version of *Mosaic*. Another popular output of GIS systems are maps such as the one shown in Figure 4.1. This particular one shows postcodes in Nottingham according to the geodemographic Group each belongs to, using the 2003 version of *Mosaic*.

The 30 case studies featured in *Changing Your World*, a promotional booklet Experian distributed to prospective clients in the late 1990s, illustrate how by this time geodemographic classification had been adopted by a much wider range of vertical markets than those featured at the Café Royale seminar and across an increasing number of European markets too. However, at this stage it is noteworthy that Figure 4.2's case studies have yet to include any instance of a public-sector application.

**Table 4.2** *Mosaic* Profile of the Catchment Area of Tavistock, Devon

|  | Tavistock | UK | Index |
|---|---|---|---|
| *Mosaic* 2009 Groups | % adults | % adults | UK base = 100 |
| A: *Alpha Territory* | 0.58 | 3.62 | 16 |
| B: *Professional Rewards* | 19.00 | 9.03 | 210 |
| C: *Rural Solitude* | 19.93 | 3.92 | 508 |
| D: *Small Town Diversity* | 21.51 | 8.76 | 245 |
| E: *Active Retirement* | 7.79 | 3.56 | 219 |
| F: *Suburban Mindsets* | 5.99 | 12.17 | 49 |
| G: *Careers and Kids* | 1.92 | 5.99 | 32 |
| H: *New Homemakers* | 2.44 | 4.36 | 56 |
| I: *Ex-Council Community* | 7.35 | 9.79 | 75 |
| J: *Claimant Cultures* | 0.00 | 5.57 | 0 |
| K: *Upper Floor Living* | 0.00 | 4.77 | 0 |
| L: *Elderly Needs* | 5.87 | 4.07 | 144 |
| M: *Industrial Heritage* | 5.87 | 7.87 | 75 |
| N: *Terraced Melting Pot* | 0.21 | 7.61 | 3 |
| O: *Liberal Opinion* | 0.73 | 8.48 | 9 |

MosaicUK by Postcode
- rural isolation
- grey perspectives
- twilight subsistence
- blue collar enterprise
- municipal dependency
- welfare borderline
- urban intelligence
- ties of community
- suburban comfort
- happy families
- symbols of success

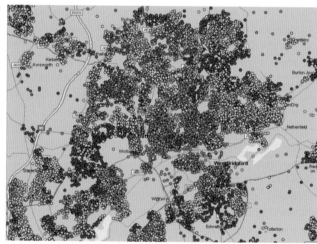

**Figure 4.1** Nottingham Postcodes by *Mosaic* Group

However, the public sector was to become the focus of a concerted Experian push during the early 2000s – local authorities, police forces, hospital trusts and fire and emergency services being their primary targets. By 2006 as many as 100 public

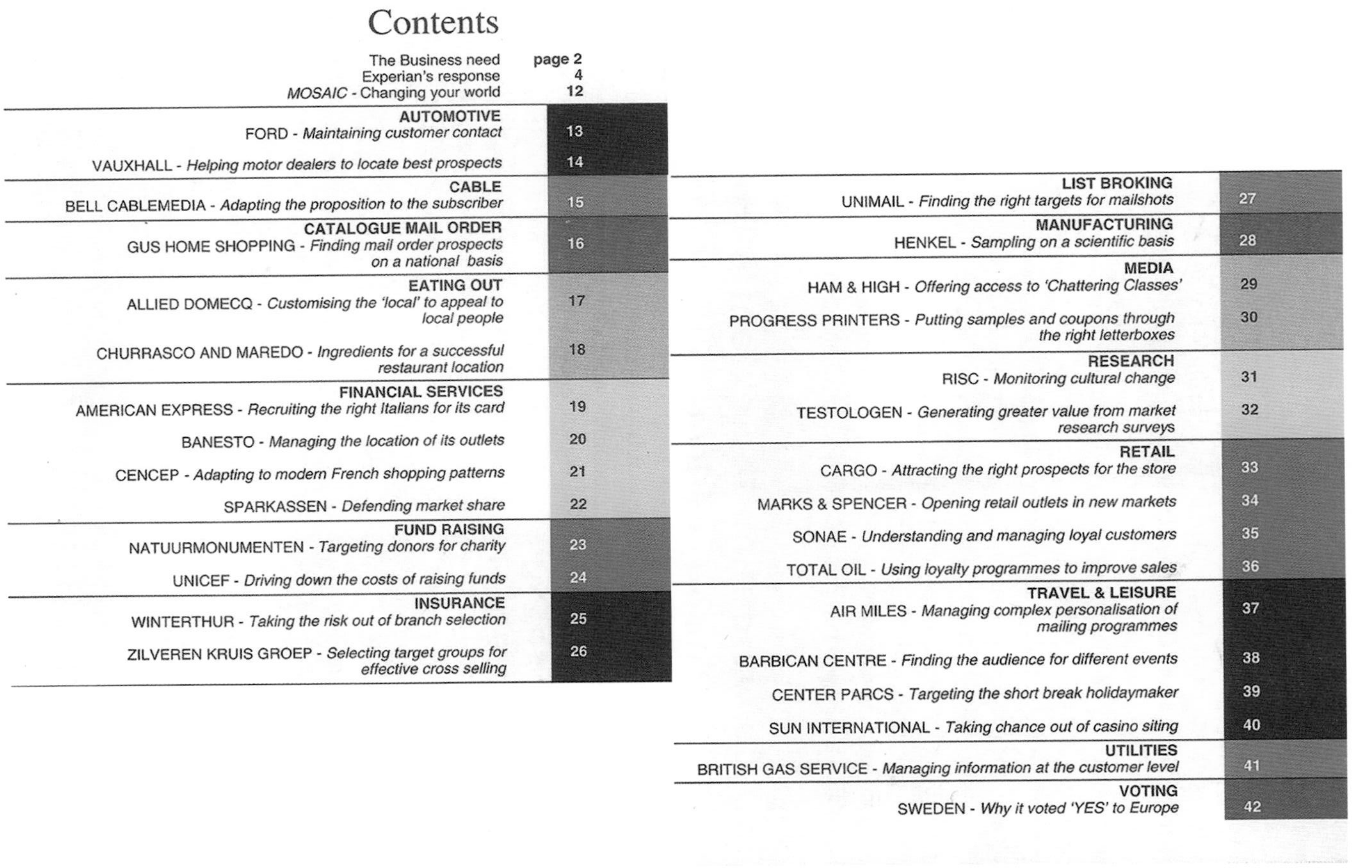

Contents

| | |
|---|---|
| The Business need | page 2 |
| Experian's response | 4 |
| *MOSAIC* - Changing your world | 12 |
| **AUTOMOTIVE** | |
| FORD - *Maintaining customer contact* | 13 |
| VAUXHALL - *Helping motor dealers to locate best prospects* | 14 |
| **CABLE** | |
| BELL CABLEMEDIA - *Adapting the proposition to the subscriber* | 15 |
| **CATALOGUE MAIL ORDER** | |
| GUS HOME SHOPPING - *Finding mail order prospects on a national basis* | 16 |
| **EATING OUT** | |
| ALLIED DOMECQ - *Customising the 'local' to appeal to local people* | 17 |
| CHURRASCO AND MAREDO - *Ingredients for a successful restaurant location* | 18 |
| **FINANCIAL SERVICES** | |
| AMERICAN EXPRESS - *Recruiting the right Italians for its card* | 19 |
| BANESTO - *Managing the location of its outlets* | 20 |
| CENCEP - *Adapting to modern French shopping patterns* | 21 |
| SPARKASSEN - *Defending market share* | 22 |
| **FUND RAISING** | |
| NATUURMONUMENTEN - *Targeting donors for charity* | 23 |
| UNICEF - *Driving down the costs of raising funds* | 24 |
| **INSURANCE** | |
| WINTERTHUR - *Taking the risk out of branch selection* | 25 |
| ZILVEREN KRUIS GROEP - *Selecting target groups for effective cross selling* | 26 |
| **LIST BROKING** | |
| UNIMAIL - *Finding the right targets for mailshots* | 27 |
| **MANUFACTURING** | |
| HENKEL - *Sampling on a scientific basis* | 28 |
| **MEDIA** | |
| HAM & HIGH - *Offering access to 'Chattering Classes'* | 29 |
| PROGRESS PRINTERS - *Putting samples and coupons through the right letterboxes* | 30 |
| **RESEARCH** | |
| RISC - *Monitoring cultural change* | 31 |
| TESTOLOGEN - *Generating greater value from market research surveys* | 32 |
| **RETAIL** | |
| CARGO - *Attracting the right prospects for the store* | 33 |
| MARKS & SPENCER - *Opening retail outlets in new markets* | 34 |
| SONAE - *Understanding and managing loyal customers* | 35 |
| TOTAL OIL - *Using loyalty programmes to improve sales* | 36 |
| **TRAVEL & LEISURE** | |
| AIR MILES - *Managing complex personalisation of mailing programmes* | 37 |
| BARBICAN CENTRE - *Finding the audience for different events* | 38 |
| CENTER PARCS - *Targeting the short break holidaymaker* | 39 |
| SUN INTERNATIONAL - *Taking chance out of casino siting* | 40 |
| **UTILITIES** | |
| BRITISH GAS SERVICE - *Managing information at the customer level* | 41 |
| **VOTING** | |
| SWEDEN - *Why it voted 'YES' to Europe* | 42 |

**Figure 4.2** Case Studies: *Changing Your World*

sector organizations were attending annual conferences focused exclusively on public sector applications of geodemographic classification. The programmes included speakers such as the Director of Transformational Government at the Cabinet Office and the Head of Customer Insight at Her Majesty's Revenue and Customs (HMRC). Attendees could choose between parallel sessions devoted to the applications of geodemographics to health, local government, community safety and education. Other speakers focused on its application to communications campaigns: Nottingham Primary Care Trust,[5] for example, on smoking cessation; Sports England on increasing participation in active sports; and Thames Valley Police on road safety. A key focus of many of the presentations was how to adapt service delivery to reflect the different communication channels that people living in particular geodemographic categories preferred to use.

Looking back 40 years later one is struck by how varied is the range of different applications for which geodemographics has been used and by the persistence of these applications. Other than public sector applications, the only application for geodemographics that was not foreseen at the outset has been in social media, an application which was not immediately obvious to observers even after its arrival.

## How do we define the extent of the neighbourhood we live in?

Freed from the constraint of having to rely on the geography of census enumeration, builders of geodemographic taxonomies were able to attend to a number of new issues, some of deep theoretical significance. For example, when you hold some information about a postcode and other information about the wider census ED of which the postcode forms a part, what relative weight should you give to the two sources of data when considering which cluster a postcode should belong to? If the postcode has, say, only four inhabitants, should the same weight be given to postcode-level data as for a postcode that has 100 inhabitants? One assumes that the finer the granularity of geographic data the more accurate the social area code returned by the algorithm. But if neighbourhood effects exist, could the classification be improved, albeit somewhat counter-intuitively, by incorporating information not just about the postcode and the census ED itself, but also about a wider geographic area? Should the information used to classify neighbourhoods be restricted to information about their residents and their residents' homes? Or should it be broadened to include measures of land use or proximity to physical or social facilities?

If the social influence of neighbourhood is expressed through the geography of social contacts, then it is evident that the pattern of most residents' contacts might be more appropriately represented by a transition gradient in which the probability of contact diminishes with distance, rather than by a bounded space within which all contact is presumed to occur, as for example in Galpin's interpretation of a natural area. A resident speaks to a neighbour over a garden fence, acknowledges other residents in the same street perhaps by name, shares opinions in the corner shop, at the school gates or in the 'local' pub, and then, from time to time, forms other acquaintances and friendships at sports clubs, gyms, places of worship or voluntary organizations at a greater distance from his or her home. Such a model of social networks would suggest that the most effective way of creating a tax-onomy of social areas would be by incorporating data for many scales of local geography, the nearer ones being given heavier weightings than the further ones.

The incorporation of data for larger geographical areas does provide conceptual and practical problems. The first of these are what are known as 'boundary' or 'edge' effects. If data values for larger geographical areas, such as local authori-ties, are included among the variables used to build a classification, the result is that postcodes on different sides of a local authority boundary, but otherwise simi-lar, are likely to find themselves assigned to different clusters. The smooth surface of neighbourhood segregation is interrupted by arbitrary decisions made hundreds of years ago regarding where administrative boundaries should be drawn.

The inclusion of data for higher level geographies, in this and other ways, results in a much greater 'regionalization' of clusters. This is not helpful. If the majority of postcodes in the London Borough of Kensington and Chelsea fall into a single geodemographic category, the classification is unlikely to prove very useful for the Council. Nor does it contribute to effective comparisons between local government areas. It is easier to compare local government areas if they all contain apples and pears, albeit in different proportions, than if some local government areas only have apples and others only have pears.

An effective method of overcoming the negative boundary effects of using data for higher order administrative levels is to use *proximity* instead. The first example of proximity being incorporated into a neighbourhood classification was in the construction of a version of the *Mosaic* classification for Australia. Here, in order to distinguish the outback, it was decided to include a measure of distance from the coast (subject to a log transformation). Proximity was next used in the construction of UK versions of *Mosaic* by introducing a measure of residential density. Such a measure would have been disruptive of the system if this measure were to have been calculated at the level of the census ED or the postcode since at this level it would have been influenced by the arbitrary allo-cation of non-residential land uses such as parks and railway land to adjoining census EDs or postcodes. Were densities to have been measured for larger geog-raphies this would then have introduced boundary effects.

The solution to these problems was to calculate a generalized measure of how far each postcode was to other postcodes, weighted by population, within a spec-ified search distance.[6] In general, the further residents of a postcode lived from other people, the lower this value would be. The measure provided a particularly helpful means of discriminating between suburbs within urban areas and relatively newly built middle class housing on the edge of commuter villages, two types of neighbourhood whose behaviour proved to be significantly more different than their demographics. Other than in these respects, builders of geodemographic classifications have been reluctant to include measures of proximity relating either to the housing stock or the demographics of local neighbourhoods.

## Neighbourhood classification adapts to the digital era

Advances in computing power make it increasingly possible for organizations to analyse large volumes of transactional information. In the 1960s and 1970s analysts in leading consumer-facing organizations would typically have access to information accumulated at the level of the individual customer, perhaps broken down by month. By 2010, as the concept of big data had begun to emerge, it had become routine for an analyst at a national retailer to be able to access the complete inventory of recent transactions for any set of customers, providing information on exactly which brands had been purchased, when, where and at what price.

The increase in the granularity at which information could be analysed, and customers targeted, led to an assumption that data disaggregated to the level of the individual customer would necessarily prove more predictive than comparatively static information describing whole neighbourhoods. Such expectations were even more widespread as social media displaced direct marketing as the most cost-effective medium for reaching individual consumers.

Paradoxically, the growth of social media has contributed more to the popularity of geodemographic classifications than to their demise. Why? First, whilst data sourced from internet visits provide an exceptionally granular representation of a consumer's behaviour, it is only by combining a number of different behavioural actions that the advertiser is able to obtain a sufficiently rounded appreciation of a customer to be able to form a judgement about the values and tastes which underlie that consumer's major buying decisions. Notwithstanding the plethora of fine-grained transactional data available, the types of people a consumer has as neighbours consistently add incremental predictive power. Geodemographics, after all, classifies people according to the types of neighbours that they have, not their own characteristics. The best models seem to combine previous purchasing patterns and social context, transactional behaviour and residential location.

Second, geodemographic classifications function as effective data-reduction tools. Users find it very helpful to be able to encapsulate in a single classification code the distillation of the myriad different behaviours that may be identifiable by different predictive models. At times it may make sense to sacrifice predictiveness for simplicity and to use a consistent classification system rather than build a series of bespoke predictive models.

Third, there are many potential targets of internet advertising that can only be identified from their geo-location, which, in many instances, is their postcode. If this is the finest level of resolution at which social media can target an identified audience, then it makes more sense to use 'external' data at the level of the unit postcode.

How are geodemographic classifications to be judged? This is a question for developers, users and, indeed, methodologists (Uprichard et al., 2009). The intention of the developer is to strike optimal positions on a number of trade-offs. Assign too much weight to housing variables and not enough to measures of age and the classification will discriminate well on some behaviours but on others not at all. Statistical discrimination will be maximized across all relevant behaviours if the widest range of indicators are input and if no individual topic is accorded undue influence.

Allow a solution with too many discrete categories and the user will find it difficult to differentiate one type of social area from another one with which it is broadly similar. Allow too few categories and the categories risk losing homogeneity. Allow too many variables from higher level geographies and the results will become excessively regionalized. Restrict yourself to data for the finest level of geography and the solution will lack statistical robustness.

Finding the optimal position on these trade-offs is in many respects an art. However, if a developer has access to a range of behavioural data (both 'big' and traditional geo-coded survey data) which has not been used to build a classification, it is possible to evaluate alternative classification solutions by measuring how predictive each one is of an entire set of 'independent' behaviours. Continuously re-evaluating incremental changes in the weights given to the inputs, the developer can 'calibrate' the classification until it reaches an optimal level of predictiveness.[7] At this point the taxonomy will be at its most efficient in statistically discriminating the widest range of possible behaviours and least likely to inherit any subjective bias from its builders.

Such has been the growth in the volumes of big data in recent years that it has become increasingly possible to progress from a classification of postcodes to a classification of individuals. Since the 2009 version of *Mosaic*, it had been the practice, whilst optimizing the classification at the level of the unit postcode, to allow different classifications to be given to different individuals within the same postcode where implied by person-level data derived from big data sources. This occurs where the known demographics of that individual are untypical of the rest of the postcode in which that person lives.

The 2014 version reversed this process. This classification was optimized at the level of the individual using a mixture of data pertaining to individuals, the postcode and the census ED. Under this new regime, postcodes are now ascribed to the categories which have been optimized at the person level using just that subset of data available at the postcode and higher level. This process has the advantage in that a multivariate person-level taxonomy will clearly be more predictive of personal behaviour than one built at postcode level. On the other hand, it is self-evident that there are many categories of neighbourhood, *Ex-Industrial Legacy* or *Summer Playgrounds* being examples, which will necessarily fail to appear when the only categories a postcode can be placed in are those based on a person-level solution. Geodemographic classification is at risk of losing its 'geo' element.

Whilst these changes benefit those using geodemographics for internet targeting, the decision to optimize a classification using person-level behaviour has not been helpful for those using geodemographics to better understand the ecology of urban areas. Clearly there are many instances in which the predictive power of a person-level classification will prove greater than that of a genuinely geodemographic one. But one should not overlook the many instances where an organization will already have access to a wealth of person-level data. Where it does, the value of a geodemographic classification will be to add incremental predictive power, not to replace already known person-level data. This incremental predictive power should arise from articulating the impact of neighbourhood effects, in other words the impact peer groups effects have on social behaviour.

The next phase in the development of geodemographics is difficult to predict, but it will almost certainly involve the utilization of ever more sources of big data (Dalton and Thatcher, 2015) at ever-greater levels of granularity. There is, for example, currently much discussion about the rhetoric and reality of using data from GPS-enabled smart phones to track and trace the movements of people from home to work and all places in-between, in order to develop a new form of ever more nuanced geo-locative geodemographics (Smith, 2017).

# Creating an international taxonomy of neighbourhoods

When at an international conference a social scientific researcher presents the results of his or her fieldwork in Bilbao or Stoke-on-Trent, one has to ask how relevant the findings are likely to be to other attendees who may be investigating similar phenomena in Dortmund or Thessaloniki, or even Bogota, Cape Town or Osaka. We would be unduly pessimistic to presume that no research findings can have applicability across national borders, but it would be equally unrealistic to suppose that every research finding enjoyed the universality of applicability that applies in the natural sciences. It would be reasonable to suppose that an international taxonomy of neighbourhoods could therefore provide a useful framework for establishing both the countries and the areas within them to which particular research findings or successful research-led interventions are likely to be relevant. Can geodemographics deliver on this ambition?

As of 2016, geodemographics had been commercially deployed in some 31 countries on six continents.[8] The initial impetus for the expansion of geo-demographics was the globalization of a little recognized supply chain, the requirement of international retailers for information in a consistent format which would enable them to optimize the location of new branch outlets. Hong Kong is one of a number of territories for which *Mosaic* classifications were built at the request of Marks & Spencer. The extent of *Mosaic's* internationalization is evident from the list of case studies contained in Figure 4.2.

However consistent the methodology used to build these various national classifications, their builders cannot count on obtaining access to a consistent set of demographic data sets or variables. Nor, perhaps more importantly, can they rely on data being made available at a consistent level of geographic granularity. As a result, there was never any expectation that the categories of neighbourhood that the algorithm produced in Norway would bear a direct correspondence to those that characterized Hong Kong, Spain or Brazil. In an increasingly globalized world it would of course be surprising if there were no consistency between the classifications, if only at a coarse level of grouping; in practice, comparison of the results of different classifications does reveal a significant level of similarity.

The 60 or so categories produced in each territory inevitably reflect local differences in climatic conditions, cultural habits, building styles and planning policies. Nevertheless, it is possible to recognize a dozen or so broad categories which consistently appear in virtually every territory. Whilst the demographic and behavioural profiles of these groupings are broadly independent of national jurisdiction, their physical appearance can be quite different. So too is the location within the urban built-up area where these types of neighbourhood are most likely to be situated.

On closer inspection, it is apparent that international differences in the form of *Mosaic* classifications are not randomly distributed. As a general rule, the differences that distinguished one Mediterranean European country from another, and the differences that characterized one northern European country from another, are far smaller than the differences between Mediterranean and northern European countries. Likewise, though patterns of residential segregation in the Americas are consistently different from those in Europe, North American patterns of residential structures are closer to those of northern European countries, and those in Latin America are closer to Mediterranean Europe.

To facilitate dialogue between its national subsidiaries and franchisees Experian formed a *Mosaic International Network*. There being overall over 1,000 different *Mosaic* categories for an international user to absorb, the network decided there

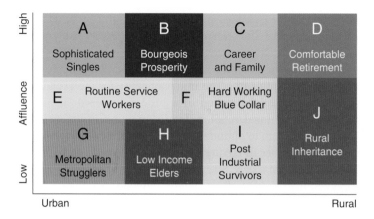

**Figure 4.3** *Global Mosaic* Schema

would be value in what was to become referred to as *Global Mosaic*, a grouping of ten higher order categories into which each of the more detailed categories in each country can be grouped (see Figure 4.3). This taxonomy was constructed using affluence and urban–rural, the two most powerful dimensions of neighbourhood differentiation and ones that emerged in every country. As with each national classification, each Group was denoted by a letter and associated with the colour traditionally used to denote it in the United Kingdom.

Initially the grouping of national categories into global categories was an entirely arbitrary process. In due course a more formal series of rules was developed using a tree structure analogous to CHAID.[9] These were based on how each national cluster compared with the rest of the country of which it was a part using indicators of age, household composition, wealth and industrial structure.

It was thought that such a system would be useful for a retailer who, having profiled their target customers in one country, would then be able to identify the shopping centres which ought to be best for their proposition when entering a new market. It would also be possible to identify how similar or how different was the appeal of an international brand in its different markets. For example a Scandinavian car manufacturer used this schema to identify that the status of its brand varied internationally almost in direct proportion to its market share, the market in which its vehicles had the least prestige being its home market.

Figure 4.4, taken from the *Global Mosaic* handbook, is the profile for Group J, *Rural Inheritance*. Among other items it lists the countries where the category is relatively under- or over-represented. It also measures the average difference between the population of this group and the average of the 16 countries included in the system.

Figure 4.4   *Global Mosaic* Group J – *Rural Inheritance*

# How consistent are patterns of urban structure of different countries?

A comparative analysis of the geographical location of the different *Global Mosaic* groupings in different countries shows that the patterns described in our discussion of the work of the Chicago School in Chapter 2 are far more characteristic of northern Europe, North America and Australia than they are of Mediterranean Europe and Latin America. In Mediterranean Europe proximity to the public spaces of the city centre is valued to a much greater extent than in the north and, though some young families settle on the urban periphery, as a rule the urban fringe is the location of public housing, of immigrants and the poor.

In Mediterranean cultures and in Latin America, perhaps because of the more powerful level of family support, it is much less common to find the types of neighbourhoods that are so much in evidence in London, Sydney and San Francisco, where spacious older houses have been divided into small flats and shared accommodation for young singles. In Spain and Italy young people are more likely to study at a local university and to live with their parents until they marry, and in some cases even longer. It is for this reason that the *Mosaic* Types *Town Gown Transition* or even *Rootless Singles*, which were so evident in the Liverpool study, tend not to be found in *Mosaics* in Mediterranean Europe.

A second difference is in the built form. Many more neighbourhoods in Mediterranean Europe than in northern Europe are characterized by high-density developments of purpose-built blocks of flats. Clearly the desire of the better-off to live close to shopping, business and entertainment areas close to the city centre cannot be accommodated other than through the construction of apartments. However, it might be argued that the climatic conditions that prevail in northwest Europe enhance the amenity value of a suburban plot which much better lends itself to the creation of a garden, as for example would be prized in the UK, Ireland, Netherlands, Belgium and northern France.

In these countries the attraction of life in a rural setting is also evident from the emergence of categories such as the UK's *Semi-Rural Seclusion* or *Greenbelt Guardians* where well-paid workers in nearby towns prefer the lifestyle and environment of what are essentially now commuter villages. This Type of neighbourhood is also particularly evident in Germany.

Another respect in which *Global Mosaic* highlights differences between the Mediterranean and northern Europe is in the rate at which the social status of a neighbourhood drops the further it lies from a city. Whereas in the nineteenth century people who lived in rural areas in northern Europe could expect to improve their standard of living by migrating to cities, it is now in those very same cities that poverty and deprivation are most highly concentrated. There is still an income gradient between metropolitan cities and the countryside but it is far less steep than it used to be. In northern Europe, *Mosaic* suggests it is very much less marked than it is in Mediterranean Europe or in North or Latin America. In northern Europe in general, and in Scandinavia in particular, physical distance presents much less of a barrier to the adoption of technological innovation and contemporary lifestyles.

There are many respects in which London is an exception to the patterns that differentiate northern from Mediterranean Europe. First, whilst London remains a great magnet for the mobile young, recent versions of *Mosaic* reveal a very marked change in the character of London's inner suburbs, the conversion of houses of multiple occupation into well-appointed self-contained flats, the construction of new apartment buildings and the displacement of rootless singles by a well-educated and typically very highly paid elite, *Liberal Opinion*.

In terms of geodemographic structure, London is beginning to take on the form of a Mediterranean city, perhaps in response to its changing ethnic profile. Additionally, although London acts as the centre for employment across a huge swathe of south east England, *Mosaic* shows that the decline in levels of affluence by distance from central London is far more pronounced than is the case with other British and northern European cities. Recent migrants to satellite communities in the south east of England tend now to be middle income groups unable to afford the high costs of housing in inner London rather than, as in earlier times, higher income families opting to live in a quieter and healthier setting.

In North America, and also to a degree in Australia, proximity to the public spaces of the city centre has much less appeal than in most of continental Europe. There the affluent classes move progressively further away from the centre of the city as new homes are built on the urban periphery, just as was posited by the theories of the Chicago School.

As a result the highest status *Mosaic* Types tend to cluster on the very edge of the built-up urban area. In the absence of historic villages and with a climate that discourages the development of gardens, there are fewer reasons for the rich to choose to live beyond the envelope of urban areas and taste directs house-buyers towards what is new and in pristine condition rather than towards heritage buildings with their inevitable blemishes. This applies not just to residential properties but also to shopping centres and commercial buildings, and, no doubt, to the buildings from which public services are provided. The New World, as a result, experiences a steeper income gradient as you move away from the city, one more typical of Mediterranean than of northern Europe.

Beneath these differences between northern and Mediterranean Europe and between the Old and New Worlds, *Global Mosaic* reveals other differences that reflect planning and social policies which are specific to individual countries. A clear divide between the status of private and social renting has been a feature of every British classification since the time of the Liverpool study. This aspect of a neighbourhood's distinction is much less evident in the *Mosaic* schemas for other countries where less stigma appears to be attached to living in socially owned housing.

Another key difference is in the proportion of households with younger children who live in the most prestigious neighbourhoods. In Britain, the Netherlands and Australia, planning constraints have resulted in a scarcity of housing with the concomitant increase in property prices. As a result, prestigious neighbourhoods are populated largely by mature families, empty-nesters and the retired. Younger people just cannot build sufficient equity in their homes to be able to gain access to these neighbourhoods. By contrast in Italy, Spain, Germany, Scandinavia, Hong

Kong, China and the Czech Republic many more of the most prestigious suburban neighbourhoods are occupied by economically successful young families engaged in new, private sector businesses.

*Mosaic* also highlights cultural differences in relation to retirement and the ownership of second homes. Swedish, Spanish and Czech Republic *Mosaics* each contain one or more categories marked by the widespread practice of urban apartment dwellers owning weekend or summer homes. In Britain, despite the increase in second home ownership in categories such as *Summer Playgrounds*, it is typically only the wealthy who own weekend or summer accommodation. Rather than retreat to the quietude of their own chalet in a forest, in the mountains or by a lake, Britain's urban populations prefer a day-trip, weekend or summer holiday at one of the many types of coastal community we describe in Chapter 10.

A visible consequence of this difference is the consistent appearance within UK *Mosaics* of various subdivisions of *Grey Perspectives*. In the US version of *Mosaic* there are categories which identify purpose-built developments for retired people, often in the form of gated and/or wardened accommodation. Such a type of neighbourhood is almost wholly absent from continental Europe. There, perhaps because people are more attached to the place where they live, there is much less of a habit of moving on retirement and much less geographical segregation between pensioners and people of working age.

Though the practice of geodemographic classification has advanced most rapidly in industrial countries, there are a number of instances where comparatively poor populations have been subjected to this form of classification. The Peruvian classification was commissioned by a door-to-door distribution business. The Ecuadorian classification was designed to investigate uneven levels of vulnerability to natural disasters. It focuses on the risk to Quito residents of an eruption of the neighbouring Guagua Pichincha volcano. By combining quantitative and qualitative survey data it was developed for use both as a decision support system and a tool for the effective communication of that risk to key stakeholders and particularly affected neighbourhoods (Willis, 2016).

As one would expect, neighbourhood classifications in Brazil, Peru and South Africa incorporate categories representing favelas and shantytowns. Perhaps the most counter-intuitive feature of these typologies is how the lack of planning controls seems to have resulted in an absence of any clear differentiation of neighbourhood types within marginal townships. The weakness of the legal process for certificating the ownership of land seems to have resulted in the more economically successful members of marginal communities using their new-found wealth to improve their existing houses, often by building additional storeys, rather than by trading up to a home in a more prestigious neighbourhood. The extent to which conditions in marginal communities can be compared internationally is hindered by census statistics not being published for the predominantly Palestinian neighbourhoods in Israel and the Andean ones in Peru and Ecuador.

In countries such as South Africa, Brazil, Peru and Ecuador, with their high levels of inequality at the household level, classifications of this sort can play an important role in enabling the state to tailor public services both to areas of need, as they did in Liverpool, and to the channels by which poorer communities engage with the state, as in Ecuador.

What value can international geodemographic comparison contribute to the research community and to the development of public policy? At the most basic, as we hinted at the start of this chapter, a consistent international taxonomy of neighbourhoods is useful for identifying the locations in any country to which findings of research undertaken in another country are likely to be most relevant. At a higher level, it provides a formal method for selecting the locations for use in comparative studies between communities in different countries.

A category such as *Industrial Grit* can be found in almost every country where communities have been affected by the global decline of smokestack industries. These, it can be believed, are the places where people are most likely to eat food which is most traditionally specific to their country and region, tripe in Lancashire and fabada in Asturias, to eat poorly and, as a result, to suffer bad health. The characterization of these neighbourhoods in a consistent manner would provide an excellent sampling frame for an international comparative study on the impact of employment in noxious industries on diet and health.

Beyond these more obvious applications, an international basis of comparison can highlight some of the external and institutional factors which contribute to patterns of urban structure differing from country to country. Climate is a particularly good example. Levels of rainfall have a major effect on what types of terrain it is attractive to live in and how appealing a country view or colourful garden is likely to be. The presence or absence of particular categories can throw light on the consequence of specific public policies. The cultural and historic tradition that British children should attend further education institutions beyond commuting distance of their parents' home has a significant impact on British geodemographics, as does the practice of relocating on retirement. The character of Mediterranean geodemographic classifications is affected by the greater role of the family in providing social support.

Then there are the consequences of public policy which, in theory, are more amenable to change. Primary among these are planning and housing policies, the designation and protection of the green belt, the provision of and rules governing access to social housing, regulations governing immigration rights and financial incentives towards home ownership or public renting.

A key motivation for the development of international geodemographics has been the need of international retailers to access a consistent decision support system for locating new outlets when entering a new international market. Despite variations in the sources of data and the level of granularity of national postcode systems, the fact that the clusters of each national system, though optimized for its market and independently built, can be placed within a consistent framework of a dozen categories does suggest that any country integrated into the world economic system is likely to develop patterns of residential structure characterized by a common set of categories.

Whilst these categories may be functionally equivalent, there are invariably interesting differences in the individual Types that appear or do not appear in particular countries. Thus, Japan sports a category based on company-owned accommodation; the United States has no categories characterized by social housing; and Hong Kong seemingly has no seaside retirement resorts. Though some of these detailed differences reflect climatic differences, the majority reflect cultural and/or institutional differences. Once they are identified these differences make us more sensitive to the impact of culture on residential structure.

What would Britain be like if students did not 'go away' to university but lived at home as they do in Italy or if, as in Belgium, the countryside around cities was not constrained by the existence of a green belt or, as in Japan, if elderly people living in rural areas lived in extended families or enjoyed exceptional life expectancy? The international comparison of neighbourhood categories can in this way throw light on the existence and impact of cultural practices which opinion-formers, accustomed as they are to the practices of the culture they belong to, can easily take for granted.

## Notes

[1] Google N-gram suggests that the first use of the string 'geodemographic' occurred in a book published in 1902. It is not possible to decipher the source. Google Scholar attributes the first unhyphenated use of the term to a journal article by Zelinsky (1970). Though the term occurs on 13 occasions in the paper, it is clear that it does not refer to the types of neighbourhood classifications being discussed here, but to a more general contraction of the geography of demography. The first published use of the string 'geodemographics', as understood here, which Google Scholar picks up is Robbin (1980).

[2] So, Chicago features prominently in the history of geodemographic classification, both as the source of academic thinking on the human ecology of the city and as the location for the development of the commercial application of early versions of the technology. It is also worth noting that from 1969 onwards Chicago was the location for the development of SPSS – an important and influential piece of statistical software (Uprichard et al., 2008) – with procedures for cluster and factor analysis and other 'data reduction' techniques.

[3] Again, these derive from the 2003 version of the *Mosaic* geodemographic classification system; their characteristics are described in what follows.

[4] For example, postcodes codified, on the one hand, as *Coronation Street* and, on the other, as *Provincial Privilege* in the 2003 version of the *Mosaic* geodemographic classification system.

[5] A primary care trust (PCT) was part of the administrative structure of the NHS in England from 2001 to 2013.

[6] The measure was constructed for each postcode by identifying all other postcodes within a given distance, dividing the population of that postcode by the square of the distance and summing for all postcodes.

[7] This process is analogous to optimizing a multiple regression model but across many separate variables simultaneously.

[8] Countries for which geodemographic classifications are known to have been built include: Australia; Belgium; Brazil; Canada; China; Colombia; Czech Republic; Denmark; Ecuador; Finland; France; Germany; Greece; Hong Kong; Israel; Italy; Japan; Malaysia; Netherlands; New Zealand; Norway; Peru; Portugal; Republic of Ireland; Romania; Singapore; South Africa; Spain; Sweden; United Kingdom; and the United States.

[9] Chi-square Automatic Interaction Detector (CHAID) was a technique created by Gordon V. Kass in 1980. CHAID is a tool used to discover the relationship between variables. CHAID analysis builds a predictive model, or tree, to help determine how the inclusion of additional variables in a model increases its ability to explain variations in the level of a given dependent variable. Further explanation is provided in Burrows and Rhodes (1998).

# 5

# WHO DO *THEY* THINK *YOU* ARE?

## Capturing the Changing Face of British Society

### How well do geodemographic classifications reflect changes in British neighbourhoods?

The year when Webber moved from the realm of public policy at the CES to the world of commerce at CACI, 1979, also happened to be the year when Margaret Thatcher's first administration was elected. One of its earliest actions was to close the CES.[1]

It would be reasonable to suppose that the manner in which geodemographic categories were labelled would be affected by this change and that whatever sociological insights that the practice of geodemographic classification had acquired would be lost. This is not how it turned out and the new cluster labels owed rather more to sociological parlance than did those by which CES had described the CRN categories. For newcomers to this arcane new science, and indeed for many established users, labels such as *Rising Materialists*, which happened to be the category that described the Dulwich postcode in which the Thatchers had recently bought a house,[2] were to become the very essence of geodemographics. Appreciation of its quasi-sociological terminology became a badge of distinction for its marketing adherents.

One test of the validity that proponents claimed for geodemographics is how well labels such as *Rising Materialists* capture the different types of residential neighbourhood that have evolved during the long period of growth of British cities. Another is how well the labels used by later versions of *Mosaic* capture the impact of the physical, political and social changes that occurred under Thatcher's premiership or during the subsequent consolidation of neo-liberal ideology during the Blair years (Davies, 2016). Before we enter these discussions, it is pertinent to ask what the considerations were that governed the choice of cluster labels?[23] And whom did they delight and whom did they offend?

Given the claims that this branch of the marketing profession has functioned as a form of shadow 'commercial sociology' (Burrows and Gane, 2006; Savage and Burrows, 2007), it is curious how little attention the literature on geodemographics has given to the features which distinguish individual geodemographic categories. Even less attention has been given to assessing how well the categories capture contemporary processes of social change. An evaluation of the validity of geodemographic categories through a review of its labels also provides a platform for Part II where we consider what insights a geodemographic perspective might contribute to a series of contemporary debates on identity politics, education, social cohesion, the preservation of the green-belt and the impact of tourism.

One of the key propositions advanced in Chapter 1 is that lay people rely to a much greater degree than professionals on visual clues for interpreting the social character of residential neighbourhoods. This is one of the reasons why the photographs of streets typical of each cluster came to play such a prominent role in the documentation of the *Acorn* and *Mosaic* categories. The photographs of houses in each cluster often reveal how narrow a period of time their houses were built in. D24 *Coronation Street,* illustrated in Figure 5.1 is a good example. Most of its postcodes were built within 15 years of the coronation of Edward VII in 1901. Though this was known at the time the label was conceived it was only later that it was discovered that no other geodemographic cluster contained as many streets named 'Coronation Street' as the one labelled *Coronation Street.* Similarly, though no question on the age of houses is asked in census questionnaires, most streets classified as C18 *Sprawling Subtopia* date from a narrow period during the 1930s when semi-detached homes were built in the Mock-Tudor style.

Whilst it would be difficult to be definitive about the patterns of residential segregation prior to 1801, the year of the nation's first census, one would imagine that the pattern would have been relatively simple. Outside the towns a distinction could be made between the nuclear villages typical of eastern England, especially in those counties affected by the enclosure movement, and the more dispersed pattern of remote homesteads that characterize the west and Wales.

Other neighbourhood Types would have emerged in small market towns serving rural hinterlands. Fishing villages and military barracks would have had their own distinctive demographics. In London, a clear distinction could have been made between the residential areas in which craft trades were practised, the ones where

Town, Bath's Georgian crescents and the stuccoed terraces and garden squares of London's West End.

The census indicators that result in their postcodes forming such a distinct cluster two centuries after their construction are a curious mix crossing many conventional dimensions of social differentiation: high educational status; terraced housing; comparatively low numbers of persons per room; high occupational status; low car ownership; few children; rapid turnover of residents; and a high proportion of residents born in other western European countries. Only in prime Georgian neighbourhoods does such a combination of demographic data occur.

Many of the nineteenth-century extensions to these neighbourhoods, in London places such as Camden Town and Brixton, fall into the category E28 *Counter-Cultural Mix*. Houses in this Type of neighbourhood were designed for social classes who at the time they were built had sufficient income to employ servants. During the inter-war years, as servants became less affordable and as the middle classes increasingly sought homes where privacy was assured by a spacious garden, new neighbourhood categories such as C19 *Original Suburbs* began to emerge. These were further from the noise and pollution of the inner city resulting in an even more rapid decline in the social status of these inner city neighbourhoods. The measures whereby the algorithm distinguishes *Counter Cultural Mix* from *Original Suburbs* include number of rooms, house tenure, family composition and car ownership.

Chapter 3 has shown how in Liverpool a similar decline had befallen streets in 'Rooming House Areas' clusters as large old houses were converted to houses in multiple occupation, their structures deteriorating and their grounds neglected. It was to such neighbourhoods that the single and unattached gravitated, as did people with experience of institutional life, the bohemian young, students and newly arrived migrants, whether from distant parts of Britain or from overseas. More recently, many streets of this sort have smartened up as well-educated young people value proximity to the vibrancy of city centres and choose to rent or buy converted flats within what were previously decaying three- or four-storey properties.

Chapter 3 referred to how Merseyside's coastal communities such as New Brighton and Southport began to sprout new Types of residential neighbourhood during the inter-war years. A new classification, J54 *Bungalow Retirement*, adds to the residential heterogeneity of seaside resorts, neighbourhoods of small, easy to manage properties marketed to elderly owner-occupiers uncertain how long they will remain able to climb stairs.

In resorts such as New Brighton, which were popular with the urban proletariat, a new form of neighbourhood was to emerge in the form of high density, three or more storey boarding houses. These accommodated summer visitors. The change in their function to neighbourhoods classified as D25 *Town Centre Refuge* has been accelerated not only by the cheap air travel that has made the

Mediterranean an affordable and attractive alternative holiday destination, but by the decanting to these neighbourhoods of the homeless and the jobless former residents of metropolitan cities.

Meanwhile the Victorian and Edwardian search for the picturesque resulted in the emergence of K56 *Tourist Attendants* – a category of neighbourhood found in places such as Ambleside and Lynton that serviced day-visitors with teas, ice-creams and crafts rather than with overnight accommodation. How evocative these place names were is attested to by the frequency with which, during the period 1880–1914, their names became used both as house names and street names in postcodes in the geodemographic Group D *Ties of Community*.

Emerging attitudes towards the picturesque are also seen in the classification K57 *Summer Playgrounds*, common in places such as Salcombe and Rock, Aldeburgh and Burnham Market. This form of neighbourhood is dominated by second homes and upmarket holiday rentals and attracts social classes that would not want to share a holiday experience with other hotel or boarding house guests.

Already, even in the earliest geodemographic classifications, the algorithms had been able to distinguish different manifestations of working class community. The older terraces in the inner parts of larger cities such as Liverpool and Middlesbrough, the previously noted *Coronation Street*, served the needs primarily of a poorly educated and unskilled population, many of whom were unemployed or employed on a casual basis. With front doors opening directly onto the street, these contrast with the terraces of a similar style and age in pit villages and other small industrial communities classified as D23 *Industrial Grit*. A key differentiator was that in the larger cities *Coronation Street* was the natural habitat of young families with a single, pre-school child, whereas residents in *Industrial Grit* were more likely to be skilled manual workers, many more of whom owned homes and cars and who moved house far less frequently. Early classifications also identify Types such as D22 *Affluent Blue Collar*, neighbourhoods of inter-war, semi-detached housing which followed the inter-war expansion of assembly plants of the automotive and aircraft industries in towns such as Birmingham, Coventry, Preston and, crucially, Luton.[4]

In the earlier geodemographic classifications, the mass of middle and better-off suburban neighbourhoods were located inside the boundary of major urban centres. Since 1979 an increasing share of the population has moved into emerging semi-rural geodemographic categories such as A07 *Semi-Rural Seclusion*, neighbourhoods which were historically rural in terms of their physical environment but which have become increasingly suburban in their demographic character as small estates of new houses have been added to established villages within easy commuter reach of centres of office employment.[5]

Initially the clustering algorithms distinguished within rural Britain between rural villages, many of whose inhabitants were employed on farms and hence classified as having 'semi-skilled' occupations, and areas of scattered own-account farmers, who, because they were self-employed, were classified by the census as 'skilled manual'. Over time this began to break down into more nuanced categories differentiated by: the attractiveness of the scenery, which resulted in, for example, a *Rural Retirement Mix* (a 1980s *Mosaic* Type); accessibility to urban employment, resulting, for example, in K58 *Greenbelt Guardians*; an *Agribusiness* cluster economically engaged in food processing as well as food production; and a residual K61 *Upland Hill Farmers*, where isolation and rural deprivation were common social problems.

Within neighbourhoods dominated by social housing factors which tend to differentiate clusters are the age of the estate, the size of town in which it is situated and whether it was built on a green-field or a brown-field site. Most of Britain's new town neighbourhoods fall within Group H *Blue Collar Enterprise*, most brown-field developments, whether high rise or high-density low rise, being classified under Group F, *Welfare Borderline*.

Sources of behavioural data demonstrate the considerable differences between the two in terms of levels of reliance on public services. It is members of the former group that have been most successful in exercising their 'right-to-buy' with the result that clustering algorithms now find it difficult to recognize this as a distinct geodemographic grouping on the basis solely of demographic and consumption data. The construction of high rise forms of development on the urban periphery produces yet another form of residential neighbourhood, differentiated both from brown-field high rise in the inner city, and the more sought after low-density estates built in established suburbs.

The disproportionate concentration of immigrant groups in London during the period since 1971 has been captured by geodemographic classification with a much more nuanced series of predominately ethnic neighbourhood Types, including the suburban C20 *Asian Enterprise*.

Though no formal measures of regionality are included in the data sets used to build geodemographic classifications, the algorithms invariably generate certain highly regionalized neighbourhood Types such as F36 *Metro Multiculture*, a Type which is virtually exclusive to inner London. Distinctive types habitually occur in Scotland, largely because Scottish properties tend to have many fewer rooms than those in England and Wales. The most striking result of the household overcrowding that results is the emergence of F37 *Upper Floor Families*, a form of public housing almost unique to Strathclyde, characterized by exceptional proportions of households with children living in cramped high rise accommodation and by levels of unemployment and lack of occupational skills of a quite different order to anywhere else in the UK.

But compared with local authorities in the south of England, Scottish municipalities have traditionally been much more active builders of social housing.

As a result, a much higher proportion of Scotland's middle classes lives in what originally was built as social housing. This is reflected in the concentration in Scotland of a number of geodemographic categories of neighbourhood characterized by better-off council tenants such as G45 *Older Right to Buy*.

The right to buy one's council property is one of a number of social trends whose impact on urban structure is very visible in recent geodemographic classifications. Another is the increase in the number and type of neighbourhoods dominated by student populations. In addition to the old-established heartlands characterized by halls of residence, E34 *University Challenge*, we find the emergence of E33 *Town Gown Transition* – neighbourhoods where students rent shared houses in streets which are equally attractive to other footloose singles. The growing interest of home builders and property companies in constructing apartments in central city locations, whether for rent or sale, is likely to add further complexity to future geodemographic classification systems (Sage et al., 2013).[6]

Another trend which has had an impact on classifications built since 2001 is the growing number of properties owned by small private landlords. This has had a particularly pronounced effect in neighbourhoods of semi-detached owner-occupied homes, built during the 1930s to accommodate the lower middle classes. This is one reason why neighbourhoods of this sort are the ones, at least whilst Britain remains a member of the European Union, which have experienced the highest growth in the number of people of eastern European origin. The growth of private landlordism and the greater difficulty young people experience in affording a home of their own is causing a number of neighbourhood types to become less socially homogenous than they used to be.

A trend which may herald the weakening of the predictive power of future geodemographic classifications is the increasingly common requirement that affordable housing should be included in new development.

A novel but effective basis for charting the historic evolution of Britain's residential neighbourhoods is created when *Mosaic* is cross analysed by the country's 'street' names. Table 5.1 evaluates a sample of *Mosaic* categories from the 2003 version on the basis of where different 'street' endings are most common. Thus, addresses ending in 'Place', 'Square' and 'Mews' are most commonly found in predominantly Georgian A01 *Global Connections*. 'Lanes' – commonest in pre-industrial Britain – gave way to 'Streets' before World War I, and 'Roads' thereafter, only to be replaced by 'Gardens' and 'Crescents' during the inter-war period. Post-war private developers attracted private buyers by choosing addresses for their estates that ended in 'Drive', 'Way', 'Close' and, most recently, 'Meadow'. Though it is understandable that residents of F38 *Tower Block Living* should find themselves living in 'Heights', E33 *Town Gown Transition* in 'Cloisters' and I48 *Old People in Flats* in 'Havens', it is also perhaps fitting that 'Retreats' should occur most often in neighbourhoods classified as E31 *Caring Professionals*.

**Table 5.1**  Characteristic 'Street' Name Endings

| Timeline | Mosaic 2003 Type of neighbourhood | Characteristic endings | | |
|---|---|---|---|---|
| Early | A01: *Global Connections* | Place | Square | Mews |
| | K58: *Greenbelt Guardians* | Lane | Green | |
| | K57: *Summer Playgrounds* | Cottages | | |
| | K61: *Upland Hill Farmers* | View | Cross | |
| | J56: *Tourist Attendants* | Terrace | Quay | Cliff |
| 1900 | D24: *Coronation Street* | Street | | |
| | D25: *Town Centre Refuge* | Parade | | |
| | D27: *Settled Minorities* | Road | | |
| | E31: *Caring Professionals* | Retreat | | |
| | E33: *Town Gown Transition* | Cloisters | | |
| Inter-war | C20: *Asian Enterprise* | Avenue | Gardens | |
| | A07: *Semi-Rural Seclusion* | Orchard | | |
| | H44: *Rustbelt Resilience* | Crescent | | |
| | A03: *Corporate Chieftains* | Chase | | |
| | G42: *Low Horizons* | Grove | | |
| | I48: *Old People in Flats* | Haven | | |
| | J51: *Sepia Memories* | Esplanade | | |
| | F39: *Dignified Dependency* | Walk | | |
| 1945 | F38: *Tower Block Living* | Court | Heights | |
| | B09: *Fledgling Nurseries* | Drive | Way | |
| | B10: *Upscale New Owners* | Close | | |
| Recent | A08: *Just Moving In* | Meadow | | |

# How did the character of British neighbourhoods change during the Thatcher years?

As we explained in Chapter 2, the labels of the first version of the *PRIZM* classification, released in the United States in 1978, were informed by references to popular culture or lay vernacular classifications of people and places. Examples were *Blue Blood Estates*, *Money and Brains*, *Furs and Station Wagons* and *Urban Gold Coast* (as enumerated earlier in Table 2.1). The labels given to the 1981 *Acorn* neighbourhood Groups and Types still smack of their origins within

**Table 5.2**  *Acorn* Neighbourhood Groups and Types, 1981 Version

| *Acorn* Groups | % hhds | *Acorn* Types | % hhds |
|---|---|---|---|
| Agricultural areas | 3.3 | Agricultural villages | 2.5 |
| | | Areas of farms and smallholdings | 0.8 |
| Modern family housing, higher incomes | 14.8 | Cheap modern private housing | 3.7 |
| | | Recent private housing, young families | 2.9 |
| | | Modern private housing, older children | 5.4 |
| | | New detached housing, young families | 2.3 |
| | | Military bases | 0.4 |
| Older housing of intermediate status | 18.7 | Mixed owner-occupied & council estates | 4.0 |
| | | Small town centres & flats above shops | 4.4 |
| | | Villages with non-farm employment | 4.7 |
| | | Older private housing, skilled workers | 5.7 |
| Poor quality older terraced housing | 4.6 | Unimproved terraces with old people | 2.8 |
| | | Pre-1914 terraces, low income families | 1.4 |
| | | Tenement flats lacking amenities | 0.4 |
| Better-off council estates | 12.2 | Council estates, well-off older workers | 3.5 |
| | | Recent council estates | 2.2 |
| | | Council estates, well-off young workers | 4.5 |
| | | Small council houses, often Scottish | 2.0 |
| Less well-off council estates | 10.4 | Low rise estates in industrial towns | 4.6 |
| | | Inter-war council estates, older people | 3.5 |
| | | Council housing for the elderly | 2.2 |
| Poorest council estates | 6.8 | New council estates in inner cities | 2.2 |
| | | Overspill estates, high unemployment | 2.7 |
| | | Council estates with overcrowding | 1.4 |
| | | Council estates with worst poverty | 0.5 |
| Multi-racial areas | 3.5 | Multi-occupied terraces, poor Asians | 0.3 |
| | | Owner-occupied terraces with Asians | 0.9 |
| | | Multi-let housing with Afro-Caribbeans | 0.7 |
| | | Better-off multi-ethnic areas | 1.7 |
| High status non-family areas | 4.9 | High status areas, few children | 2.3 |
| | | Multi-let big old houses and flats | 1.9 |
| | | Furnished flats, mostly single people | 0.7 |
| Affluent suburban housing | 15.9 | Inter-war semis, white collar workers | 6.1 |
| | | Spacious inter-war semis, big gardens | 4.9 |
| | | Villages with wealthy older commuters | 2.8 |
| | | Detached houses, excusive suburbs | 2.1 |
| Better-off retirement areas | 4.8 | Private houses, well-off elderly | 2.7 |
| | | Private flats with single pensioners | 2.1 |
| Unclassified | 0.1 | | 0.1 |
| Total Great Britain | 100.0 | | 100.0 |

the discourse of central and local government. They are terse and quite formal descriptors almost all grounded in six key dimensions of differentiation: location, rural–suburban–urban; housing, type and tenure; prosperity; life stage; household structure; and ethnicity. Britain was segmented into just 38 different Types nested within 11 broader Groups. Table 5.2 shows the original classification and the proportion of households falling into each Group and Type.

Table 5.2 shows a socio-spatial structure of British society as pertained at the time that Margaret Thatcher came to power. It is a geodemographic description that was to change markedly over subsequent decades. The most prevalent Type of neighbourhood – containing some 6.1 per cent of all households – was described as *Inter-war semis, White collar workers* nesting within a broader Group of neighbourhoods designated as *Affluent suburban housing*.[7] The next most prevalent Type of neighbourhood – containing some 5.7 per cent of all households – was described as *Older private housing, Skilled workers* nested within the largest of all Groups of neighbourhoods labelled as *Older housing of intermediate status –* containing some 18.7 per cent of all households.

These neighbourhoods were largely the preserve of semi-skilled and skilled manual workers with a foothold in the lower end of owner occupation.[8] What were termed *Multi-racial areas* accounted for just 3.5 per cent of all households. What was still then referred to as *Council housing* was so differentiated that it required as many as 11 different Types of neighbourhood nested into three different Groups in order to fully account for its diversity; almost 30 per cent of all households lived in one or other of these 11 different Types of neighbourhood.

The earliest *Acorn* classification did not offer a particularly granular differentiation of people and places located in more rural areas. It differentiated between two neighbourhood Types located within *Agricultural areas* (some 3.3 per cent of all households) and two further Types with a rural inflection: *Villages with non-farm employment* (4.7 per cent), part of the *Older housing of intermediate status* Group; and *Villages with wealthy older commuters* (2.8 per cent) nested within the *Affluent suburban housing* group.

The specificities of coastal living were also implicit in this original classification. But the complex intersections between race, ethnicity, class and urban culture were not as apparent in the classification as they would later become. Concepts such as 'gentrification' and 'industrial legacy' did not yet appear in the labels, nor did words indicative of taste or ideology, such as 'Conservative' or 'Opinion'.

# Cluster labels offend the sensibilities of some social scientists

By the time Webber had moved to CCN not only had he access to results from the 1981 census, but for the first time he was able to supplement census statistics with various other measures derived from transactional data to which CCN had access as well as links to the wealth of behavioural data contained in the TGI.

The labels of the first version of *Mosaic*, which appeared in the late 1980s, had much more of the feel of the *PRIZM* categories. Although the 12 Groups of neighbourhood identified in the classification still had a semi-formal quality to them – *High Income Families, Council Flats, Mortgaged Families, Country Dwellers* and so on – the *Mosaic* labels begun to draw upon various social and cultural tropes of the time, some of them borrowed from academic urban and cultural studies, in order to better encapsulate some of the most fundamental characteristics of the people and places being described.

As shown in Table 5.3, in just two, or at most three, cleverly selected words such as *Pebble Dash Subtopia, Suburban Mock Tudor, Bohemian Melting Pot* and *Chattering Classes*, and using a maximum of 20 characters, *Mosaic* attempted to envision what by now were 52 (up from 38) different Types of neighbourhood. Underpinning statistically robust categories designed to efficiently account for statistical variation in all manner of other variables, these labels were primarily designed to communicate the essence of each Type to commercial users and marketers. Those more respectful of the political mores of the time, and they included much of the academy, never the most ludic of environments, were often not so sympathetic to what they felt to be analytic playfulness and frivolous disrespect for established modes of discourse (Curry, 1998; Goss, 1995a; 1995b; Graham, 2005; Pickles, 1994).

The objection to the naming of the clusters in this way perhaps diverted attention from a more judicious consideration of the actual patterns of neighbourhood differentiation that these labels described (Parker et al., 2007). To meet the needs of users each label was now accompanied by a plethora of statistical data showing how each neighbourhood differed from the national average; these data were also narrated – often drawing from extant social scientific literature – and accompanied by photographs, collages, statistics, maps, area rankings and even the personal names most over-represented in that Type of neighbourhood. The inclusion of popular names in the documentation proved a source of great entertainment to lay users.

However, it was not just the labels to which these analysts objected – there were also accusations that such classifications were potentially static, essentialist, reductionist, reifying, unable to deal with local specificities (Voas and Williamson, 2001) and potentially generative of a hardening of spatial patterns of segregation (Curry, 1998; Goss, 1995a; 1995b; Graham, 2005; Pickles, 1994).

Because of this, there were a number of years during which the geodemographic research tradition in academic research did not develop at the pace which might otherwise have been anticipated (Reibel, 2011: 310).[9]

Some of these concerns were misplaced and others not. However, as it has become more and more apparent that *all* methods of social research – academic and commercial – have become ever more subject to on-going processes of digitization (Ruppert et al., 2013) – as manifest, in particular, in the turn to big

**Table 5.3**  *Mosaic* Neighbourhood Groups and Types, Original 1980s Version

| *Mosaic* Groups | % hhds | *Mosaic* Types | % hhds |
|---|---|---|---|
| A: High Income Families | 9.8 | A01: Clever Capitalists | 1.5 |
| | | A02: Rising Materialists | 1.5 |
| | | A03: Corporate Careerists | 2.4 |
| | | A04: Ageing Professionals | 1.7 |
| | | A05: Small-Time Business | 2.7 |
| B: Suburban Semis | 11.0 | B06: Green Belt Expansion | 3.4 |
| | | B07: Suburban Mock Tudor | 3.2 |
| | | B08: Pebble Dash Subtopia | 4.4 |
| C: Blue Collar Owners | 13.1 | C09: Affluent Blue Collar | 2.9 |
| | | C10: 30s Industrial Spec | 3.8 |
| | | C11: Low-Rise Right to Buy | 3.3 |
| | | C12: Smokestack Shiftwork | 3.1 |
| D: Low-Rise Council | 14.4 | D13: Co-op Club and Colliery | 3.4 |
| | | D14: Better-off Council | 2.1 |
| | | D15: Low-Rise Pensioners | 3.2 |
| | | D16: Low-Rise Subsistence | 3.5 |
| | | D17: Problem Families | 2.2 |
| E: Council Flats | 6.9 | E18: Families in the Sky | 1.3 |
| | | E19: Graffitied Ghettos | 0.3 |
| | | E20: Small Town Industry | 1.4 |
| | | E21: Mid-Rise Overspill | 0.7 |
| | | E22: Flats for the Aged | 1.4 |
| | | E23: Inner City Towers | 1.8 |
| F: Victorian Low Status | 9.3 | F24: Bohemian Melting Pot | 2.3 |
| | | F25: Victorian Tenements | 0.1 |
| | | F26: Rootless Renters | 1.5 |
| | | F27: Sweatshop Sharers | 1.1 |
| | | F28: Depopulated Terraces | 0.8 |
| | | F29: Rejuvenated Terraces | 3.5 |
| G: Townhouses and Flats | 8.5 | G30: Bijou Homemakers | 3.5 |
| | | G31: Market Town Mixture | 3.8 |
| | | G32: Bedsits and Shop Flats | 1.2 |
| H: Stylish Singles | 6.2 | H33: Town Centre Singles | 2.1 |
| | | H34: Studio Singles | 1.7 |
| | | H35: College and Communal | 0.5 |
| | | H36: Chattering Classes | 1.9 |
| I: Independent Elders | 7.4 | I37: Solo Pensioners | 1.9 |
| | | I38: High Spending Greys | 1.3 |

*(Continued)*

| Mosaic Groups | % hhds | Mosaic Types | % hhds |
|---|---|---|---|
| | | I39: Aged Owner Occupiers | 2.7 |
| | | I40: Elderly in Own Flats | 1.5 |
| J: Mortgaged Families | 6.2 | J41: Brand New Areas | 1.0 |
| | | J42: Prenuptial Owners | 0.8 |
| | | J43: Nest-making Families | 1.7 |
| | | J44: Maturing Mortgages | 2.7 |
| K: Country Dwellers | 7.0 | K45: Gentrified Villages | 1.5 |
| | | K46: Rural Retirement Mix | 0.6 |
| | | K47: Lowland Agribusiness | 1.8 |
| | | K48: Rural Disadvantage | 1.2 |
| | | K49: Tied/Tenant Farmer | 0.6 |
| | | K50: Upland & Small Farms | 1.3 |
| Institutional Areas | 0.4 | L51: Military Bases | 0.3 |
| | | L52: Non-Private Housing | 0.1 |
| Total Great Britain | 100.0 | | 100.0 |

data, 'predictive analytics' and so on (Burrows and Savage, 2014; Uprichard et al., 2008) – such concerns have tended to wane as academic researchers, as well of those from a commercial background, have to confront the realities of how best to respond to the inundation of digital data.[10]

Whatever the objections to the labels used, the first version of the *Mosaic* classification gave a clear indication of how much things were changing under Thatcherism. The more granular set of neighbourhood Types meant that no one Type accounted for any more than 4.4 per cent of households. It was, in fact, the previously mentioned *Pebble Dash Subtopia* that hit this threshold. As a neighbourhood Type it also provides an excellent illustration of how a summary label is able to encapsulate a complex assemblage of attributes – cultural, demographic, economic, material, political, social and so on – that, nevertheless, come together to generate the distinctive socio-spatial amalgam that differentiates such places from other Types of neighbourhood. A summary from the guide[11] that accompanied the release of a slightly later version of the classification gives a good sense of what underpins such a designation:

*Pebble Dash Subtopia* consists of housing that was built during the owner occupier boom of the 1920s and early 1930s, when low density estates of three bedroom semis mushroomed across new London suburbs such as Wembley, Surbiton, Bexleyheath and Hornchurch. This was a period when 'pebble dash' was preferred to traditional brick as a material for the outer facing of such houses.

With bow windows and half-timbered gables, these houses were originally built to meet the demand of white-collar workers for a place of their own, close to the fresh air and delights of the country. With gardens and a space for a car, such estates represented escape from the grime, congestion and confusion of the inner city, and were advertised by the speculative builders who built them as a kind of suburban utopia offering benefits of both town and country living.

Today these suburbs are rather further than they were from the delights of the country and are often suffering from a lack of investment, not just in the dwellings themselves but in schools, shops and public services. Absent are the trendy young singles who are attracted by the more lively and cosmopolitan atmosphere of the Victorian and Edwardian terraces close to town or wish to escape the city altogether to live in modern estates in rural villages.

The ageing population of *Pebble Dash Subtopia* makes for a rather conservative and unfashionable lifestyle, but some of these areas are now becoming significantly younger and more cosmopolitan than they were. The absence of the old community spirit may be less of a problem for the younger generation and new fashions don't have to be bought locally. In areas where people need to make the most of limited incomes, people will know the latest market value of their houses, the comparative prices of petrol at different supermarket filling stations or the recent retail promotions advertised in the local newspaper.

*Pebble Dash Subtopia* comprises people who are careful and reliable about their money; they have practical good sense, keep their wilder emotions under control and find glamour in the cinema, the TV or the weekly magazine.

*Pebble Dash Subtopia* is a good market for first time mortgages, many of which are large in relation to the value of the property. These people are heavy users of most forms of credit and rely on personal loans and credit cards, which they can have difficulty in repaying.

Leisure activities focus around 'going out'; *Pebble Dash Subtopia* are avid restaurant users and are interested in mainstream arts but will also attend the minority events advertised in 'listings' sections of local newspapers. Leisure is particularly focused on mind broadening experiences, for example at the cinema, rather than at family-oriented venues. These people buy packaged holidays, typically a week at a resort in the Mediterranean.

There is strong readership of newspapers such as The Mail and The Express as well as special interest magazines. Foreign newspapers sell well in these neighbourhoods. *Pebble Dash Subtopia* are heavy viewers of TV and prefer human interest programmes, soaps and comedies, as opposed to programmes on antiques, gardening or history. Magazines with a strong low-cost fashion element sell well.

People shop regularly and often for quite small amounts as and when they need to. They pop regularly to the off-licence, buy convenience foods from petrol stations and frequent the cheaper local restaurants. They like experimenting with new and ethnic recipes and try out unusual cocktails and designer branded beers.

*Pebble Dash Subtopia* do not have the budget to buy other than basic household durables, which they buy at the lowest prices they can find. In these neighbourhoods, many households devote substantial amounts of their time to decorating and improving their houses.

Objections to seemingly facile 20-character labels such as *Pebble Dash Subtopia* would be more justifiable were the categories not merely the headings which summarized these more detailed descriptions. These are no more than titles, used in the same way one might title a book, an article, a chapter, or a lecture. There are of course many operational reasons, the layout of the Table 1.3 profiling supporters of a human rights charity and a right-wing political party being examples, why it is impractical to use longer labels, especially where as many as 67 different Types need to be clearly differentiated. It is inevitable that what necessarily becomes an 'ideal type' will do some violence to the specificity of any concrete neighbourhood but such a trade-off is an inevitable and, indeed, inherent feature of much social science research. Indeed, it is an integral feature of any cluster algorithm that it is charged with keeping this variability to the absolute minimum possible.

*Mosaic* also offered up a more highly differentiated set of neighbourhood Types for those at the top end of the income distribution – *High Income Families* were classified into five different Types. Those living in more rural parts of the country were also more finely differentiated; there were now six Types of *Country Dwellers*. Those living in coastal areas were still not clearly differentiated but 11 different neighbourhood Types were still needed to fully describe the span of circumstances of those living in what was still termed 'council' accommodation.

Complex patterns of urban living were beginning to emerge in the classification but, interestingly, a decision was taken that race and ethnicity should no longer be foregrounded in the labels used and that categories with significant minority populations should be subsumed instead within neighbourhood Groups stressing more generalized patterns of cultural diversity such as *Bohemian Melting Pot*. What today are popularly referred to as a *Liberal Metropolitan Elite* are apparent in embryonic form amongst the *Chattering Classes* (just 2 per cent of households at the time).

The next version of *Mosaic*, released in the mid-1990s, retains very similar Groups and Types to the original version but there are some subtle changes whereby some of the labels hint of social and economic processes of change as, for example, where the process of pit closure causes *Co-op Club and Colliery* to become *Coalfield Legacy* and the emergence of a *Rejuvenated Terraces*, hinting at gentrification. Concessions to political correctness appear when *Problem Families* becomes *Peripheral Poverty* though *Sweatshop Sharers* become more explicitly raced as *Asian Heartland*; and *Rejuvenated Terraces* move from the *Victorian Low Status* Group to the more upmarket *Townhouses and Flats* displacing *Bedsits and Shop Flats*, which shifts into the *Stylish Singles* Group (more on account of their single person status than their style as it turns out).

# The emergence of new types of neighbourhood in the twenty-first century

The next version of *Mosaic*, released in 2003, drew upon 2001 census statistics as well as a broader range of transactional data sources. It was a major revision of the classification.[12] Competition between vendors of geodemographic systems resulted in pressures to increase the number of categories, in this instance to as many as 64 distinct Types nested within 11 Groups – a somewhat illogical demand of a methodology developed as a *data reduction* tool. Each Group and Type continued to be given a label that would appeal to commercial and marketing users.

However, the Experian account managers who oversaw the use of the system by the growing number of local authority, public health and police services users successfully lobbied for the creation of a parallel set of labels that would be more acceptable to those working in the public sector. For this category of user, the Group *Symbols of Success* became *Career professionals living in sought-after locations*, within this Group the Type *Cultural Leadership* became *Highly educated senior professionals, many working in the media, politics and law*. Likewise, the parallel label for the Group *Welfare Borderline* became *People living in social housing with uncertain employment in deprived areas*, and within this Group the Type *Metro Multiculture* became *High density social housing, mostly in inner London, with high levels of diversity*; the *Rural Isolation* Group became *People living in rural areas far from urbanization*. Within this Group the *Summer Playgrounds* Type became *Communities of retired people and second homers in areas of high environmental quality*, and so on.

As Table 5.4 shows, by 2003 patterns of differentiation within the urban cores of the country now needed seven different types to describe them. The further expansion of higher education and the accompanying 'studentification' (Sage et al., 2012; 2013) caused the emergence of more neighbourhood Types defined primarily by the presence of students.

**Table 5.4** Mosaic Neighbourhood Groups and Types, 2003 Version

| Mosaic Groups commercial and public sector | % hhds | Mosaic Types | | % hhds |
|---|---|---|---|---|
| | | Commercial | Public sector | |
| A: *Symbols of Success*<br><br>Career professionals living in sought-after locations | 9.6 | A01: *Global Connections* | Financially successful people living in cosmopolitan inner city locations | 0.7 |
| | | A02: *Cultural Leadership* | Highly educated senior professionals, many working in the media, politics and law | 0.9 |
| | | A03: *Corporate Chieftains* | Successful managers living in very large houses in outer suburban locations | 1.1 |
| | | A04: *Golden Empty Nesters* | Financially secure couples, many close to retirement, living in sought-after suburbs | 1.3 |
| | | A05: *Provincial Privilege* | Senior professionals and managers living in the suburbs of major regional centres | 1.7 |
| | | A06: *High Technologists* | Successful, high-earning couples with new jobs in areas of growing high-tech employment | 1.8 |
| | | A07: *Semi-Rural Seclusion* | Well paid executives living in individually designed homes in rural environments | 2.0 |
| B: *Happy Families*<br><br>Younger families living in newer homes | 10.8 | B08: *Just Moving In* | Families and singles living in developments built since 2001 | 0.9 |
| | | B09: *Fledgling Nurseries* | Well-qualified couples typically starting a family on a recently built private estate | 1.2 |
| | | B10: *Upscale New Owners* | Financially better-off families living in relatively spacious modern private estates | 1.4 |
| | | B11: *Families Making Good* | Dual income families on intermediate incomes living on modern estates | 2.3 |
| | | B12: *Middle Rung Families* | Middle income families with children living in estates of modern private homes | 2.9 |
| | | B13: *Burdened Optimists* | First generation owner-occupiers, many with large amounts of consumer debt | 2.0 |
| | | B14: *In Military Quarters* | Military personnel living in purpose-built accommodation | 0.2 |

Table 5.4  (Continued)

| Mosaic Groups commercial and public sector | % hhds | Mosaic Types | | % hhds |
|---|---|---|---|---|
| | | Commercial | Public sector | |
| C: Suburban Comfort<br><br>Older families living in suburbia | 15.1 | C15: Close to Retirement | Senior white collar workers, many on the verge of a financially secure retirement | 2.8 |
| | | C16: Conservative Values | Low density private estates, now with self-reliant couples approaching retirement | 2.8 |
| | | C17: Small Time Business | Small business proprietors living in low density estates in smaller communities | 2.9 |
| | | C18: Sprawling Subtopia | Inter-war suburbs, many with less strong cohesion than they originally had | 3.1 |
| | | C19: Original Suburbs | Singles and childless couples increasingly taking over attractive older suburbs | 2.4 |
| | | C20: Asian Enterprise | Suburbs sought-after by the more successful members of the Asian community | 1.0 |
| D: Ties of Community<br><br>Close-knit, inner city and manufacturing town communities | 16.0 | D21: Respectable Rows | Mixed communities of urban residents living in well-built, early 20th-century housing | 2.7 |
| | | D22: Affluent Blue Collar | Comfortably-off manual workers living in spacious but inexpensive private houses | 3.1 |
| | | D23: Industrial Grit | Owners of affordable terraces built to house 19th-century heavy industrial workers | 3.8 |
| | | D24: Coronation Street | Low income families living in cramped Victorian terraced housing in inner city locations | 2.8 |
| | | D25: Town Centre Refuge | Centres of small market towns and resorts containing many hostels and refuges | 1.1 |
| | | D26: South Asian Industry | Communities of lowly paid factory workers, many of them of South Asian descent | 0.9 |
| | | D27: Settled Minorities | Inner city terraces attracting second generation Londoners from diverse communities | 1.6 |

(Continued)

**Table 5.4** Mosaic Neighbourhood Groups and Types, 2003 Version

| Mosaic Groups commercial and public sector | % hhds | Mosaic Types | | % hhds |
| --- | --- | --- | --- | --- |
| | | Commercial | Public sector | |
| E: Urban Intelligence | 7.2 | E28: Counter Cultural Mix | Neighbourhoods with transient singles living in multiply occupied large old houses | 1.4 |
| Educated, young, single people living in areas of transient populations | | E29: City Adventurers | Economically successful singles, many living in small inner London flats | 1.3 |
| | | E30: New Urban Colonists | Young professionals and their families who have 'gentrified' older terraces in inner London | 1.4 |
| | | E31: Caring Professionals | Well-educated singles and childless couples colonising inner areas of provincial cities | 1.1 |
| | | E32: Dinky Developments | Singles and childless couples in small units in newly built private estates outside London | 1.1 |
| | | E33: Town Gown Transition | Older neighbourhoods increasingly taken over by short-term student renters | 0.8 |
| | | E34: University Challenge | Halls of residence and other buildings occupied mostly by students | 0.3 |
| F: Welfare Borderline | 6.4 | F35: Bedsit Beneficiaries | Young people renting hard to let social housing, often in disadvantaged inner city locations | 0.7 |
| People living in social housing with uncertain employment in deprived areas | | F36: Metro Multiculture | High density social housing, mostly in inner London, with high levels of diversity | 1.7 |
| | | F37: Upper Floor Families | Young families living in upper floors of social housing, mostly in Scotland | 1.7 |
| | | F38: Tower Block Living | Singles, childless couples and older people living in high rise social housing | 0.5 |
| | | F39: Dignified Dependency | Older people living in crowded apartments in high density social housing | 1.3 |
| | | F40: Sharing a Staircase | Older tenements of small private flats often occupied by highly disadvantaged individuals | 0.5 |

**Table 5.4** (Continued)

| Mosaic Groups commercial and public sector | % hhds | Mosaic Types | | | |
| | | Commercial | Public sector | % hhds |
|---|---|---|---|---|
| G: Municipal Dependency | 6.7 | G41: Families on Benefits | Families, many single parent, in deprived social housing on the edge of regional centres | 1.2 |
| Low income families living in estate-based social housing | | G42: Low Horizons | Older people living in very large social housing estates on the outskirts of provincial cities | 2.6 |
| | | G43: Ex-industrial Legacy | Older people, many in poor health from work in heavy industry, in low rise social housing | 2.9 |
| H: Blue Collar Enterprise | 11.0 | H44: Rustbelt Resilience | Manual worker, many close to retirement, in low rise houses in ex-manufacturing towns | 3.0 |
| Upwardly mobile families living in homes bought from social landlords | | H45: Older Right to Buy | Older couples, mostly in small towns, who now own houses once rented from the council | 2.7 |
| | | H46: White Van Culture | Residents in 1930s and 1950s London council estates, now mostly owner-occupiers | 3.2 |
| | | H47: New Town Materialism | Social housing, typically in 'new towns', with good job opportunities for the poorly qualified | 2.2 |
| I: Twilight Subsistence | 3.9 | I48: Old People in Flats | Older people living in small council and housing association flats | 0.8 |
| Older people living in social housing with high care needs | | I49: Low Income Elderly | Low income older couples renting low rise social housing in industrial regions | 1.6 |
| | | I50: Cared for Pensioners | Older people receiving care in homes or sheltered accommodation | 1.4 |

(Continued)

**Table 5.4** Mosaic Neighbourhood Groups and Types, 2003 Version

| Mosaic Groups commercial and public sector | % hhds | Mosaic Types | | % hhds |
| --- | --- | --- | --- | --- |
| | | Commercial | Public sector | |
| J: Grey Perspectives | 7.9 | J51: Sepia Memories | Very elderly people, many financially secure, living in privately owned retirement flats | 0.8 |
| Independent older people with relatively active lifestyles | | J52: Childfree Serenity | Better off older people, singles and childless couples in developments of private flats | 1.3 |
| | | J53: High Spending Elders | Financially secure and physically active older people, many retired to semi-rural locations | 1.5 |
| | | J54: Bungalow Retirement | Older couples, independent but on limited incomes, living in bungalows by the sea | 1.3 |
| | | J55: Small Town Seniors | Older people preferring to live in familiar surroundings in small market towns | 2.7 |
| | | J56: Tourist Attendants | Neighbourhoods with retired people and transient singles working in the holiday industry | 0.3 |
| K: Rural Isolation | 5.4 | K57: Summer Playgrounds | Communities of retired people and second homers in areas of high environmental quality | 0.3 |
| People living in rural areas far from urbanisation | | K58: Greenbelt Guardians | Well off commuters and retired people living in attractive country villages | 1.7 |
| | | K59: Parochial Villagers | Country people living in still agriculturally active villages, mostly in lowland locations | 1.6 |
| | | K60: Pastoral Symphony | Smallholders and self-employed farmers, living beyond the reach of urban commuters | 1.3 |
| | | K61: Upland Hill Farmers | Low income farmers struggling on thin soils in isolated upland locations | 0.4 |
| Total Great Britain | 100.0 | | | 100.0 |

Also of note is the manner in which neighbourhoods previously defined in terms of different types of *council housing* have not only become described in terms of *social housing* – a linguistic re-designation consequent upon increasing state-subsidized housing provision being provided by housing association and other registered social landlords outside local authority control – but now existing in close juxtaposition with other neighbourhoods displaying high levels of social need but where residents predominantly live in the private rented sector and/or houses now in owner-occupation purchased through the 'right-to-buy' scheme. Patterns of rural living are also now more clearly differentiated with the specificity of coastal living now apparent. The neighbourhoods in which older residents predominate are now differentiated in greater detail with nine different neighbourhood Types identified.

A further version of the schema, still using 2001 census statistics but now supplemented with ever more sources of transactional data, was developed and released in 2009. With this release, there was an even clearer differentiation between the commercial and public sector versions of the product; now it was not just the labels that described the neighbourhood Groups and Types that were different, so too were the ordering of the categories and the manner in which they nest into Groups. Table 5.5 lists the commercial and Table 5.6 the public sector versions.[13]

The 2009 release featured a record number of 67 neighbourhood Types, nested into 15 Groups within the 'commercial' version, whilst the 'public sector' version identified 69 Types. Many of the trends identified in the 2003 version continue. Patterns of differentiation between neighbourhoods dominated by wealthy elites become even more nuanced (Burrows et al., 2017), the complexities of both metropolitan and rural cultures are also foregrounded, as are changes in the lifestyles of older residents and those living in what were previously areas of council housing. The role of students in the restructuring of urban space continues to be recognized but now the specificities of recent-graduate life are also featured within neighbourhood Types such as *Bright Young Things* and *Urban Cool*. A Type of neighbourhood where recently arrived migrants have been found accommodation by local councils is also featured and the changing forms of suburban living are also embedded within the classification.

The most recent version of *Mosaic*, released in 2014, not only includes statistics from the 2011 census for the first time but, as we noted in Chapter 4, it also marks a significant methodological departure. For the first time the classification has been optimized at the level of the *individual* using a mixture of data pertaining to individuals, the postcode and the census ED. As ever more granular big data becomes available it becomes possible to ever more accurately classify individual addresses.

Thus, rather than producing classifications at the postcode level and making exceptions at an address level where and when data were available that suggested

**Table 5.5** *Mosaic* Neighbourhood Groups and Types, 2009 Version

| *Mosaic* Groups | % hhds | *Mosaic* Types | % hhds |
|---|---|---|---|
| A: *Alpha Territory* | 3.5 | A01: *Global Power Brokers* | 0.3 |
| | | A02: *Voices of Authority* | 1.2 |
| | | A03: *Business Class* | 1.5 |
| | | A04: *Serious Money* | 0.6 |
| B: *Professional Reward* | 8.2 | B05: *Mid-Career Climbers* | 2.3 |
| | | B06: *Yesterday's Captains* | 1.8 |
| | | B07: *Distinctive Success* | 0.5 |
| | | B08: *Dormitory Villages* | 1.3 |
| | | B09: *Escape to the Country* | 1.1 |
| | | B10: *Parish Guardians* | 1.0 |
| C: *Rural Solitude* | 4.4 | C11: *Squires Among Locals* | 0.9 |
| | | C12: *Country Loving Elders* | 1.3 |
| | | C13: *Modern Agribusiness* | 1.4 |
| | | C14: *Farming Today* | 0.5 |
| | | C15: *Upland Struggle* | 0.3 |
| D: *Small Town Diversity* | 8.8 | D16: *Side Street Singles* | 1.2 |
| | | D17: *Jacks of All Trades* | 2.0 |
| | | D18: *Hardworking Families* | 2.6 |
| | | D19: *Innate Conservatives* | 3.0 |
| E: *Active Retirement* | 4.3 | E20: *Golden Retirement* | 0.7 |
| | | E21: *Bungalow Quietude* | 1.8 |
| | | E22: *Beachcombers* | 0.6 |
| | | E23: *Balcony Downsizers* | 1.3 |
| F: *Suburban Mindsets* | 11.2 | F24: *Garden Suburbia* | 2.1 |
| | | F25: *Production Managers* | 2.6 |
| | | F26: *Mid-Market Families* | 2.7 |
| | | F27: *Shop Floor Affluence* | 2.7 |
| | | F28: *Asian Attainment* | 1.0 |
| G: *Careers and Kids* | 5.8 | G29: *Footloose Managers* | 1.7 |
| | | G30: *Soccer Mums and Dads* | 1.3 |
| | | G31: *Domestic Comfort* | 1.1 |
| | | G32: *Childcare Years* | 1.5 |
| | | G33: *Military Dependents* | 0.2 |
| H: *New Homemakers* | 5.9 | H34: *Buy-to-Let Territory* | 1.8 |
| | | H35: *Brownfield Pioneers* | 1.4 |
| | | H36: *Foot on the Ladder* | 2.4 |
| | | H37: *First to Move In* | 0.4 |

| Mosaic Groups | % hhds | Mosaic Types | % hhds |
|---|---|---|---|
| I: Ex-Council Community | 8.7 | I38: Settled Ex-Tenants | 2.1 |
| | | I39: Choice Right to Buy | 1.7 |
| | | I40: Legacy of Labour | 2.7 |
| | | I41: Stressed Borrowers | 2.2 |
| J: Claimant Cultures | 5.2 | J42: Worn-Out Workers | 2.3 |
| | | J43: Streetwise Kids | 1.1 |
| | | J44: New Parents in Need | 1.8 |
| K: Upper Floor Living | 5.2 | K45: Small Block Singles | 1.8 |
| | | K46: Tenement Living | 0.8 |
| | | K47: Deprived View | 0.5 |
| | | K48: Multicultural Towers | 1.1 |
| | | K49: Re-housed Migrants | 1.0 |
| L: Elderly Needs | 6.0 | L50: Pensioners in Blocks | 1.3 |
| | | L51: Sheltered Seniors | 1.1 |
| | | L52: Meals on Wheels | 0.9 |
| | | L53: Low Spending Elders | 2.7 |
| M: Industrial Heritage | 7.4 | M54: Clocking Off | 2.3 |
| | | M55: Backyard Regeneration | 2.1 |
| | | M56: Small Wage Owners | 3.1 |
| N: Terraced Melting Pot | 7.0 | N57: Back-to-Back Basics | 2.0 |
| | | N58: Asian Identities | 0.9 |
| | | N59: Low-Key Starters | 2.7 |
| | | N60: Global Fusion | 1.4 |
| O: Liberal Opinion | 8.5 | O61: Convivial Homeowners | 1.7 |
| | | O62: Crash Pad Professionals | 1.1 |
| | | O63: Urban Cool | 1.1 |
| | | O64: Bright Young Things | 1.5 |
| | | O65: Anti-Materialists | 1.0 |
| | | O66: University Fringe | 0.9 |
| | | O67: Study Buddies | 1.1 |
| Total Great Britain | 100.0 | | 100.0 |

that this would be more accurate, as had begun to happen in the 2003 and 2009 versions of the classification, the 2014 release starts with the classification of individuals and households. The postcode classification is the result of aggregating these results 'up'.

The demarcation between the commercial and public sector versions has also altered; although different versions are marketed to the two user groups, the Group and Type labels are now the same for both. Perhaps it is the case that the world

**Table 5.6** Mosaic Neighbourhood Groups and Types, Public Sector Version 2009

| Mosaic Groups | % hhds | Mosaic Types | % hhds |
|---|---|---|---|
| A: Residents of isolated rural communities | 4.4 | A01: Rural families with high incomes, often from city jobs | 0.9 |
| | | A02: Retirees electing to settle in environmentally attractive localities | 1.3 |
| | | A03: Remote communities with poor access to public and commercial services | 0.9 |
| | | A04: Villagers with few well paid alternatives to agricultural employment | 1.4 |
| B: Residents of small and mid-sized towns with strong local roots | 8.8 | B05: Better off empty nesters in low density estates on town fringes | 3.0 |
| | | B06: Self-employed trades people living in smaller communities | 2.0 |
| | | B07: Empty nester owner-occupiers making little use of public services | 2.6 |
| | | B08: Mixed communities with many single people in the centres of small towns | 1.2 |
| C: Wealthy people living in the most sought-after neighbourhoods | 3.5 | C09: Successful older business leaders living in sought-after suburbs | 1.5 |
| | | C10: Wealthy families in substantial houses with little community involvement | 0.6 |
| | | C11: Creative professionals seeking involvement in local communities | 1.2 |
| | | C12: Residents in smart city centre flats who make little use of public services | 0.3 |
| D: Successful professionals living in suburban or semi-rural homes | 8.2 | D13: Higher income older champions of village communities | 2.3 |
| | | D14: Older people living in large houses in mature suburbs | 1.8 |
| | | D15: Well-off commuters living in spacious houses in semi-rural settings | 1.8 |
| | | D16: Higher income families concerned with education and careers | 2.3 |
| E: Middle income families living in moderate suburban semis | 11.2 | E17: Comfortably-off suburban families weakly tied to their local community | 2.1 |
| | | E18: Industrial workers living comfortably in owner-occupied semis | 2.7 |
| | | E19: Self-reliant older families in suburban semis in industrial towns | 2.6 |
| | | E20: Upwardly mobile South Asian families living in inter-war suburbs | 1.0 |
| | | E21: Middle aged families living in less fashionable inter-war suburban semis | 2.7 |
| F: Couples with young children in comfortable modern housing | 5.8 | F22: Busy executives in town houses in dormitory settlements | 1.7 |
| | | F23: Early middle aged parents likely to be involved in their children's education | 2.4 |
| | | F24: Young parents new to their neighbourhood, keen to put down roots | 1.5 |
| | | F25: Personnel reliant on the Ministry of Defence for public | 0.2 |

**Table 5.6** *(Continued)*

| Mosaic Groups | % hhds | Mosaic Types | % hhds |
|---|---|---|---|
| G: *Young, well-educated city dwellers* | 8.5 | G26: Well educated singles living in purpose built flats | 1.1 |
| | | G27: City dwellers owning houses in older neighbourhoods | 0.6 |
| | | G28: Singles and sharers occupying converted Victorian houses | 0.5 |
| | | G29: Young professional families settling in better quality older terraces | 1.7 |
| | | G30: Diverse communities of well-educated singles living in smart, small flats | 0.5 |
| | | G31: Owners in smart purpose built flats in prestige locations, many newly built | 1.0 |
| | | G32: Students and other transient singles in multi-let houses | 0.9 |
| | | G33: Transient singles, poorly supported by family and neighbours | 1.0 |
| | | G34: Students involved in college and university communities | 1.1 |
| H: *Couples and young singles in small modern starter homes* | 5.9 | H35: Childless new owner-occupiers in cramped new homes | 2.4 |
| | | H36: Young singles and sharers renting small purpose built flats | 1.8 |
| | | H37: Young owners and rented developments of mixed tenure | 1.4 |
| | | H38: People living in brand new residential developments | 0.4 |
| I: *Lower income workers in urban terraces in often diverse areas* | 7.0 | I39: Young owners and private renters in inner city terraces | 0.3 |
| | | I40: Multi-ethnic communities in newer suburbs away from the inner city | 0.6 |
| | | I41: Renters of older terraces in ethnically diverse communities | 0.5 |
| | | I42: South Asian communities experiencing social deprivation | 0.9 |
| | | I43: Older town centre terraces with transient, single populations | 2.7 |
| | | I44: Low income families occupying poor quality older terraces | 2.0 |
| J: *Owner occupiers in older-style housing in ex-industrial areas* | 7.4 | J45: Low income communities reliant on low skill industrial jobs | 3.1 |
| | | J46: Residents in blue collar communities revitalized by commuters | 2.1 |
| | | J47: Comfortably-off industrial workers owning their own homes | 2.3 |
| K: *Residents with sufficient incomes in right-to-buy social houses* | 8.7 | K48: Middle aged couples and families in right to buy homes | 1.7 |
| | | K49: Low income older couples long established in former council estates | 2.1 |
| | | K50: Older families in low value housing in traditional industrial areas | 2.7 |
| | | K51: Often indebted families living in low rise estates | 2.2 |

*(Continued)*

**Table 5.6** Mosaic Neighbourhood Groups and Types, Public Sector Version 2009

| Mosaic Groups | % hhds | Mosaic Types | % hhds |
|---|---|---|---|
| L: Active elderly people living in pleasant retirement locations | 4.3 | L52: Communities of wealthy older people living in large seaside houses | 0.7 |
| | | L53: Residents in retirement, second home and tourist communities | 0.6 |
| | | L54: Retired people of modest means commonly living in seaside bungalows | 1.8 |
| | | L55: Capable older people leasing/owning flats in purpose built blocks | 1.3 |
| M: Elderly people reliant on state support | 6.0 | M56: Older people living on social housing estates with limited budgets | 2.7 |
| | | M57: Old people in flats subsisting on welfare payments | 1.3 |
| | | M58: Less mobile older people requiring a degree of care | 0.9 |
| | | M59: People living in social accommodation designed for older people | 1.1 |
| N: Young people renting flats in high density social housing | 5.2 | N60: Tenants in social housing flats on estates at risk of serious social problems | 0.8 |
| | | N61: Childless tenants in social housing flats with modest social needs | 1.8 |
| | | N62: Young renters in flats with a cosmopolitan mix | 0.5 |
| | | N63: Multicultural tenants renting flats in areas of social housing | 0.5 |
| | | N64: Diverse home-sharers renting small flats in densely populated areas | 0.6 |
| | | N65: Young singles in multi-ethnic communities, many in high rise flats | 0.5 |
| | | N66: Childless, low income tenants in high rise flats | 0.5 |
| O: Families in low-rise social housing with high levels of benefit | 5.2 | O67: Older tenants on low rise social housing estates where jobs are scarce | 2.3 |
| | | O68: Families with varied structures living on low rise social housing estates | 1.1 |
| | | O69: Vulnerable young parents needing substantial state support | 1.8 |
| Total Great Britain | 100.0 | | 100.0 |

**Table 5.7** Mosaic Neighbourhood Groups and Types, 2014 Version

| Mosaic Group % hhds | Mosaic Type | Description | % hhds |
|---|---|---|---|
| A: City Prosperity | A1: World-Class Wealth | Global high flyers and families of privilege living luxurious lifestyles in London's most exclusive boroughs | 0.6 |
| 3.6 | A2: Uptown Elite | High status households owning elegant homes in accessible inner suburbs where they enjoy city life in comfort | 1.1 |
| | A3: Penthouse Chic | City suits renting premium-priced flats in prestige central locations where they work hard and play hard | 0.5 |
| | A4: Metro High-Flyers | Ambitious 20- and 30-somethings renting expensive apartments in highly commutable areas of major cities | 1.3 |
| B: Prestige Positions | B5: Premium Fortunes | Influential families with substantial income established in distinctive, expansive homes in wealthy enclaves | 1.0 |
| 7.4 | B6: Diamond Days | Retired residents in sizeable homes whose finances are secured by significant assets and generous pensions | 1.1 |
| | B7: Alpha Families | High-achieving families living fast-track lives, advancing careers, finances and their school-age kids' development | 1.4 |
| | B8: Bank of Mum & Dad | Well-off families in upmarket suburban homes where grown-up children benefit from continued financial support | 1.7 |
| | B9: Empty-Nest Adventure | Mature couples in comfortable detached houses who have the means to enjoy their empty-nest status | 2.1 |
| C: Country Living | C10: Wealthy Landowners | Prosperous owners of country houses including the rural upper class, successful farmers and second-home owners | 1.3 |
| 6.1 | C11: Rural Vogue | Country-loving families pursuing a rural idyll in comfortable village homes while commuting some distance to work | 1.5 |
| | C12: Scattered Homesteads | Older households appreciating rural calm in stand-alone houses within agricultural landscapes | 1.4 |
| | C13: Village Retirement | Retirees enjoying pleasant village locations with amenities to service their social and practical needs | 1.8 |

*(Continued)*

**Table 5.7** Mosaic Neighbourhood Groups and Types, 2014 Version

| Mosaic Group % hhds | Mosaic Type | Description | % hhds |
|---|---|---|---|
| D: Rural Reality 5.9 | D14: Satellite Settlers | Mature households living in expanding developments around larger villages with good transport links | 1.9 |
| | D15: Local Focus | Rural families in affordable village homes who are reliant on the local economy for jobs | 1.8 |
| | D16: Outlying Seniors | Pensioners living in inexpensive housing in out of the way locations | 1.7 |
| | D17: Far-Flung Outposts | Inter-dependent households living in the most remote communities with long travel times to larger towns | 0.5 |
| E: Senior Security 8.5 | E18: Legacy Elders | Time-honoured elders now mostly living alone in comfortable suburban homes on final salary pensions | 1.9 |
| | E19: Bungalow Haven | Peace-seeking seniors appreciating the calm of bungalow estates designed for the elderly | 1.9 |
| | E20: Classic Grandparents | Lifelong couples in standard suburban homes enjoying retirement through grandchildren and gardening | 2.2 |
| | E21: Solo Retirees | Senior singles whose reduced incomes are satisfactory in their affordable but pleasant owned homes | 2.5 |
| F: Suburban Stability 8.4 | F22: Boomerang Boarders | Long-term couples with mid-range incomes whose adult children have returned to the shelter of the family home | 2.0 |
| | F23: Family Ties | Active families with teens and adult children whose prolonged support is eating up household resources | 2.1 |
| | F24: Fledgling Free | Pre-retirement couples with respectable incomes enjoying greater space and spare cash since children left home | 1.9 |
| | F25: Dependable Me | Single mature owners settled in traditional suburban semis working in intermediate occupations | 2.4 |
| G: Domestic Success 6.9 | G26: Cafés and Catchments | Affluent families with growing children living in upmarket housing in city environs | 1.3 |
| | G27: Thriving Independence | Well-qualified older singles with incomes from successful professional careers in good quality housing | 1.9 |

**Table 5.7** *(Continued)*

| Mosaic Group % hhds | Mosaic Type | Description | % hhds |
|---|---|---|---|
| | G28: *Modern Parents* | Busy couples in modern detached homes juggling the demands of school-age children and careers | 1.7 |
| | G29: *Mid-Career Convention* | Professional families with children in traditional mid-range suburbs where neighbours are often older | 2.1 |
| H: *Aspiring Homemakers* | H30: *Primary Ambitions* | Forward-thinking younger families who sought affordable homes in good suburbs which they may now be out-growing | 2.0 |
| | H31: *Affordable Fringe* | Settled families with children owning modest, three-bed semis in areas where there's more house for less money | 2.2 |
| 8.8 | H32: *First-Rung Futures* | Pre-family newcomers who have bought value homes with space to grow in affordable but pleasant areas | 2.1 |
| | H33: *Contemporary Starts* | Fashion-conscious young singles and partners setting up home in developments attractive to their peers | 1.3 |
| | H34: *New Foundations* | Occupants of brand new homes who are often younger singles or couples with children | 0.2 |
| | H35: *Flying Solo* | Bright young singles on starter salaries choosing to rent homes in family suburbs | 1.2 |
| I: *Family Basics* | I36: *Solid Economy* | Stable families with children renting better quality homes from social landlords | 1.7 |
| | I37: *Budget Generations* | Families supporting both adult and younger children where expenditure can exceed income | 1.5 |
| 7.2 | I38: *Childcare Squeeze* | Younger families with children who own a budget home and are striving to cover all expenses | 2.0 |
| | I39: *Families with Needs* | Families with many children living in areas of high deprivation and who need support | 2.0 |

*(Continued)*

**Table 5.7** Mosaic Neighbourhood Groups and Types, 2014 Version

| Mosaic Group % hhds | Mosaic Type | Description | % hhds |
|---|---|---|---|
| J: Transient Renters | J40: Make Do & Move On | Yet to settle younger singles and couples making interim homes in low cost properties | 2.0 |
| | J41: Disconnected Youth | Young people endeavouring to gain employment footholds while renting cheap flats and terraces | 1.4 |
| 6.5 | J42: Midlife Stopgap | Maturing singles in employment who are renting short-term affordable homes | 1.6 |
| | J43: Renting a Room | Transient renters of low cost accommodation often within subdivided older properties | 1.5 |
| K: Municipal Challenge | K44: Inner City Stalwarts | Long-term renters of inner city social flats who have witnessed many changes | 0.8 |
| | K45: Crowded Kaleidoscope | Multi-cultural households with children renting social flats in over-crowded conditions | 1.2 |
| 6.5 | K46: High Rise Residents | Renters of social flats in high rise blocks where levels of need are significant | 0.4 |
| | K47: Streetwise Singles | Hard-pressed singles in low cost social flats searching for opportunities | 1.8 |
| | K48: Low Income Workers | Older social renters settled in low value homes in communities where employment is harder to find | 2.2 |
| L: Vintage Value | L49: Dependent Greys | Ageing social renters with high levels of need in centrally located developments of small units | 1.2 |
| | L50: Pocket Pensions | Penny-wise elderly singles renting in developments of compact social homes | 1.3 |
| 6.8 | L51: Aided Elderly | Supported elders in specialized accommodation including retirement homes and complexes of small homes | 0.9 |
| | L52: Estate Veterans | Longstanding elderly renters of social homes who have seen neighbours change to a mix of owners and renters | 1.6 |
| | L53: Seasoned Survivors | Deep-rooted single elderly owners of low value properties whose modest home equity provides some security | 1.8 |

**Table 5.7** *(Continued)*

| Mosaic Group % hhds | Mosaic Type | Description | % hhds |
|---|---|---|---|
| M: Modest Traditions | M54: Down-to-Earth Owners | Ageing couples who have owned their inexpensive home for many years while working in routine jobs | 1.8 |
| | M55: Offspring Overspill | Lower income owners whose adult children are still striving to gain independence meaning space is limited | 1.7 |
| 5.9 | M56: Self-Supporters | Hard-working mature singles who own budget terraces manageable within their modest wage | 2.4 |
| N: Urban Cohesion | N57: Community Elders | Established older households owning city homes in diverse neighbourhoods | 1.1 |
| | N58: Cultural Comfort | Thriving families with good incomes in multi-cultural urban communities | 1.4 |
| 4.8 | N59: Asian Heritage | Large extended families in neighbourhoods with a strong South Asian tradition | 1.0 |
| | N60: Ageing Access | Older residents owning small inner suburban properties with good access to amenities | 1.4 |
| O: Rental Hubs | O61: Career Builders | Motivated singles and couples in their 20s and 30s progressing in their field of work from commutable properties | 1.6 |
| | O62: Central Pulse | Entertainment-seeking youngsters renting city centre flats in vibrant locations close to jobs and night life | 1.0 |
| 7.0 | O63: Flexible Workforce | Self-starting young renters ready to move to follow worthwhile incomes from service sector jobs | 1.3 |
| | O64: Bus-Route Renters | Singles renting affordable private flats away from central amenities and often on main roads | 1.8 |
| | O65: Learners & Earners | Inhabitants of the university fringe where students and older residents mix in cosmopolitan locations | 0.7 |
| | O66: Student Scene | Students living in high density accommodation close to universities and educational centre | 0.5 |
| Total Great Britain | | | 100.0 |

of commerce is now as fearful of generating consumer backlash from the use of politically incorrect language as the public sector has been in the past. The convergence of the labels used certainly makes easier the presentation of what are again 67 neighbourhood Types (albeit rather different to the ones in the 2009 version) nested into 15 Groups. Table 5.7 shows this most recent release although now, of course, the labels refer to individual household addresses rather than postcodes. Gentrification is one of a number of forms of social change that can only be identified at a postcode level which inevitably become lost when the classification system is optimized at a person level.

This, probably the most nuanced of the classifications yet to be released, shows very clearly just how different a country Britain has become compared to the 1980s. Patterns of differentiation across class, tenure, race and ethnicity, urban–suburban–rural, stage of life-course and so on have become ever subtler. However, major new dimensions of differentiation are also beginning to emerge. As we discuss below, perhaps the clearest of these is the decline in home ownership, the rise of 'buy-to-let' and the formation of distinct new private rental hubs – now accounting for a full 7 per cent of all households.

# Conflicting opinions regarding the validity of methods

So far in this chapter we have considered the ability of geodemographic classification to capture the historical evolution of Britain's residential areas. We have also considered how clearly the categories created in successive versions of *Mosaic* capture the impact of political and social change. Assuming *Mosaic* is successful in these regards some reference should be made to how much of its success is due to the wealth of input data it has access to, how much to the intelligence embedded in the clustering algorithms and how much to operator intervention. Should such classifications be viewed as 'objective' or as 'subjective' representations of the social world?

One common criticism of geodemographic classifications is that they fail to advance any real understanding of the social processes which cause neighbourhoods to change. The account of the historical evolution of different forms of neighbourhood with which this chapter begins does suggest that this is not an inherent feature of the methodology used, more a concession to the requirements of the organizations by which vendors expect the product to be purchased. But it may be a legitimate complaint about how the categories are named, described and visualized. There is no reason why underpinning social processes should not be incorporated into the labels, as in neighbourhoods labelled as *Ex-Industrial Legacy* or *New Urban Colonists*. However, we would argue, careful inspection of the statistical profiles of the clusters should provide plenty of evidence of the changing role and demographic composition of all neighbourhood types even where this has not been reflected in the label. In retort, promoters of *Mosaic* argue that it is precisely because of social change that the geodemographic classifications are updated on a regular basis, perhaps more frequently than the theories of some of their critics.

Another common and not unreasonable criticism is the lack of clarity regarding what elements of cluster descriptions are based on statistical evidence and what are based on more tacit knowledge. There is no easy answer to this question. The statistical clusters are clear and robust, and a wide range of profile data is used to document how one cluster differs from another. However, the 'art of geodemographics' comes in the ability of the developer to describe and narrate this wealth of statistical data in a manner that is understandable and, critically, *useful* to users of the classification.

However, an inability to cite sources or to replicate results has also sometimes deterred academic researchers from considering these taxonomies as serious and reliable. The use of commercially sensitive information in the construction of the classifications – and in the profiles, often based on commercially sponsored survey questionnaires, routinely used to demonstrate significant socio-economic and cultural differences between the categories – often means that there is little opportunity to replicate them. So, although the classifications themselves can often be used in academic research, the data used in their construction are not available.[14]

From the earliest development of geodemographic taxonomies people have argued about the appropriateness of the different forms of description that should be used to label them. We have already seen that in the Liverpool study labels were given to the higher level categories but not to the finer level ones. Since *PRIZM* was launched in the United States and *Acorn* in the UK, the developers of neighbourhood taxonomies have sought to encapsulate the 'essence' of each cluster in terms brief enough to fit in a column of a table, 'catchy' enough to be memorable and specific enough for the cluster to be distinguishable from others. Achieving all three objectives is no easy task.

In the United States, *PRIZM* was initially developed to serve the needs of advertising and media buying agencies and it was no accident that the person tasked with devising appropriate labels for the *PRIZM* Types should have extensive experience within the advertising industry. As we saw in Table 2.1, *Blue Blood Estate*, *Furs and Station Wagons* and *Shotguns and Pickups* are three of the more memorable labels developed to describe the first generation of *PRIZM* codes.

Subsequently, on both sides of the Atlantic, some of the more recently devised labels have been neither memorable nor specific; labels have been devised which retreat into the terminology of individual demographic variables used to build the classification. *Higher Income Older People* may describe the dominant demographics of a cluster but not its characteristic intersectional emergent properties.

As we detailed previously, especially in Tables 5.4 and 5.6, on occasion a parallel set of labels has been developed to describe the *Mosaic* Types, more aligned to the argot of public sector users and, perhaps, academic researchers. In the United States political correctness has, at various times, required that every one of the clusters in a taxonomy should be described in the language of 'winners'. Obeisance to political correctness has also sometimes affected the ability of users to properly understand the specific characteristics of spatial clusters of those living in different types of poverty.

A common misunderstanding is to suppose that, because the users of such systems are likely to be targeting consumers or clients rather than the buildings in which they live, it makes more sense to describe neighbourhoods in terms which describe their residents rather than their physical appearance. This is exemplified in the labels used in the most recent versions of *Mosaic*.

In practice however, and as we have discussed, other than in the countryside, most streets will have been built during a narrow window of time and most postcodes contain buildings of relatively similar appearance. As a result, most streets are more uniform with respect of the age and type of their houses than they are in respect of the ages of their inhabitants. Thus, using a label such as *Coronation Street* provides a clearer and more accurate understanding of the cluster than describing it as a *neighbourhood of low incomes and settled older people*. Moreover, as we have discussed in relation to people looking in the windows of an estate agency, the physical appearance of a street is more likely to register with a user than the age or income of its less visible inhabitants.

Clearly then there are limits to which circles can be squared. To be memorable labels need to be constrained to a maximum of 20 or so characters. To do justice to what is essentially a multivariate taxonomy they should not focus exclusively on any one or two specific demographic variables. Labels which imply processes, such as *Hard Scrabble* (in the USA), *Summer Playgrounds*, *Ex-Industrial Legacy* or *New Urban Colonists* are likely to work better than more specific monikers, even if initially they do involve the users in some effort to understand the distinctive features that underlie such terms. Achieving agreement on the names that should describe a set of clusters can be the most arduous and disheartening stage in the build of a new system.

## How objectively can a computer algorithm classify residential neighbourhoods?

It is easy for debate over the labelling to detract from discussion of the many methodological decisions that need to be taken in order to generate meaningful clusters in the first place. The generation of the clusters themselves is by no means a merely mechanical process. Whilst in general terms cluster analysis techniques give data the opportunity to self-organize in the most efficient way, as we have discussed, it would be a mistake to suppose that the construction of geodemographic typologies is a process over which the developer has or should have no control (Uprichard et al., 2009).

Clearly a taxonomy of neighbourhoods can only be constructed using information which is available at the level of granularity at which it is built or higher. Nevertheless, it is uncommon for the set of variables available for use in building a solution to be as balanced between different topics as the developer would ideally want it to be. Questions included in the decennial census are inevitably those requested by government departments and, for this reason, are more likely to identify vulnerable groups than those with high levels of income or wealth. Without any operator intervention, a classification which gives an equal weight to all available census variables is likely to differentiate disadvantaged neighbourhoods with greater precision than it does wealthy ones. One way of addressing this concern is rather than clustering neighbourhoods on the basis of their values on individual input variables, as *Mosaic* does, cluster them on the basis of their scores on the dimensions created by factor analysis. There may have been a time when it was desirable to maximize discrimination among different types of disadvantaged neighbourhood. However, given recent increases in income and wealth inequalities, a clear understanding of patterns of differentiation amongst the wealthy is now becoming an equally important requirement of these systems (Burrows et al., 2017).

Given the limitations of variables available for inclusion in the clustering process, a prudent developer will organize available variables into particular domains such as rurality, ethnicity, housing, age and so on. The developer will then consider the relative influence on the solution that it would be appropriate to allow each domain to contribute. If it is decided that 'rurality' should be given an influence equal to 10 per cent of the total influence, and if only two out of the 100 usable variables distinguish rurality, then it may be appropriate, software functionality permitting, to up-weight by a factor of five the influence given to each of the indicators of rurality, reducing the relative weight given to the other available variables.

It can easily be supposed that once a cluster analysis algorithm begins to iterate it will necessarily improve its ability to distinguish different types of area until it achieves a level of performance beyond which no further improvement in statistical discrimination can be achieved. This is not necessarily the case. 'Hill climbing' algorithms often settle on a local optimum, not a global one. From analysis of the output statistics of a solution it is usually possible, by combining and splitting different clusters, to modify a local optimum in such a way that the algorithm works through a new cycle of iterations thereby achieving a new, higher-performing optimum.

As a general rule, a desirable solution is one where the clusters each contain a broadly similar share of the overall population. Given that the data values pertaining to individual postcodes are not spread around equally in 'n'-dimension space, the most practical solution is more likely to be one in which the clusters with the highest share of the national population have higher levels of internal homogeneity, the smaller clusters the lower degree of internal homogeneity.

But how should the optimal number of clusters be arrived at? Cluster analysis can be considered as a form of data reduction, the object of which is to maximize the retention of the variability of the input data but with the smallest possible number of categories. Pick too many clusters and it becomes difficult at the margins to tell one cluster from another. Pick too few and the clusters are in danger of losing internal coherence.

From experience building classifications for different countries, Experian settled on a rule of thumb that the optimal number of clusters is likely to occur when one would lose some 0.25 per cent of the total variance if the two most similar clusters were merged into one. The smaller the loss of variance by merging any two clusters the more difficult it becomes to remember what it is that makes them different. The higher the loss of variance by merging two clusters the more likely they are to contain postcodes which are inadequately described by any of the clusters in the solution.

As another general rule, there is a limit to the number of different categories that the mind can distinguish at any one time and it is many fewer than the number of clusters in most geodemographic classifications. It thus makes sense to organize the clusters hierarchically with a lower level of between say 25 and 65 Types, nesting into a higher level of around ten Groups. Whilst it is possible to identify categories which are relevant to virtually any application at the lower 'Type' level, the decision as to how these lower level categories are then grouped is necessarily more arbitrary. What constitutes an optimal higher level grouping for one user is not necessarily the same as what will best suit another.[15]

It is important not to overlook cognitive limitations. Few people's eyes are sharp enough to differentiate more than ten colours on a map. Thus, as well as the labels being a matter of much debate, the consistent association of colours with groups – although perhaps initially seeming to be a trivial matter – is also crucial if one is concerned to optimize pattern recognition.

Although the report of the Liverpool study provided statistics both for the 25 individual clusters and for the five Groups as described in Chapter 3, the report also demonstrated the way in which a hierarchic form of cluster analysis could be used to group the 25 clusters into a number of different higher order groupings in such a way as to maximize the ability of these alternative groupings to discriminate on different topics such as housing, age structure and use of public services.

This combination of a fixed taxonomy of finer level categories and a customized set of higher level groupings was adopted later by commercial developers such as Experian who created alternative groupings for different categories of user such as motor distributors and financial services companies. From time to time, higher order groupings were optimized to meet the needs of individual users. In such cases it was often decided that the hierarchic grouping process should be optimized not on the basis of the data variables used to build the classification but on client-specific data which had been pre-summarized at cluster level rather than having been used to build *Mosaic*.

As we reported in relation to the Liverpool study, it may be appropriate for some categories to be associated with particular colours. Specific colours have long associations with particular cultural and political identifications: for the ancients the colour purple symbolized extreme wealth; in the UK blue is associated with conservatism; red with socialism and, perhaps, social housing; yellow with the *Ties of Community* neighbourhoods in which the Liberal Democrats do well; grey with the elderly; and green with young metropolitans who, statistical profiles tell us, are the most sensitive to the challenge of global climate change. Adopting a common and consistent colour system proves critical to helping users immediately recognize the different major groupings whether they are represented in the form of maps, charts, tables or other forms of visualization.

In our opinion it is easy to underestimate the extent to which the construction of geodemographic systems can benefit from deep professional experience. Clearly the effectiveness with which a classification picks up visible differences in urban structure is hugely affected by the data available to the classification builder, and the level of granularity at which they are made available. But quite small improvements in methodology, though each one not likely to be hugely influential on its own, can in aggregate have a significant impact not just on the apparent veracity of the categories but also on their usability.

## Notes

[1] An unintended consequence of this was that it generated a diaspora of academics who went on to contribute greatly to the growth of marketing consultancies.

[2] The details of which can be found here: www.telegraph.co.uk/news/politics/margaret-thatcher/margaret-thatcher-biography/11908691/margaret-thatcher-biography-retirement-home.html. The neighbours among whom politicians choose to purchase a property often reveal the groups among whom they feel themselves most at home, Theresa May homing in on *Semi-Rural Seclusion*, David Cameron on *Greenbelt Guardians*, George Osborne on *Global Connections* and John Major on *Conservative Values*. We believe *Caring Professionals* describes Jeremy Corbyn's choice of neighbours.

[3] We will go through the development of these labels systematically in what follows. However, we will introduce a number of them here, ahead of this, by way of illustration of the historical development of the neighbourhoods we go on to describe more generally.

[4] The label is, of a course, a play on the classic *Affluent Worker* studies (Goldthorpe et al., 1968a; 1968b; 1969) – concerned to explore the supposed embourgeoisement of the skilled manual working classes in Luton in the 1960s (see Savage, 2005, for a pithy overview).

[5] See the classic account of Pahl (1965).

[6] As are clusters of new developments that seem to be designed to extend the student lifestyle further into adulthood through co-living and upmarket communal style arrangements, such as that advertised as The Collective in North West London – www.thecollective.co.uk. For an interesting commentary on such developments see: http://elliotsnook.com/blog/index.php/2017/01/25/even-the-laundrette-makes-doing-laundry-a-less-lonely-experience-twodios-the-introduction-of-21st-century-tenements.

[7] Such neighbourhoods were the setting for much of the popular entertainment of the time. BBC programmes in the 1970s and 1980s such as *The Fall and Rise of Reginald Perrin*, *Terry and June* and *The Good Life* were comedic attempts to examine the prevailing culture of such locales.

[8] At the time only 56 per cent of all households were living in the owner-occupied sector. It was still largely a tenure that was the preserve of the middle and upper classes (Burrows, 2003).

[9] The work of Kandt (2015: 16–22) provides a useful summary of these critical literatures and more recent social research utilizing geodemographic classifications as central features of their analysis.

[10] Abbott (2000: 298–9) still provides the most pithy summary of what is at stake: '[a]s more and more behavior is conducted electronically, more and more things can be measured more and more often…[requiring us to]…rethink data analysis from the ground up'.

[11] This, it turns out, is still available online via the UK Data Service at the University of Essex: http://doc.ukdataservice.ac.uk/doc/5289/mrdoc/pdf/5289userguide.pdf.

[12] As we explained at the outset, it is this version of *Mosaic* that we draw upon most in this book, finding it the most analytically satisfying and probably the most closely aligned with social scientific categories of the various versions available.

[13] An excellent interactive visualization tool is still available at: http://guides.business-strategies.co.uk/mosaicpublicsector2009/html/visualisation.htm.

[14] Whether this matters or not is in many respects a matter of trust. After all, it is as much on the basis of trust as on performance that a user prefers one vendor to another, knowing that as a user it will never be possible to justify the expense and time of independent replication.

[15] Thus, for example, the final report of the Liverpool study set out six alternative ways in which the 25 clusters could be optimally grouped into five higher order groupings. These alternative groupings were constructed using different subsets of data known for the clusters: house tenure, age structure, housing deficiencies, vulnerable minorities, social malaise and socio-economic status. Perhaps the most interesting of these criteria was social malaise. This alternative grouping was based on the 20 non-census indicators derived from the city's departmental records. The basis for examining the geographical structure of Liverpool in terms of demand on council services was quite novel. It was that census areas be grouped together on the basis of similarities to create a set of 25 different types of residential neighbourhood; that these 25 different types of residential neighbourhood would then be sufficiently large in terms of population to be statistically valid categories for the level of service demand to be measured; and that these 25 different types be then organized into a five-fold division of the city in such a way as to maximize the differences in service demand between these five-fold divisions.

# Part II
## A Geodemographic Account
## of Social Change

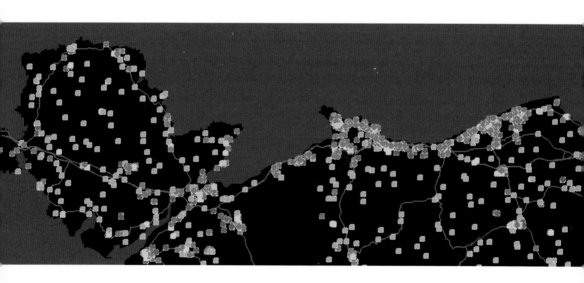

# 6

# THE LIBERAL METROPOLITAN ELITE
## 'Citizens of Nowhere'?

Today too many people in positions of power behave as though they have more in common with an international elite than with the people down the road, the people they employ, the people they pass in the street. But if you believe you are a citizen of the world you are a citizen of nowhere. You don't understand what the very word 'citizenship' means.

Theresa May, British Prime Minister, 5th October 2016

## The Liberal Metropolitans – a powerful new elite

In this chapter, we focus on the following *Mosaic* Types listed originally in Table 5.4.

| Code | *Mosaic* Type label | UK % | Top local authorities |
|------|------|------|------|
| A02 | *Cultural Leadership* | 0.9 | Richmond |
| E28 | *Counter Cultural Mix* | 1.4 | Islington |
| E29 | *City Adventurers* | 1.3 | Wandsworth |
| E30 | *New Urban Colonists* | 1.4 | Richmond |
| E31 | *Caring Professionals* | 1.1 | Norwich |
| E33 | *Town Gown Transition* | 0.8 | Oxford |
| E34 | *University Challenge* | 0.3 | Ceredigion |

'Citizens of Nowhere' – no soundbite from Theresa May's address to the 2016 Conservative Party Conference registered more strongly with the British media. Devised by her speechwriters, it is a pithy categorization. Brief enough to qualify as a *Mosaic* label, its three short words capture the essence of a socio-political group whose concise definition had eluded even the most experienced of media commentators.

What at that time had particularly attracted the venom of Brexiteers was the low value in which 'Citizens of Nowhere' were thought to hold Britain's sovereignty, rendering them as 'enemies of the people'[1] and on a par with the bureaucrats in Brussels. But in 2016 it was not just in the UK that this group found itself in the public spotlight. Both in the United States and in continental Europe, popular opinion railed against a cadre that appeared to have captured control of the media and business as well as politics and used it for its own advantage. This *Liberal Metropolitan Elite* (LME), the more neutral term we use to describe this Group, is the subject of this chapter.

It is not its wealth that defines this new 'Elite', nor is it its occupational profile. The attribute which the *Mosaic* labels such as *Chattering Classes*, *Cultural Leadership*, *Voices of Authority* and *Liberal Opinion*[2] so tellingly capture is this group's uncanny ability to make its opinions heard and, at least until recently, its expectation that its voice will be listened to. It is this group that appropriates to itself the decision regarding what subjects it is legitimate to debate in the higher reaches of journalism, politics and the arts. Its members are 'Metropolitan' in that they gravitate towards London and those provincial British cities where Russell Group universities engage in academic exchange. They are 'Liberal' in their claim to embrace diversity, whether in terms of ethnic, religious or gender identities or tolerance of sexual mores, foods, languages and customs. The twist which May's conference speechwriter adds to this portrayal is that their orientation is international rather than national.

However widely it's recognized, however distinctive its values and however significant its cultural influence may be, the term Liberal Metropolitan Elite has modest value in its own right as a social scientific category. After all, what share of the national population do its members comprise? Where is it physically located? What are its lifestyles, values and behaviours? What does it eat and drink? Answering questions of this sort is the aim of this chapter. In doing so, we hope to demonstrate the ability of geodemographic categorization to capture – or in the parlance of social research methods *operationalize* – its essential character and, perhaps even more importantly, to quantify the respects which distinguish it from other population groups and to explain the processes by which it sustains its cultural dominance.

Table 5.4, in the previous chapter, contains the seven *Mosaic* neighbourhood Types which could be described as belonging to the LME. Six of them fall within Group E, *Urban Intelligence* from the 2003 version of *Mosaic*, and one, *Cultural*

*Leadership*, from Group A, *Symbols of Success*, which is often the ultimate destination of the more 'successful' members of those currently residing in the other Types considered here. They are described below.

1.  A02 *Cultural Leadership* – 'Highly educated senior professionals, many working in the media, politics and law' as described in the public sector version.
2.  E28 *Counter Cultural Mix* – 'Neighbourhoods with transient singles living in large old houses in multiple occupation'.
3.  E29 *City Adventurers* – 'Economically successful singles, many living in small inner London flats'.
4.  E30 *New Urban Colonists* – 'Young professionals and their families who have "gentrified" older terraces in inner London'.
5.  E31 *Caring Professionals* – 'Well-educated singles and childless couples colonizing inner areas of provincial cities'.
6.  E33 *Town Gown Transition* – 'Older neighbourhoods increasingly taken over by short-term student renters'.
7.  E34 *University Challenge* – 'Halls of residence and other buildings occupied mostly by students'.

Here is an edited extract from the documentation of 2003 *Mosaic* that describes Group E: *Urban Intelligence*.

*Urban Intelligence* people are young, well-educated and open to new ideas and influences. They are cosmopolitan in their tastes and liberal in their social attitudes. Few have children. Many are in further education while others are moving into full-time employment. Most do not feel ready to make permanent commitments, whether to partners, professions or to specific employers. As higher education has become internationalized, the *Urban Intelligence* group has acquired many foreign-born residents, which further encourages ethnic and cultural variety.

These neighbourhoods typically occur in inner London and the inner areas of large provincial cities, especially those with popular universities. The growth in student numbers has led to their dispersal from halls of residence into older working class communities and the areas of large Victorian houses that typically surround the older universities.

Other inner city areas have also been taken over by recent graduates and young professionals who want to live close to their work and the facilities of the inner city. Demand for flats is outstripping supply, and developers are now building new flats as well as refurbishing older houses, particularly in locations close to old canals and docklands. In London, this extends into previously lower middle class suburbs such as Wandsworth and Hammersmith...

**Table 6.1** Differences between the *Liberal Metropolitan Elite* (*LME*) and *Symbols of Success* (excluding the *Cultural Leadership Type*)*

| Topic | Response | Index *LME* | Index Symbols of Success | Difference |
|---|---|---|---|---|
| Occupation | Higher manager | 160 | 216 | 56 |
| Occupation | Higher professional | 223 | 200 | 23 |
| Occupation | Intermediate | 100 | 103 | 3 |
| Occupation | Lower managerial and professional | 139 | 141 | 2 |
| Occupation | Lower supervisory | 60 | 56 | 5 |
| Occupation | Admin and secretarial | 97 | 105 | 8 |
| Occupation | Personal service | 70 | 70 | 0 |
| Occupation | Sales and customer service | 81 | 67 | 13 |
| Occupation | Skilled trades | 51 | 61 | 10 |
| Occupation | Process, plant operatives | 40 | 37 | 2 |
| Magazines subscribed to | New Statesman | 334 | 67 | 267 |
| Magazines subscribed to | Which? | 142 | 213 | 72 |
| Magazines subscribed to | Women's interests | 151 | 214 | 63 |
| Newspapers read | Daily Mail | 108 | 143 | 35 |
| Newspapers read | Daily Telegraph | 132 | 269 | 137 |
| Newspapers read | Financial Times | 261 | 260 | 1 |
| Newspapers read | Guardian | 396 | 146 | 250 |
| Newspapers read | Independent | 313 | 166 | 146 |
| Newspapers read | Observer | 353 | 151 | 202 |
| Newspapers read | Sunday Express | 83 | 143 | 60 |
| Newspapers read | Sun | 72 | 32 | 40 |
| Newspapers read | Times | 238 | 247 | 9 |

* So, to be clear, the *LME* is operationalized here as: A02 + E28 + E29 + E30 + E31 + E33 + E34, whilst the remaining six categories of *Symbols of Success* are: A01 + A03 + A04+ A05 + A06 + A07.

In terms of values, this is the most liberal group; it also has the most catholic tastes and the most International orientation.

Learning how to use financial products, surviving on a budget and managing debt are concerns for many in this group. But others have high levels of disposable income – mindful of career uncertainties, this creates an interesting market for various forms of high risk investment, whether in short term trading or in the buy-to-let market.

Table 6.1 shows a striking *similarity* between the occupational profile of these seven Types (the six from *Urban Intelligence* plus *Cultural Leadership* from the *Symbols of Success* Group) – what from now on we summarize as the LME – and that of the remaining six clusters within the *Mosaic* Group A, *Symbols of Success*. By contrast the same table shows how *different* are their magazine and newspaper readership profiles.

While the LME read The *New Statesman*, The *Guardian*, The *Independent* and The *Observer*, the six remaining *Symbols of Success* Types read *Which?*, The *Daily Telegraph*, The *Mail*, The *Sunday Express* and women's interest magazines.

Differences in value systems are equally evident in terms of charitable support – survey respondents in LME postcodes being five times more likely to give to Aids charities, three times more likely to give to human rights charities and twice as likely to give to charities for the homeless. The causes favoured by the rest of *Symbols of Success* are religious charities and ones supporting birds.

Of the many aspects of the LME that we could examine, the one this chapter focuses on is its political orientation. This, we believe, can contribute to a better understanding of the fault-lines that have emerged during the past half-century both within and between Britain's main political parties.

# The shift in the heartlands of Conservatives and Labour

Any analysis of the political impact of the growth of the LME needs to start with a discussion of the decline that has occurred during the past 50 years in the ability of social class to predict voting behaviour. Though the alignment between class and political identification has declined in every type of neighbourhood, it is in neighbourhoods characterized as LME that this misalignment began earliest (Franklin, 1985) and has advanced furthest. Until the 1960s most people could be placed in social space on the basis of visible manifestations of social class such as dress, mode of speech, manners and so on. The 'swinging 60s' were responsible for the demise of many of these distinctions and it was presumed that in the supposedly 'class-less society' which the 1960s would usher in, class, on its own, would no longer be as reliable a predictor of values and opinions as it used to be.

By contrast since the 1960s, knowing whether a Londoner lived in Hampstead or Blackheath, as opposed, for example, to Pinner or Coulsdon, became a correspondingly better predictor of their social values. When Ken Baker linked *Acorn* to the behavioural data held on the TGI, it was this difference that intrigued him most, how one could identify the parts of the city in which readers of two middle class organs, The *Daily Telegraph* and The *Guardian*, were likely to live. Indeed, as we reported in Chapter 4, it was this distinction that was chosen as the subject of a presentation at the pivotal Café Royale seminar in 1980.

Such media preferences were of course reflections of more deep-seated social values and party political identification. Perhaps the first indication of the political significance of the LME occurred in the 1966 general election when Ben Whittaker was returned as the first ever Labour MP for Hampstead. In an earlier era, it would have been unthinkable that Labour could win so middle class a seat. The LME is the Group whose various neighbourhood Types comprise the largest proportion of Hampstead's neighbourhoods.

During the 50 years since 1966 there has been a huge growth in the size, confidence and influence of this particular geodemographic group. A radical minority, once fabled for its eccentric habits – shopping at Habitat, reading *Private Eye*, wearing sandals, eating muesli and supporting human rights – and visible only in what in the US *PRIZM* would describe as *Upper Bohemia*, has now come to dominate large swathes of inner London and significant parts of the high status Victorian inner suburbs of Britain's provincial cities. Such is the growth in size and influence of this group that it has arguably come to dominate not just the higher echelons of the Labour Party, but the media, entertainment, education and caring professions. Its prevailing ethos is that one should not be seen to be advancing one's own class interests, should be observing due process rather than gut instinct and guard against mistreatment of groups disadvantaged by imbalances in power. These orientations apply to members of the LME in both their professional and private lives.

What was once marginal has now mainstreamed, personal opinions have transmogrified into sometimes uncritical assumptions about the world and a form of political correctness that has come to dominate much cultural and political discourse. In recent years however, the pervasiveness of the influence of this group has become a target for the anger of an increasingly large population of non-metropolitan voters, ironically for the seemingly illiberal restrictions it can appear to impose on the opinions and languages which non-members of this elite may express.

Whilst the divisions arising from the referendum on Britain's membership in the European Union may have surprised many members of the LME, the trajectory of this geodemographic group in the 50 years since Ben Whittaker's election suggests that the shift in the party-political alignment of the LME has been occurring for many decades. We would argue that the practice of analysing voting intention through the prism of traditional representations of social class is the principal reason why this result has come as a surprise to so many political scientists, media commentators and researchers. Had they used geo-demographics as a basis for analysing opinion surveys we believe that the political divergence between the LME and the traditional working class might have been apparent much earlier.

Until quite recently, social class was considered by many commentators to be the bedrock on which political parties based their appeal. Many still do. But it is important to recognize that social class has by no means been the exclusive grounds for the emergence of and competition between Britain's political parties. For much of the nineteenth century, tariff reform constituted a more potent source of conflict pitting the economic interests of urban industrialists, pioneers of modern methods of production and international in their outlook, against the interests of a rent-seeking landed gentry concerned about the economic decline of a sector progressively more exposed to international competition.

This fault-line between economic liberals and economic conservatives coincided with a parallel division between social reformers and social conservatives. Reformers, many of whom like Charles Booth were non-conformists and lived in industrial cities, favoured tolerance of minority groups and campaigned for increased freedoms, whether of worship, trade or the extension of the franchise. This was in opposition primarily to supporters of the status quo, the established church ('of England') and the predominantly rural property-owning classes. Towards the end of the century identity emerged as a third source of political division, Liberals being relaxed about the prospect of Irish Home Rule, their Unionist opponents attaching greater importance to maintaining the nation state in its current form.

It is our contention that it was only during the twentieth century that these sources of social fracture, modernity, internationalism, sovereignty and tolerance of religious diversity, became subordinate to class as the primary basis for political affiliation as the Conservative and Labour parties came to represent the interests of the middle classes and the working classes respectively. Arguably the alignment between class and party preference reached its apogee during the elections of 1951 and 1955 when all but 4 per cent of voters voted for a candidate from one of the two main class-based parties.

In an age when party affiliation was routinely passed down from generation to generation, the principal object of election campaigners was to maximize turnout among members of their own tribe. By 2010 the (supposed) allegiance of voters to the party of their parents' class had become much weaker. Elections were now won by projecting an image and establishing a political position which gained traction among the ever-increasing number of politically and class-unaligned electors.

Finding and using language which would resonate with these 'floating' voters was held to be the key to electoral success and, since the 1990s, using geodemographics to vary this message on a geographical basis has become a key part of the campaigns of each of the main political parties.

One effect of the widening of access to higher education and the growth of new professions was that many more young people found themselves working in occupations and living in neighbourhoods that put them in a different social grouping to that which was ascribed to their parents, based on their occupation if not their behaviour. Should they vote on the basis of an inherited political identification or on the basis of the economic interests of the new class they that they now belonged to?

Many social changes contributed to problems with accepted definitions of social class. People whose parents may have had no realistic option other than to rent their home from the local council now aspired to and often succeeded in becoming the first generation of their family to own a home of their own. As property owners should they now vote Conservative? Where previously a family's social position might have been defined by the occupation of a male principal 'breadwinner', it became increasingly common practice for both partners to work full-time, and not necessarily in occupations categorized by the same social class. Longer life expectancy made it increasingly difficult to allocate a social class to the growing share of the population who were retired. Meanwhile the decline of the manufacturing industry, which followed from improvements in productivity and from globalization, progressively weakened the bargaining power of trade unions, reduced their membership and made it more difficult for union leaders to communicate to working people messages based on class positions and class interests.

The advent of television broadcasting, and more recently social media, exposed electors to a greater diversity of political influences, freeing them from peer group pressures. Unlike previous forms of communication, these new communications channels were no longer mediated by the interests and opinions of the social groups to which their recipients belonged, such as a church, a trade union or a golf club.[3]

Where at one time electors made unthinking decisions at the ballot box based on historical identities and class allegiances, an increasing proportion now expressed their preference in a manner that they felt increasingly encouraged to adopt as consumers in a market economy. How credible were the campaign messages of the different parties and which one's policies were most likely to benefit them financially? The conclusion of political scientists was that though class, as measured by occupation, continued to be important, its effect on how people voted was becoming progressively weaker than it used to be (Heath, 2015). Table 6.2 shows the declining salience of social class – as measured by the categories market researchers use – in the 2015 British general election.

**Table 6.2**  How Britain Voted in 2015

| Social class | % Conservative | % Labour | Conservative lead |
|---|---|---|---|
| AB | 45 | 26 | 19 |
| C1 | 41 | 29 | 12 |
| C2 | 32 | 32 | 0 |
| DE | 27 | 41 | −14 |

*Source*: IPSOS/MORI *How Britain voted in 2015*

Though these emerging trends impacted all sectors of the population, we would contend that each of them contributed particularly to the growth of the LME, to the development of its distinctive set of social values and to its political divergence from other segments of the middle classes. Career advancement for the LME increasingly depended on employees, typically graduates, being reflective in their mental attitudes, international in their approach, transformative in their manner of working and sensitive to the existence of the less privileged in their social attitudes. Such attitudes would no doubt have struck a chord with Charles Booth and the fellow philanthropists and reformers who dominated the Liberal Party in Victorian Britain.

For this reason it is no longer meaningful today to interpret Labour's success in constituencies such as Hampstead or Hornsey and Wood Green as a reflection of the social classes or class interests of their electors. On the contrary, for many of its residents the decision to live in Hampstead, provided they can afford the financial cost (Webber and Burrows, 2016), became an expression of a chosen identity, one which asserts to priority of tastes and cultural capital over narrowly defined financial success.

## How you vote is better predicted by where you live than what job you do

When it became apparent how strongly social media might influence the opinions of its most active users, many observers predicted a rapid decline in the influence of local friends and neighbours. People would now truly live in what Melvyn Webber (1964) had described as a 'non-place urban realm'. Voting for a particular party would become one of the many behaviours that would now be predicted by personal circumstances and dispositions and by social media affinities rather than by the opinions of local others.

This, and the convergence of the voting intentions of different social classes which we have discussed in the previous pages, presents an interesting conundrum. If, as clearly is the case, social classes have been converging in terms of how they vote and residents have been increasingly exposed to the influence of social media, should we not be witnessing a convergence in the share of the votes cast for Conservative and Labour candidates in different parliamentary constituencies? Should not the margins by which victorious candidates are elected begin to narrow? After all, if social media displaces the influence of the local and if class ceases to exert its former influence, why should people in any one constituency vote in a very different way from how they vote in any other?

The analysis of results in recent general elections provides no evidence for the convergence in election outcomes that would be expected from such reasoning. The winners' margins in individual constituencies in the 2017 election were no smaller than they had been in 1964. That this convergence has not occurred is significant: it implies that the place in which a voter lives continues to affect not just the way in which they vote but also the way in which electors belonging to any *particular class* cast their vote.

How can we demonstrate the continuing effect of place on how people vote? One way of doing this involves us imagining a scenario whereby, in the 2015 general election, individual voters in each constituency cast their votes for Conservatives and Labour candidates in proportions similar to the national averages for their class. In other words, professionals, managers and unskilled workers in every single constituency in Britain voted in exactly the same proportions for each party as they did in every other constituency. On this assumption, using the findings of Table 6.2, it follows logically that in any individual constituency the Conservative Party could never exceed a ceiling of the 45 per cent share of the vote they did actually achieve among professionals and managers, nor fall below the 27 per cent share they then obtained from social groups D and E.

In this scenario, the largest majority by which the Conservatives could ever defeat Labour would be in a seat in which every voter was a professional or manager and would be equivalent to 19 per cent of the votes cast. Likewise, even in the extreme case that every single voter in a seat belonged to social classes D and E, no Labour MP would could expect to win a majority over his or her Conservative opponent by more than 14 per cent.

Comparing the outcomes that would have resulted from these assumptions with the actual results in the 2015 general election provides interesting evidence of the existence of peer group effects.[4] Of the 632 contested seats, fewer than 30 per cent of constituencies, 178, produced a result within the range of possible outcomes based on this condition (that members of a social class would vote in each seat in the same way as they did nationally). There were also 204 seats where Labour had a higher majority over the Conservatives than its 14 per cent majority among members of social classes D and E. In 250 seats the Tories beat Labour by a larger share than their 19 per cent majority among voters in social class AB. In total, therefore, in seven out of every ten constituencies the winning party's majority was greater than their lead even in the social class that favoured them the most. This can leave us in no doubt that there have to be reasons other than just differences in their social class which affect the way in which individual electors vote. Given that in recent elections the average swings in safe seats have been similar to those in marginals, it is safe to say that little if any convergence is taking place. Table 6.3 shows some extreme examples.

**Table 6.3** Conservative Lead over Labour in Selected Constituencies and Social Classes, 2015

|  | % Conservative lead |
| --- | --- |
| North East Hampshire | 56 |
| Harlow | 19 |
| *Social Class AB* | 19 |
| *Social Class DE* | −14 |
| York Central | −14 |
| Liverpool Walton | −77 |

That 70 per cent of constituencies had majorities beyond the range of parties' variation in support among individual social classes is surprising enough. What is perhaps even more striking is how large some of the majorities were. The 56 per cent majority achieved by the Conservatives in North East Hampshire – the seat with the highest Tory majority over Labour – was almost three times its majority among professionals and managers (19 per cent). In Liverpool Walton Labour's majority was over five times that among social classes D and E nationally. Clearly voters continue to be influenced not just by their own personal circumstances but also by the attitudes of the other members of the local community with whom they come into contact on a day-to-day basis. In a strongly working class seat, all social classes are more likely to vote Labour, in strongly middle class seats, all social classes are more likely to vote Conservative. But this is not the sole explanation for this phenomenon.

If, from the results in North East Hampshire and Liverpool Walton, we can deduce the existence of very powerful local peer effects, the results in Harlow and York Central suggest that the source of these peer group effects is something other than just social class. Harlow, a new town some 30 miles from London, is an archetypal example of a town with a population group described by *Mosaic* as *White Van Culture*. Yet it divides its support between Conservative and Labour in similar proportions to the 'professionals and managers' social class. York Central is a constituency with far higher social and educational status than Harlow, a major religious centre with a successful university and with an electorate which provides professional and retail services to an extensive and prosperous rural hinterland.

Yet in 2015 York Central's electors voted for the two main parties in the same proportions as social classes D and E did nationally.[5] So, given that the social class of individual voters explains only a modest amount of the variation in the outcomes of elections at constituency level, what role can geodemographic classification play in accounting for that part of the variance that remains unexplained?

One reason why the members of any specific social class might vote differently in different types of neighbourhood follows from the inevitability that no measure of social class can be wholly consistent as an operational representation of the concept. Doubtless the types of worker who live in Liverpool Walton who are categorized as C2, semi-skilled, will on average be different to the types of people given the same social categorization who live in North East Hampshire. Accepting this line of thinking it is conceivable that social class may be a rather better predictor of voting behaviour than is implied by these statistics, it is just that we have a problem ascribing people to social classes in a consistent and accurate way. In other words, class is still an accurate predictor, it is just that the proxy we use for inferring class is not as reliable at is used to be or as we would like it to be.[6]

Alternatively, it could be that in the contemporary world, or indeed in just certain *Mosaic* Types, it is a person's cultural attitudes, even taste, which forms a better basis than occupation for determining social status and hence political affiliation. As occupations become more specialized, and as even friends and family find it difficult to understand the nature of the job that a family member does when he or she goes to work, it is easy to understand why occupation becomes less effective as a criterion for conveying a person's social status. In such situations social status can only be communicated by other measures of behaviour such as choice of car, style of house, private rather than state schooling and neighbourhood of residence. Groups based on taste will almost certainly be difficult groups for political parties to appeal to with any meaningful manifesto. However, if we were to abandon occupation altogether as a measure of social class, and to ascribe class exclusively on the basis of behaviour, we are in danger of circularity – if social classes are defined on the basis of behaviour then it is almost inevitable that behaviour will be predicted on the basis of social class. Since behaviour is so influenced by local social norms and relative access to opportunities, whatever effect we would otherwise have ascribed to a neighbourhood, becomes built into this new definition of social class. It can no longer be considered as an autonomous effect and can't play a very useful role in any predictive model.

This dilemma can perhaps be usefully resolved in Weberian terms by distinguishing between social status, which is largely acquired through behaviour and consumption, and social class, a concept which gives greater weight to a person's role in the field of economic production (Gane, 2005). We believe that the categories in which people are placed by the current occupation-based classification are, in terms of lifestyles and life opportunities, not as uniform across different geographical areas as most analysts tend to assume. However, it is our belief that these errors have only a modest impact on voting habits compared with other sources of difference.

A possible explanation for the surprisingly large amount of variation in the relative share of the Tory and Labour vote at the level of individual constituency is what might be described as *peer group* effects. A credible hypothesis is that each individual voter will be influenced both by his or her own objective circumstances, as represented by his or her social class, and by the opinions of the circle of people that person comes into contact with in the local community. Sometimes these will be congruent but some electors will experience a conflict between the two.

Imagine a person who teaches in a primary school in Bexhill and who is in daily contact with the social attitudes of parents. He or she may well be more disposed to vote Conservative than a counterpart in a similar school in Birkenhead, where children are likely to experience different needs and their parents to share different values. It is possible that a teacher with right of centre tendencies might be more minded to apply for a teaching position in Bexhill than in Birkenhead, and vice versa. Social values, according to this line of argument, both influence where people choose to live and are affected by the prevailing ethos of the geographical area in which a person lives. If election results were to be affected by peer group effects of this sort, and they are, the effect would be to increase Conservative majorities in middle class seats and to increase Labour majorities in working class seats. But peer group effects, or at least those contingent on social class, do not explain why some middle class constituencies, such as Hampstead and York Central, return Labour MPs, whilst some working class constituencies, such as Harlow and Basildon, return Conservative ones.

To demonstrate that peer group effects are at work, but which do not involve under-represented social classes adopting the political views of those that are over-represented in the constituency, we have ranked the 632 UK constituencies according to the relative share of the Conservative and Labour parties' vote at the 2015 election. We then ranked them according to the relative proportions of social groups AB and DE based on the results of the 2011 census. Comparing the ranking based on actual voting and the ranking based on occupational status yields a correlation of only 0.62. Under 40 per cent of the variation in the relative share of the Tory–Labour vote at the level of the constituency is accounted for by the socio-economic make-up of the constituency.

So, although pressures to conform to the prevailing political viewpoint may explain some of the variation in the shares of the two parties at constituency level, it is evident from Table 6.4 that there are many constituencies where the 2015 result deviated significantly from what might have been predicted on the basis of their social class ranking. What insight can geodemographics give into the reasons for misalignment between a constituency's social class and parties' share of the vote?

**Table 6.4** Constituencies Whose Rank on the Basis of Tory/Labour Share of the Vote Was Least Consistent with Their Rank in Terms of Occupational Status – Seats Where Labour Over-performed

| Constituency | Voting rank | Social rank | Deviation |
| --- | --- | --- | --- |
| Hornsey and Wood Green | 595 | 24 | –571 |
| Islington North | 600 | 62 | –538 |
| Manchester, Withington | 605 | 80 | –525 |
| Dulwich and West Norwood | 544 | 53 | –491 |
| Islington South and Finsbury | 530 | 51 | –479 |
| Sheffield, Hallam | 483 | 12 | –471 |
| Holborn and St Pancras | 540 | 85 | –455 |
| Streatham | 524 | 73 | –451 |
| Vauxhall | 511 | 72 | –439 |
| Bermondsey and Old Southwark | 543 | 106 | –437 |

Table 6.4 lists the ten constituencies where Labour out-performed expectations by the largest amount when taking into account their social class profile. These essentially were (now) high status seats which had nevertheless returned Labour MPs. The Liberal Democrats had held four of these seats in 2010. However, in two of these cases, Hornsey and Wood Green and Bermondsey and Old Southwark, the level of divergence from the expected result is no different from that in neighbouring constituencies so we cannot adduce the local success of the Liberal Democrats as being the reason. The ranking reveals a very clear pattern of geographical clustering and, outside London, the presence of inner city constituencies with exceptionally large numbers of university students. Though it could be questioned whether the presence of sitting Liberal Democrat MPs and of young electorates appear to explain the difference, the list contains other seats in inner London such as Islington North, Islington South, Dulwich, Streatham and Vauxhall, which have become highly sought after residential locations for young professionals and indeed even older 'gentrifiers' in the liberal and caring professions. Evidently there is a strong pro-Labour influence in these seats which does not lend itself to an explanation based either on socio-economic status or on peer group effects.

The *Mosaic* neighbourhood type E28 *Counter Cultural Mix* is the most over-represented in these constituencies. In an earlier paper, Webber (2007: 193–4) described it thus:

> [M]ostly older, high-density residential neighbourhoods that are located in parts of London in which many of the older tenements have been replaced with what were originally local authority run estates. These therefore are,

or were, located in unfashionable neighbourhoods and have traditionally afforded accommodation to young single people arriving in London from the regions, students, and immigrant groups. Many of these areas are now losing second-generation immigrants to the smaller, self-contained terraces that are common further from the centre of London. Many of the three-storey houses have been converted from multiple occupation to self-contained flats. In the better parts, some have been converted to single-family ownership. These, therefore, are neighbourhoods close to the frontier with the gentrifying *avant garde* and, when they are first gentrified, are colonised by slightly bohemian cadres typically endowed with more education than money. This, therefore, is a type of neighbourhood in which one finds large numbers of students, foreign as well as British, and large numbers of professionals working in the public sector, many of whom are happier to live among people of occupational classes different from their own. It is in these areas in particular that one finds the highest readership of left or centre-leaning middle class media such as The *Independent*, The *Guardian*, and The *Observer*... In these classic melting pots, a key factor that attracts many residents is the tolerance of diversity. Such people are mostly pleased to be able to go about their own business free of social pressures towards conformity. Although residents lead parallel lives, there is greater communication between different social and ethnic groups than in almost all other types of neighbourhoods, which is reflected in a high proportion of the residents of mixed ethnic background. Countercultural views tend to extend towards the adoption of many anti-corporate attitudes...where anti-globalisation activists are most likely to live, and where alternative remedies and diets are most likely to be adopted. These are neighbourhoods where nonstandard family relationships are relatively common. Whilst there are clear disadvantages of living in such neighbourhoods, such as high levels of crime, noise, pollution, lack of usable open space...

Table 6.5 lists seats at the other end of the spectrum. These are constituencies which, despite their low occupational status, nevertheless returned Conservative MPs to Westminster in 2015. These are the constituencies in which the Conservatives managed to achieve much higher majorities over Labour than would be expected on the basis of their social profile. In the 2017 General Election, the Conservatives improved their majority over Labour in these ten constituencies by an average of 4.2 per cent, whereas in the ten constituencies in which Labour had already over-performed by the largest margin in 2015, the Labour majority over the Conservatives increased on average by a further 12.9 per cent. This polarization is increasing.

Table 6.5   Constituencies Whose Rank on the Basis of Tory/Labour Share of the Vote Was Least Consistent with Their Rank in Terms of Occupational Status – Seats Where Conservatives Over-performed

| Constituency | Voting rank | Social rank | Deviation |
| --- | --- | --- | --- |
| South Holland and The Deepings | 20 | 489 | 469 |
| North East Cambridgeshire | 65 | 530 | 465 |
| Boston and Skegness | 194 | 600 | 406 |
| South West Norfolk | 137 | 455 | 318 |
| Clacton | 237 | 551 | 314 |
| Bognor Regis and Littlehampton | 101 | 413 | 312 |
| North West Norfolk | 179 | 491 | 312 |
| Banff and Buchan | 231 | 541 | 310 |
| North Cornwall | 81 | 384 | 303 |
| Great Yarmouth | 275 | 577 | 302 |

In Table 6.5 we once again find a high level of geographical clustering, in this case around the Fens. Characteristics of many of these constituencies are large-scale agricultural production and food processing enterprises, operations which in recent years have become particularly reliant on workers recruited from eastern Europe. Though Clacton, Bognor and Skegness were once moderately desirable retirement resorts, none of these constituencies now attract sophisticated retirees or second-homers, nor are any within easy reach of university towns, centres of public administration or sources of high-tech employment.

In *Mosaic* parlance, these are areas dominated by neighbourhoods of the Type K59, *Parochial Villagers*. The *Mosaic* documentation describes such neighbourhoods as follows:

*Parochial Villagers* is found in lowland Britain, in communities that have been relatively unaffected by the attentions of urban commuters, wealthy pensioners, weekenders or summer holiday-makers. The countryside, whilst pleasant, lacks the undulation, which would make it attractive for picnickers or weekend walkers. The architecture of the village housing lacks the quality and the use of attractive building materials that would make it attractive to people choosing to retire to a rural community. These are local market towns, serving local farming communities rather than providing jobs for well paid executives in large national companies who might otherwise be eager to find attractive village environments in which to raise their children. These therefore are old established villages, often dating from medieval times... Here, as elsewhere in the British countryside, young people are increasingly required to move to the town to acquire the technical or university education that is the prerequisite for a remunerative career and, having left home villages for this reason, often lack any particular motivation for returning other than to visit their parents. On some farms sons may take over from fathers but many of the farms in these areas are owned by large syndicates rather than by owner managers and most of the people who live in these villages are employed in rural support industries and do not have jobs that they can pass down to their children. Though these are areas where housing is relatively affordable and whilst councils are often happy to allow new building, much of the housing is not suited to the needs of young families and children. Unless they have been born in the villages young couples often find it difficult to build networks of local friendships especially where their children have to travel some distance to school as many do... These therefore are parochial communities in the sense that the parish and its church provide the defining sense of local identify to the residents but also in the sense that these are not areas which are practised in accepting outsiders. Indeed it is often this parochial nature of the local population that deters would-be urban commuters and retirees who, unless they have been born locally, fear that it could take many years before they were accepted into the local community... Parochial Villagers contains people who are well integrated in their local communities and whose consumption focuses around daily necessities. Metropolitan lifestyle accoutrements are more likely to cause local amusement than envy and few people are particularly interested in the finer nuances of high street fashion. Tastes, whether in food, clothing or cars are for old fashioned and well-known brands and though people like to purchase face to face from small businesses that they trust, these are not neighbourhoods where people place a high value on craft production and individual designs

Of the seven district councils with the highest concentration of *Parochial Villagers*, six contain some or all of the constituencies listed in Table 6.5. They are South Holland, East Lindsey, North Norfolk, Breckland, Kings Lynn and West Norfolk and Boston.[7]

The constituencies at either end of this ranking are, in effect, mirror opposites of each other in respect of openness to new ideas and diversity, willingness to embrace new technologies and new forms of household and industrial organization. This pattern of results is of course highly relevant to the immediate post-Brexit criticism of the Labour Party regarding its over-identification with the LME and apparent disconnect with people living in small towns and provincial communities.

## *Mosaic* Types where each party does better than one might expect

In order to explain the analysis that follows, further evidence of how a geodemographic classification may help to throw light on the relationship between social class and voting, it may be useful to flesh out in a little more detail the twin concepts of a profile and a profile library briefly introduced in Chapters 1 and 5.

A 'profile' is the name conventionally given to the statistical output created when either the postcodes on a customer file or the respondents to a behavioural question recorded on a research survey are cross-tabulated by a geodemographic classification. Typically, a profile would compare the percentage of consumers, residents or citizens on a particular file falling within each *Mosaic* Type with the corresponding proportions of UK adults or households. Two such profiles were introduced in Table 1.3, one of the supporters of a human rights charity the other of the supporters of a far-right political party. In this instance a value of 100 in the index column indicates a proportion of supporters identical to the national average, a score of 150 a level 50 per cent above the national average, a score of 80 a level 20 per cent below the national average and so on.

Over time a library has been created storing the profiles of some 1,200 demographics and behaviours which have been tabulated against 2003 *Mosaic*. The distribution of respondents in each *Mosaic* Type intending to vote Conservative or Labour are just two of these 1,200. Other profiles include the percentage of households belonging to each social class as defined by market researchers.

Though the profiles of Conservative and Labour voters were created using a different set of survey respondents from those from which the profile of social classes is produced, this does not inhibit us from comparing the two sets of profiles for the purpose of investigating whether the misalignment between social status and party support occurs within particular Types of neighbourhood.

To this end, just as the 632 parliamentary constituencies were, the 61 *Mosaic* Types were first ranked by the differences in the proportion of census respondents belonging to two groups, one professionals and managers (ABs), the other semi-skilled workers (D). To create a social rank score for each of the 61 Types, each *Mosaic* Type's numeric rank order on semi-skilled workers was subtracted from its rank order on professionals and managers. An identical process was used to rank the 61 *Mosaic* categories according to the relative support for the Conservatives and Labour.

Were social class the sole dimension influencing how people vote, and were any departure from this established relationship random (rather than systemic), then one would expect the ranking based on Conservative/Labour leaning to be exactly aligned with the ranking based on social class. In practice, though the two rankings are strongly correlated, there are a number of types of neighbourhood where each of the two parties performs very much better, or worse, than would have been anticipated solely on the basis of social class.[8]

Given our earlier discussion, it perhaps comes as no surprise that Labour tends to over-perform (in relation to social class) in neighbourhoods in the *Urban Intelligence* Group such as E33 *University Challenge* and E34 *Town Gown Transition* – two Types often found in close proximity to leading universities in large cities whose buoyant economies are often based on new knowledge-based and creative industries. It also over-performs among those well-off, middle aged members of the middle classes who have colonized what were once working class neighbourhoods, E30 *New Urban Colonists* and E31 *Caring Professionals*. The previously discussed *Counter Cultural Mix*, along with F35 *Bedsit Beneficiaries* and D27 *Settled Minorities*, are less well-off neighbourhoods, in many respects similar to these other clusters demographically, where Labour performs much better than one would expect on the basis of social class.[9] These *Mosaic* Types are marked in red on the visualization contained in Figure 6.1.

At the other end of the spectrum we can identify other types of neighbourhood whose position on the Labour/Conservative ranking is much more favourable to the Conservatives than would be expected if all we knew about them was their social class profile.

As do the Labour over-performing areas, these also form solid blocks of adjacent clusters. Conservatives over-perform (at least in relation to Labour) in four of the five Types within Group K, *Rural Isolation*, but less so among environmentally aware K58 *Greenbelt Guardians*. They also significantly over-perform in adjoining clusters of Group J, *Grey Perspectives*, in particular J54 *Bungalow Retirement*, J55 *Small Town Seniors* and J56 *Tourist Attendants*, all of them located principally in small town and rural areas.

Another contiguous grouping of Conservative over-performing clusters is formed by B13 *Burdened Optimists*, C18 *Sprawling Subtopia*, D22 *Affluent Blue Collar* and D23 *Industrial Grit*. These are also marked in blue in Figure 6.1. Here we find middle income families, most with relatively limited educational qualifications, but with strong aspirations towards property ownership and financial self-sufficiency – a group of swing voters politicians have at various times referred to as 'Hard-Working Families' and the 'Just About Managing'.

The evidence of such strong residuals does seem to support the proposition that, as regards the conduct of political campaigning, factors other than class have become increasingly salient in the past 50 years. These forms of analysis help to account for the success and failure of the parties in retaining and winning key marginal constituencies. Thus Labour, despite polling weakly in 2015, achieved a higher share of the vote than 30 years ago in many constituencies rich in the neighbourhoods of *Urban Intelligence* we have detailed: Exeter;

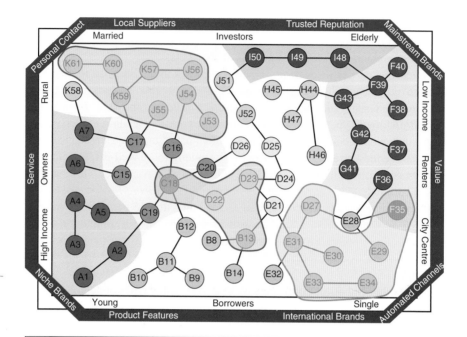

**Visualizing the *Mosaic* classification using a 'Minimum Spanning Tree'**

The *Mosaic* tree is a representation of a statistical device which enables researchers to visualize in multi-dimensional space the regions where particular behaviours are most common. Each one of the 61 *Mosaic* Types, as represented by its Group and Type code, is placed on the grid adjacent to the other *Mosaic* Types to which its demographics are most similar. Solid black lines link each cluster to whichever other one(s) it is most similar to. Around the inner frame of the tree are marked six key demographic dimensions that differentiate the 61 categories. For instance, residents in the *Mosaic* Types in the 'north west' corner tend to be married and to live in rural neighbourhoods whilst in the 'south east' corner they tend to be single and to live close to city centres. Around the outer frame are marked five other dimensions relevant to marketing and communications. For example, residents in the 'north west' corner value personal contact when shopping, those in the 'south east' corner are the most likely to use automated channels when interacting with government or commercial organizations. The tree provides an excellent basis for locating regions in multi-dimensional space where particular behaviours are concentrated or, as in this instance, where the two main parties do better or worse than would be expected on the basis of social class.

Figure 6.1 Minimum Spanning Tree

Lancaster; Hove; Streatham; Hampstead; Hornsey and Wood Green; and so on. By contrast the formerly relatively safe seats which Labour is now some way from winning – places such as Camborne and Redruth, Gloucestershire West, Nuneaton, Loughborough and Basildon – have large numbers of electors in neighbourhoods such as *Burdened Optimists*, *Sprawling Subtopia*, *Affluent Blue Collar*, *Industrial Grit*, *Rural Isolation* and *Grey Perspectives*.

This analysis lends support to the contention that both main parties are themselves fracturing into coalitions of communities with increasingly distinct values. For example, the appeal of the Conservatives to 'One Nation' values are likely to resonate especially with voters in geodemographic categories common in smaller, stable communities who retain a sense of obligation to assist those less fortunate than themselves. By contrast the appeal to 'hard-working families', lower taxes and less deregulation is one which will resonate most in neighbourhoods of a very different character as described above.

Likewise, the emerging division within the Labour party between the LME and the more socially conservative clusters of traditional Labour values is reflected in the neighbourhood Types where Labour over-performs, which are also the ones where Labour has been more effective in retaining its share of the vote and in recruiting new party members. This emerging division was clearly illustrated by the inopportune reaction and subsequent resignation from her position of Shadow Attorney General of the Labour MP for Islington South, Emily Thornberry, when visiting the Rochester and Strood constituency during the 2014 by-election. Used in her home constituency to canvassing in the multicultural and internationally oriented neighbourhoods of *Urban Intelligence* and F36 *Metro Multiculture*, she was shocked to find a display of national identity in the form of a large England flag in a neighbourhood of B13 *Burdened Optimists* (or possibly H46 *White Van Culture*), Types in which such display of national identity is consistent with the prevailing culture. The culture of such neighbourhoods is one from which many other leading Labour leaders, not least Jeremy Corbyn, have been accused of becoming increasingly remote.[10]

## The political significance of the New Metropolitan Elite

This chapter has described the emergence, growth and geographical spread of a Liberal Metropolitan Elite, which, over the past 50 years, has demonstrated an increased sympathy not just with the Labour Party but with that wing of the party most engaged in political issues involving the protection of the disadvantaged and the unempowered. By contrast with traditional Labour supporters, this emerging influence is not employed in heavily unionized occupations, does not engage in manual work and benefits only to a very modest degree from policies of redistribution. It does not work disproportionately in the public sector. Its class interest appears to be only weakly advanced by Labour.

In the manner of its daily existence the group is significantly more exposed to people from different backgrounds, whether it terms of race, religion, housing tenure or deprivation than its equivalents in suburban or rural locations. And, though it is not especially dependent on state benefits, its well-being is particularly dependent on the collective provision of services, public transport, clean air and access to parks in particular. Market research data show it is a group which, on account of its high income, lack of time and often cramped housing, is among the pioneers of personal outsourcing – eating in restaurants, being entertained in the cinema or theatre, having clothes dry-cleaned. Its ethos contrasts with the self-reliance practised particularly in the countryside, which we discuss in Chapter 9, and its preference for physical and practical activities such as DIY, cooking, gardening and the exercising of pets.

In terms of its employment this group is disproportionately involved in highly specialized professional activities often of a normative or affective nature, in the media and entertainment for example, in politics, charities or lobbying, or in the arts. Career advancement within each of these occupational groupings often depends on an ability to identify with the emotional demands of a range of different demographic groupings, not just an ability to accurately apply rule-based professional standards.

The argument that this elite is disproportionately involved in cutting edge innovation could be contested. To a degree its reliance on traditional media at the expense of social media is one of the common reasons advocated for the success both of the Brexit campaign and of Donald Trump.

The features which provide coherence to this elite are ones which appear to be common across post-industrial western societies and ones which it is difficult to attribute to the economic elements of class interest. Explanations based on these traditional forms of social division seem to struggle. It is our surmise that the key to interpreting the coherence of this group lies more in terms of educational and behavioural differences, many of which reflect differences in tastes and values and, indirectly, social experiences.

In these respects, the group, it could be argued, is in the vanguard of a return to the situation which pertained a hundred or more years ago, when political divisions were based to a much greater extent than they were in the twentieth century on ethical values, on international versus national identification, reform versus conservatism and on reflective consideration based on evidence rather than on gut instinct.

## Notes

[1] The Lord Chief Justice and two senior colleagues were branded with this moniker by The *Daily Mail* on 3 November 2016 when they ruled Brexit could not be triggered without a Westminster vote.

[2] The first two of these labels come from the 2003 version of *Mosaic* whilst the last two come from the 2009 version.

[3] Of course, the advent of social media seems to be changing things yet again (Burnap et al., 2016).

[4] It is worth noting that this method is the one used to create standardized mortality rates so it is by no means an untested methodology.

[5] The 2017 General Election resulted in even greater polarization between these two seats, Labour achieving a swing of 10.4 per cent in York Central, and only 1.6 per cent in Harlow.

[6] We discovered in Chapter 3 that as far back as the early 1970s unskilled workers in Liverpool's inner city council estates had an unemployment rate significantly higher than did their counterparts in other areas of the city. If the unskilled workers in the inner city estates were current or former dockers, and those in other areas were railway porters, then it may be that the category 'unskilled' lacked the homogeneity analysts need it to have for it to be useful in an application of this sort.

[7] It is not on account of the performance of UKIP that the East Anglian seats fall within the second group. UKIP performed well in these seats because of the difficulty Labour has in appealing to *Parochial Villagers* despite the presence in their local economies of so many jobs for people of lower socio-economic status. We will discuss this further in Chapter 9 on the countryside.

[8] Given that there are 61 *Mosaic* Types the largest deviation possible between a cluster's rank on social class and voting is 60. This would occur were the most Conservative leaning cluster to be the one with the lowest proportion of professionals and managers.

[9] Note the absence of E32 *Dinky Developments*: neighbourhoods of recently built housing occupied by young, first-time buyers, most not yet with children. The typical resident in such neighbourhoods is not dissimilar in age and education to residents in the Labour-leaning categories but tends to have different career, material and household aspirations and tends to live in quite different types of location. Politically they constitute a very different tribe.

[10] It is no coincidence that the *Mosaic* Type of Jeremy Corbyn's home postcode in Hornsey and Wood Green, the profile of his constituency, Islington North, and the neighbourhoods from which he has been successful in recruiting new Labour members should be so similar.

# 7

# MUNICIPAL OVERSPILL ESTATES
## Educational Under-Achievement among the 'Left Behinds'?

Job Centre Floor Manager: 'There's a special number if you've been diagnosed as dyslexic.'
Daniel: 'Right, can you give us that 'coz with computers, I'm dyslexic.'
Job Centre Floor Manager: 'You'll find it online, sir.'

Scene from *I, Daniel Blake*, 2016

## Provincial low rise municipal estates

In this chapter we focus on life in the following five *Mosaic* Types selected from Table 5.4.

| Code | *Mosaic* Type label | UK % | Top local authorities |
|------|---------------------|------|----------------------|
| G41 | Families on Benefits | 1.2 | Nottingham |
| G42 | Low Horizons | 2.6 | Knowsley |
| G43 | Ex-Industrial Legacy | 2.9 | South Tyneside |
| H46 | White Van Culture | 3.2 | Barking and Dagenham |
| H47 | New Town Materialism | 2.2 | Redditch |

A major focus of Chapter 6 was the way the result of the 2016 referendum on membership of the European Union raised awareness of the existence and influence of a Liberal Metropolitan Elite. Since the referendum, media and political attention has switched to what has variously been described as the 'left behinds'[1] or the 'somewheres' (Goodhart, 2017). The sprawling municipal estates found in the outer suburbs of many of the UK's largest provincial cities constitute one of the principal heartlands of this socio/political group. It was territory such as this, as well as the *Parochial Villagers*, which we will describe in more detail in Chapter 9, that proved particularly fertile ground for UKIP during the 2015 election campaign (although not so much so during the 2017 campaign).

These estates can be considered as the mirror image of the Brexit-opposing *Mosaic* categories described in Chapter 6. It is perhaps the *Mosaic* 2003 neighbourhood Group G, *Municipal Dependency* – described in the public sector version as 'Low income families living in estate-based social housing' – that most clearly embodies these characteristics. This Group is composed of three distinct neighbourhood Types:

1.  G41 *Families on Benefits* – 'Families, many single parent, in deprived social housing on the edge of regional centres'.
2.  G42 *Low Horizons* – 'Older people living in very large social housing estates on the outskirts of provincial cities'.
3.  G43 *Ex-Industrial Legacy* – 'Older people, many in poor health from work in heavy industry, in low rise social housing'.

For the first three quarters of the twentieth century the term 'municipal' enjoyed far more positive associations than it does today. Officers employed by county boroughs took pride in their initiatives to improve public health. They enacted bylaws which imposed high standards on newly built streets, they channelled and discharged sewerage, they collected and disposed of refuse, and they paved and lit residential streets. Urban households cleansed their clothes and bodies in municipal baths, exercised their limbs on municipal sports grounds and courted potential partners in municipal parks. After a healthy lifetime their bodies were taken to rest in municipal crematoria. Children were educated in municipal schools and returned home each afternoon to homes in municipal estates on the upper deck of municipally run buses.

Today it is difficult to credit that between the two world wars gas and electricity, and in Hull even telephones, were delivered by municipally owned utilities. In this context it is easy to forget that even when the first UK geodemographic systems were built there were many neighbourhoods in Britain's cities where most of the basic needs of residents were still being met by services delivered by municipalities. It is these neighbourhoods that the *Mosaic* Group G *Municipal Dependency* distinguishes and that are the focus of this chapter.

As was noted in Chapter 3, the algorithm used by the Liverpool study distinguished these overspill estates as quite different types of social area from the city's inner city council estates. The low rise outer estates that belong to the national cluster were built at a time when there was no presumption against the use of green-field sites for new housing development and when municipal housing was built at much lower densities than today's new housing. Today, notwithstanding generous gardens and plentiful provision of grass, greenery and public open space, many of these estates appear tired and generally lacking in vibrancy, not least due to the planners' deliberate efforts to physically separate homes from shopping, industrial and commercial land uses.

Linking *Mosaic* to administrative data on school pupils' performance at Key Stage 2 and GCSE, central government's IMD and young offender data, this chapter identifies low educational attainment and youth offending as a particular problem in neighbourhoods of this sort. Key Stage test results are well below and petty crime well above what might be expected had deprivation been the sole driver of pupil performance and teenage crime. Can geodemographics help us identify what specific aspects of disadvantage contribute to this educational under-performance and to behavioural problems with young people? Whilst there is no doubt that the demise of the heavy industries that once employed the skilled manual workers for whom this sort of housing was built contributes to the generally low aspirations of many pupils, we conclude that another critical factor is the sheer size, social uniformity and physical and cultural remoteness of these municipal estates.

The Pupil Level Annual School Census (PLASC), which reveals how the performance of pupils in such neighbourhoods compares with that of other geodemographic Types, provides further evidence of the 'neighbourhood effects' described in earlier chapters. This chapter showcases a series of statistical techniques which make it possible to quantify the impact of these effects. It also demonstrates how geodemographics might be used to deliver a fairer evaluation of school performance than current league tables.[2]

In addition to separating out the city's dock front from its suburban council estates, the Liverpool study demonstrated the tendency for its better-off tenants to gravitate towards its 'better' estates. Other than in its housing department, many of the council's officials were surprised to discover that it was not just in the private housing sector that one could find finely nuanced distinctions between 'better' and 'worse' estates. Council tenants were certainly very aware of them and of the procedures used by the Liverpool housing department which resulted in this 'social sorting'. This process could have profound effects on theirs and others' lives. There is no doubt that the differences in the social composition of the different neighbourhood categories that arose from the classification process were also caused in part by the changes in government policy regarding the level of public subsidy that was offered to councils when building social housing.

But these were not the only processes at work. The records held by the municipal housing department allowed officers to form judgements about each of their tenants. Did they pay their rent on time? How well did they look after their property? When homes became available on the 'better' estates, it was common for a first right of refusal to a transfer to be offered to tenants considered to be 'better' on these and other evaluation criteria. Likewise, as it became harder to find tenants for homes on the estates with the worst reputations, these were the properties that the council offered to and were accepted by people in the most desperate circumstances and whose need for council accommodation was most urgent.

The political decision to grant council tenants the 'right-to-buy' (Dunn et al., 1987) hugely accelerated these processes. This entitlement was clearly more problematic in developments of flats since no single occupier had responsibility for the maintenance of common areas. But in the low rise estates tenants were less likely to have either the means or the motivation to buy their properties if they lived on the less sought-after ones. If they did not live on what buyers perceived to be a desirable estate, there was much less chance that they would benefit from a substantial capital gain if and when they sold their property.

When, as it inevitably would, the proportion of tenants taking advantage of their new entitlements began to vary depending on the type of estate they lived on, this impacted even more strongly on the esteem in which estates were viewed. Properties on estates with a high proportion of new owners tended to be kept in better repair. Replacement front doors and new extensions signified to the outside world that their current occupiers should not be mistaken for council tenants despite the layout of the estate and the design of its houses (Saunders, 1989).

Since the early 1970s, when the Liverpool study was undertaken, the result of this process of sortation has been visible in every UK geodemographic classification system. Indeed, so great has been the impact of 'right-to-buy' legislation that contemporary classifications often struggle to distinguish between neighbourhoods whose properties were originally built for sale to private owners and the more desirable municipal estates most of whose properties have been sold to former municipal tenants.[3]

As we have seen in Chapter 5, the 2003 version of *Mosaic* distinguishes three broad social areas of social housing. Group F, *Welfare Borderline*, consists mostly of mid and high rise social housing, typically but not exclusively in neighbourhoods that have been subjected to slum clearance and reconstruction. Group G, *Municipal Dependency*, the focus of this chapter, is especially common in the suburbs of large provincial cities and in maritime industrial areas, and comprises low rise, low density estates still mostly municipally owned. The third Group, H, *Blue Collar Enterprise*, also consists of neighbourhoods of low rise housing, but much of this has been purchased through 'right-to-buy' legislation. Many of its residents work in high demand non-graduate employment. Group H is particularly prevalent in smaller towns and in the 'New Towns' built during the 1950s and 1960s.

The first of these Groups – described in the public-sector version of *Mosaic* as 'People living in social housing with uncertain employment in deprived areas' – houses many of the new immigrant communities which we will describe in Chapter 8. These neighbourhoods possess a very different ethos and set of challenges to those categorized under *Municipal Dependency*. Of the three included in this latter heading, perhaps the most emblematic neighbourhood type is G42 *Low Horizons*. The *Mosaic* handbook describes it as follows:

> *Low Horizons* contains large numbers of people in large provincial cities, who are on low incomes and are particularly dependent on city councils for housing and for transport. Low Horizons neighbourhoods are mostly found in large Northern cities, where the majority of the population remains particularly dependent on local authorities for their housing and transport. Though not necessarily areas of acute social deprivation and still having the benefit of active family and community support networks, these are nevertheless communities where horizons are low and where few people have been converted to the culture of optimistic self-reliance that has characterised lower occupational groups living in small towns and southern regions of the country. In these communities those who have exercised the right to buy their homes from the council are still in a minority. The majority of the population works in semi-skilled, routine jobs which demand few qualifications and offer modest wages. Though many residents are unemployed, sick or bringing up children on their own, there is not the same degree of reliance on state welfare benefits as there is on services provided by the local council.

These areas consist mostly of low rise council housing, often dating from the early post-war period, which originally provided adequate though not spacious accommodation for blue-collar workers moving out from decaying inner city terraces. These estates are distinctive for the ambitious scale at which many of them were built, often over long periods of time, typically very distant from any local centres of employment. The tearing up of local communities that was involved in this 'decanting' of populations to suppos-edly more healthy peripheral estates has led to an environment whose scale and uniformity is now a critical liability since it affords few opportunities for newer land uses as well as poor access to the places where people naturally congregate and build the networks that constitute a genuine community.

This uniformity contributes to low levels of contact with other social groups, owner-occupiers, people who are self-employed, students, people with qualifications, and to limited opportunities for new social experimentation. In these environments older couples on better incomes are more likely to purchase a new house on a private estate than to buy their own homes... These processes contribute to the concentration in these neighbourhoods of families with children who are particularly likely to be of school age. Very few people in these neighbourhoods come from minority ethnic groups.

The highest concentrations of this type of neighbourhood are found in northern cities such as Hull, Middlesbrough and Sunderland, which have been largely by-passed by the expansion of professional public sector jobs or the professional service functions associated with the Liberal Metropolitan Elite. Many others are situated in former coalfield communities, though to a lesser extent than neighbourhoods described as G43 *Ex-Industrial Legacy*. Unlike their counterparts in inner cities, especially in London, these are communities which often feel a sense of almost tribal identity, and this tribe – the white working class English – feels it has been overlooked by Westminster politicians.[4]

## 'Low Horizons': its problem with young offenders

One of the key findings of the Liverpool study was the level of nuisance caused to older residents by the large number of older children living on these estates. The problem was caused in part by the higher than average numbers of children contained in households in these outer estates and the fact that most of the leisure and cultural facilities these young adults would normally gravitate to were not located anywhere near their homes. That the issue of anti-social behaviour among young adults is still a particular problem in this type of neighbourhood is evident from the tabulation of respondents to the British Crime Survey (BCS) by type of area as shown in Table 7.1.

Table 7.1 gives results from the BCS for 12 questions relating to safety and anti-social behaviour. These questions are those where the experiences of respondents in the *Municipal Dependency* Group as a whole, and those in the *Low Horizons* Type in particular, differ most significantly from those of the population at large.[5] From these results it would seem that the problems that residents in *Low Horizons* are most concerned about compared with residents in other Types of neighbourhood are vandalism and graffiti.

Burnt out cars and dealing in drugs are other sources of dissatisfaction that *Low Horizons* experiences to an even greater degree than *Municipal Dependency*

**Table 7.1** Questions from the British Crime Survey by Selected *Mosaic* Groups and Types

| British Crime Survey – question | Group G: *Municipal Dependency* | Type G42: *Low Horizons* |
|---|---|---|
| Vandalism and graffiti is a 'very big problem' | 269 | 284 |
| Burnt out cars are 'very common' | 247 | 274 |
| People using or dealing in drugs is a 'very big problem' | 262 | 266 |
| A fairly bad place to live | 279 | 245 |
| Rubbish and litter is a 'very big problem' | 225 | 237 |
| Police rated as 'very poor' | 218 | 235 |
| Teenagers hanging around is a 'very big problem' | 235 | 216 |
| Teenagers hanging around on the streets having a bad effect on my life | 171 | 207 |
| Crime type: Defacing | 195 | 183 |
| Crime type: Stealing | 199 | 175 |
| 'Very worried' about having things stolen from car | 156 | 170 |
| How worried about mugging? 'Very worried' | 150 | 163 |

as a whole. It is on these estates that residents are particularly concerned by teenagers 'hanging around'. In all likelihood, it is this that contributes to the poor rating that respondents give when asked how nice a place their neighbourhood is to live in. It is probably the lack of vigour in addressing low-level crimes such as stealing and defacing, rather than organized crime, that causes respondents in this cluster to hold such a poor opinion of police effectiveness. No doubt much of this might be a consequence of the relatively poor standards of education in neighbourhoods of this sort and the lack of challenging job opportunities provided by the local economy.

Nottinghamshire Police found similar patterns in a study of young offenders. Their study covered 12,310 offences over a three-and-a-half-year period to June 2003. Even at the level of the 11 *Mosaic* Groups, Table 7.2 shows that offender rates varied by a factor of over ten to one. The 4.5 per cent of the county's households living in *Low Horizons* were responsible for 9.9 per cent of the recorded offences.

The purpose of the study was to assess whether different policies strategies were appropriate in different types of high crime neighbourhood. When

**Table 7.2**   Relative Incidence of Young Offender Offences per 1,000 Households by *Mosaic* Group, 2003

| *Mosaic* neighbourhood group | % Nottinghamshire households | Index |
|---|:---:|:---:|
| A: *Symbols of Success* | 6.8 | 27 |
| B: *Happy Families* | 8.3 | 43 |
| C: *Suburban Comfort* | 14.6 | 29 |
| D: *Ties of Community* | 22.6 | 98 |
| E: *Urban Intelligence* | 6.3 | 106 |
| F: *Welfare Borderline* | 6.7 | 209 |
| G: *Municipal Dependency* | 9.9 | 257 |
| H: *Blue Collar Enterprise* | 12.0 | 153 |
| I: *Twilight Subsistence* | 4.6 | 30 |
| J: *Grey Perspectives* | 5.5 | 25 |
| K: *Rural Isolation* | 2.6 | 38 |

records were broken down in more detail, it did become evident that the strategies that would suit the peripheral estates might be quite different from those appropriate for the inner city estates and areas of minority populations. Offenders in the outer estates were less likely to live independently of their parents or in single-parent households, and more likely to live in conventional household structures. They were generally younger. Many were still at school. They were more likely to be involved in arson and theft of and from cars, and less likely to be apprehended for robbery, assault, drugs, shoplifting and fraud. When caught they were more likely to plead guilty. The results supported the findings of the BCS, that the criminality in these areas was more opportunistic, less violent and more due to boredom and lack of meaningful career opportunities than to the breakdown in family relationships more typical of offenders in town and city centre neighbourhoods. Both schools and parents were therefore seen as more important targets for police communications and intelligence.

The high levels of youth offending in this sort of area, it was concluded, was largely a consequence of the relatively poor standards of education and the lack of challenging apprenticeships and job opportunities provided by the local economy.

# It is not just deprivation that explains variations in pupil performance

A common response of Europhile members of the Liberal Metropolitan Elite to the Brexit result was that the electorate voted the 'wrong' way because its members were somehow 'uneducated'. The reaction does have some empirical justification in so far that it is in this type of neighbourhood that levels of pupil attainment remain the most stubbornly low. This becomes evident when the information on pupils' attainment contained in PLASC is linked to postcode data to construct a new data set able to explore the social granularity of the variation in pupil attainment.

The PLASC data[6] contain records for all children attending state schools in England. The database from which the following results have been obtained relates to the cohort of pupils who took various Key Stage tests in summer 2003.[7] Though their performance at Key Stage tests constitutes the largest block of data held against each pupil, these data are collected in such a way as to encourage cross tabulation against a range of what are known as 'contextual' variables.

One such example is whether a pupil receives free school meals, a measure commonly used by the Department for Education and Skills as a proxy for household poverty. The capturing of the pupil's home postcode allows pupil performance to be analysed also by the IMD. The identity of the school the pupil attends also makes it possible to analyse pupil performance by various attributes of the school population. Finally, the comparison of the scores of pupils in each year's test to their scores in tests in previous years makes it possible to identify factors associated with the relative improvement or decline in pupil performance at different points in time.

Table 7.3 uses the PLASC data to measure how well the *Mosaic* classification predicts a school's performance at GCSE level and how its predictive power compares with that of other indicators of disadvantage.[8] It should be no surprise that the best predictor of pupils' GCSE results is their performance in a previous Key Stage test. After this it is evident that measures relating to the pupil's neighbourhood of residence, whether the postcode or the census ED, are the most useful predictors. Measures relating to the school are the next most predictive. The least predictive measures are those relating to the pupil.

Among the area-based measures linked to the PLASC data it is evident that both *Mosaic* and *Acorn* are significantly better predictors than the IMD, the criterion used in the formula for determining the funding of each local education authority. Equally significant is that the geodemographic profile of a school's pupils is as effective a predictor as the proportion of pupils taking free school meals.

It is important to recognize that most of the attributes held against individual pupils in the PLASC database – whether or not they speak English at home, are refugees, are from minority ethnic groups or take free school meals – are ones which identify relatively small population groups. Gender is the principal exception. Whilst members of these small groups may do much worse (or better) than average at GCSE, such differences clearly can't explain the significant variations in performance that occur in the majority of schools where the broad mass of pupils are English, not refugees and are not eligible for free school meals.

**Table 7.3** How Well Different Variables Predict GCSE Points Score

| | Pupil | | | | Postcode | | Output area | School | |
| --- | --- | --- | --- | --- | --- | --- | --- | --- | --- |
| | KS2 level | Free school meals | Gender | Ethnicity | Mosaic | Acorn | Deprivation | Free school meals | School Demographics |
| Average points deviation weighted by size of segment | 12.8 | 3.8 | 2.8 | 1.1 | 7.3 | 7.2 | 6.3 | 5.7 | 5.6 |
| Average deviation squared | 164.1 | 14.8 | 7.6 | 1.2 | 53.2 | 51.2 | 40.2 | 32.1 | 30.9 |
| Deviation squared, averaged | 256.0 | 30.5 | 7.6 | 6.1 | 71.0 | 69.2 | 52.9 | 74.0 | 44.5 |

Attributes pertaining to neighbourhoods and schools differ from these indicators of disadvantaged groups in that they lend themselves to being organized into class bands of roughly equal size. As a result, they have the benefit of being able to predict high as well as low achievers. It is the particular ability of geodemographic classifications to discriminate right across the poverty–affluence continuum that causes them to act as better predictors of school performance than the IMD.

The objective of the IMD was to identify the locations where the population of multiply disadvantaged people live. It was not designed to differentiate pupils in the upper 70 per cent of the performance range. It is easy for public servants, such as those responsible for the PLASC data, to overlook the distinction between the use of the index as a tool for the geographic targeting of 'at risk' groups as against its use for discriminating across the entire pupil range and inclusion in a school funding formula.

This can be seen particularly clearly from Table 7.4. Here we rank the 62 *Mosaic* categories in descending order according to the average deprivation score of the home postcodes of pupils recorded on the PLASC database.

One would expect pupils in the less multiply deprived types of neighbourhood to achieve higher average GCSE scores than pupils from disadvantaged areas, and so they do. But there are 27 *Mosaic* clusters where there are no pupils on PLASC who live in a multiply deprived postcode. It is therefore possible to identify correspondence between deprivation and pupil performance only in the remaining 34.

The practice of evaluating schools by the incidence of deprivation among their pupils fails to take into account the difference in performance one would typically expect between a school whose pupils live in Types of neighbourhood of average status, where average GCSE results are obtained, and a school whose pupils live in Types of neighbourhood of very high status, where exceptional results would not be unexpected. As with other pupil level attributes, the use of the IMD for funding tends to be appropriate only at the lowest end of the status distribution.

Focusing only on the more disadvantaged neighbourhoods reveals a striking misalignment between the levels of deprivation and pupil performance among geodemographic categories characterized by inner city social housing. In each of these categories pupils perform consistently better at GCSE than would have been anticipated if all one knew about them was the level of multiple deprivation of their home postcode. This is shown in Figure 7.1.

A similar pattern is evident in neighbourhoods of Asian owner-occupiers, where GCSE results are much higher than would have been anticipated on the basis of multiple deprivation alone. By contrast some of the neighbourhood Types with the very worse GCSE performance are characterized by predominantly white pupils living on very large overspill housing estates in England's larger provincial cities of the type discussed above. Though struggling academically, these neighbourhoods are not recognized by the IMD as experiencing extreme levels of disadvantage.

**Table 7.4** Average GCSE Points Score by Type of Neighbourhood

| Rank | Code and Mosaic Type | Number of pupils | Average GCSE score | Average score on IMD |
|---|---|---|---|---|
| 1 | A02: Cultural Leadership | 3,648 | 55.44 | 0.00 |
| 2 | A03: Corporate Chieftains | 6,226 | 56.29 | 0.00 |
| 3 | A04: Golden Empty Nesters | 6,439 | 55.34 | 0.00 |
| 4 | A05: Provincial Privilege | 9,075 | 53.32 | 0.00 |
| 5 | A06: High Technologists | 17,173 | 52.61 | 0.00 |
| 6 | A07: Semi-Rural Seclusion | 12,063 | 51.10 | 0.00 |
| 7 | B09: Fledgling Nurseries | 4,877 | 44.51 | 0.00 |
| 8 | B10: Upscale New Owners | 10,580 | 50.24 | 0.00 |
| 9 | B11: Families Making Good | 16,577 | 45.68 | 0.00 |
| 10 | B12: Middle Rung Families | 25,352 | 43.45 | 0.00 |
| 11 | B14: In Military Quarters | 879 | 38.98 | 0.00 |
| 12 | C15: Close To Retirement | 20,667 | 49.73 | 0.00 |
| 13 | C16: Conservative Values | 13,560 | 46.66 | 0.00 |
| 14 | C17: Small Time Business | 17,777 | 44.85 | 0.00 |
| 15 | C18: Sprawling Subtopia | 23,434 | 44.47 | 0.00 |
| 16 | C19: Original Suburbs | 16,646 | 49.25 | 0.00 |
| 17 | D21: Respectable Rows | 13,361 | 41.22 | 0.00 |
| 18 | J51: Sepia Memories | 437 | 43.48 | 0.00 |
| 19 | J52: Childfree Serenity | 3,086 | 46.38 | 0.00 |
| 20 | J53: High Spending Elders | 5,138 | 50.28 | 0.00 |
| 21 | J54: Bungalow Retirement | 2,774 | 43.03 | 0.00 |

**Table 7.4** *(Continued)*

| Rank | Code and Mosaic Type | Number of pupils | Average GCSE score | Average score on IMD |
|------|----------------------|------------------|--------------------|----------------------|
| 22 | J55: Small Town Seniors | 12,051 | 41.26 | 0.00 |
| 23 | K57: Summer Playgrounds | 728 | 44.85 | 0.00 |
| 24 | K58: Greenbelt Guardians | 9,027 | 49.56 | 0.00 |
| 25 | K59: Parochial Villagers | 7,287 | 43.87 | 0.00 |
| 26 | K60: Pastoral Symphony | 5,335 | 46.96 | 0.00 |
| 27 | K61: Upland Hill Farmers | 1,412 | 47.33 | 0.00 |
| 28 | B13: Burdened Optimists | 10,884 | 36.79 | 0.01 |
| 29 | D22: Affluent Blue Collar | 20,524 | 42.05 | 0.01 |
| 30 | D23: Industrial Grit | 27,637 | 37.02 | 0.01 |
| 31 | E30: New Urban Colonists | 3,850 | 47.42 | 0.01 |
| 32 | E31: Caring Professionals | 3,943 | 41.55 | 0.01 |
| 33 | J56: Tourist Attendants | 878 | 43.44 | 0.01 |
| 34 | C20: Asian Enterprise | 11,286 | 43.66 | 0.02 |
| 35 | E32: Dinky Developments | 2,017 | 38.77 | 0.02 |
| 36 | H45: Older Right To Buy | 10,627 | 35.38 | 0.02 |
| 37 | A01: Global Connections | 556 | 43.22 | 0.03 |
| 38 | H46: White Van Culture | 24,009 | 34.26 | 0.03 |
| 39 | I49: Low Income Elderly | 6,096 | 37.28 | 0.04 |
| 40 | I50: Cared For Pensioners | 1,120 | 30.95 | 0.06 |
| 41 | A08: Just Moving In | 1,870 | 41.20 | 0.08 |
| 42 | D25: Town Centre Refuge | 3,613 | 35.72 | 0.08 |
| 43 | H44: Rustbelt Resilience | 18,900 | 30.96 | 0.08 |

*(Continued)*

**Table 7.4** Average GCSE Points Score by Type of Neighbourhood

| Rank | Code and Mosaic Type | Number of pupils | Average GCSE score | Average score on IMD |
|---|---|---|---|---|
| 44 | H47: New Town Materialism | 25,270 | 28.10 | 0.09 |
| 45 | L99: Unclassified | 1,477 | 37.14 | 0.09 |
| 46 | D24: Coronation Street | 16,230 | 32.07 | 0.10 |
| 47 | E29: City Adventurers | 1,162 | 40.89 | 0.10 |
| 48 | E34: University Challenge | 485 | 37.88 | 0.12 |
| 49 | E33: Town Gown Transition | 1,796 | 38.52 | 0.14 |
| 50 | D27: Settled Minorities | 11,444 | 36.07 | 0.16 |
| 51 | I48: Old People In Flats | 537 | 29.14 | 0.17 |
| 52 | G43: Ex-Industrial Legacy | 14,528 | 29.39 | 0.20 |
| 53 | F35: Bedsit Beneficiaries | 559 | 32.80 | 0.21 |
| 54 | D26: South Asian Industry | 12,832 | 34.99 | 0.23 |
| 55 | E28: Counter Cultural Mix | 4,766 | 35.13 | 0.29 |
| 56 | F37: Upper Floor Families | 8,555 | 26.67 | 0.37 |
| 57 | F39: Dignified Dependency | 2,801 | 27.74 | 0.46 |
| 58 | G42: Low Horizons | 23,617 | 25.81 | 0.48 |
| 59 | G41: Families On Benefits | 13,560 | 24.15 | 0.50 |
| 60 | F38: Tower Block Living | 580 | 25.87 | 0.61 |
| 61 | F36: Metro Multiculture | 12,074 | 32.98 | 0.62 |
| 62 | F40: Sharing A Staircase | 195 | 29.52 | 0.75 |

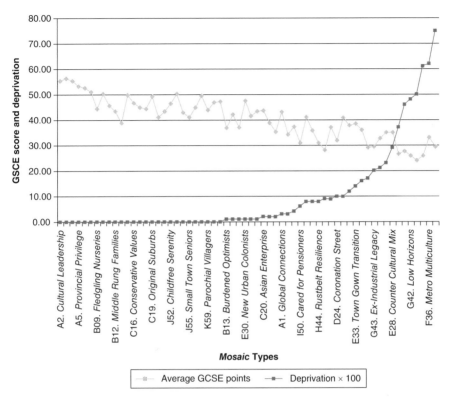

**Figure 7.1** Alignment between Index of Multiple Deprivation and Pupil Attainment

# The *Mosaic* Types where low educational attainment is particularly problematical

There are two categories where this misalignment between pupil performance and deprivation (as measured by the IMD) is particularly visible.[9] We have already described the characteristics of one of them, *Low Horizons*. The other is H47 *New Town Materialism*, a member of Group H, *Blue Collar Enterprise*. The 2003 *Mosaic* guide describes it as follows:

> *New Town Materialism* contains young families living in recently constructed council and new town housing. Most people have poor qualifications which results in the majority of the population working in lower status occupations. Levels of unemployment can be quite high bearing in mind there are plentiful job opportunities at nearby light industrial estates. Others find it difficult

to secure jobs with good enough pay to meet their consumer aspirations. High proportions of these young families then resort to consumer credit to fund the purchases necessary to sustain their materialist lifestyles and quite a few have now been taken to court to recover their debts. Typically, people get by with one car.

Many of these families may be second-generation new town dwellers, their grandparents having spent their lives in nearby cities whilst their parents may have moved to new towns during the 1950s and 1960s. Most *New Town Materialism* neighbourhoods were built in the last 30 years and now incorporate a mix of age groups from adults in their late 20s and 30s and others in older working age groups. By contrast there are few very old people in these areas. There are few members of ethnic minority groups.

Particularly few subscribe to any religious faith. Many couples are co-habiting rather than married and quite a few relationships end in divorce or single parenthood. A striking feature of these estates is the large number of children in the average families, children thereby making up a very high proportion of the total population.

It also happens to be exceptionally fertile territory for finding readers of The *Sun*. Traditionally these have been places where it has been possible for people with energy and drive to achieve material success without the need for formal educational qualifications. It is because of the high material expectations in these types of neighbourhood that so many people allow themselves to get into debt. Living in areas of low unemployment, they are confident in their ability to repay whatever they borrow because there is a plentiful supply of local jobs requiring modest qualifications and an insufficient number of people with modest qualifications to fill them.

What can these findings contribute to our understanding of the obstacles to improved educational performance? And what do they illustrate about the contribution that geodemographic analysis can make to the research process?

In the absence of detailed qualitative evidence,[10] it would not be unreasonable to hypothesize that a particular obstacle to pupils' educational advancement in neighbourhoods of *Low Horizons* is that its pupils tend to live in environments where, other than the teachers, doctors and social workers who administer to them, they have only the most fleeting contact with people who have received any benefit from further education. So large are the estates that many pupils live on – the City of Manchester's Wythenshawe estates are said to have housed over 100,000 inhabitants – that many have become self-sufficient single class communities.

To be clear, these are not 'sink' estates, populated by dysfunctional families exclusively reliant on benefits. They are places, often in regions suffering from the decline of heavy industry, where there is an almost complete absence of an educated middle class living nearby.[11] What work is locally available is mostly in routine occupations for which only modest qualifications are required. Many residents have lived in their homes or on the estate for many years so the networks of association that have been built up, though largely informal, are denser than their counterparts in inner city estates. Relatives tend to live nearby and can often be relied on for support in time of need. Networks link together people who tend to share similar social positions and tastes but do not tend to foster social mobility. The converse is that few residents have experienced life anywhere other than in their own locality. Unlike the chaotic melting pots of inner London estates, with their sprinkling of bohemians and impecunious graduates, these are places where many children have never seen the sea, let alone a passport desk.

The diagnosis of the mismatch between deprivation and performance in *New Town Materialism* is rather different. Here, it could be hypothesized, pupils come from communities in which there are historical reasons why material advancement has not been so dependent on their investment in educational qualifications, the absence of which has been only a modest obstacle to earning good money. Greater returns are believed to arise from flexibility, industry and low-level entrepreneurship than from diligent adherence to bureaucratic or academic norms.

At the other end of the educational spectrum the *Mosaic* Types of pupils whose performance at GCSE is consistently much better than would be expected on the basis of multiple deprivation statistics are ones that contain high proportions of ethnic minorities. F36 *Metro Multiculture* and D26 *South Asian Industry* are examples. The inference that can be drawn from the relationship between Types of neighbourhood, deprivation and average GCSE scores is that low educational attainment tends to occur in many different contexts and for quite different reasons, of which low incomes, poor housing conditions and lack of fluency in the English language are just three. The IMD certainly captures some of these contexts, but by no means all of them. In particular it captures measurable and physical manifestations of disadvantage more effectively than cultural ones.

Such conjectures are necessarily speculative. However, the provision of detailed qualitative descriptions of neighbourhood Types does make it possible to home in on explanations which are likely to resonate in very specific contexts (unlike the generalized explanations which drive much political thinking) and, especially important, define the geographic territories where specific ethnographic or qualitative investigations need to be undertaken or where specific policy interventions should be trialled.

The social scientific community is familiar with the process of data collection and analysis which explores the validity of previously generated hypotheses. What this process is less well suited to is the collection and organization of data in ways which facilitate the generation of new hypotheses. These two examples from educational performance illustrate the contribution that geodemographics can make to the quest for fresh understandings of familiar problems.

Geodemographic classifications are legitimately criticized for providing 'snapshots in time', divorced from consideration of the processes of temporal change. But there is no reason why this need be the case. Just as they can be used to link data from different sources, so geodemographics can be used to link data from different points in time. By way of illustration, Table 7.5 provides evidence of the distinctive performance of pupils within the South Asian community. It shows that when *Mosaic* neighbourhood Types are used to compare the relative performance of pupils both at Key Stage 2 and at GCSE, it is pupils from predominantly South Asian postcodes and from rural postcodes that display the highest relative improvement. It is in high status inner city neighbourhoods that the deterioration is greatest, at least among those attending state schools.

It may well be that in areas of *Liberal Opinion* a significant proportion of higher performing pupils at Key Stage 2 are lost from the system by the time they take GCSEs, perhaps because they transfer to independent schools after Key Stage 2 or their parents relocate to suburban or rural neighbourhoods where their children take their GCSEs.

That there are *Mosaic* neighbourhood Types where there is a systematic tendency not just for pupils' absolute performance to differ but for their relative performance to rise or fall as they get older, has clear relevance to the processes and criteria used to evaluate school performance. For example, if one were simply to use 'value added' as a criterion for evaluating school performance, then we would be likely to find a large cluster of ostensibly 'high performing' schools whose catchment areas were dominated by South Asian neighbourhoods.

**Table 7.5** Neighbourhood Types Where Pupils' Relative Score Improves/ Deteriorates Most

| | *Mosaic* Types: improvement and decline | | |
| --- | --- | --- | --- |
| | Current year | Current year | |
| Selected *Mosaic* Types | KS2 rank | GCSE rank | Improvement/ decline |
| C20: *Asian Enterprise* | 37 | 23 | 14 |
| D26: *South Asian Industry* | 55 | 46 | 9 |
| K59: *Parochial Villagers* | 30 | 22 | 8 |
| F40: *Sharing a Staircase* | 58 | 53 | 5 |
| K57: *Summer Playgrounds* | 23 | 18 | 5 |
| E28: *Counter Cultural Mix* | 39 | 45 | −6 |
| E31: *Caring Professionals* | 24 | 30 | −6 |
| I48: *Old People in Flats* | 49 | 55 | −6 |
| E29: *City Adventurers* | 26 | 34 | −8 |
| A01: *Global Connections* | 7 | 27 | −20 |

Achieving high value added is less challenging for those accountable for school performance where these are the Types of neighbourhood from which a school draws the majority of its pupils since this is where pupils' relative performance tends to improve as they grow older.

## Measuring the impact of peer group effects on education performance

In Chapter 6 we were able to demonstrate the considerable impact on parliamentary election results of what we variously refer to as 'peer' and 'neighbourhood' effects. In other words, we find that behaviours typically explained on account of a person's social class tend also to be influenced by the behaviours of near neighbours. Combining *Mosaic* with PLASC data it is possible to demonstrate, as Table 7.6 does, that a similar process occurs in education. Pupils' performance is affected by the *mix* of neighbourhoods from which their school draws its other pupils as well as by the Type of neighbourhood in which each individual pupil lives.

The rows of the matrix of Table 7.6 indicate the average GCSE scores of pupils based on the geodemographic category of their home postcodes. The columns indicate the extent to which the school they attend attracts pupils from high or low performing *Mosaic* Types. To allocate pupils to the five rows we have rank ordered the *Mosaic* Types into five approximately equal bands according to the average GCSE score of their pupils. Pupils in the *Mosaic* Types with the highest average GCSE scores are assigned to the top row ('highest') whilst those who live in postcodes in Types of neighbourhood which tend to perform worst are shown in the 'lowest' row.

**Table 7.6** Influence of Neighbourhood Type and of School Geodemographics on Pupils' GCSE Points

Average GCSE Points – non-SEN Pupils by Geodmeographics of Postcode and of School

|  | | Geodemographics of the school | | | | | |
|---|---|---|---|---|---|---|---|
|  | | Highest | High | Average | Low | Lowest | Mean |
| Geodemographics of home postcode | Highest | 57.2 | 53.8 | 52.3 | 51.7 | 47.8 | 55.6 |
|  | High | 53.4 | 49.9 | 47.9 | 45.4 | 44.1 | 49.8 |
|  | Average | 50.0 | 46.9 | 44.9 | 42.7 | 41.5 | 45.3 |
|  | Low | 45.3 | 41.5 | 39.9 | 37.7 | 35.7 | 38.6 |
|  | Lowest | 41.3 | 37.1 | 35.0 | 32.3 | 29.8 | 32.7 |
|  | Mean | 53.0 | 47.4 | 43.9 | 39.5 | 35.2 | 44.3 |

In a similar manner, the schools covered by the PLASC data are placed in five class bands with equal numbers of GCSE candidates. The left-hand column ('highest') contains those 20 per cent of candidates from schools whose pupils are drawn predominantly from *Mosaic* neighbourhood Types where pupils typically do best at GCSE. The right-hand column ('lowest') contains schools that admit pupils predominantly from *Mosaic* neighbourhood Types where fewest perform well at GCSE.[12]

Table 7.6 shows that many children from neighbourhood Types with lowest educational performance are doubly disadvantaged. First, they live in neighbourhoods where it is not expected they will do well. Then they attend schools where they are surrounded by other pupils with below average expectations. Likewise, those middle class children who attend predominantly middle class schools enjoy a double benefit – the advantage of their home is reinforced by a school peer group with high aspirations.

This supports the contention that a particular disadvantage of children living in *Low Horizons* is not just the financial and social disadvantage of multiple deprivation or entitlement to free school meals, but the absence of contact with pupils from homes in more aspirational Types of neighbourhood. Pupils from poor neighbourhoods who, for some reason or other find themselves among a school peer group from predominantly better-off homes, perform less well than their school contemporaries at GCSE but nevertheless much better than their neighbours who attend schools dominated by pupils from other poor neighbourhoods.

These findings therefore confirm that it is very rational for middle class parents to seek to move into middle class neighbourhoods if they can afford to do so, but especially to move into neighbourhoods with large concentrations rather than lonely pockets of affluence. However well or badly their children are taught, they have a much higher probability of performing well in tests than if they attend a school containing pupils from a socially representative mix of neighbourhoods.

Of course, this finding has great relevance to attempts to increase social mobility by intervening in the criteria used to award places both in grammar schools and universities.

# Using *Mosaic* to evaluate school performance

When we correlate the performance of a school (as measured by the attainment level of its pupils at GCSE) with what would be expected given the geodemographic categories from which it draws its pupils, we obtain a correlation coefficient of +0.71. In other words, almost exactly half[13] of the variation in the average GCSE scores of English state schools is 'explained' by the differences in the geodemographics of their intakes. When one considers that only half the variation in school performance is accounted for by all the other factors which are under the control of the local authority, school governors or head it becomes evident that the league table position of many schools does little more than indicate the social profile of their pupils' parents.

What might be a fairer, more robust and a more appropriate measure of a school's relative performance would therefore be to compare its actual average GCSE points score with the average score that would have been achieved had each of its pupils attained the average score for the *Mosaic* neighbourhood Type in which they lived.

By way of illustration, Figure 7.2 maps schools in the Bristol by average GCSE points that might be expected given the geodemographics of their intakes. The warmer the shading the higher the target/benchmark score of the region's secondary schools. These are essentially schools with an intake predominantly from better-off *Mosaic* categories. Figure 7.3 maps primary schools around Plymouth by average score at Key Stage 2 English compared with the target calculated in this manner. Schools with warmer shading are ones which perform more highly than might be expected on the basis of the geodemographic profile of their pupils; schools with cooler shading are those performing less well than might reasonably have been expected.

One of the benefits of using geodemographics for evaluations of this sort is that the results can be summarized at any level of geography. Table 7.7 demonstrates this by listing the local education authorities in which average pupil performance at GCSE compared most and least favourably with the target of what might be expected given the geodemographic profile of pupils under their control.

In summary therefore the concept of misalignment, when used to identify Types of neighbourhood that perform much better or worse than one would expect given their position on the IMD, does help to pick out very specific urban cultures where educational achievement is particularly undervalued by local parents. By isolating these Types of neighbourhood *Mosaic* guides researchers and policy-makers towards geographical types of area which warrant more in-depth ecological or qualitative assessment. However provisional such conclusions may be, they do facilitate the development of potential explanations for under- or over-performance based on a more in-depth understanding of local cultural norms than could be adduced from classifications based merely on theoretical concepts, of which the IMD is just one.

**Expected average GCSE score**

- Highest
- Above average
- Average
- Below average
- Lowest

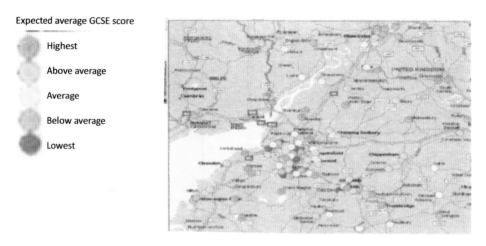

**Figure 7.2** 'Expected' Performance of Schools around Bristol based on GCSE Scores

**Key Stage 2 performance**

- Overperforming
- Average
- Underperforming

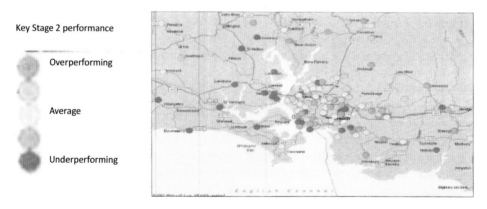

**Figure 7.3** Performance of Primary Schools around Plymouth based on Differences between 'Expected' and 'Actual' Average Scores at Key Stage 2, English

**Table 7.7** 'Performance' Against Benchmark: Selected Local Education Authorities

Average GCSE Points Score: Actual, Expected and Performance of Selected Local Education Authorities (LEAs)

| LEA | Actual | Expected | Under-Performance | LEA | Actual | Expected | Over-Performance |
|---|---|---|---|---|---|---|---|
| Kingston upon Hull | 29.97 | 33.71 | -3.78 | Torbay | 40.09 | 38.09 | +1.96 |
| Hillingdon | 36.75 | 39.83 | -3.12 | Slough | 40.78 | 38.75 | +1.99 |
| Bristol | 33.87 | 36.91 | -3.08 | Gloucestershire | 42.21 | 39.91 | +2.36 |
| Greenwich | 33.76 | 36.73 | -3.01 | York | 40.96 | 38.65 | +2.27 |
| Bracknell Forest | 38.06 | 40.76 | -2.74 | Kingston upon Thames | 46.06 | 42.63 | +2.39 |
| Blackpool | 34.30 | 36.80 | -2.54 | Redbridge | 42.73 | 40.27 | +2.42 |
| Lewisham | 34.53 | 36.91 | -2.42 | Trafford | 41.80 | 39.29 | +2.47 |
| Islington | 33.26 | 35.62 | -2.40 | Isles of Scilly | 44.00 | 41.43 | +2.53 |
| Luton | 34.51 | 36.87 | -2.40 | Camden | 39.77 | 36.91 | +2.82 |
| Doncaster | 33.56 | 35.81 | -2.29 | Sutton | 44.17 | 41.04 | +3.09 |
| Merton | 37.32 | 39.52 | -2.24 | Gateshead | 38.89 | 35.46 | +3.39 |
| Nottingham | 31.75 | 33.82 | -2.11 | Kensington & Chelsea | 41.71 | 37.77 | +3.90 |

# Notes

[1] See www.theguardian.com/commentisfree/2017/feb/22/politicians-love-left-behind-cliche-brexit.

[2] An earlier example of this type of analysis can be found in Webber and Butler (2007).

[3] Prime examples are the neighbourhood Types that fall within the *Blue Collar Enterprise* Group in the 2003 version of *Mosaic*.

[4] Although a very uncomfortable read, the work of criminologists Steve Hall and Simon Winlow offers forceful ethnographic and theoretical insights into this world; a recent example is Winlow et al. (2016).

[5] As explained in relation to Table 1.3, and elsewhere, the numbers contained in the table are, again, indices such that a value of 100 indicates a proportion identical to the national average. A value of 200 indicates twice the national average, a value of 150 a level 50 per cent above the national average and so on.

[6] The interested reader can find more details in Webber and Butler (2007).

[7] Given the results that follow one can only hope that things have improved since this time. As already explained, in this, and much of the analysis we present in the book, the primary aim is demonstrate how geodemographic classifications can be utilized within social research in various ways rather than to provide the most contemporary analysis possible. In this instance we are concerned to show how *administrative* data from PLASC can be usefully meshed with *Mosaic* in order to produce new forms of knowledge.

[8] It should be noted that the analysis is restricted to those pupils who were not recorded as having any special educational needs (SEN).

[9] It is easy to suppose that the task of interpreting the distinctive features of a cluster should proceed by examining the respects in which it differs from the national average. A more telling set of statistics measures the respects in which any particular cluster differs from those of the other clusters to which it is in general most similar. Thus the concept of misalignment is critical to the accurate interpretation of the distinctive character of a cluster. The use of principal component analysis necessarily obscures such misalignments, treating them as random errors.

[10] Warrington (2005) provides a reasonable overview of the evidence that does exist.

[11] McKenzie (2015) in her *Getting By* offers a rich qualitative account of such a place. Perhaps even more powerful is her account in The *Guardian* – www.theguardian.com/society/2015/jan/21/estate-working-class-problem-st-anns-nottingham.

[12] It is noteworthy that the range of average scores for the five classes based on home location (55.6 to 32.7) is broadly similar to the range of scores when based on school geodemographics (53.0 to 35.2).

[13] Because the square of 0.71 is 0.5051.

# 8

# MINORITY COMMUNITIES
## Melting Pots or Parallel Lives?

In many cases, the report acknowledges that the available data are already feeling out of date (for example where we rely on the Census which, while comprehensive and rich, is only conducted every decade, with the most recent results coming from 2011). In others, data are not available at a sufficiently granular level to pick out trends that might exist or be emerging in smaller or newer groups in society. In general, better data and research are needed across a range of issues relating to integration.

Executive Summary, *The Casey Review: A Review into Opportunities and Integration*, p.7, December 2016

## The UK's minority communities – expansion and fragmentation

Of the Types listed in Table 5.4, the UK's minority population is mostly found in the following five *Mosaic* Types.

| Code | *Mosaic* Type label | UK % | Top local authorities |
|------|------|------|------|
| A01 | *Global Connections* | 0.7 | Kensington and Chelsea |
| C20 | *Asian Enterprise* | 1.0 | Harrow |
| D26 | *South Asian Industry* | 0.9 | Newham |
| D27 | *Settled Minorities* | 1.6 | Waltham Forest |
| F36 | *Metro Multiculture* | 1.7 | Tower Hamlets |

The broad categories of neighbourhood which we have described in the previous two chapters are ones whose demographics are very different, but it is in respect of their attitudes towards modernity and socio-cultural change that they are most dia-metrically opposed.[1] One set of attitudes where these differences are most evident is in relation to the issues of race, migration and identity. Clearly the geography and the social mobility of Britain's minority populations is highly relevant to this debate. It is this that is the subject of this chapter.

For the purpose of this examination, rather than restrict ourselves to main-stream geodemographic classifications we make use of an additional form of classification based on big data. In combination, these classifications suggest that the composition of the non-white British population is considerably more complex and nuanced than would appear from the statistics currently used to inform this debate. A key theme of Chapter 6 was the increased fragmentation of Britain's middle class. In this chapter, we find the existence of a similar but perhaps even more complex fragmentation within Britain's ethnic minority population.

Of the reasons for this fragmentation one is undoubtedly the increase in the number of overseas-born people living in Britain in recent years. Rienzo and Vargas-Silva (2017: 2), using data from the Labour Force Survey, calculate that between 1993 and 2015 the overseas-born population in the UK more than doubled from 3.8 million (about 7 per cent of the population) to about 8.7 million (about 13.5 per cent). The spatial distribution of this growth and diversity has been any-thing but even. Of the 8.7 million in 2015, 1.4 million were living in inner London, 1.8 million in outer London and the rest distributed – very unevenly – throughout the UK. The smallest number of overseas-born individuals were in Tyne and Wear

**Table 8.1**  The Top 10 'Sender' Countries as Measured by their Percentage Share of the Overseas-born Population

| Country | % |
| --- | --- |
| Poland | 9.5 |
| India | 9.0 |
| Pakistan | 5.9 |
| Ireland | 4.5 |
| Germany | 3.3 |
| Romania | 2.6 |
| Nigeria | 2.3 |
| Bangladesh | 2.3 |
| South Africa | 2.2 |
| Italy | 2.1 |

*Source*: Rienzo and Vargas-Silva (2017: 6)

and the rest of the north east. However, generally, it has been in regions with the smallest number of overseas-born residents in 1995 that the rate of growth has been the greatest. In Tyne and Wear, for example, the population has increased by some 200 per cent from just 24,000 in 1995 to some 68,000 in 2015. Over the same period the population in inner and outer London combined has grown by just 94 per cent, from 1.6 million in 1995 to 3.2 million in 2015.

A second reason is the ever more diverse set of countries from which these migrants have been drawn. The top ten 'sender' countries in 2015, as measured by their percentage share of the overseas-born population (Rienzo and Vargas-Silva, 2017: 6) are shown in Table 8.1.

A third is the way in which minority ethnic populations that have had time to establish themselves in Britain have developed very distinctive pathways in order to achieve economic security and social acceptance. Recently arrived migrants, of course, are only the most recent in a historic series of migrant populations to have been attracted to Britain's urban centres[2] and a comparison of recently arrived and long-settled communities can provide a useful sense of historical perspective.

One problem for much research on minority populations, as Louise Casey found, is that the most recent official data on the demographics of this population rely on a census which, depending on where one is in the census cycle, can

**Table 8.2**  Ethnic Composition of United Kingdom, 2011

| Ethnicity | % |
|---|---|
| All white ethnic groups | 86.0 |
| Asian/Asian British | |
|     Indian | 2.5 |
|     Pakistani | 2.0 |
|     Other Asian | 1.5 |
|     Bangladeshi | 0.8 |
|     Chinese | 0.7 |
| Black/African/Caribbean/Black British | |
|     African | 1.8 |
|     Caribbean | 1.1 |
|     Other black | 0.5 |
| Mixed/multiple ethnic groups | |
|     White and Black Caribbean | 0.8 |
|     White and Asian | 0.6 |
|     Other mixed | 0.5 |
|     White and Black African | 0.3 |
| Other ethnic group | |
|     Any other ethnic group | 0.6 |
|     Arab | 0.4 |

be between two and 13 years out of date. The figures contained in Table 8.2 are already in need of significant revision.[3]

Although these demographic changes are important in accounting for complex patterns of fragmentation, there are also perhaps subtler cultural forces that only become apparent when it is possible to examine more detailed patterns of socio-spatial residential settlement at a finer level of granularity than is normally possible within social research.

In order to do this, we foray into the realm of what has come to be known as big data (Burrows and Savage, 2014). The particular classification we employ here is Origins, the big data from which it is derived being a database containing the names and postcodes of virtually all UK adults. Whereas a geodemographic classification groups postcodes into clusters on the basis of their demographics, *Origins* contains an algorithm which infers the ethno-cultural background that most effectively describes each person based on a combination of personal and family name (Webber and Phillips, 2016). The advantage *Origins* has over conventional measures of self-identification or country of birth employed in survey questionnaires is that the data can be summarized at a much finer level of geographic resolution than survey data, the categories are more detailed and, of course, the data can be updated in real time. The ability to highlight patterns as they are now rather than as they were at the time of the last census is particularly relevant when considering minority populations, whose numbers and locations can change very rapidly within comparatively short periods of time.

A feature of the Liverpool study that strikes contemporary readers is the almost complete absence of any discussion of race. Not a single one of its 25 clusters is described in terms of the immigrant populations that live in it. In the descriptions of the clusters the study makes reference to immigrant populations just once. A few non-white residents were noted, almost in passing, as living in the *Rooming House* Group. In this respect immigrants are included along with other non-conforming groups such as students, single parents, ex-prisoners, drug addicts and those discharged from institutions as being geographical or social 'outsiders', excluded from the family and community structures which affirmed the identity of the rest of Liverpool's population, however precarious its financial circumstances.

This pattern was quite unlike the schema described by Park and Burgess in Chicago, discussed in Chapter 2. Many of their inner city neighbourhoods were labelled exclusively according to the communities that dominated them. In Chicago, most inner city neighbourhoods were dominated by single communities whose cohesion was based on the sharing of common languages, religious affiliations and culinary traditions. These communities delivered a high level of social support to the migrants that arrived in the city in such large numbers from different European countries.

Whereas in Chicago, as in inter-war Britain, immigrant groups were predominantly white and European, Britain's post-war settlers, initially at least, were predominantly people of colour. It was from just two regions within the former British Empire, the West Indies and South Asia, that new arrivals first sought permanent status as British citizens. Subjected as they then were to discrimination in the housing and employment markets, and at risk of physical assault from the majority population, it was colour that at this time became the defining feature of these immigrants. This perception applied just as strongly in the minds of those responsible for public policy as it did among the population at large. The dominance of colour as the basis for classification operated to the virtual exclusion of any other form of difference and was sufficient without any further qualification to define the population that was the object of what became to be considered unacceptable forms of prejudice.

In the early years of immigration, emerging 'black' communities tended to be found almost exclusively in geodemographic categories characterized by the large Victorian houses which were becoming increasingly difficult for middle class families to manage in the absence of domestic servants. The *Rooming House* districts of the Liverpool study were typical of such neighbourhoods. It was not just the physical structure of the housing in such neighbourhoods that lent itself to multiple occupation. Equally important was the loss of whatever degree of community cohesion such neighbourhoods had formerly enjoyed, a loss which lowered the social barriers to admittance of minority populations.

As these 'reception areas' filled up, and as migrants became more established, successive geodemographic classifications revealed the disposition of a number of minority communities to relocate to new types of neighbourhood characterized by affordable but often cramped terraced housing. Other communities found their way into what at the time had become 'hard to let' council (later social) housing. Members of communities more adept at climbing available ladders of opportunity used their new-found wealth to buy their way out of the inner city and to establish footholds in suburbs that previously had been both exclusively white and exclusively middle class. Classifications of neighbourhoods based on ethnicity no longer coincided so precisely with classifications of neighbourhood based on class.

In North London, for example, the Greek Cypriot community became increasingly successful in distancing itself from the neighbourhoods it previously shared with the Turkish community. Likewise, in South London, Tamil communities have succeeded in physically separating themselves from neighbourhoods popular with people of West Indian or Pakistani descent. The result of these trends was twofold. First, there was a progressive weakening of the relationship between the social status of a neighbourhood and the size of its minority population. The second was a separation of ethnic neighbourhoods into ones associated with different fractions of the immigrant population and its descendants, some of whom were far more economically successful than others.

*Origins* data reveal that the tendency for particular minorities to cluster together in particular neighbourhoods is far more pronounced among larger communities than it is within smaller ones: among Somalis rather than Ethiopians, and among Jews rather than Armenians, for example. The tendency is also more common among groups which are – on some measure – 'culturally distant' from the majority white British population, such as Bangladeshis and Pakistanis, than among those less differentiated by religion, language and customs, such as people of West Indian origin.

## Victims of prejudice or inheritants of distinctive cultures?

From just two principal sources of immigration, London has, within 50 years, become a veritable 'Tower of Babel', home to minority groups speaking over a hundred different languages. The ethnic, linguistic and religious variety makes it far more problematic than it used to be to decide how best to codify the members of these communities for analytic purposes. Should Turks and Iranians be categorized as people of colour or, as they are classified in the US census, white? Since the accession of eastern European countries to the European Union, and in particular since the terrorist attacks in the US and continental Europe, is skin colour any longer adequate on its own as a basis for defining vulnerability to racial prejudice or religious intolerance?

Further complexity is added to the process of classification as many British-born children of first generation migrants choose to identify themselves with the country of their birth rather than that of their parents or grandparents. What had originally been conceived in broadly binary terms increasingly took on a character closer to that of a kaleidoscope. Inevitably the standard classifications which policy-makers have adopted and which those who research vulnerable populations feel obliged to use, struggle to reflect these changes.

As a result, the majority of public servants, and indeed many members of the research community, continue to see colour as the most salient distinguishing feature of the immigrant community and one which continues to define a 'protected group' in equality and human rights legislation. The implicit justification is that it is this characteristic that most accurately defines the disadvantage which results from the historic prejudice against, and exploitation of, people of colour. The narrative that justifies public policy and guides politically acceptable discourse focuses on historic injustices, whether in the British Empire or more recently in Britain itself. This is held to contribute to discrimination and the unequal access to power and the ladders of opportunity that enable individuals or communities to achieve economic success.

Such narratives may have been compelling at a time when many new arrivals were the direct descendants of people who, only a few generations earlier, had been subjected to the evils of slavery. It is understandable, but is it any longer acceptable that so little consideration is given to narratives which foreground cultural differences grounded in histories and practices that long preceded the experience of colonial oppression or which are relatively independent of it?[4]

As we have already discussed, during the debate on whether or not Britain should remain a member of the European Union, the narrative most common in neighbourhoods closer in character to *Low Horizons* than to *Urban Intelligence* was rather different from that of the Liberal Metropolitan Elite to which most policy-makers belonged. Here, so it would seem, the primacy of physical characteristics, such as the colour of a person's skin, has increasingly given way to judgements based on perceived *behavioural* differences, such as an inability to speak English (perceived by some members of the public to be a drain on local authority resources) or religion (perceived by some as providing a recruitment pool for terrorists) and behaviours or cultural traditions, such as female genital mutilation, forced marriages, repressive domestic control and so on. Although members of *Urban Intelligence* opposed such practices, many who lived in categories such as *Low Horizons* felt public authorities pursued these practices on far too half-hearted a basis.[5]

# The different types of minority neighbourhood

Of the 61 categories identified in the 2003 version of the *Mosaic* classification, the four with the highest proportion of ethnic minorities are described as C20 *Asian Enterprise*, D25 *South Asian Industry*, D26 *Settled Minorities* and F36 *Metro Multiculture*. These go some way, but as we shall see later, only so far in providing some statistical justification for what may have appeared to some readers to have been an otherwise overly subjective interpretation contained in the previous section of this chapter.

Both in terms of size and ethnic composition these four clusters are very different. In *Asian Enterprise* we find a significant immigrant population, mostly Hindu South Asian, who, because of the emphasis they place on educational qualification and entrepreneurship, have succeeded in buying access to relatively highly sought-after neighbourhoods. Common features are spacious, semi-detached houses, many of them developed during the 1930s in Mock-Tudor style for suburban owner-occupiers. The street scene in Figure 8.1 illustrates a practice common in this *Mosaic* Type, the paving over of front lawns to accommodate residents' cars.

**Figure 8.1** *C20 Asian Enterprise*

The Victorian terraced streets of Birmingham, Oldham, Blackburn and Bradford present some of the largest concentrations of *South Asian Industry*. This is the cluster in which we find the most people of Pakistani and Bangladeshi heritage. Born as many of them were in rural villages, whatever technical skills they entered Britain with were of little practical value and, compared for example with immigrants from Turkey or Ugandan Asians, few had experience in trade. With too poor a command of English to find work in the service sector most worked, initially at least, in unskilled factory jobs. By tradition they worked the night shift and found accommodation in inexpensive, poorly maintained terraced housing. During their first years in the country, many shared cramped accommodation with members of their extended families. Some still do. Others rented houses from longer established members of their own community.

*Settled Minorities* is a type of neighbourhood more prevalent in multi-ethnic communities in inner London. In neighbourhoods of relatively spacious two- and three-storey Victorian dwellings, some have been divided into bedsits or self-contained flats. Others provide single-family accommodation to a generation of immigrants for whom, at the time they arrived, a pre-1914 terraced house was much more affordable than it is today. The ethnic profile of this *Mosaic* category is much more diverse than that of the two South Asian clusters. Members of many smaller ethnic communities have joined people of predominantly West Indian and Turkish origin. Dalston and Walthamstow are London suburbs which contain many neighbourhoods of this sort. Immigrant communities in this category are now more likely to live cheek by jowl with well-educated single people and childless couples attracted to these areas by their proximity to central London employment, the cache of living in a multicultural neighbour-hood and their relative affordability (Davison et al., 2012).

*Metro Multiculture* describes a type of neighbourhood that occurs almost exclusively in London. The ill-fated Grenfell Tower in north Kensington is an example of such housing where residents from many different minority communities rent flats in medium or high rise blocks of social housing. Diversity is assured by the practice whereby most local councils house families in particular estates on the basis of need rather than ethnicity. That many are on benefits or unemployed does not preclude up-market marques being seen in communal parking lots. If for no other reason than their proximity to richer neighbours, tenants in these estates tend to display a much greater level of cultural sophistication than their counterparts in *South Asian Industry*.

These four types of neighbourhoods are by no means the only ones with a significant minority representation. A01 *Global Connections* attracts the wealthy and powerful from around the world to neighbourhoods in Kensington, Chelsea and Notting Hill and ranks among the highest for non-white British residents. Both it and A03 *Corporate Chieftains* have a huge over-representation of people with Jewish or Armenian backgrounds as well as an above average number of people with Greek Cypriot, Cantonese or Hindu Indian forebears.[6]

## Using big data to reveal patterns among minority populations

Their access to big data is a critical reason why commercial organizations often approach behavioural research differently to university researchers or civil servants. Consider, for example, a retail bank which manages data in such a way as to meet its requirement to record the balances in its customers' current accounts, mortgage accounts or credit cards. Or a retailer who uses electronic point of sale technology not just to compute the amount owed by customers passing through its checkouts but to manage stock control. The cost of collecting very large and complex data can seldom be justified other than for operational reasons of this sort.

Government of course also invests in the development and maintenance of complex operational systems, whether to collect taxes, to licence vehicles or recover student loans. Where transactions were once recorded manually, the drive for efficiency requires that they now be captured digitally, for example by the use of credit cards, swipe cards or by having customers key in data via an internet connection or via a telephone keypad. These data sets provide an excellent resource for analysing behavioural data on a geographical basis.

The digital transformation of operational systems has had less impact on the research methods of academics and public servants, most of whom continue to rely on survey questionnaires for answers to most research questions. By contrast in the commercial sector, management consultants, for better or worse, have been increasingly successful in persuading management that one of the most critical sources of a company's competitive advantage is its ability to convert the data contained in transactional records that support operational systems into business intelligence (Burrows and Savage, 2014).

Support for this proposition comes from the argument that although operational systems seldom capture data which precisely match the specifications required by the researcher, there are occasions where qualities that are peculiar to such data combine to make them as useful or, in some cases, even more useful for generating behavioural insight than questionnaire-based surveys. These qualities are the *volume* of data, the *variety* of data fields and the *velocity* of data updates.

Indeed, there can be instances, it could be argued, where the fields and categories that researchers assume they require access to are not necessarily the optimal ones for the research project that they are engaged on. Representations of key constructs can easily reflect modes of thinking which have themselves arisen long ago as a result of historic reliance on particular data-gathering methods. Obvious examples are the questions which it is practical to include on a survey questionnaire, and the method of data collection on which researchers have been traditionally dependent (Savage and Burrows, 2007). Using occupation as a basis for inferring social class is one such example, using self-identification as the basis for inferring ethnicity another.

Of the many thousands of uses to which operational big data sets are used by commercial organizations, one is to remove from high-volume mailings the names of people who have recently died or who have moved from a former address. To meet this need, a number of specialist data processing companies maintain and regularly update comprehensive registers containing the names, current addresses and postcodes of as complete a set of UK adults as they can muster.

Just as in the manner that the postcode field in each customer's address record provides a useful indication of the types of neighbours they are likely to live among, the personal and family name fields provide a potentially valuable proxy for their cultural background. Whereas the occurrence of N6 6DJ in the postcode field indicates a person living in a neighbourhood dominated by A02 *Voices of Authority* the appearance of the values *Wolfgang* and *Wagner* in the personal and family name fields of a customer address record suggest that the subject of that record is likely to be person with a German background. The *Origins* classification system which makes these inferences relies on two reference files, one listing some four million different family names, the other some 800,000 different personal names. These reference files are constructed using a file containing the names of some 900 million individuals in around 30 different countries.

Just as *Mosaic* categories are the product of algorithms, and not categories pre-conceived by researchers, so too is the case with the *Origins* categories. Left to its own devices and taking no account of pre-existing categorizations, an algorithm creates categories which, as it then becomes apparent, can be effectively interpreted only in terms of a combination of factors including: country of origin, such as Iranian; language, such as Greek; religion, such as Sikh; and culture, such as Armenian.

Why should it be preferable to infer a person's ethno-cultural background from their name rather than asking them to select an ethnicity from a self-completion questionnaire?[7] Or, perhaps more to the point, in what circumstances would it be more practical to use a representation of ethnicity based on big data rather than self-reported ethnicity, as the census does? Two arguments are often advanced against the use of names as a proxy for ethnicity. One is that no one is better placed than the data subject to know his or her ethnicity. The other is that it is disrespectful or even unethical not to allow a person to assert the identity by which he or she wishes to be classified and subsequently be treated.

The principal justification for the use of names as a proxy is where the research objective is not to consider the ethnic origin of any *single* data subject, only the *aggregate* distribution of (*Origins*) codes in a population of data subjects. These data subjects could be residents, employees or customers. In respect of accuracy it is argued that in many instances self-identification is problematic because it often only indicates the group that a person would like to become a member of, the model for his or her behaviour or not infrequently the legal status to which that person feels entitled. This is an essentially forward-looking view which does not, in every instance, correspond with the identity of the community from which that person originated. It is particularly among second- and third-generation immigrants that there is likely to be such a misalignment of identities, which is the reason why one previous census has included a question on where a respondent's parents were born as well as where they themselves were born.

Such judgements obviously apply in circumstances where it is possible to ask and to expect to obtain a response from a survey questionnaire. But there are many instances in which it is not realistic to achieve the defining attributes of big data: volume, variety and velocity. In a big data environment, the *Origins* taxonomy can achieve volume (being applied to all adults), can achieve variety (classifying names into one of 259 categories) and can achieve velocity (codes being appended on a continuous and 100 per cent sample basis). This is unlike questionnaire-based surveys where, for reasons of cost and respondent fatigue, results can only be collected on an occasional or sample basis and where there will inevitably be respondent bias due to the tendency for response to vary by ethnicity.[8]

# Combining *Origins* and *Mosaic* to track social mobility

Information on the types of neighbourhood in which minorities tend to live ought to be capable of revealing how members of different communities have adapted to life in Britain. This adaptation can be considered in terms of the degree to which the minority has been successful (or otherwise) in respect of material advancement and also the extent to which they have become 'integrated'.

The relationship between adaptation and ethnicity is illustrated by Table 8.3, which gives the proportion of people from 15 different ethno-cultural backgrounds who live in categories created by the 2003 *Mosaic* classification. The 15 *Origins* groupings were selected from a longer list of over 100 and the six *Mosaic* categories shown are the ones where the largest proportion of adults with

**Table 8.3** Percentage of Ethnic Minorities by Selected *Mosaic* Type

| *Origins* Type | Other *Mosaic* Types | Global Connections | Corporate Chieftains | Asian Enterprise | South Asian Industry | Settled Minorities | Welfare Borderline |
|---|---|---|---|---|---|---|---|
| Malta | 81.23 | 1.27 | 1.48 | 2.45 | 0.69 | 4.21 | 8.66 |
| Cantonese Chinese | 80.47 | 2.08 | 2.16 | 2.55 | 0.71 | 4.53 | 7.50 |
| Mauritius | 73.06 | 3.18 | 1.94 | 5.97 | 1.53 | 9.03 | 5.28 |
| Cyprus | 72.89 | 2.40 | 4.97 | 6.25 | 0.27 | 7.08 | 6.14 |
| Armenian | 72.68 | 7.09 | 8.87 | 4.02 | 0.17 | 3.75 | 3.41 |
| Jewish | 72.38 | 5.24 | 7.90 | 3.35 | 0.35 | 5.11 | 5.67 |
| Black Caribbean | 63.68 | 0.76 | 0.53 | 5.42 | 2.23 | 11.44 | 15.96 |
| Turkey | 58.74 | 1.63 | 1.59 | 4.97 | 1.58 | 12.50 | 19.00 |
| Vietnam | 55.75 | 0.88 | 0.38 | 1.99 | 3.33 | 9.26 | 28.42 |
| Sikh | 55.27 | 0.41 | 2.37 | 27.91 | 6.94 | 4.04 | 3.07 |
| Indian Hindi | 54.08 | 0.93 | 3.82 | 24.82 | 7.15 | 5.72 | 3.47 |
| Eritrea | 50.10 | 1.53 | 0.51 | 2.45 | 0.82 | 8.57 | 36.02 |
| Ghana | 46.82 | 0.94 | 0.47 | 4.53 | 0.84 | 15.89 | 30.51 |
| Pakistan | 42.16 | 0.79 | 1.27 | 10.86 | 30.51 | 7.24 | 7.16 |
| Bangladesh | 38.23 | 0.67 | 0.68 | 5.73 | 30.17 | 7.63 | 16.89 |
| UK adults | 89.96 | 0.64 | 1.63 | 1.15 | 0.88 | 1.38 | 4.36 |

non-white British names live. The 15 *Origins* groupings are ranked in descending order according to their presence in 'other' *Mosaic* Types, in other words Types of neighbourhood without a significant minority presence. The 'ethnic' *Mosaic* Types are organized left to right in descending order of social rank. As can be seen from the top row, over 81 per cent of people with Maltese names live in neighbourhoods which, according to *Mosaic*, are predominantly white British, that is to say in Types of neighbourhood which contain few adults who bear other than what are classified as white British names. This contrasts with people with Bangladeshi names, at the foot of the list, only 38 per cent of whom live in predominantly white British *Mosaic* neighbourhood Types.

By contrast, the mix of people living in the prestigious *Global Connections* Type gives a clearer indication of the *Origins* categories that have been most successful in climbing ladders of opportunity. Thus, whilst the Maltese have been more likely than any other group to make their way into predominantly white British neighbourhoods, they have been much less successful in gaining entry to Britain's most prestigious neighbourhoods than have people classified from their names as Jewish or Armenian. Similarly, people whose names suggest a West Indian heritage have been more successful in gaining entry to predominantly white British neighbourhoods than they have in gaining entry to neighbourhoods of highest status.

Table 8.3 also reveals the very considerable differences in the levels of socio-economic advancement that have been experienced by different minority populations, at least as defined from their names. Jewish populations are eight times more likely than adults in general to live in the prestigious *Global Connections* Type and five times more likely than average to live in a neighbourhood characterized by *Corporate Chieftains*. The spectacularly low-profile Armenian community has been even more successful in buying into the most prestigious neighbourhoods. But it is not just members of a white diaspora who have been 'successful' on this criterion. So too have the Hindu Indians, Sri Lankans and Cantonese Chinese. Evidently it is possible for a group that has experienced severe discrimination in the past, such as British Jews, to become highly successful in terms of access to economic and cultural power.[9]

On the other hand, it is evident from Table 8.3 that members of other minorities such as the Vietnamese, Ghanaians and Eritreans have become disproportionately reliant on local councils and housing associations for meeting their housing needs. Despite finding it equally difficult to establish a foothold on the ladders of financial opportunity, members of the Bangladeshi and Pakistani communities depend far less on the state to provide them with accommodation, preferring instead to own or rent from other members of their own communities.

Language also appears to be a barrier. A limited ability to communicate in English is probably one factor that accounts for Pakistani and Bangladeshi populations being the most likely to cluster together in their own communities. It limits the employability of many older community members to factory work or to the servicing of other members of their own community. By contrast, members of smaller immigrant groups, such as people from Mauritius, not being sufficient in number to live in neighbourhoods where they can interact exclusively with other members of their own community, have perhaps a greater incentive to learn to converse in English. Many find it more convenient to live in melting pots with a rich diversity of other immigrant groups rather than in neighbourhoods of 'parallel lives', dominated by a single group, whether white British, Pakistani or Hindu Indian.

Cross analysis of *Origins* by *Mosaic* makes it possible not just to identify which minorities live in which Types of neighbourhood but how this is changing through time. Examples can be found in Table 8.4. Here 15 *Mosaic* categories from the more recent 2009 version of the classification are ordered according to the proportion of their adults whose names were classified as white British in 2011. Whereas nationally some 15 per cent of adults bear non-white British names, this figure rises to over 30 per cent in three *Mosaic* categories: *Upper Floor Living* – tenants in purpose-built blocks of social housing; *Liberal Opinion*, whose general character we have discussed in Chapter 6; and *Terraced Melting Pot* – high density neighbourhoods of less prestigious late-nineteenth-century terraced housing. Types of neighbourhoods where people from non-British backgrounds are least likely to live are rural areas, small towns and neighbourhoods with large numbers of elderly people.

As we would expect during the five years since 2011 the proportion of people with non-white British names has risen most in neighbourhoods where the proportion of adults with non-white British names was already high. What is indicative of social change are the two exceptions. First from their original heartlands in areas of multiple occupation and terraced housing, immigrant populations have disproportionately settled in the less expensive and prestigious of Britain's inter-war suburbs. Then in neighbourhoods of *Liberal Opinion*, after decades of steady growth, the proportion of non-white British names appears to have plateaued. It is possible these two trends are connected, escalating property prices and rents in central city areas forcing immigrants to obtain better value for their money further away from the inner city.

Table 8.4 can also be used to identify differences in the trajectories of different minority communities over these five years. For example, there are some communities, the Cantonese Chinese (note how *Origins* can distinguish them from the Mandarin Chinese), Greek Cypriots, Hindu Indians, Iranians and Vietnamese, for whom the biggest increase in their population has been in the most prestigious of the 2009 *Mosaic* Groups, the *Alpha Territory*. Significantly for the Mandarin Chinese, the biggest increase has been in the more suburban but also prestigious grouping *Professional Rewards*. Overall these communities seem to be doing well.

**Table 8.4**   Change in Non-White British Names by *Mosaic* Groups, 2009
Version, Between 2011 and 2016

| *Mosaic* Group | White British names 2011 % | White British names 2016 % | Change 2011–16 % | Biggest increase in *Origins* categories |
|---|---|---|---|---|
| *Upper Floor Living* | 64.29 | 61.42 | –2.87 | Black Africans<br>Black South Africans<br>Ethiopians<br>Somalis<br>Turks<br>West Indians |
| *Liberal Opinion* | 67.07 | 66.55 | –0.52 | |
| *Terraced Melting Pot* | 67.13 | 62.64 | –4.50 | Albanians<br>Bangladeshis<br>Lithuanians<br>North Africans<br>Pakistanis<br>Romanians |
| *Alpha Territory* | 78.25 | 76.13 | –2.12 | Cantonese Chinese<br>Greek Cypriots<br>Hindu Indians<br>Iranians<br>Vietnamese |
| *New Homemakers* | 80.46 | 77.41 | –3.05 | Nigerians |
| *Suburban Mindsets* | 84.47 | 80.74 | –3.73 | Sikhs<br>Tamils<br>Sri Lankans |
| *UK Average* | 84.97 | 82.56 | –2.40 | |
| *Careers and Kids* | 89.61 | 88.00 | –1.61 | |
| *Claimant Cultures* | 89.73 | 86.32 | –3.41 | Czechs<br>Ghanaians<br>Poles<br>Russians |
| *Ex-Council* | 92.10 | 89.95 | –2.15 | |
| *Industrial Heritage* | 92.34 | 90.68 | –1.65 | |
| *Professional Rewards* | 92.64 | 91.43 | –1.21 | Mandarin Chinese |
| *Active Retirement* | 92.82 | 91.56 | –1.26 | |
| *Small Town Diversity* | 93.65 | 92.65 | –1.00 | |
| *Elderly Needs* | 93.87 | 92.10 | –1.78 | |
| *Rural Solitude* | 94.88 | 94.64 | –0.24 | |

Table 8.4 shows significant but more modest upward mobility among Sikhs and Sri Lankans. Not necessarily for them are the risky entrepreneurial careers favoured by other South Asian groups but reliable middle class occupations that enable them to afford living in areas of *Suburban Mindsets*. These are typically neighbourhoods of inter-war, owner-occupied semi-detached houses in outer London suburbs with garages and reasonably sized gardens.

By contrast with the Hindus and the Sikhs, the Muslim South Asian population has expanded most in streets of *Terraced Melting Pot*, largely because these are areas where they had originally settled. Whether to be close to places of worship or because they lack the financial means to move, this is a well-established group whose aspirations do not appear to involve moving to more modern property in an outer suburb. It is in areas of older terraced houses of this sort that the North African population has expanded most and where more recently arrived eastern Europeans from Lithuania and Albania have tended to settle.

Table 8.4 also shows that Poles and Czechs have tended to gravitate towards low rise neighbourhoods of low-income social housing, which tend to be found outside London. This is by contrast with the experience of most Black African minorities, Turks and West Indians, who have found accommodation in high rise social housing in inner London. None of these groups – so far – seems to display the upward social mobility characteristic of Sikh, Hindu Asian and East Asian communities.

## Metrics for distinguishing different patterns of minority living

Much has been written about the manner in which members of certain communities are at risk of living to what amount to 'parallel lives'.[10] They may live in geographic proximity to the white British population but culturally they live far apart. The concept of 'cultural distance' is simple to understand. Two people from different cultures become neighbours. Two people from different cultures become work colleagues. Two people from different cultures become partners. What additional effort needs to be expended in such relationships for these people to recognize and appreciate each other's cultures and mental processes so as to enable them to better understand each other, resolve conflicts and collaborate in order to complete important tasks? Simple though the *concept* may be to understand, it is not necessarily easy to understand how such cultural distance could be measured or *operationalized*.

A near universal file of names, coded by the ethno-cultural background of each member, does make it possible to devise a crude proxy measurement for this concept and, to the extent that one trusts it, form a useful view of how culturally distant different communities are from each other. For our purposes, here we consider how one might create a measure of the 'cultural distance' between the white ethnic majority of the population and other ethno-cultural groups. In general, one would assume that in Britain people named *Smith* or *Jones* would be more likely to bear personal names such as *John* or *Mary* than people who bore family names such as *Patel* or *Rossi*. The metric displayed in Table 8.5 applies this reasoning across 15 illustrative *Origins* types. It ranks them according to the propensity of adults with family names associated with these different ethno-cultural communities to bear *personal* names classified by *Origins* as white British.[11]

What then are the factors one might suppose would cause members of a particular ethno-cultural group to bear a British personal name? One of course would be cross-cultural marriage, where a woman from a minority community bears the family name of a white British husband. A second would be the children who are the product of such a union. Sharing a common religion improves the chances of sharing a common set of surnames. Though the name *Matthew* will be spelt differently in different Christian countries, the spelling of names of apostles and saints such as *Peter*, *Thomas* and *Michael* is the same in many different European countries. Sharing a common language contributes to the shared use of a common set of popular names as does admiration for a common set of international celebrities. In addition, cultures which share a broadly similar heritage to Britain are also likely to share common names, or indeed to borrow them from each other.

**Table 8.5** Proportion of Adults with Family Names of Different *Origins* Whose Personal Names are White British

| *Origins* of family name | % bearing British personal name | *Origins* of family name | % Bearing British personal name |
| --- | --- | --- | --- |
| Scottish | 95.1 | Black South African | 42.0 |
| English | 94.7 | Korean | 40.7 |
| Welsh | 94.4 | Polish | 38.9 |
| Irish | 94.1 | Cantonese Chinese | 38.2 |
| Black Caribbean | 86.0 | Finnish | 32.4 |
| Maltese | 82.4 | Nigerian | 32.2 |
| Jewish | 80.0 | Maronite Christian | 25.4 |
| French | 78.4 | Japanese | 20.9 |
| Danish | 78.2 | Iranian | 19.8 |
| German | 75.6 | Turkish | 19.4 |
| Dutch | 75.6 | Mandarin Chinese | 18.9 |
| Spanish | 58.2 | Hindu Indian | 7.5 |
| Italian | 54.5 | Bangladeshi | 6.9 |
| Hungarian | 49.0 | Sikh | 6.7 |
| Latvian | 46.7 | Pakistani | 6.0 |

*Bruno* and *Boris* are examples of names which are common throughout Europe, not just in Britain. Likewise, *Jacqueline* and *Karl* are personal names that the British have borrowed from their geographic and cultural neighbours.

Each of these factors are indicative of cultural proximity and help to explain why it is people who bear Black Caribbean, Maltese, Jewish and French family names who are, in the UK, the most likely to bear British personal names. At the opposite end of the ranking it is people with family names from South Asian communities who are least likely to bear British personal names.

When the names of members of South Asian communities are analysed in more detail, it becomes apparent that those who live in postcodes character-ized by 'parallel lives', and in particular in ones where their own community is the largest one, are significantly less likely to bear British personal names than their counterparts living in more mixed neighbourhoods or predominantly white British ones. How reliably can we infer from this that it is members of South Asian communities who live in their own heartlands that tend to be the least well integrated into the cultural practices of the majority population?

Rather than the view, based on a binary coding of respondents to survey ques-tionnaires into 'white' and 'non-white' populations, that integration is a generic issue for non-white British communities that have been the object of discrimi-natory or other forms of disadvantage, it might be more appropriate to consider various communities as each uniquely located on a continuum between cultur-ally close and culturally distant. It is entirely understandable that members of those minorities that are culturally most distant from the majority population should tend to cluster into neighbourhoods where their own community is the largest non-white British one. By contrast, one would expect that minorities that are culturally more integrated would tend to be geographically more dispersed. This hypothesis is consistently supported by evidence that within their heart-lands members of a minority community are less likely than elsewhere to bear a British personal name, in other words to be more culturally distant, and hence less integrated.[12]

Whereas Table 8.3 uses the *Origins* classification to highlight the different Types of neighbourhood in which certain ethno-cultural minorities live, Figure 8.2 illustrates how big data can be used to reveal how they have each populated dif-ferent parts of London. Maps of this sort are created by colouring each individual postcode (such as N6 5SB) according to the *Origins* category which, in 2016, com-prised the largest proportion of the postcode's adult population. The absence of a coloured dot indicates either a non-residential area or a neighbourhood where fewer than 20 per cent of adults bore a non-white British name.

Notwithstanding the fact that in almost every postcode there is quite a high level of mixing, this method of visualization shows very clearly the propen-sity of London's larger immigrant communities to settle in very specific parts

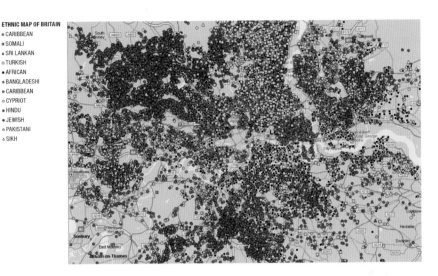

**ETHNIC MAP OF BRITAIN**
- CARIBBEAN
- SOMALI
- SRI LANKAN
- TURKISH
- AFRICAN
- BANGLADESHI
- CARIBBEAN
- CYPRIOT
- HINDU
- JEWISH
- PAKISTANI
- SIKH

**Figure 8.2**  Dominant Minorities by Postcode, London, 2016

of the city. Though some groups live closer and others further from the centre of London – the Sikh population tend to live in the suburbs, the Bangladeshis close to the centre – the overall pattern of segregation is by no means as concentric as was the case in Chicago in the 1930s. Nor is it necessarily the most recently arrived immigrant groups that live most centrally. The feature of the Chicago model that is more evident is that individual communities tend to dominate particular radial sectors, suburbanizing themselves from their inner London heartlands along specific transport corridors.

For example, the heartland of the Hindu Indian community, which first settled in and around Wembley to the north west of London, has moved further out to the north west in the direction of Pinner. The Jewish community, one of whose original heartlands was in North London's Marylebone and Hampstead, has moved further north, first to Golders Green and then to Hendon, Mill Hill and Radlett. Greek Cypriots, who first settled in Camden Town, have also moved out northwards to Palmers Green and the western suburbs of Enfield. The Turkish community, early residents of Dalston and Stoke Newington, have migrated to Edmonton and in the direction of Waltham Cross to the north east of London. Afro-Caribbeans have migrated from Brixton further south to Streatham and to Thornton Heath, whilst Black Africans have moved in a south easterly direction from Deptford to Woolwich, Thamesmead and Erith. This at least is what appears to have happened from a map based on data for a five-year period. We shall see in due course how big data can also provide detailed information on how these patterns are changing over time.

Though this is not necessarily evident from the map, the underlying data from which it is built suggest that most parts of London are 'dominated' by a single minority. The intensity of this dominance of the minority is almost certainly less strong than it was in 1930s Chicago. In postcodes where, for example, Greek Cypriots, Turks or Jews form the largest group, plenty of space is left for other minorities to live. This is not so much the case in northern England, in towns such as Oldham and Blackburn where Muslims typically constitute a much larger proportion of the population of the postcodes that they dominate.

Another interesting feature of the data shown in Figure 8.2 is the degree to which the number of dots of different colour correlate with actual size of that minority population. There are many postcodes where the Hindu Indians, the Pakistanis, the Sikhs and the Bangladeshis constitute the largest minority population but what we find is that a higher proportion of these South Asian communities live in neighbourhoods where they are the largest group than is the case among, for example, the Chinese, the West Indians, Turks and Black Africans. This is because the principal South Asian groups, the Hindu Indians, the Sikhs, the Pakistanis and the Bangladeshis, tend to group together on a geographical basis to a much greater extent than do other communities.

By contrast, bearing in mind the relative size of its population, there are relatively few postcodes where West Indians are the largest community despite their historic association with neighbourhoods such as Brixton and Notting Hill.[13] And, despite the existence of distinctively Chinese business districts, such as Soho, the Chinese do not cluster residentially to a sufficient degree to result in there being more than a handful of postcodes where Chinese names are more common than any other group (Knowles and Burrows, 2017).

Different levels of social and financial advancement by no means explain variations in the extent to which different communities cluster together geographically. The Jewish community, though as we have seen the most successful as measured by the Types of neighbourhood in which its members live, is nevertheless highly concentrated at postcode level, as is evidenced by the density of purple dots in Figure 8.2 around Golders Green and, in Figure 8.3 below, around Stamford Hill. Indeed, this community is much more successful – on this measure at least – than West Indians who, by contrast with the situation when they first arrived in Britain, have become very much more dispersed. The desire of members of a community to live in a neighbourhood where their ethnic group is already well established can perhaps be perceived as an indication of that community's commitment to maintaining its cultural distinctiveness, the Jews (highly concentrated) and the West Indians (highly dispersed) illustrating that this distinctiveness is only tangentially correlated either with social status or absence of colour.

That London's black communities, West Indian and Black African, should be so much more dispersed than other immigrant groups is notably different from the situation in most cities in the United States, where the boundary between white and black neighbourhoods is far more sharply defined. It is a curious paradox that in London the geographic dispersion of West Indians is as great as that of second- and third-generation Italian immigrants whose forebears arrived in the early post-war years in such numbers to work in the market gardens of the Lea Valley.

The term 'diversity' is used in many different contexts. In the context of this chapter it is used to describe a melting pot neighbourhood, in which many different non-white British people co-exist whether harmoniously or not, as opposed to a 'parallel lives' neighbourhood in which, if there is a non-white British population, its members belong predominantly to a single minority group.

The review of social cohesion in Britain produced by Louise Casey in 2016, a quote from which opened this chapter, is one of a number that have alerted the government to the existence of communities whose members have only modest contact with the majority population and who live what she, not uncontroversially, referred to as 'parallel lives'.[14] Such communities are characteristic of 'undiverse' or 'mono-cultural' neighbourhoods in the context of this discussion.[15]

Diverse and mono-cultural neighbourhoods each deliver benefits and dis-benefits in terms of community organization, cohesion and representation. In very diverse neighbourhoods the police and providers of other public services often find it difficult to establish links with leaders of the local community, to involve the community in consultation exercises and to engage with them to work out local solutions to local problems. The corollary of such diversity is that minorities tend to have to learn to co-exist with members of the other minorities with whom they share the neighbourhood. Their children will mix with those of other groups at school. They will get used to encountering other cultures when they go shopping, or to the bank or to the doctor's surgery. They may not speak English at home but need to use it as a 'lingua franca' in the Tower of Babel. Communities that tend to be present in diverse neighbourhoods tend to have lower levels of cultural distance than those who live in mono-cultural neighbourhoods, their lives perhaps less subject to control by religious elders and self-appointed community leaders. But, as was evident after the Grenfell Tower disaster in North Kensington in June 2017, that does not mean that residents in such neighbourhoods are incapable of community organization.

By contrast, life in a mono-cultural neighbourhood has the benefit of providing social and emotional support to its members. They can operate much more easily without the need to use the English language. They can, if they wish, remain unchallenged by the need to engage with practices considered as day-to-day obligations outside their restricted world. The strength of cultural tradition in places of this sort can be oppressive and there are many young people whose lives are frustrated by not being allowed to participate in the cultural practices of a wider society. These are places where marriages are more likely to be arranged and where, when violence occurs within the family, it is most likely to go unreported.[16]

The technical task of devising a metric for measuring diversity of this sort is not difficult if one has access to a database giving the distribution of *Origins* categories within each of Britain's 1.8 million postcodes. The one used in this chapter uses the probability with which two adults, chosen at random from the non-white British population within the area, would belong to different non-white British *Origins* sub-groups, a sub-group being a 50-level grouping of individual *Origins* categories.

In situations where the proportion of the population which is white British is high and the size of the non-white British population low, it is not appropriate to calculate measures of diversity. But in areas of high immigration the value can be low where a single grouping is overly dominant. Highest values of diversity occur in postcodes where no overly dominant minority is present irrespective of the concentration of white British adults.

As can be seen from Figure 8.3, mapping values for this metric in areas with significant immigrant populations highlights the very different conditions that exist in London compared with the north of England. London is a true melting pot. It is not just the city as a whole either, individual streets tend to be far more diverse than streets anywhere else in Britain. So, although – as we have seen – most individual minorities do favour particular parts of the city, few postcodes are dominated by any single minority. South Tottenham, shown in Figure 8.3, is a case in point.

Outside London we find less mixing between minorities and in former Pennine mill towns such as Batley, Oldham and Blackburn, hardly any. In the latter towns labour was at one time recruited from very localized areas within South Asia. Other than people from these places, very few other migrants came to live in these towns. The expansion of minority neighbourhoods in towns of this sort is due almost entirely to higher than average levels of fertility and/or to extended family members being granted permission to settle in Britain.

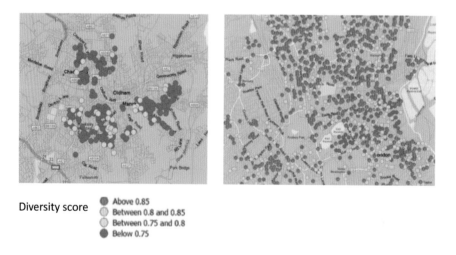

Diversity score
● Above 0.85
◔ Between 0.8 and 0.85
○ Between 0.75 and 0.8
● Below 0.75

Figure 8.3   Diversity in Oldham and South Tottenham

# Tracking migration patterns among minorities

Of the three 'v's that distinguish big data – 'volume', 'variety' and 'velocity' – it is often the combination of 'volume' and 'velocity' that provides the type of insight that it is most difficult to obtain from survey sources.

For many decades it seemed that inner London was the prime magnet for immigrant groups, the white British moving not just to the outer London suburbs but also to commutable locations beyond the boundary of the Greater London Authority area. After tentative beginnings older properties started to be 'done up' by new generations of gentrifiers and inner London became hollowed out by a loss of skilled manual and junior white collar workers. More recently the increasing population of London and the limits to its commutable journey-to-work area have resulted in an acceleration of brown-field development and the replacement of Victorian industrial buildings with high specification developments for singles and childless couples. What impact have this and the increased pressure on London's housing had on the ethnic composition of central, inner and outer London?

Given that the big data used to generate the figures we have already discussed is updated on an annual basis, in other words has high velocity, it is possible to answer some of these questions by comparing the *Origins* names of adults in local areas in 2011 and 2016. When each of the 50 *Origins* subgroups are examined at the level of the postcode sector (such as N6 4) it appears that most minority communities, not just the more affluent ones such as Jews, Hindu Indians and Greek Cypriots, are experiencing a rapid process of *suburbanization*, moving to more affordable accommodation both in outer London and beyond the Greater London boundary.

Figure 8.4 shows the shift in the concentration of the population with Nigerian names between 2011 and 2016. There is clear evidence not just that Nigerians (or people with Nigerian names to be more specific) are moving further out from London, in particular along the corridor formed by the south bank of the Thames and as far as Dartford, but that Nigerians are moving towards their established heartlands rather than dispersing. The Nigerian populations of inner north London and inner east London are both in decline. Nigerians are not just suburbanizing themselves but tending to concentrate along a favoured radial sector along the south bank of the Thames, especially in the section between Thamesmead and Erith.

When we look at the distribution of people with white British names in inner London we see the reverse of this pattern. Despite the increased role of London as a global city, there is evidence of the 're-colonization' of central London by the British, a pattern equally evident in the centres of Birmingham and Manchester.

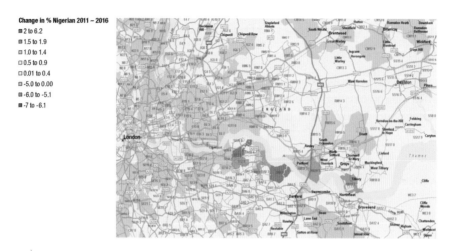

**Figure 8.4**  Change in % of adults with Nigerian names

In all three cases, it is likely that the expansion of higher education is an important consideration as is the number of new private developments in parts of London which, until recently, were given over almost exclusively to social housing.

## Different Cultures, Different Trajectories

In this chapter we have used big data sources and novel taxonomies to highlight the very heterogeneous nature of the British minority ethnic community. We have sought to downplay colour to being just one of a number of different criteria on which communities can be differentiated and we have highlighted what we see as critical behavioural differences between people from different cultural backgrounds.

What surprises us is that the different metrics that differentiate one community from another appear not to be as correlated with each other as strongly as mainstream theories of disadvantage would suggest. For example, within South Asian communities, which are the most culturally distant and the most likely to live parallel lives, there are nevertheless much higher levels of entrepreneurial success than among groups such as the Turkish community and West Indians, who are far more dispersed and less culturally distant from the host population.

Despite their experience of persecution, Jews have an outstanding track record in gaining access to Britain's most prestigious neighbourhoods, yet, though they marry freely with the gentile population, they nevertheless continue to cluster in residential enclaves. The Armenians, who some would argue have suffered equally from persecution, have also been successful in terms of residential advancement. Why the Greek Cypriot and Iranian communities should have been so much more successful than the Turks or the Pakistanis, despite no obvious comparative advantages, is difficult to understand.

Just as there are metrics which highlight the contrasting fortunes of different immigrant groups, so measures of diversity and population change highlight the uneven way in which immigrant communities populate the country, the South Asian communities of northern cities conducting their lives in a highly segregated environment whilst the citizens of inner London co-exist, seemingly without great community tension, in a veritable melting pot.

Compared to the black population of the United States, Britain's West Indian and Black African populations appear to be among the most willing of any immigrant group to select a white partner and to live in white and other diverse communities. Unlike in America, the rapid suburbanization of the immigrant communities is being driven by the search for less expensive neighbourhoods and not so much by upward social mobility.

Though many second- and subsequent-generation migrants are experiencing upward social mobility, data sets to which *Origins* has been appended suggest that they have been quicker to adopt the lifestyles and behaviours of the majority population than their underlying values. Despite living together in diverse neighbourhoods, minorities continue to display the very distinct values that their forbears arrived with, sometimes to a much greater degree than they themselves realize.

What then can we deduce from this use of big data to identify how more widespread immigration is altering the patterns of residential segregation in Britain? The prime one is that, just as Chapter 6 reveals the growing fragmentation within the middle classes, big data reveals increased differentiation within the immigrant community.

Different minority groups vary greatly in the success of their members in climbing ladders of economic opportunity and achieving sufficient economic success to move to more sought-after residential neighbourhoods. Some groups are more likely than others to form partnerships across racial divides and to be comfortable living in neighbourhoods where their own community is not the dominant one. The position of a minority on the dimension of cultural distance is a poor predictor of the level of economic advancement of its members but neither colour nor experience of colonial rule are entirely reliable predictors of deprivation or advancement. We need to pay more attention to the aspects of the culture which distinguish ethnic groups if we are to better understand the contrasting trajectories of different fractions within the immigrant community and its descendants. These cultural attributes persist for much longer than the effects of colonial rule and perhaps need to displace some of the emphasis currently given to historic discrimination as an explanation of social disadvantage.

## Notes

[1] See the arguments of Goodhart (2017) and also the blog in support of the paper by Jennings and Stoker (2016) – www.pqblog.org.uk/2016/06/the-bifurcation-of-politics-two.html – where it is argued that: 'In cosmopolitan areas we find an England that is global in outlook, liberal and more plural in its sense of identity, while in provincial backwaters we find an England that is inward looking, relatively illiberal, negative about the EU and immigration, nostalgic and more English in its identity…'

[2] This is not the place to rehearse the history of immigration to Britain, but it is worth noting that Panayi (2010) estimates that some 2.4 million migrants entered Britain before 1945 – 1.5 million of them Irish, 240,000 Belgians, 220,000 Jews, 100,000 Germans, 70,000 Americans, 40,000 Italians, 40,000 French, 20,000 Chinese, 20,000 South Asians, 10,000 Africans, 10,000 Arabs, 10,000 West Indians, 5,000 Poles, 2,000 Cypriots, 2,000 Hungarians and 50,000 from elsewhere on the planet.

[3] These data, from the 2011 census, are derived from the classification of ethnicity discussed in Chapter 3.

[4] This is no small matter politically of course. As Knowles (1996) argues, in many of the practices of social workers and those working in health and community settings – 'caring professionals' in the parlance of *Mosaic* – there is often a complex tension about how best to come to terms with evidence of cultural differences between different ethnic groups, whilst avoiding accusation of 'stereotyping'. Some argue that such differences have arisen primarily as a result of the different levels and forms of discrimination in different colonial environments. Others argue that such a perspective does not give enough credit to the proposition that many such cultural differences have a history much longer than that of European colonialism.

[5] *The Independent Inquiry into Child Sexual Exploitation in Rotherham, 1997–2013* provides an emblematic, if not uncontroversial, illustration of many of these issues. Tufail (2015) provides an interesting examination of this and other similar cases.

[6] Burrows et al. (2017) provide a more detailed analysis using a later version of *Mosaic*.

[7] Consider again the data shown in Table 8.2.

[8] It should be noted that the development of *Origins* was initially in response to the need for a more sophisticated basis for establishing equal opportunities monitoring in a number of health care settings. It was found that, despite best efforts, service users tended not to respond to equal opportunity monitoring

forms of various types and thus the achievement (or otherwise) of equity targets was impossible to ascertain.

[9] Such a possibility is difficult to square with traditional interpretations of the impact of historic disadvantage on social mobility, a contradiction that caused serious divisions within the Labour Party during 2016. For some Labour Party members, the Jewish community are perceived as the historical victims of a horrendous level of discrimination and oppression, for other members they are perceived as an extremely powerful elite. See, for example, www.newstatesman.com/politics/uk/2016/10/anti-semitism-and-left-something-rotten-state-labour.

[10] Much of it summarized in *The Casey Review* with which we opened this chapter, see: www.gov.uk/government/uploads/system/uploads/attachment_data/file/575973/The_Casey_Review_Report.pdf.

[11] Note that, membership of that community in this instance is determined solely on the basis of the origin of the family name.

[12] If cultural distance, using this metric as a proxy, appears to be highly correlated with neighbourhood separation, it would be a mistake to suppose that it has more than a very weak association with social mobility and financial success. In other words, there are many factors other than cultural distance that render some ethno-cultural communities more successful than others once they arrive in Britain.

[13] The size of this community is up-weighted in the analysis to account for the presence – for well-known historical reasons – of so many British names among people of West Indian descent. One thinks, obviously, of people such as Bernie Grant, Trevor Phillips and Stuart Hall.

[14] An earlier more critical review can be found in Camina and Wood (2009).

[15] In Chapter 7 we discussed the implications of mono-cultural British whiteness; here we focus on minority ethnic populations.

[16] See, for example, the vivid testimonies of Jasvinder Sanghera: https://www.karmanirvana.org.uk/about.

# 9

# THE BRITISH COUNTRYSIDE
## Playgrounds for the Middle Classes?

Early association with country solitudes had bred in him an unconquerable, and almost unreasonable, aversion to modern town life, and shut him out from such success as he might have aspired to by following a mundane calling in the impracticability of a spiritual one ... Farming, at any rate, after becoming well qualified for the business by a careful apprenticeship – that was a vocation which would probably afford an independence without the sacrifice of what he valued even more than a competency – intellectual liberty.

Description of Angel Clare in Thomas Hardy's
*Tess of the d'Urbervilles* (1892)

## The growth in the appeal of country living

Of the 61 *Mosaic* Types listed in Table 5.4 this chapter focuses on the following five.

| Code | Mosaic Type label | UK % | Top local authorities |
|------|-------------------|------|-----------------------|
| K57 | Summer Playgrounds | 0.3 | North Cornwall |
| K58 | Greenbelt Guardians | 1.7 | Cotswold |
| K59 | Parochial Villagers | 1.6 | South Holland |
| K60 | Pastoral Symphony | 1.3 | South Shropshire |
| K61 | Upland Hill Farms | 0.4 | Powys |

Thus far, in our substantive examples, our focus has tended to be on primarily urban phenomena. In this chapter we turn our attention to the less densely populated parts of the country, which, as we shall see, have been subject to no less complex patterns of change over the past few decades: their demographics have been transformed; their economic base has been restructured; and old established members of the community have been displaced (Shucksmith, 2012). However, despite some bold historical attempts to typify *quantitatively* different types of rural neighbourhood (Shucksmith et al., 1995) most of the contemporary knowledge we have about rural life is *qualitative* in nature (Shucksmith and Brown, 2016), much of it focused on detailed studies of specific communities. What conclusions are of general applicability to other rural communities is not clear, nor is it clear to which other communities, or types of community, their findings are relevant. In the absence of any agreed taxonomy for identifying rural areas, or indeed any basis for differentiating different types of rural neighbourhood, it has not been easy to replicate for rural areas the more coherent and systematic theories of change that have been constructed in the field of urban studies (Marsden et al., 2012).

It is perhaps not surprising that rural neighbourhoods have attracted much less attention than their urban counterparts. Policy is formulated mostly in the city. Most academic commentators live and work in neighbourhoods which cluster around the urban locations where most British universities are located. The countryside, represented at Westminster almost exclusively in England by Conservative Members of Parliament, is perhaps perceived as less worthy of detailed study than urban areas, which suffer from more recognizable manifestations of deprivation. By their very nature urban neighbourhoods tend to display greater inequalities and higher levels of social segregation. As a result, they are far more likely to experience multiple forms of disadvantage.

In the nineteenth and twentieth centuries it was in towns that social change appeared to be and probably was most manifest, the countryside remaining as it were an unchanged constant whose function was to supply the town with food and, in times of urban expansion, satisfy its demand for migrant labour. Yet since 1945 it is in the countryside that population has grown fastest. This growth, and the associated demographic change that marks the contemporary countryside, could not have occurred without a persistent exodus of urban residents, a population group which is particularly skewed towards specific demographic groupings. It is easy to forget that this differential exodus will have had a reciprocal, though often less visible, impact on the social fabric of the towns from which these people have migrated.

What then is the countryside and how is it to be defined? And at what level of granularity? Is rural Britain to be defined: economically, in terms of agricultural or other rural land uses; physically, in terms of population density;

or socially, in terms of the persistence of traditional networks of association that find expression in institutions such as the parish church, pub, community hall and local store? Until 1945 there is no doubt that such different criteria for defining rural Britain would have produced broadly similar results. Today those who enjoy living in a seemingly rural landscape no longer necessarily participate in traditionally rural networks of association, nor do they live in communities where agriculture is necessarily the mainstay of the local economy. The absence of an agreed framework for defining contemporary rural Britain may be one contributor to the relatively low awareness – at least in academic literature, not in rural areas themselves or among the editors of *The Archers* – of the social change it has been experiencing. The purpose of this chapter is therefore to focus on the changes that have been experienced by Britain's rural communities and how the evidence for these changes can be inferred from geodemographic classifications.

The gentrification of country villages by what we might now call financially successful urban 'entrepreneurs' is nothing new. Since at least as far back as the sixteenth century members of London's merchant classes saw merit in exchanging the more noxious features of city life for the fresh air and unpolluted water of what until then had been modest agricultural settlements (Richardson, 1992). Old houses still standing in Blackheath, Clapham, Dulwich and Highgate attest to this desire. Thackeray makes reference to a 'banking colony' whose villas in Roehampton acted as leisure retreats from their London town houses. By Thackeray's time the villa had become an important new architectural design, offering allusions to older or continental housing forms. It was so arranged as to avoid views of neighbours but to maximize sightlines across open country so as to appropriate the illusion of the country house and to emulate the qualities proposed by influential landscape designers such as Repton towards the end of the eighteenth century. A key feature of these emerging semi-rural enclaves was their rejection of the uniformity of urban housing for more informal layouts.

Rookeries – slums that emerged during the nineteenth century and contributed greatly to the level of criminality – gave further impetus for country living and provided the first recognition that poverty, which was previously considered a household phenomenon, could also be manifested at the neighbourhood level. It required the publication by William Cobbett of his rural rides across southern England from 1821 onwards and, later, an exposure of the condition of labourers on the estates of the great philanthropist the seventh Earl of Shaftesbury, to raise awareness that poverty could exist in rural as well as urban locations. The repeal of the laws restricting the import of grain in 1815 and 1846 contributed not just to rural poverty but to the destabilization of the historic social fabric of rural communities recorded by Thomas Hardy in novels such as *Tess of the d'Urbervilles* and *Jude the Obscure*.

Their fates notwithstanding, the early decades of the twentieth century witnessed a popular renewal of interest in the sense of community imagined to have existed in the fabled rural 'Merrie England'. This revival was expressed in the aesthetics of the Arts and Crafts movement and by the revival of vernacular architectural styles (Miller, 2006). The maypole on the village green was symbolic of a variety of activities which sought to reconnect Britain with its rural past. Railway companies pursued their own interests by promoting rural lifestyles on poster adverts and it was not out of altruism that the Shell petroleum company launched a series of guides to the countryside. *Country Life*, founded in 1917, used photographs to extol country living and publishers such as Batsford broadened awareness of the architectural treasures of rural Britain. Architects and interior designers provided the urban middle classes with advice on how to live in the country with style. And no greater distinction could be acquired than a weekend invitation to an English country house party (Tinniswood, 2016). Perhaps at no other time in British history had the image and reality of rural living been further apart.

When creating a small residential development for her staff on the grounds of her Holly Lodge estate in north London, Angela Burdett-Coutts, said to be the second richest woman in Britain after Queen Victoria, had her cottages constructed in an elaborate neo-gothic style arranged around an imaginary village green (Healey, 1978). The homes built for the workers of the Levers and Cadburys at Port Sunlight and Bournville were among the first to adopt the vernacular half-timbered Mock-Tudor style which was to become the dominant aesthetic of suburban domestic architecture in the inter-war period (Nicholson-Lord, 1987).

When commissioned by Henrietta Barnett to develop plans for Hampstead Garden Suburb, Raymond Unwin not only developed these building styles but consciously arranged artisan cottages as though they were situated in a rural village. Meanwhile Henrietta Barnett, who had extensive experience in community development in the east end, insisted that Unwin's design should include numerous places for association. Churches, an educational institute, allotments, parks and tennis courts, she believed, would enable residents to recreate the powerful networks of association of rural England that were so sadly absent in the unplanned suburbs by which speculative developers disfigured cities in the early years of the twentieth century (Watkins, 2011). Gardening was sufficiently aligned with the ethos of the time that Henrietta initiated an annual suburb gardening competition as well as an annual sports day.

It is no accident that in the 1930s it became fashionable for developers to choose English trees as names for the new streets they built. Any occurrences of 'Oakdene Avenue' and 'Elmhurst Gardens' can be dated to this period with a high degree of confidence just as any streets named after writers such as 'Pepys Street' and after battles such as 'Inkerman Terrace' are almost certain to have been laid out by Victorian or Edwardian developers.

The imaginary rediscovery of 'Merrie England' contributed greatly to the increasingly diverse set of types of rural community which, as we saw in Chapter 5, are visible in the geodemographic clusters thrown up by the *Mosaic* system. In particular it has resulted in an emerging set of ostensibly rural neighbourhoods which lie within commuting reach of major centres of employment, or ones which provide environmentally attractive locations for the footloose or the retired, or ones which have been bought up as second homes. These may be rural in terms of landscape and land use but not in terms of employment structure or networks of association. The number and share of the national population living in these categories continue to grow.

At the same time, we see from *Mosaic* continued evidence of a 'deep countryside', still economically dependent on agriculture and too remote from corporate office parks to be viable as locations for middle class commuters. Subsequent classifications show the decline in the geographical extent of this category over the last 50 years. Now it is restricted to the most remote, peripheral regions of the country. It is only comparatively recently that this deep countryside has ceased to lose population. However, it continues to receive very little investment in new homes or infrastructure and it harbours serious levels of poverty and of social isolation, often well concealed.

The transformation of the countryside – from a place where landed gentry were surrounded by tenants and retainers with too little motivation to move to the town, to a tolerably attractive and for many a highly desirable place to live – owes more than we often care to remember to a series of technological innovations which flourished during the first two thirds of the twentieth century. These include the connection to the electric grid and the telephone, the television and, perhaps most important of all, the private car. Maybe by 2003 it was no longer necessary to append the word 'Isolation' to 'Rural' as a descriptor of this *Mosaic* Group. For it was these technological innovations that caused rural communities to lose their isolation and for their lower classes to become integrated for the first time into the nation's mainstream culture.

A second engine of rural change, the effects of which are equally evident from geodemographic classification, has been in the growth in agricultural productivity, especially in the grain-producing counties of eastern England. Here it had previously been possible to run large landholdings only with the help of a large, locally resident labour force. Unlike seaside resorts and mining communities, which have suffered so grievously from the loss of their economic base, there are few settlements whose erstwhile function was to supply inexpensive labour to local landowners that have not succeeded in finding a new role. Some have become communities of choice for commuters to nearby towns, others places suited to the needs of artists and other footloose, self-employed 'brainworkers', or as destinations for retirees or as providers of second homes for the more prosperous strata within the urban middle classes.

This transformation may not necessarily have been any less painful than the process of urban gentrification about which so much has been written (Lees et al., 2010). As late as the 1960s the stock of public housing in rural areas, though lower as a proportion of the total housing stock than urban areas, was still sufficient to meet the needs of its lower income groups. Since then the proportion of public housing stock that has been acquired under 'right-to-buy' legislation is even higher than in urban areas and hardly any new social housing has been added (Chaney and Sherwood, 2000; Sturzaker and Shucksmith, 2011).

In 1945 most agricultural workers had modest skills and limited horizons. Their descendants increasingly find themselves beleaguered by the decline in rural employment and by the poor local provision of rural public services. Most tenancies of cottages owned by local farmers have been terminated. The disproportionate number of them that lacked baths or inside toilets, often right up until the 1960s, have now been bought and modernized by incoming middle class families and the rural working classes are increasingly obliged to turn for their housing needs to more affordable properties in nearby market towns.

# The different types of rural neighbourhood

The extent of these social changes does of course vary. They are most evident in those parts of rural Britain that have the easiest access to urban centres and indeed it is in these areas that these patterns of change first became evident. It is places closer to towns, and even more particularly to motorway access points, that we find rural landscapes populated by the homes of A07 *Semi-Rural Seclusion* for example. It is a moot point as to whether their residents have made a deliberate choice to live in a rural environment or whether they have been obliged to by the constraints on urban expansion imposed by the Town and Country Planning Act of 1947 which enabled local authorities to designate green belts. Further from urban centres we find the more economically self-sufficient communities, where pressure for new housing has been less and population growth lower. K60 *Pastoral Symphony* and K61 *Upland Hill Farmers*, as we have suggested, tend to be located in the more distant extremities of the country. Their valued landscapes are more likely to be maintained by self-employed small farmers than by business syndicates.

Within the belt of commutable countryside surrounding Britain's major cities, *Mosaic* distinguishes between 'estate' villages, where from time to time major house-builders construct crescents of identical homes affordable for families on middling incomes, and the category K58 *Greenbelt Guardians*, which, when it was built, owed much to the cultural (if not the political) legacy of William Morris, a rejection of the mechanical uniformity of urban dwellings and the regimentation of urban living. Often built in what prior to the 1974 reorganization of local government were classified as 'rural districts', homes were built beyond the limits of municipal building standards such as pavements and street lighting. Quite a few are still accessed by roads that have still not been adopted by the local council. In places of this sort it is a badge of distinction that one's street has yet to be asphalted and that one's address should be denoted by the name of one's house rather than a number. Pioneers for whom this sort of neighbourhood was built were ones for whom signs of cultural distinction might include being a knowledgeable gardener, an ability to distinguish a sparrowhawk from a kestrel or seemingly effortless competence on one's own tennis court or outdoor swimming pool. Such neighbourhoods are still among the most fertile grounds for recruiting members to the National Trust or to local wildlife and conservation societies. These are among the most vociferous and effective objectors to developments that might threaten the local natural environment.

The great agricultural depression of the inter-war years and loose planning policies contributed to developments in this *Mosaic* Type tending to have some of the lowest residential densities and highest average plot sizes especially on land of low agricultural value. This, combined with the acidic soils on which many of these houses were built, contributes to a legacy of space hungry vegetation such as laurels, rhododendrons and conifers, which were planted during a period when seclusion was more highly valued than it is today.

In places further from urban centres, geodemographic classifications are successful in distinguishing arable from pastoral Britain, areas of small-holders and own-account farmers living in scattered settlements by contrast with areas of more intensively mechanized 'prairie' agriculture. By and large, this distinction reflects the geological and climatic divide between the east and west of Britain and the distinction between nuclear villages, where agricultural labourers once lived, and the pattern of scattered farmsteads typical of dairy farming and stock raising landscapes. As we first noted in Chapter 5, algorithms are assisted with this distinction by the practice of census authorities of assigning the socio-economic designations 'skilled manual' to self-employed farmers, 'professionals or managers' to owners of large farms and 'semi-skilled' to the agricultural labourers whom they employ.

The influence of geology is evident from the distribution of *Rural Retirement Mix* in the 1980s version of *Mosaic*. Just as the village containing housing estates is progressively displacing urban leafy suburbs as a home for middle class families, so *Rural Retirement Mix* increasingly attracts a cadre for whom Worthing, Colwyn Bay or Swanage would have been natural retirement destinations in earlier times. Whilst these rural settlements are still far from acquiring the accoutrements of an American retirement community, the presence of a significant population of older newcomers provides the social milieu and the networks of association that gives villages of this sort an enviable reputation as a suitable retirement location for active elders. Here residents themselves only recently retired will greet newcomers with an insistence that they must play an active role in a range of voluntary organizations for which new volunteers are needed. Villages on the edge of National Parks or within Areas of Outstanding Natural Beauty are particularly likely to fall within this *Mosaic* classification. Ideal conditions are good drainage – no damp clay soils – an undulating landscape, the use of vernacular building materials and, if possible, a stretch of unspoiled coastline within a 45-minute drive. Comfortably-off incomers avoid villages whose population growth is caused by the modern estate developments that turn villages into dormitories for commuters. Dorset is the county with the largest percentage of its population in this *Mosaic* Type.

Remoteness, if not isolation, contributes to the networks through which residents who fall within these *Mosaic* classifications form associations. Distance from the specialist services offered by urban centres encourages people to be more self-reliant. One drives or is driven, rather than travels on public transport or by taxi, cooks one's own meals rather than orders via Deliveroo. Eating out is reserved for special occasions. Where townspeople would visit the cinema or theatre, villagers club together to organize their own forms of entertainment. Spacious gardens and even grounds allow them to grow their own food and gather fuel with which to heat their own homes. Distinction is conferred on those whose gardens reach the standard that justifies being opened to the public.

Remoteness and established networks of association also encourage diversification of income generation – there is insufficient demand for a full-time window-cleaner or a dedicated kennel – and the remoteness from high street chains encourages more people than just local farmers to enter self-employment. Lifestyles adapt not just to the field sports and leisure pursuits offered by the surrounding countryside but to the fact that space is no longer at a premium. It is in neighbourhoods of this sort that consumers are among the most likely to own freezers, dishwashers, motor mowers, conservatories, a second car, a boat or a caravan. Unlike the trend in metropolitan inner cities, money is relatively more likely to be spent on consumer products than on experiences.

## Using *Mosaic* to track longitudinal change in rural Britain

Virtually every geodemographic classification, certainly every one in Britain, creates a series of clusters which can be interpreted as 'rural'. The most obvious marker of a rural cluster is the proportion of the workforce engaged in agriculture. But this may be just one of many hundreds of demographic measurements used to build the classification. The rural, as we have seen above, differs from the non-rural in so many different ways.

The census office has its own criteria for classifying localities as 'rural' but the units it uses are rather clumsy and it is not clear that this definition is sufficiently precise or sufficiently long lasting in its application to make it possible to undertake analysis of longitudinal changes in the characteristics of rural Britain.

Clearly there are two different strategies that can be used to measure such change over a period of time. One is to classify areas which are rural at the start of the period and to compare their population profile with that of the same set of areas at the end of a period. This method effectively identifies changes in the population make up of places that were at one time classified as rural.

An alternative is to allow neighbourhoods to form themselves into distinct clusters at the start of a period and again at the end of a period, identifying ones which are essentially rural in character at each point in time and then measuring changes in the profile of the category rather than that of its individual members. The first method identifies population changes for a fixed set of areas. The second method identifies population changes for what might be described as a functional set of areas. It is the second method that we now use to compare the profile of rural areas 40 years apart, in 1971 and 2011.

The earliest set of national classifications, as we have explained in Chapter 3, were built by the OPCS using information from the 1971 census. The particular classification on which the following results are based is one based on information for the 16,700 wards and parishes which contained 50 or more inhabitants. These were grouped into 36 clusters using a set of 40 census indicators. The 36 clusters were organized into a set of seven 'families', the third one of which, with 6.2 per cent of the national population, was described as 'Rural Areas'.

The most salient feature of rural Britain at that time, not surprisingly, was its reliance on agriculture. Over 59 per cent of all people employed in agriculture or fisheries lived in one of these rural clusters, a level nearly ten times the national average. Because of their comparative isolation, rural households were just over twice as likely than average to own two or more cars. But the influence of wealthy landowners and the unimproved condition of much rural housing was evident in the proportion of homes without an inside toilet and without a bath. This was not much lower than in areas of older terraced housing of a sort which, were it in Liverpool or other large cities, would have been designated fit only for slum clearance.

Other indicators that were distinctive of rural Britain were large numbers of semi-skilled workers, a categorization attributed to agricultural labourers, and of households renting unfurnished accommodation from private landlords, in many cases the very people who employed them. People living in rural Britain tended to have the most spacious houses and not to live in over-crowded conditions or in just one or two rooms.

In all these respects the rural Britain identified at the time of 1971 can be compared with a definition of rural Britain using the results of Experian's *Mosaic* classification built using the 2011 census. Though this classification was built at postcode level, the corresponding statistics are based on data published for census

EDs, a level intermediate between the postcode and the 1971 wards and parishes. To make the comparison we have defined as 'rural' not just the five *Mosaic* clusters falling into the Group *Rural Isolation* but two others as well, A07 *Semi-Rural Seclusion* and J56 *Tourist Attendants*. In total some 7.7 per cent of the British population fell within one of these seven 'rural' categories in 2011. This figure is then slightly higher than the 6.2 per cent in 1971 but not unreasonably so given the drift of population towards the countryside during the intervening 40 years.

Table 9.1   Change in Age Profile of Rural Britain, 1971–2011

| Age band | 1971 | 2011 | Change over time | Change from previous cohort |
|----------|------|------|------------------|------------------------------|
| 0–4      | 93   | 82   | −9               | –                            |
| 5–14     | 94   | 97   | +3               | +12                          |
| 15–24    | 89   | 74   | −15              | −18                          |
| 25–44    | 98   | 82   | −16              | −1                           |
| 45–64    | 105  | 131  | +26              | +42                          |
| 65+      | 117  | 106  | −11              | −37                          |

*Note*: Figures are normalized against the UK average, where a value of '100' indicates a level equivalent to the national average.

Table 9.1 suggests that whereas in 1971 most rural residents would have been born, brought up, lived and died in a rural community, by 2011 rural residency had for many more people become more a life-stage decision than an affirmation of identity. Young people, when they reached an age of independence, left the countryside for life in towns and cities. It had become increasingly common for families, once children had reached secondary school age, to move to the countryside for a better quality of life. Most stayed there for the rest of their lives but more detailed age break data shows that, compared to 1971, an increasing number now decide once they reach their 80s to move back into towns where they can be assured of better access to shops and medical facilities.

Table 9.2   Change in Occupational Status of Rural Britain, 1971–2011

| Social status | 1971 | 2011 | Change over time |
|---------------|------|------|------------------|
| Professionals and managers | 87  | 133 | +46 |
| Non-manual                 | 45  | 109 | +66 |
| Skilled manual             | 94  | 102 | +8  |
| Semi-skilled               | 153 | 62  | −91 |
| Unskilled                  | 83  | 72  | −11 |

That this migration of mature families has been led by the better-off is suggested by the statistics in Table 9.2. By 2011 rural Britain had become the preserve of the middle classes. It is not only in terms of occupations and earnings that rural Britain was becoming more affluent relative to other types of neighbourhood. Relative to other types of neighbourhood, households are even more likely to own a car than they were in 1971, even less likely to be unemployed and even more likely to live in a home with seven or more rooms. As in the past, rural Britain continues to attract people with the very highest incomes. Company directors – directors of large companies in particular – have replaced the pre-industrial landed gentry.

In 1971 Britain's rural communities were still relatively self-sufficient in employment and only loosely integrated within a larger travel to work zone. Farm managers and own-account farmers purchased services from local suppliers rather than distant businesses, they and their staff were served in village shops and they sent their children to village schools. Some people commuted to office jobs in larger towns but these were the exception rather than the rule. Today the commuter to a nearby town has displaced the local employee. Since 1971 it is in rural Britain that the proportion of people walking to work has dropped by the largest amount, from 75 per cent to 56 per cent of the national average by 2011. Compared with the national average even fewer than in 1971 rely on public transport.

On the other hand, the countryside has benefitted very considerably from the growth of non-farm self-employment, attracting footloose professionals able to serve their clients over the internet, notwithstanding problems with rural broadband, and technical consultants needing a UK base between foreign assignments.

**Table 9.3**   Change in Housing Tenure of Rural Britain, 1971–2011

| House tenure | 1971 | 2011 | Change over time |
|---|---|---|---|
| Owner-occupier | 114 | 115 | +1 |
| Social housing tenant | 61 | 27 | −34 |
| Private renter | 131 | 117 | −14 |

It is not just occupational change that has placed pressures on workers with more modest skills whose forebears would have been employed on local country estates. Their role is compounded by the progressive diminution of what was, even in 1971, a very modest stock of social housing. Most rural settlements contained a small development of social housing built between the wars. But since 1971 much of this has been lost under 'right-to-buy' legislation and it is very rare that any more is added – councils no longer seeming able to add new stock other than on a volume basis. Though properties are still available for private rent, housing pressures in rural Britain are exacerbated by it having seven times the average proportion of second homes. Some of the results of this are shown in Table 9.3.

Once it would have only been the children of professional classes who left the countryside on leaving school. Now rural Britain has become a very lonely place for single non-pensioners, whether young, divorced or widowed. For the younger singles on lower incomes the local market town has become a much more affordable and convivial a place to live.

## Using *Mosaic* to identify the behavioural traits of rural inhabitants

In earlier chapters we have made reference to the existence of a profile library; a database containing many hundreds of behaviours that have been cross tabulated by Type of neighbourhood. The 600 or so profiles in this library make it possible to depict the attitudes and behaviours which distinguish people who live in rural Britain. These profiles are not based on responses from rural local authorities or even rural wards and parishes. Here we are grouping people by the character of the individual postcodes they live in, units typically containing 20 or so households, and which are identified as the most distinctively rural with reference to the wide range of indicators used to build the *Mosaic* classification.

For many urban dwellers tempted to move to a home in the country, the idea of living in a community where neighbours know and look out for each other is a powerful attraction. This attraction is something rather different from conviviality – that can be enjoyed in the *Bohemian Melting Pot* of an early version of *Mosaic* – since it also involves elements both of safety and physical separation from the supposed disorderliness of urban society. That this is not mere imagination is confirmed by statistics from the BCS, which consistently show rural respondents being far more likely to agree that theirs is a 'very nice place to live' and that they and their neighbours 'look out for each other'. These statistics are consistent across all five of the categories that make up the Group *Rural Isolation*.

Thus, people are 2.28 times more likely than in urban areas to say that they are not worried about the risk of having their cars stolen [228[1]]. Despite the absence of street lighting, twice as many say they feel safe walking alone after dark [199]. They are among the least likely to cite drugs as being a serious problem [36] or to be aware of domestic violence [32]. If they are to encounter criminality it is most likely to be the result of a false sense of security when they fail to secure their car in an (urban) car park [142] or look after their wallet in an (urban) entertainment centre [209].

For many people of course, the attraction of a home in the countryside is a close-ness to nature, which is why respondents in the Group *Rural Isolation* come out as the highest in citing country pursuits [248], birdwatching [226], pets [133] and gardening [135] as interests. These cultural preoccupations, as one might expect, are reflected in the charities that residents in such neighbourhoods are most likely to support, those relating to birds [180], wildlife and the environment [162].

Contrary to old-fashioned assumptions about the parochial nature of rural Britain, *Rural Isolation* offers a particular attraction to people interested not just in walking but also hiking, motoring, sailing and skiing [154]. Whilst the majority may be happy to potter around in their gardens and walk their pets, the modern countryside provides an environment suitable for more dedicated outdoor enthusiasts and endurance fanatics. It is not clear how much this is the result of differential in-migration or of the lifestyle opportunities presented by access to so much open space. Data from the University and Colleges Admissions Service (UCAS) reveal that children brought up in rural areas are the most likely to choose veterinary science or agriculture as their preferred subject of study when they apply to university [192].

As the source of much of Britain's food, Britain's countryside is associated with fresh produce and healthy eating. No other *Mosaic* Group equals *Rural Isolation* in its disdain for white bread or in reporting such high levels of purchase of wholemeal [133] or granary [143] loaves. People are not in such a hurry that they are do not have the time to make freshly ground coffee [131] but, if they do use instant, it is more likely to be decaffeinated [131]. They are more likely to be heavy consumers of yoghurt [131] than cream and are heavy drinkers of cider [172] rather than draught lager [75]. A result of their disinclination to eat processed foods means that residents in *Rural Isolation* are among the least likely to buy a ready meal [70] or, in part as a result of lack of access, to use a take away [42] or to be a heavy user of a fast food restaurant [16].

Supplemented no doubt by the produce of local gardens and orchards, this group is among the most avid purchasers of fresh vegetables [117] and fresh fruit [114]. By contrast more money is spent on frozen meat [115] than in other *Mosaic* Type, no doubt from the freezer cabinet of the local supermarket residents visit, perhaps on a weekly basis. Partly for this reason and partly on account of the disproportionate size and number of outbuildings of homes in this *Mosaic* Type, residents are among the most likely to own a stand-alone freezer.

Thomas Hardy was one of the most assiduous chroniclers of rural habits and it is the view of P.N. Furbank in his introduction to a Pan Macmillan edition of *Tess of the D'Urbervilles* that he took great delight in recording the self-sufficiency of rural people:

He (Hardy) is fascinated by contrivance: how exactly Angel contrives to carry the dairymaids across the flooded road, or how the weary Fanny Robin ingeniously contrives to employ a dog as a crutch; how Clym as a boy makes pigments out of flower-pollen, and the gamblers in the *Return of the Native* use glow-worms as lamps. In a rural existence the suggestion is, everything has to be made out of the material at hand. Not only is this true in practical matters, it is equally true in moral ones. Eustacia has to construct a romantic lover out of the poor material of Wildeve, who is all that there is available; and Tess, rebuffed by church and society, improves her own baptismal ceremony for her dying baby. Out of the given materials, however unpromising, these underprivileged humans make up complete lives, complete self-expression.

Evidence from the profile library suggests that the countryside is still a heartland of self-sufficiency and self-control. What people achieve is largely due to their own efforts, not the consequence of chance. This predisposition is reflected in the low level of support for Labour [66], even after allowing for social class. When giving to charity, rural Britain is relatively unsympathetic to those who might be expected to help themselves. Little is given to charities for the homeless [84], for Aids [57] or for mental health. People are more willing to donate for disaster relief [150] than to support human rights [84].

That it is a common view that advancement comes through one's own endeavours rather than through a lucky break is supported by disinclination towards betting [49] and bingo [39], neither of which are popular rural pastimes. *Rural Isolation* is among the most sceptical about astrology [53] and shows little interest in computer games [63] and fantasy and sci-fi [67].

Conservative social attitudes are reflected in the disproportionate lack of interest in what may be perceived to be ephemeral concerns with hair and beauty and with fashion. In environments where very many people live in old buildings, it is understandable that they should tend to be more interested in the legacy of the past, in antiques [178] and visiting historic properties owned by the National Trust. Curiously the one respect in which rural residents, or at least their younger members, appear not to be mindful is a disproportionate reluctance to purchase condoms [69] and, surprisingly given the social profile of the area, a higher than average level of teenage pregnancy [104].

How far people's leisure interests cause them to move to the countryside and how far their distinctive interests reflect their greater opportunity to indulge in new activities – and less in old ones – is very difficult to judge. From lifestyle data it does seem that newcomers are willing to sacrifice networks of association based on common professional experience or political views for ones much more based on physical proximity. Likewise, emotions tend to be invested in hobbies and interests of a practical nature rather than introspection, an orientation which is reflected in choices for charitable giving. Whilst communitarian values of inter-dependency are expressed in terms of practical assistance in meeting the day-to-day needs of people who are known, lack of day-to-day experience of the diversity of sufferings associated with the city does appear to inure residents from a sense of responsibility for those who, it is felt, should apply to their lives the degree of self-reliance which is taken for granted in a rural community.

## Note

[1] The figures in brackets from now on indicate how the response of rural people compares with that of the population as a whole – a value of 100 indicating an average response to the question, one of 200 a level twice the national average and one of 50 one half of the national average.

# 10

# COASTAL COMMUNITIES
## All Victims of Low-Cost
## Airline Travel?

To Lyme they were to go – Charles, Mary, Anne, Henrietta, Louisa and Captain Wentworth… After securing accommodations, and ordering a dinner at one of the inns, the next thing to be done was unquestionably to walk direct down to the sea. They were to come too late in the year for any amusement or variety which Lyme, as a public place, might offer; the rooms were shut up, the lodgers almost all gone, scarcely any family but the residents left – and as there is nothing to admire in the buildings themselves, the remarkable situation of the town, the principal street almost hurrying to the water, the walk to the Cobb, skirting around the pretty little bay, which in the season is animated with bathing machines and company, the Cobb itself, its old wonders and new improvements, with the very beautiful line of cliffs stretching out to the east of the town, are what the stranger's eye will seek.

Visit to Lyme Regis in Jane Austen's *Persuasion* (1817)

## The different types of coastal neighbourhood

The focus of this chapter is on coastal communities[1] many of which are captured by the following five *Mosaic* Types listed in Table 5.4.

| Code | *Mosaic* Type label | UK % | Top local authorities |
|------|--------------------|------|----------------------|
| J51 | *Sepia Memories* | 0.8 | Christchurch |
| J53 | *High Spending Elders* | 1.5 | Christchurch |
| J54 | *Bungalow Retirement* | 1.3 | Tendring (Clacton) |
| J56 | *Tourist Attendants* | 0.3 | Penwith (Penzance) |
| D25 | *Town Centre Refuge* | 0.3 | Hastings |

Jane Austen, William Thackeray, Charles Dickens – in all three of their works, visits to the seaside, such as this account of the Musgroves to Lyme Regis in *Persuasion*, have a transformative effect on their characters. From the eighteenth century, drinking sea water, and then sea bathing, were believed to have curative powers and, following the patronage of Brighton by the Prince Regent later George IV, a sojourn at a coastal 'watering place' conferred a social distinction previously accorded to a visit to a spa. But even in Jane Austen's time different resorts had developed what we would now call different brand 'values'. What her characters get up to in Brighton, Ramsgate and Lyme Regis all subtly reflect these resorts' different reputations for different forms of pleasure and relaxation (Mullan, 2012: 91).

During the 200 years since *Persuasion* was written, coastal communities have become even more variegated in terms of their attractions and reputations. In recent years there has been a growing awareness of the legacy problems associated with these communities, particularly in relation to low educational attainment, low wages and seasonal unemployment. But some of the distinctions *Mosaic* makes, as for example between D25 *Town Centre Refuge*, J54 *Bungalow Retirement* and J56 *Tourist Attendants* neighbourhoods, is a salutary reminder that many seaside towns are home to just as diverse a set of neighbourhoods and residents as their inland counterparts. Consider how different are the cultures of the following two Types of neighbourhood, as described in the *Mosaic* documentation, both of which are found predominantly in coastal communities:

### J53 *High Spending Elders*

In earlier generations the epithet 'energetic' would seldom have been used to describe pensioners who, on their retirement, were expected to spend their declining health sitting in deckchairs in quiet seaside 'resorts'. Today a more healthy and a more demanding generation of empty nesters often see the immediate post-retirement years as an exciting period of liberation from work and family, a period which enables them to re-engage with a wider variety of leisure activities which may have had to be deferred during their hectic working lives. This, together with the advent of the car, has opened up a whole new range of possible retirement locations for the wealthy and healthy younger pensioner.

Besides old coastal favourites such as Christchurch, Worthing and Bexhill, these neighbourhoods are increasingly located in inland regions of high landscape value, in the Cotswolds, in the beautiful stone villages in the west of Dorset, in Georgian Bath or on the shores of Lake Windermere. These prestige areas are ones which retirees share with wealthy local people many of whom will have moved into them only in later middle age. At the top end of the market these will be areas of large detached houses, often of some architectural merit, employing traditional building materials, which were originally constructed to meet the needs of a regional industrial elite. Whilst such a profile may adequately describe more recent choice destinations for the prosperous active elderly, many premium seaside suburban locations continue to fall into this category in select seaside 'watering places' such as Frinton and Budleigh Salterton, which host international croquet tournaments, as well as in the larger retirement centres such as Eastbourne and Bournemouth.

Once established in these neighbourhoods, many of these new wealthy retirees will set about joining local historical associations and amenity groups as well as bridge circles and golf clubs and start planning overseas visits to distant relatives they have not seen for years. Many will make an attack on overgrown gardens or draw up plans for upgrading their new residences to meet the needs of an increasing number of young grandchildren.

In these neighbourhoods it will be assumed, often correctly, that the people are married rather than single or co-habiting, that they own their homes outright, have a private index linked pension, have grown-up children, are in good enough health to drive a car and have private medical insurance.

### D25 *Town Centre Refuge*

Whereas the central areas of large cities are mostly surrounded by rows of Victorian terraces or council flats, the areas separating the commercial districts of smaller towns and seaside resorts are more likely to consist of small rented flats and big old houses many of which have fallen into multiple occupation. Particularly in declining seaside resorts, *Town Centre Refuge* is comprised of young adults on low incomes and divorced people, with significant minorities living in hostels and in shared accommodation. Though many of these people were born in the town, such neighbourhoods are likely to accommodate people from surrounding middle class communities who, for one reason or another, can't or prefer not to engage in mainstream consumerist lifestyles. *Town Centre Refuge* is in certain locations accommodation of last resort attracting an aimless population many of whom drift in and out of employment. Particularly where they are located by the coast (though not in inland market towns) such neighbourhoods are also selected as locations for accommodating asylum seekers and may acquire a reputation among local residents for drugs and prostitution, despite the fact that many of them border on areas of good quality housing. Transient lifestyles lead to higher levels of crime in the more suburban areas of smaller towns and many perpetrators are petty criminals living locally. It is in these areas that noise is often cited as a source of environmental nuisance. The population of *Town Centre Refuge* is mostly made up of young single people, a large number of whom are still in their late teens and many more in their 20s, most in partnerships of varying degrees of durability. There are fewer people in older working groups but often a substantial number of very elderly people accommodated in the larger houses that have been converted by local authorities to provide sheltered accommodation for those on lower incomes.

Catering for the needs of weekenders and summer tourists is the major source of employment in seaside resorts whilst in inland centres many young people serve in local shops. Levels of unemployment are well above the national average and relatively few people own a car.

What residents of the types *High Spending Elders* and *Town Centre Refuge* have in common is that both are more common in coastal resorts than in any other part of Britain. But there the similarity ends. From Table 10.1 it is evident that there is little else these two manifestations of the British seaside have in common, at least in terms of demographics, values and behaviours.

So great are these differences that it is difficult to sustain the argument that there should be a uniform set of prescriptive policies that are appropriate for all those coastal communities which have traditionally relied on attracting retirees and summer visitors.

One explanation of why the social structure of seaside communities is so much more varied than that of former coalfield communities or textile towns is that different seaside resorts developed during different periods of time to satisfy the needs of a very different clientele. The reasons why people visit the seaside, the types of facility that attract them and the way they fill their leisure time are all in a constant state of flux. Some people visit with the aim of improving their physical or spiritual well-being, others in the pursuit of hedonist enjoyment. For others still the seaside offers a quite different form of escape – one of rest, quietude and reflection.

Which of these motivations will be uppermost in visitors' minds clearly depends on their life-stage – are they young and single, do they have children or have they reached retirement age? This will have a bearing on the length of time they stay and, if it is for more than a day, on the form of accommodation which the local market has developed to meet their needs and budgets. Change in the overall

**Table 10.1** Indices of Behavioural Differences Between Two Types of Neighbourhood Common in Coastal Communities (UK Average = 100)

| Behaviour | J53 *High Spending Elders* | D25 *Town Centre Refuge* |
|---|---|---|
| Shareholdings: high value | 358 | 18 |
| Type of residence: Detached | 280 | 29 |
| Read: *Daily Telegraph* | 282 | 104 |
| Shop at Waitrose | 227 | 69 |
| Hold equity or share ISA | 208 | 83 |
| Household income: £50,000+ | 152 | 46 |
| Interest: Gardening | 132 | 65 |
| Interest: Grandchildren | 135 | 74 |
| Read: *Guardian* | 104 | 161 |
| Reason for supermarket choice: Opening hours | 65 | 131 |
| Interest: Rock music | 47 | 150 |
| Employment status: Unemployed | 49 | 155 |
| Value of County Court Judgments: £1–1,000 | 23 | 137 |
| Interest: Personal astrology | 40 | 173 |
| Employment: Hotels and catering | 93 | 238 |
| Support: Aids charities | 47 | 202 |
| Type or residence: Converted or shared house | 57 | 519 |

balance of these motivations necessarily calls for change in the way individual resorts promote themselves. Change often requires new uses to be found for obsolete forms of accommodation and involves new demographic groups colonizing legacy forms of residential neighbourhood.

Earlier chapters have interpreted patterns of residential structure of British cities, towns and villages in terms of long-term changes, for example the growth of the liberal intelligentsia, the decline of heavy industry, the arrival of immigrant communities and the attraction of rural lifestyles to the urban middle classes. Neighbourhoods in coastal communities have been no less affected by changes in technology and consumer tastes. Developments in transport technology, longer life expectancy due to advances in public medicine and the demise of the British Empire have all had an impact. So too, in a less heralded way, have changes in the level of engagement visitors want to have with the local population.

During his tenure of 10 Downing Street in the 1960s, Harold Wilson was wont to holiday each summer in the Scilly Isles. The Scillies formed part of the parliamentary constituency of St Ives. Had his preference been for a seaside holiday in a resort represented by a Labour MP his choice would have been extremely limited, even after the Labour landslide of 1966.

One option might have been Falmouth, which at that time was joined with the former tin-mining communities of Redruth and Camborne to create the Falmouth and Camborne constituency, or Sheringham or Cromer in North Norfolk, which returned a Labour MP thanks to the local strength of the National Union of Agricultural Workers. Other than these, most Labour politicians visited the seaside only when it was the turn of Blackpool, Bournemouth or Brighton to host the annual party conference.

By the time of Labour's landslide victory of 1997 Tony Blair, were he to have holidayed by the British seaside rather than in the villas his political or personal friends lent his family in Tuscany or Barbados, would have been spoiled for choice. During the years since 1966 the Conservatives had succumbed to defeat not just in Blackpool and Brighton. Voters in Weymouth, Hove, Hastings, Ramsgate, Yarmouth, Cleethorpes, Scarborough, Morecambe, Rhyl, Colwyn Bay, Llandudno and Tenby all returned Labour MPs to Westminster. Those living in Torquay, Eastbourne, Southport, Weston-super-Mare, the Isle of Wight, Teignmouth, Ilfracombe, Newquay, Falmouth and St Ives (including the Scillies) had at various times been represented by Liberal Democrat MPs and in Frinton and Clacton by the country's only UKIP MP.

Just as the emergence of the geodemographic category *Liberal Opinion* has transformed the electoral complexion of established middle class neighbourhoods in Britain's largest cities, so too have the changing tastes of the British holidaymaker transformed the electoral complexion of Britain's Victorian seaside resorts.

## A historical explanation of coastal diversity

The term 'residential' appears as a critical term in the categorization of British parliamentary constituencies in the compilation of British election statistics between 1963 and 1992 (Crewe et al., 1995). The use of this term to differentiate seats from other categories such as 'rural' and 'urban' highlights the importance that the middle classes once attached to living in a community physically separated from centres of industrial and commercial employment. Maybe some of the motivation was also physical separation from the types of people who relied on these forms of employment. It may have been the healing properties of salt water that made the seaside a place to *visit* initially. But from late Victorian times it was its physical separation from areas of industrial activity that made a resort a desirable place to *live* in and, even more, to *retire* to. These became no longer just places which people visited for a day or when on holiday. Such were their supposed health-giving properties that it was to institutions in such places that young boys were sent to boarding school[2] and infirm old people to recuperate.

In time the economic and population growth of many of these towns became as dependent on supporting their retired populations as on the servicing of temporary visitors. But the two were not necessarily unrelated. It was understandable that people should retire to the places with which they had formed a strong emotional attachment during many happy years of holidaying there. Were the Scillies not so inaccessible the Wilsons might well have chosen them as their retirement home.

In due course, the precise location of these two functions within a resort began to separate. People who sought fun in Blackpool during their working lives chose a quiet street in adjacent Lytham St Annes when they retired. Bexhill, which for some reason was favoured by returnees from India, provided a similar role in respect of Hastings. So too did Herne Bay in relation to Margate, and Frinton in relation to Clacton. The geodemographic category K56 *Tourist Attendants* – neighbourhoods which serviced visitors – would be found in the same towns, though seldom in the same wards, as K54 *Bungalow Retirement*, illustrated in Figure 10.1, or K53 *High Spending Elders* to which more well-heeled visitors later retired.

Nottingham Road, Clacton on Sea, Essex, CO15 5PG

Hazeldown Road, Teignmouth, Devon, TQ14 8QR

Fife Road, Herne Bay, Kent, CT6 7RE

Haysom Close, New Milton, Dorset, BH25 6PN

**Figure 10.1**   *J45 Bungalow Retirement*

The Blairs were typical of many British families whose response to the vagaries of the British summer weather and variable quality of the British dining experience was to head for the airport rather than, as earlier generations would have done, the railway station, the coach pick-up point or the motorway access junction. But it would be an over-simplification to suggest that the growth of Mediterranean and long-haul holidays was the sole reason for the changing geodemographics of the British seaside resort.

Geodemographic change has been most striking in what from the time of the Napoleonic Wars until the 1870s were described as 'watering places' and more recently as 'seaside resorts'. Destinations on the railway map of Britain, these were places important enough to have achieved the status of a municipal borough or urban district if not that of a county borough. Their councils competed for custom by the construction of sea-front esplanades, often enhanced by shelters for the elderly against inclement weather, and well-tended horticultural displays. Commercial enterprises obtained licences to hire deck chairs to the less active and to attract younger family members with Punch and Judy, donkey rides and ice creams. The municipal bus company offered tours on open-top buses. Councillors in the larger resorts agonized over the cost of restoring the pier whilst at the same time encouraging 'attractions' which could compete with Margate's 'Dreamland' and Blackpool's 'Tower'. Catering for visitors was a relatively labour-intensive activity in places of this sort.

The decline in the residential status of this sort of resort, and especially the larger ones, arose not just from competition from the Mediterranean but from the increased privatization of the holiday experience. Whereas in the early twentieth century the journey there would have been by collective forms of transport, private railway companies and coach firms, the advent of the car increasingly liberated the tourist from the formalities, inflexibility and cost of the traditional resort holiday experience and made it possible during the family holiday to explore smaller, initially less visited settlements, bays and coves. Whereas accommodation might previously have been provided on a weekly half-board basis, car-borne tourists increasingly sought accommodation in farm-stays and bed and breakfasts or toured with a caravan or their own tent, preferring to manage their own itineraries and save money by preparing their own meals.

An increasingly common means by which the middle classes achieved this independence and flexibility was through the rental of a holiday cottage. Those with sufficient capital by-passed this practice altogether by buying a second home, those of more modest means provided opportunities for developers of residential caravan sites and holiday parks to build and offer private chalets for sale.

The type of holiday experience that became most popular in any specific holiday region was often determined by the topography and geology of the local area. For families with young children a condition of a successful holiday would be tidal rock-pools surrounding a safe, sandy beach where a seasonal shop would sell buckets and spades, plastic balls and fishing nets. Pebbled shorelines, shunned by families with young children, became sanctuaries for older couples with grown-up children, anxious to maintain physical distance as well as social distinction between themselves and the less sophisticated 'trippers'. Hence *High Spending Elders* selected Budleigh Salterton over Exmouth, Frinton over Clacton and Sheringham over Cromer.

Places with extensive sand dunes, such as Perranporth, Hayle and Wells-next-the-Sea, specialized in the development of holiday camps and residential chalets whilst rocky cliffs protecting good surfing beaches, such as Polzeath, David Cameron's holiday favourite, and St Davids offered favourable returns to investors in holiday rentals. Small towns beside once sleepy estuaries, such as Padstow, Fowey, Salcombe, Dartmouth and Aldeburgh, became the preserve of the boating fraternity. A local yacht club and what to others seemed an absurdly over-priced clothing store signified a neighbourhood that had achieved the status of a *Summer Playground*.

The geodemographic types J56 *Tourist Attendants* and J53 *High Spending Elders* tended to cluster in places that, up until the local government reorganization in 1974, had the designation urban district or municipal borough (rather than rural district). These were run by councils which imposed higher standards of building control and provided their residents, albeit at higher cost, with higher standards of service such as street lighting and roadside pavements. Many of the places where the geodemographic categories *Bungalow Retirement* and, from an earlier version of *Mosaic, Rural Retirement Mix* are more common are in former 'rural districts', in places such as Milford-on-Sea in Hampshire, Jaywick in Essex or Peacehaven near Brighton, a retirement resort originally established for the benefit of recuperating veterans of World War I. It was in these places that developers could create new homes at the lowest costs. Predominantly bungalow developments, these places attracted people disenchanted by the growing diversity of big cities and by the decline in civility they felt was occurring in the suburban neighbourhoods in which they had been brought up.

Whilst when they were first built these estates would have attracted retirees from Conservative-supporting suburbs of large cities, newer arrivals are of a social class and geodemographic category much less likely to exhibit strong political partisanship and between 1997 and 2015 were easy prey for populist campaigning by Liberal Democrats and UKIP.

In recent years, changes in retirees' locational preferences has contributed to the decline in the status of these locations. In the days they were built, retired people were expected to be less physically mobile and less self-supporting than they are today. A small garden, the absence of stairs and proximity to newsagents, grocery shops, a pharmacy and a doctor's surgery would have been strong selling points for a bungalow in Herne Bay or Bridlington. They still are, but only for some, certainly not for as many retired people as it used to be and least of all for the upper middle classes.

Many contemporary retirees, who like to think of themselves as fit and active, don't want to be reminded of their advancing years by living in a neighbourhood dominated by the elderly and often by the infirm elderly, particularly where the neighbourhood has no claim to architectural or cultural distinction. As we showed in the previous chapter, down-sizers in recent years have been increasingly willing to exchange proximity to the supposedly health-enhancing properties of the British coastline for the heritage buildings and the imagined community of a country village at least until they reach a riper age. In the past 20 years, geodemographic classification has also charted the increased disposition of better-off retirees to choose more urban inland locations which enjoy a historical and cultural legacy, places such as Bath, Cheltenham, Chester, Chichester and York.

Cheap foreign holidays and increased car ownership has presented the larger seaside resorts such as Blackpool, Margate, Hastings and Torquay with a serious problem – what to be done with an over-supply of spaces in traditional boarding houses. These are seldom suited for conversion to family dwellings and are buildings for which there are few obvious alternative uses. With the fall in the construction of new social housing, a new role has been discovered for many of the former boarding house areas, expressed in the category D25 *Town Centre Refuge*. This Type of neighbourhood is often one of last resort for people on various forms of benefit, many of whom lack support from an extended family. Substance abuse, alcoholism, litter and lack of maintenance, which are common in these neighbourhoods, exert their influence on a wider geographical area, resulting in reduced house prices, the flight of the upwardly aspirational and, in many instances, deficiencies in local political leadership.

In 2012, according to a government survey, Blackpool scored lowest on an overall 'Happiness Index', notwithstanding the presence of its 'Pleasure Beach'. In 2013, based on the percentage of its pupils achieving five GCSEs at level C or above (including Maths and English), Blackpool performed better only than Knowsley among England's 150 Local Education Authorities. In 2017 it was reported to have taken over from Merthyr Tydfil as the town with the highest proportion of the UK working age population on incapacity benefit.

By 2012 this manifestation of disadvantage had become sufficiently visible for the government to set up the Coastal Communities Fund to promote tourism through the refurbishment of coastal heritage infrastructure. The Turner Gallery in Margate and the Tate in St Ives are examples of attempts at coastal community regeneration which, in Margate, has already led to some improvement, if only of a highly localized area. Indeed, investment in new railway infrastructure may have done more for Margate. In Hastings, property prices had fallen so far below those of neighbouring towns that a sizeable bohemian artist population has now established itself. The town's transformation is now believed to be self-sustaining.

At the other end of the social spectrum is J53 *Childfree Serenity*, typically privately owned developments of high specification flats set in landscaped gardens. It attracts a wealthy, childless population which values quietness, order and security. This Type of neighbourhood clusters in very specific locations around the coast, in the western part of Southend, in Hove and on the pine-clad sandy heaths separating Bournemouth and Poole. Each of these enclaves has a very significant Jewish population, an ethnic group which, it seems, is culturally disposed to the lifestyle of living in privately owned apartments within a secure development.

# Regional differences in the presence of different types of coastal community

Geodemographics points to a considerable divergence between northern and southern seaside communities. Taking just post towns with more than 20,000 inhabitants in 2011, we find that six of the ten which have been most successful in attracting wealthy retirees, *Golden Retirement* in the parlance of the 2009 version of *Mosaic*, are in and around Bournemouth. Uniquely in Britain, this area of sandy beaches has discovered a strategy for avoiding the decline normally associated with large numbers of day-trippers. Three others, Bexhill, Eastbourne and Worthing, also face the English Channel. The only substantial northern coastal community to have retained an ability to attract wealthy retirees is Southport.

The degree to which day-trippers deter wealthy older people from retiring to a resort is evident in those coastal communities where there is an almost complete absence of *Golden Retirement*. Other than Southsea, these are all in the north, places such as Blackpool, Rhyl, Cleethorpes and Skegness, which, being unable to attract middle class retirees, are all in serious decline.

Lower-middle income families continue to retire to coastal communities both in the north and the south, settling in J45 *Bungalow Quietude*. These postcodes are most often found in secondary locations and in smaller, less busy resorts, for instance in the coastal communities surrounding Blackpool such as Lytham St Annes, Thornton Cleveleys and Poulton-le-Fylde. Bridlington, Cleethorpes, Skegness, Clacton and Rhyl still contain a large amount of housing stock of this type. Unlike *Golden Retirement*, which attracts long distance retirees from other regions of the UK, new retirees to *Bungalow Quietude* will discover, if they did not know it in advance, that many of their neighbours have made the move from the same city, from Liverpool to Rhyl, from Leeds to Bridlington, Sheffield to Cleethorpes and Nottingham to Skegness.

Clacton, Bridlington and Skegness also have significant developments of what in 2009 *Mosaic* parlance is referred to as *Beachcombers* – typically

**Table 10.2** Resorts by Different Types of Coastal Neighbourhood

| Post town | County | Number of adults 2011 | % Golden Retirement | % Bungalow Quietude | % Beachcombers |
|---|---|---|---|---|---|
| New Milton | Dorset | 20,417 | **21.11** | 4.74 | 9.83 |
| Sidmouth | Devon | 13,349 | **23.85** | 2.02 | 15.40 |
| Frinton-on-Sea | Essex | 10,407 | **16.06** | 16.46 | 12.74 |
| Budleigh Salterton | Devon | 5,536 | **28.94** | 1.21 | 19.74 |
| Aldeburgh | Dorset | 2,143 | **23.47** | 0.00 | 39.15 |
| Clacton-on-Sea | Essex | 59,246 | 1.45 | **12.70** | 11.47 |
| Prestatyn | Clwyd | 16,742 | 0.48 | **15.92** | 2.53 |
| Abergele | Clwyd | 14,840 | 3.18 | **15.75** | 4.45 |
| Birchington | Kent | 9,699 | 9.82 | **13.82** | 11.10 |
| Walton-on-the-Naze | Essex | 5,769 | 1.65 | **27.53** | 19.33 |
| Mablethorpe | Lincolnshire | 11,140 | 0.91 | 8.30 | **50.34** |
| Winchelsea | East Sussex | 1,929 | 1.14 | 0.00 | **57.44** |
| Salcombe | Devon | 1,892 | 0.00 | 0.00 | **64.59** |
| Aberdovey | Gwynedd | 729 | 0.00 | 0.00 | **74.62** |
| Bamburgh | Northumberland | 380 | 0.00 | 0.00 | **93.95** |
| UK average | | | 0.56 | 1.44 | 0.67 |

neighbourhoods whose economies rely on the summer servicing of visitors. *Beachcombers* make up an even more important part of the population of smaller coastal communities, such as Dartmouth and Newquay, that provide the infrastructure to accommodate weekly or fortnightly vacations, not merely the amusements that entertain day or weekend visitors. Table 10.2 shows that the towns which serve these different segments of the tourism and retirement market are situated on very different parts of the coastline.

## Neighbourhood segregation within coastal communities

Morecambe and Margate are as physically distant as it is possible for two English resorts to be. Nevertheless they have had similar histories and now confront similar economic challenges. Both resorts were to become popular destinations for the industrial working class once they were connected by rail to London (in the case of Margate) and Bradford (in the case of Morecambe). Whilst citizens of Leeds looked to Scarborough and citizens of Lancashire to Blackpool, the rail link via Settle and Carnforth was particularly successful in linking Bradford to what became known affectionately as 'Bradford-on-Sea' and, on the northern shore of Morecambe Bay, to Grange-over-Sands (Figure 10.2).

**Figure 10.2** Morecambe, 1960s

Morecambe and Margate both expanded during the second half of the nine-teenth century in response to the development of the railway network; and both specialized in serving the needs of a very specific clientele – the urban working class – with a very similar leisure proposition: donkey rides, deck chairs, a pier, amusement arcades, souvenir shops and light entertainment. It is therefore not surprising that the residential pattern of the two towns developed in a similar way.

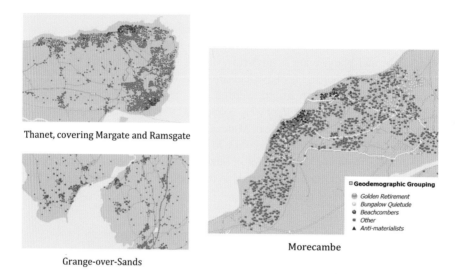

Thanet, covering Margate and Ramsgate

Grange-over-Sands

Morecambe

**Figure 10.3** *Mosaic* 2009, Maps of Morecambe, Thanet and Grange-over-Sands

Both towns contain a legacy of high density streets of three- or four-storey terraced houses, each of which was built to be managed by a single proprietor to provide weekly board for the visitors that arrived at the town's nearby railway station. Close to the railway station and the town centre, typically within a couple of min-utes' walk of the seafront and the various entertainments the resorts used to offer, these now form an area described by *Mosaic* 2009 as *Anti-Materialists*. Welfare payments form the principal source of financial support for many residents who occupy individual rooms or small flats in houses in multiple occupation. These neighbourhoods fulfil a function very similar to that of the rooming house areas identified in the 1971 Liverpool study report described in Chapter 3. The pres-ence of a cluster of neighbourhoods of this sort deters better-off visitors from the town centre and the well-educated young people who have been so instrumental in re-populating the central areas of other British cities.

Such residents incur substantial costs not just to central government but to local councils, generating disproportionate use of the social, health and police services and contributing to the low average levels of educational attainment which currently distinguish Britain's seaside communities. A map of Thanet shows a similar cluster of postcodes in the centre of Ramsgate, a town which in the nineteenth century appealed to a similar clientele as Margate. This, and what is described in what follows, is shown in Figure 10.3.

By contrast *Bungalow Quietude* occupies sites further back from the seafront in streets from a later stage of each town's development. Located further from attractions and amenities, land in these locations was less valuable. In both Morecambe and Thanet these streets were built shortly before the introduction of planning policies limiting the further expansion of the town and often lie close to open land. These postcodes tend to be tightly clustered, physically separated from other geodemographic categories, and not the product of opportunistic infill.

Though in their heyday there may have been many privileged neighbourhoods in both Morecambe and Thanet, today *Golden Retirement* is virtually absent from both, other than along the seafront where it takes advantage of direct views out to sea. Rather than retiring to Margate or Ramsgate the wealthy retired prefer to live in smaller, more characterful resorts such as the St Peters area of Broadstairs and Whitstable. Wealthy retirees from Bradford are no longer found in Morecambe itself but in Arnside further north and, more particularly, in Grange-over-Sands, a retirement community whose muddy foreshore and sea-front railway track provides an effective deterrent to would-be users of buckets, spades and fishing nets. Morecambe's seafront illuminations are just seven miles by sea, over 20 miles by road but light years away in terms of geodemographic character.

The holiday parks, bed and breakfasts, inns and restaurants that cater for the holiday trade are today situated some way away from the major seaside resorts and are particularly associated with the geodemographic Type *Beachcombers*. This is almost wholly absent from the maps of Thanet and Morecambe but present in large numbers in the small coastal communities around Grange-over-Sands and on the eastern bank of the Kent estuary.

## The impact of changes in transport technology

Changes in taste and technology, particularly the growth in car ownership, have resulted in a level of demographic and economic change in coastal communities which is arguably at least as significant as that experienced by inner cities and the countryside. The demand for what resorts traditionally used to offer has been affected by changes in technology which have brought a foreign holiday within the financial reach of members of almost every social class. More predictable weather and the provision of different and more appealing leisure activities have led to the offerings of many traditional British resorts seeming tired by comparison. This decline has resulted in places such as Margate and Morecambe appealing even less to their traditional clientele, as the shops and amusements they offer become geared towards the requirements of visitors with ever lower incomes and ever more modest tastes, those who cannot afford a foreign holiday. As the number of boarding house proprietors declines and the number of amusement arcade attendants grows, it is not unreasonable to suppose that the decline in the social status of visitors itself contributes to a parallel decline in the social status of the occupations of those who serve them, this being reflected in the long-term shift in voting behaviour.

However, there are many other social changes which have played an equally significant role even if their effects are less spatially concentrated. These too are picked up by the growth of categories such as *Summer Playgrounds* and *Rural Retirement Mix*. Besides preferring the more reliable weather of a Mediterranean resort, social trends are resulting in visitors looking for holiday arrangements that provide greater scope for freedom and greater value for money. Not only is the private car a more convenient means of transporting the paraphernalia needed to enjoy a holiday at the seaside, it liberates the visitor from reliance on whatever food it is the custom of the half-board or full-board establishment to serve. It allows greater freedom to visit attractions – the Eden Project or the variety of safari parks that have been established in the past 50 years being good examples – which, unlike the Blackpool Pleasure Beach, no longer need to be located within walking distance of the places where people stay.

The independence offered by the private car also meshes with the increased preference for natural rather than artificial attractions, of the open countryside, heritage villages and off-the-beaten track fishing villages such as Port Isaac featured in the TV series *Doc Martin*, which could otherwise be visited only as part of an organized coach excursion. As a result, serving the needs of visitors has become an increasingly important contributor to the economy of the geodemographic Group K *Rural Isolation* and one of the reasons for the high level of self-employment in rural areas notwithstanding the decline of agricultural employment.

The expansion of private car ownership and quest for autonomy has resulted in an increased demand for rentable self-catering accommodation. For the middle classes this desire is more likely to be met by a country cottage, discovered via the internet, than an urban flat. For the impecunious, a holiday park, a fixed caravan site or a camping site provides children opportunities to enjoy the company of others of a similar age and to make new friends in an outdoor setting.

In addition to cheap flights and the demand for greater independence, there has been an increase in the number of short breaks that people take in addition to their annual holiday. These breaks are increasingly likely to be taken during the off-season, periods in the year when the attractions that have traditionally attracted visitors to established resorts look even more forlorn in the unlikely event that they are not closed for business.

Changes in holiday destinations are reflected in the changing popularity of different retirement destinations. As life expectancy on retirement increases, many of those who plan to move away from cities as they reach their 60s feel in too good a physical shape to live comfortably in a bungalow. Instead, so long as they are not infirm and can still drive, they increasingly opt to retire to a rural community in a sufficiently attractive part of the country to offer companionship with other middle class retirees or, if to the seaside, to smaller communities, less affected by what early versions of *Mosaic* referred to as *Rootless Renters*, the presence of whom has damaged the reputation of larger resorts. But the biggest source of change is that when people cease to visit a particular resort they no longer retire to it. Those who now holiday in different British (or even continental) destinations now choose to spend their retirements in them instead of traditional retirement resorts.

These changes in taste and preference are gradually reflected by the market for residential properties, declines in relative prices affecting the social profile of people who decide to retire to places such as Clacton, Yarmouth and Rhyl. It also makes these places more affordable for younger local people and gradually communities that had traditionally been considered as places of retirement have become an affordable option for those on the lowest rung of the housing ladder, for the recently separated or divorced and for those who in the Liverpool study would have found refuge in the *Rooming House* clusters. Thus, whilst rural Britain increasingly adopts many of the functional characteristics that formerly characterized the suburbs of small and medium-sized towns, parts of the traditional seaside resort, which were once grouped alongside high status affluent suburbs, are now coming to adopt many of the deprivations we have traditionally associated with the inner city.

## Notes

[1] We have been struck by the relative paucity of social scientific work concerned with such localities compared to others we have examined in this book.

[2] In the 1960s, Sutton Avenue, Seaford in East Sussex, is reputed to have had a road sign warning '7 schools in next mile'.

# Part III
## Coda

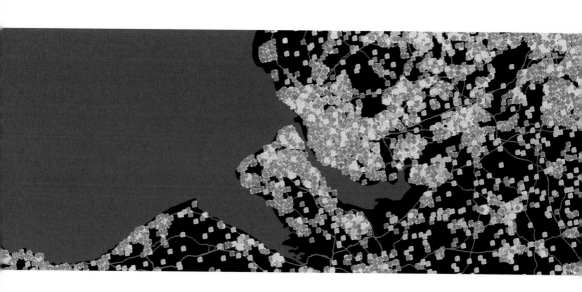

# 11

# A GEODEMOGRAPHIC TRAVELOGUE

The aim of the previous five chapters has been to demonstrate how fresh insights into important socio-political issues can be achieved by using neighbourhood type as a basis for organizing data. But what relevance does this method have to the conduct and results of the classic community studies that have been so influential in shaping our understanding of social processes?

There is no doubt that when they commissioned the three studies of Liverpool, Birmingham and Lambeth in 1973, officials in the (then) Department of the Environment believed that the new insights yielded by these studies would be relevant to any city with a decaying inner area. The impact on social scientific thinking of their three studies may not have compared with that of Young and Willmott's (1957) study of family and kinship in East London, or of Jackson and Marsden's (1962) enquiry into educational aspirations in Huddersfield, or of Goldthorpe and Lockwood's study of Luton's affluent car workers (Goldthorpe et al., 1968a; 1968b; 1969), but whether they did so overtly or implicitly, these studies sought to draw conclusions whose general applicability extended beyond the particular limitations of where and when they were conducted. Each assumed implicitly that their findings would be more relevant to some sorts of community than to others.

Influential though each study undoubtedly has been, the absence of a generally agreed taxonomy of neighbourhoods continues to make it difficult to know which communities these are. As we have discussed earlier, this was a criticism made by David Eversley (1973) of the studies that filled his bookshelves when he was Chief Planner at the Greater London Council.

No less difficult is the task of establishing how applicable the findings of these and other iconic studies are to the same communities today. Were we to return to where Goldthorpe and Lockwood conducted fieldwork in Luton, to where Rex and Moore (1967) studied the impact of immigration in Sparkbrook or to Ray Pahl's (1984) self-provisioning denizens of the Isle of Sheppey, what evidence would we find of the persistence of the social processes described in these studies? So great has been the social and ethnic transformation of London's East End over the past 40 years that in the case of Young and Willmott's work the answer must be very little. Likewise with Luton.

Yet it may be that the implications of the social relationships they observed are not confined to the particular era when their fieldwork was undertaken. Maybe they are still relevant in other places, similar in character to where their fieldwork was undertaken, where social change has been less extreme. Maybe matriarchal family networks continue to thrive on the council estates in Bootle that house the families of former Liverpool dockers. Maybe the embourgeoisement of the *Affluent Worker* persists in those communities in Flintshire where the wings of the Airbus are assembled. A visit to Liverpool would almost certainly conclude that despite the investment in its centre, most of the divisions identified in the Liverpool study of the 1970s are as evident today as they were 40 years ago. Given the importance of Liverpool in the historical development of geodemographics, it might be of interest, as we come towards the end of the book, to revisit the city and examine its contemporary circumstances in more detail.

Table 11.1 profiles the 546,261 adult residents of the Liverpool post town.[1] Any number of observations could be made about this particular area profile. First, there is a significant under-representation of those living in Group A: *Alpha Territory*, with not a single adult being classified in the most affluent Type: A01 *Global Power Brokers*. People living in A02 *Voices of Authority* are significantly under-represented (just 0.4 per cent of the Liverpool population compared to some 1.2 per cent of the British population as a whole). Second, there is also significant under-representation in Group B: *Professional Rewards* and, less surprisingly, given its profoundly urban character C: *Rural Solitude*, D: *Small Town Diversity* and E: *Active Retirement*. Third, within the neighbourhood Types most closely associated with the suburban, middle and lower-middle classes, there are quite distinctive patterns of settlement with significant over-representation in neighbourhood Types such as: F25 *Production Managers*, F26 *Mid Market Families* and H37 *First Moved In*. Those living in neighbourhood Types nested within Group G: *Careers and Kids* are significantly under-represented. Fourth, people who have historically purchased their council homes are over-represented, especially those classified as I38 *Settled Ex-Tenants*, as are those, often poorer households still predominantly living in social housing. Neighbourhood Type J42 *Worn-Out Workers*[2] are over seven times more likely to be found in Liverpool than they are in Britain as a whole. This is now the most over-represented group in Liverpool. Others are: Type J44 *New Parents in Need*, who are over three times more likely to be found in Liverpool compared to the rest of the country; Type K45 *Small Block Singles*, who

**Table 11.1** Neighbourhood Groups and Types, Mosaic 2009 Version for Liverpool Compared to the UK

| Mosaic Groups | Mosaic Types | Liverpool | Liverpool % | UK % | Type Index | Group Index |
|---|---|---|---|---|---|---|
| A: Alpha Territory | A01: Global Power Brokers | 0 | 0.0 | 0.3 | 0.0 | 45.2 |
| | A02: Voices of Authority | 2,270 | 0.4 | 1.2 | 34.6 | |
| | A03: Business Class | 4,174 | 0.8 | 1.5 | 50.9 | |
| | A04: Serious Money | 2,493 | 0.5 | 0.6 | 76.1 | |
| B: Professional Rewards | B05: Mid-Career Climbers | 5,743 | 1.1 | 2.3 | 45.7 | 42.3 |
| | B06: Yesterday's Captains | 7,670 | 1.4 | 2.0 | 70.2 | |
| | B07: Distinctive Success | 978 | 0.2 | 0.6 | 29.8 | |
| | B08: Dormitory Villages | 4,673 | 0.9 | 1.7 | 50.3 | |
| | B09: Escape to the Country | 885 | 0.2 | 1.4 | 11.6 | |
| | B10: Parish Guardians | 924 | 0.2 | 0.9 | 18.8 | |
| C: Rural Solitude | C11: Squires Among Locals | 67 | 0.0 | 1.0 | 1.2 | 1.9 |
| | C12: Country Loving Elders | 85 | 0.0 | 1.0 | 1.6 | |
| | C13: Modern Agribusiness | 146 | 0.0 | 1.3 | 2.1 | |
| | C14: Farming Today | 105 | 0.0 | 0.6 | 3.2 | |
| | C15: Upland Struggle | 0 | 0.0 | 0.4 | 0.0 | |
| D: Small Town Diversity | D16: Side Street Singles | 1,390 | 0.3 | 1.2 | 21.2 | 37.7 |
| | D17: Jacks of All Trades | 2,196 | 0.4 | 2.5 | 16.1 | |
| | D18: Hardworking Families | 5,476 | 1.0 | 2.1 | 47.7 | |
| | D19: Innate Conservatives | 8,963 | 1.6 | 2.9 | 56.6 | |

(Continued)

**Table 11.1** Neighbourhood Groups and Types, Mosaic 2009 Version for Liverpool Compared to the UK

| Mosaic Groups | Mosaic Types | Liverpool | Liverpool % | UK % | Type Index | Group Index |
|---|---|---|---|---|---|---|
| E: Active Retirement | E20: Golden Retirement | 1,495 | 0.3 | 0.6 | 45.6 | 47.0 |
| | E21: Bungalow Quietude | 3,665 | 0.7 | 1.4 | 47.9 | |
| | E22: Beachcombers | 47 | 0.0 | 0.7 | 1.2 | |
| | E23: Balcony Downsizers | 3,935 | 0.7 | 0.9 | 80.0 | |
| F: Suburban Mindsets | F24: Garden Suburbia | 19,522 | 3.6 | 2.8 | 127.6 | 145.0 |
| | F25: Production Managers | 40,051 | 7.3 | 3.0 | 244.4 | |
| | F26: Mid-Market Families | 28,082 | 5.1 | 2.8 | 183.6 | |
| | F27: Shop Floor Affluence | 8,385 | 1.5 | 2.3 | 66.7 | |
| | F28: Asian Attainment | 343 | 0.1 | 1.3 | 4.8 | |
| G: Careers and Kids | G29: Footloose Managers | 2,577 | 0.5 | 1.6 | 29.5 | 49.0 |
| | G30: Soccer Mums and Dads | 2,725 | 0.5 | 1.2 | 41.6 | |
| | G31: Domestic Comfort | 6,122 | 1.1 | 1.5 | 74.7 | |
| | G32: Childcare Years | 4,618 | 0.8 | 1.5 | 56.4 | |
| | G33: Military Dependents | 0 | 0.0 | 0.2 | 0.0 | |
| H: New Homemakers | H34: Buy-to-Let Territory | 1,689 | 0.3 | 1.1 | 28.1 | 54.4 |
| | H35: Brownfield Pioneers | 4,397 | 0.8 | 1.1 | 73.2 | |
| | H36: Foot on the Ladder | 5,380 | 1.0 | 2.0 | 49.2 | |
| | H37: First to Move In | 1,486 | 0.3 | 0.2 | 136.0 | |
| I: Ex-Council Community | I38: Settled Ex-Tenants | 17,562 | 3.2 | 1.9 | 169.2 | 102.3 |
| | I39: Choice Right to Buy | 13,183 | 2.4 | 2.1 | 114.9 | |
| | I40: Legacy of Labour | 20,110 | 3.7 | 3.2 | 115.0 | |
| | I41: Stressed Borrowers | 3,868 | 0.7 | 2.6 | 27.2 | |
| J: Claimant Cultures | J42: Worn-Out Workers | 95,832 | 17.5 | 2.4 | 731.0 | 129.5 |
| | J43: Streetwise Kids | 1,184 | 0.2 | 1.2 | 18.1 | |
| | J44: New Parents in Need | 34,387 | 6.3 | 1.9 | 331.3 | |

**Table 11.1** (Continued)

| Mosaic Groups | Mosaic Types | Liverpool | Liverpool % | UK % | Type Index | Group Index |
|---|---|---|---|---|---|---|
| K: Upper Floor Living | K45: Small Block Singles | 22,667 | 4.1 | 1.4 | 296.4 | 110.8 |
| | K46: Tenement Living | 3,019 | 0.6 | 0.9 | 61.4 | |
| | K47: Deprived View | 1,774 | 0.3 | 0.3 | 108.3 | |
| | K48: Multicultural Towers | 209 | 0.0 | 1.1 | 3.5 | |
| | K49: Re-housed Migrants | 1,199 | 0.2 | 1.1 | 20.0 | |
| L: Elderly Needs | L50: Pensioners in Blocks | 10,659 | 2.0 | 1.0 | 195.1 | 88.9 |
| | L51: Sheltered Seniors | 4,008 | 0.7 | 0.7 | 104.8 | |
| | L52: Meals on Wheels | 1,400 | 0.3 | 0.4 | 64.1 | |
| | L53: Low Spending Elders | 3,692 | 0.7 | 1.9 | 35.6 | |
| M: Industrial Heritage | M54: Clocking Off | 12,231 | 2.2 | 2.3 | 97.3 | 76.9 |
| | M55: Backyard Regeneration | 6,870 | 1.3 | 2.4 | 52.4 | |
| | M56: Small Wage Owners | 13,980 | 2.6 | 3.1 | 82.6 | |
| N: Terraced Melting Pot | N57: Back-to-Back Basics | 13,985 | 2.6 | 2.2 | 116.4 | 122.3 |
| | N58: Asian Identities | 224 | 0.0 | 1.1 | 3.7 | |
| | N59: Low-Key Starters | 35,863 | 6.6 | 2.6 | 252.5 | |
| | N60: Global Fusion | 789 | 0.1 | 1.7 | 8.5 | |
| O: Liberal Opinion | O61: Convivial Homeowners | 2,982 | 0.5 | 1.7 | 32.1 | 96.6 |
| | O62: Crash Pad Professionals | 1,763 | 0.3 | 1.4 | 23.1 | |
| | O63: Urban Cool | 226 | 0.0 | 1.3 | 3.2 | |
| | O64: Bright Young Things | 6,257 | 1.1 | 1.5 | 76.4 | |
| | O65: Anti-Materialists | 10,849 | 2.0 | 1.1 | 180.5 | |
| | O66: University Fringe | 14,205 | 2.6 | 1.1 | 236.4 | |
| | O67: Study Buddies | 8,482 | 1.6 | 0.5 | 310.5 | |
| Unknown | | 45 | 0.0 | 0.0 | 0.0 | |
| Total Great Britain | | 546,261 | 100.0 | 100.0 | 0.0 | |

are almost three times more likely; and Type L50 *Pensioners in Blocks*, who are almost twice as likely. Fifth, those living in the multi-ethnic urban core in Group N: *Terraced Melting Pot* are also over-represented, Type N59 *Low-Key Starters* in particular. Finally, although Liverpool has a significant over-representation of student (and post-student) neighbourhoods, as would be expected with so many higher education institutions within its environs, it is significantly under-represented within other categories of Group O: *Liberal Opinion*.

In 2002 Mike Savage was funded by the Leverhulme Trust to carry out a study that aimed to go back to the original materials that underpinned some of the classic sociological studies of the 1950s and 1960s in order to explore 'what would happen if these archived sources were themselves used as primary material for an historical sociology of post-war Britain?' (Savage, 2010: vii). The book that resulted – *Identities and Social Change in Britain Since 1940* – was hugely successful in mapping out, both literally and metaphorically, the critical importance of a small number of key sociological studies, including those described above, not just for the development of the discipline, but for far broader cultural and political understandings of social change. A map of the fieldwork sites he discusses appears on page 2 of Savage's book.

These studies, although located within particular places, all came to have a profound impact on broader understandings of social issues more generally. We could perhaps think of such studies as being located within 'touchstone' places; fieldwork sites that might be worth revisiting if one were on a sojourn in search of a contemporary sociological understanding of the state of the nation; a geodemographic travelogue.[3] If we were interested in developing a nuanced sociological understanding of post-Brexit Britain we might undertake a journey visiting a range of such touchstone field study places across the nation.[4]

Table 11.2 maps out some of these possibilities, locating them not as Savage does in terms of their geographic location but, in the spirit of this book, in terms of the Types of neighbourhood that characterize each of them today. For each of the 15 Groups, we have identified emblematic locations that were once the location of major community studies.[5] Table 11.3 provides the summary details of the original studies, their locations and the key geodemographic features of each.

However well these studies anchor social scientists' understanding of different types of neighbourhood, their reach among lay people and indeed many other professionals is modest compared with the influence of popular media. We have already mentioned the way in which historic perceptions of the seaside have been influenced by the work of Jane Austen, of *Rural Isolation* by Thomas Hardy and of *Alpha Territory* by William Thackeray. Through what lenses are the different *Mosaic* Types currently mediated to contemporary viewers, listeners and readers? It is curious how by contrast with the popularity of American soap operas such as *Dallas* and *Dynasty*, which were situated in *PRIZM's* equivalent of *Serious*

**Table 11.2** Stops on the Route Ordered by Mosaic Groups

| | London W8 | Banbury | Llangollen | Sheerness | Clacton-on-sea | Cheadle | Milton Keynes | Luton | Pontefract | Liverpool | Glasgow G45 9 | Kirkcaldy | Port Talbot | Sparkbrook | London N1 |
|---|---|---|---|---|---|---|---|---|---|---|---|---|---|---|---|
| A: Alpha Territory | 1,662.5 | 35.0 | 0.0 | 8.3 | 0.0 | 183.2 | 50.9 | 22.1 | 11.0 | 45.2 | 0.0 | 33.3 | 0.0 | 6.9 | 101.1 |
| B: Professional Rewards | 0.0 | 220.7 | 106.4 | 25.7 | 23.3 | 249.6 | 113.2 | 49.1 | 60.8 | 42.3 | 0.0 | 88.6 | 16.2 | 0.0 | 0.0 |
| C: Rural Solitude | 0.0 | 211.3 | 802.8 | 63.5 | 123.2 | 0.0 | 25.8 | 6.8 | 16.5 | 1.9 | 0.0 | 18.2 | 0.7 | 0.0 | 0.0 |
| D: Small Town Diversity | 0.0 | 129.8 | 336.0 | 288.9 | 291.0 | 105.7 | 61.7 | 37.7 | 76.5 | 37.7 | 0.0 | 69.5 | 68.9 | 0.0 | 0.0 |
| E: Active Retirement | 0.0 | 58.0 | 97.4 | 84.5 | 735.3 | 117.1 | 19.5 | 43.1 | 42.5 | 47.0 | 0.0 | 119.7 | 39.5 | 0.0 | 0.0 |
| F: Suburban Mindsets | 0.0 | 85.0 | 1.9 | 69.0 | 20.1 | 261.8 | 82.0 | 176.6 | 79.7 | 145.0 | 3.0 | 65.6 | 54.6 | 25.6 | 0.4 |
| G: Careers and Kids | 0.0 | 112.5 | 6.5 | 43.5 | 1.4 | 125.4 | 317.1 | 61.4 | 96.8 | 49.0 | 0.0 | 99.4 | 77.6 | 0.0 | 0.0 |
| H: New Homemakers | 0.0 | 205.8 | 43.4 | 59.0 | 12.3 | 44.4 | 352.4 | 265.5 | 71.3 | 54.4 | 38.1 | 158.2 | 19.7 | 2.1 | 8.4 |
| I: Ex-Council Community | 0.0 | 81.9 | 98.8 | 169.1 | 109.1 | 35.0 | 78.9 | 99.6 | 275.9 | 102.3 | 78.7 | 164.3 | 344.3 | 7.4 | 0.0 |
| J: Claimant Cultures | 0.0 | 11.2 | 0.0 | 35.9 | 21.5 | 3.4 | 45.2 | 23.3 | 49.0 | 129.5 | 100.0 | 37.7 | 86.1 | 29.4 | 0.0 |
| K: Upper Floor Living | 41.3 | 12.6 | 0.0 | 70.4 | 56.9 | 7.9 | 52.0 | 63.2 | 19.6 | 110.8 | 1,356.0 | 200.1 | 36.3 | 123.9 | 1,095.1 |
| L: Elderly Needs | 0.0 | 78.1 | 72.7 | 79.3 | 166.7 | 70.8 | 55.5 | 48.4 | 164.8 | 88.9 | 172.7 | 380.0 | 82.5 | 9.5 | 2.7 |
| M: Industrial Heritage | 0.0 | 102.4 | 94.1 | 136.5 | 94.7 | 77.8 | 78.3 | 108.2 | 174.7 | 76.9 | 0.0 | 75.4 | 232.7 | 0.0 | 0.0 |
| N: Terraced Melting Pot | 0.0 | 69.0 | 0.0 | 153.0 | 60.6 | 21.6 | 88.7 | 248.5 | 114.2 | 122.3 | 0.0 | 16.0 | 72.9 | 1,090.1 | 18.3 |
| O: Liberal Opinion | 445.7 | 45.5 | 1.6 | 9.4 | 24.8 | 12.0 | 32.0 | 75.9 | 5.2 | 96.6 | 0.0 | 43.1 | 2.9 | 13.0 | 497.3 |
| Total | 19,953 | 64,759 | 6,660 | 27,230 | 59,246 | 44,855 | 173,442 | 151,187 | 72,015 | 546,261 | 7,287 | 47,503 | 40,467 | 52,588 | 67,787 |

**Table 11.3**  Field Sites and Study Narratives in 15 Emblematic Geodemographic Groups

| Field site | Study narrative |
| --- | --- |
| London W8 – an example of<br><br>A: *Alpha Territory* | Notting Hill Gate bounds W8 to the north, Holland Park to the west, Knightsbridge to the east and Cromwell Road to the south. Kensington High Street, which transects it, forms its main commercial artery. The almost 20,000 adults who live in this neighbourhood are amongst the very wealthiest in the world. Over 60 per cent of the population is classified as being part of A: *Alpha Territory*, the great bulk of them being A01 *Global Power Brokers* – the neighbourhood Type within the *Mosaic* schema with the highest incomes in the UK. This, then, is the very epicentre of 'super-rich' London where those living in the *Alpha Territory* are almost 17 times more likely to be found than they are in the UK as a whole. Our own recent study of the *Alpha Territory* (Atkinson et al., 2016a; 2016b; Burrows et al., 2017; Webber and Burrows, 2016) provides an illustrative study. |
| Banbury – an example of<br><br>B: *Professional Rewards* | Banbury has long been viewed as providing privileged sociological insights into British town life (Frankenberg, 1966; Savage, 2010) because of the enduring influence of the *Tradition and Change* studies led by Meg Stacey (Stacey, 1960; Stacey et al., 1975). The geodemographics of Banbury have altered radically since these studies were undertaken. For our visit we are primarily interested in those neighbourhoods classified as B: *Professional Rewards*, which are over twice as prevalent here as they are in the UK as a whole. In particular we might explore the life-worlds of those residing in *Mosaic* Type B09 *Escape to the Country* within which over 5 per cent of Banbury residents now live. |
| Llangollen – an example of<br><br>C: *Rural Solitude* | Across the Welsh border we could revisit the environs of Glyn Ceiriog, within the Llangollen area, the location of the classic anthropological study, *Village on the Border: A Social Study of Religion, Politics and Football in a North Wales Community*, by Ronnie Frankenberg (1957). Here those living within *Mosaic* Group C: *Rural Solitude* are over eight times more likely to be found than in the UK as a whole. *Mosaic* Types C12 *Country Loving Elders* and C13 *Modern Agribusiness* play a particularly significant role in this part of the UK, as do people living in D17 *Jacks of All Trades* within the D: *Small Town Diversity* Group. |

**Table 11.3**   *(Continued)*

| Field site | Study narrative |
|---|---|
| Sheerness – an example of<br><br>D: *Small Town Diversity* | The Isle of Sheppey in Kent, and the town of Sheerness in particular were the location of Ray Pahl's *Divisions of Labour* (Pahl, 1984) and were recently the subject of a major revisiting (Crow and Ellis, 2017). *Divisions of Labour* was a study of 1980s small town white working class entrepreneurship and self-provisioning developed in the face of the economic realities of Thatcher's Britain. Today the upper and middle classes are still significantly under-represented and all of the neighbourhood Types in Group D: *Small Town Diversity* are over-represented, those in the (now, within political discourse, emblematic) D18 *Hardworking Families* Type especially so. The less affluent of those seeking E: *Active Retirement* are also over-represented here, as are those of modest means living in terraced housing: N57 *Back-to-Back Basics* and, especially, N59 *Low-Key Starters*. |
| Clacton-on-Sea – an example of<br><br>E: *Active Retirement* | The traditional seaside town of Clacton-on-Sea has quite a diverse geodemographic profile, but the *Mosaic* Group that is the most over-represented here are those living in E: *Active Retirement*. Such people are over seven times likely to be found here than they are in the country as a whole, with those living neighbourhoods classified as E21 *Bungalow Quietude* and E22 *Beachcombers* being especially significant. It is a reflection on the biases and prevailing interests of social scientists that studies of such places are thin on the ground. However, Clacton (along with Bexhill–on-Sea in East Sussex) were the subject of an excellent study by the urban sociologist Valerie Karn (1977), *Retiring to the Seaside*. |
| Cheadle – an example of<br><br>F: *Suburban Mindsets* | *Globalization and Belonging* by Savage et al. (2005) is a study of four predominantly middle class neighbourhoods in the Manchester conurbation: Cheadle; Chorlton; Ramsbottom; and Wilmslow. It is quite a rare sociological study in the manner that it explicitly draws up geodemographic forms of analysis (Savage et al., 2005: 19–20). Here we would focus on Cheadle because of its over-representation of F: *Suburban Mindsets*, which are over two and a half times more likely to be found here than across the country as a whole, with some 10 per cent of the population living within *Mosaic* Type F24 *Garden Suburbia* in close juxtaposition with over 15 per cent living in neighbourhoods classified as being dominated by F25 *Production Managers*. Cheadle is a good place to visit if one wants to understand the concerns of the 'ordinary' provincial lower middle classes. |

*(Continued)*

**Table 11.3**  Field Sites and Study Narratives in 15 Emblematic
Geodemographic Groups

| Field site | Study narrative |
| --- | --- |
| Milton Keynes – an example of<br><br>G: *Careers and Kids* | Milton Keynes – the archetypical British new town – has been the subject of various social scientific studies located within its environs over the years, a number of which are summarized in Clapson (2004). Here we are particularly interested in the often unremarkable domains of the *Mosaic* Group G: *Careers and Kids* which are over three times more prevalent here than in the UK as a whole. |
| Luton – an example of<br><br>H: *New Homemakers* | Luton – the site of the *Affluent Worker* study in the 1960s and of a more recent re-study by Devine (1992). Luton now has a complex geodemographic structure, with a number of *Mosaic* Groups significantly over-represented. However, the group that will interest us most here is H: *New Homemakers*, those in *Type* H36 *Foot on the Ladder* in particular. Luton now provides an excellent place for coming to terms with the sensibilities of younger people in mid-range employment in the early stages of their housing careers, many of whom commute to London. |
| Pontefract – an example of<br><br>I: *Ex-Council Community* | The Pontefract area in West Yorkshire, the town of Featherstone in particular, was the location of one of the most famous community studies ever carried out in the UK: *Coal is our Life: An Analysis of a Yorkshire Mining Community* by Dennis et al. (1956). The coalmines are now long gone, but their impact endures in many aspects of the contemporary life and times of such places. Here we are particularly interested in the Mosaic Group I: *Ex-Council Community*, the members of which are 2.75 times more likely to be found here than across the country as a whole. Within this Group, *Mosaic* Type I40 *Legacy of Labour* is particularly over-represented, with over 17 per cent of the population being classified as residing in such neighbourhoods. If we want to understand the mores of ex-mining communities then this is obviously an excellent place to visit. |
| Liverpool – an example of<br><br>J: *Claimant Cultures* | Liverpool we have already discussed in great detail. It is included here not only because it was the location where geodemographics were first developed in the UK but also because it was the location for a very early study of urban neighbourhoods and communities in the 1950s (Lupton and Mitchell, 1954; Mitchell et al., 1954). Although only just over 24 per cent of its adult population is classified in Group J: *Claimant Cultures* (with Group Index of 129.5), this represents some 131,403 people, the largest number in the UK. As we have already seen from Table 11.1, if we wanted to examine the life-worlds of this Group, those classified as J42 *Worn-Out Workers* and J44 *New Parents in Need* in particular, Liverpool would be an ideal location. |

**Table 11.3** *(Continued)*

| Field site | Study narrative |
|---|---|
| Glasgow G45 9 – an example of K: *Upper Floor Living* | The geodemographics of Scotland in general, and its urban centres in particular, are often quite distinctive. Glasgow was the field site of the classic *A Glasgow Gang Observed*, by sociologist Frank Coffield – later revealed as the educational sociologist – using the pseudonym James Patrick (1973). However, the geodemographics of the city as a whole are obviously highly complex; even including a significant over-representation of those living in A: *Alpha Territory*. Thus, if we want to get a better sense of some of the distinctive aspects of the city, and of localities of the type that featuring predominantly in the Patrick volume, then we could focus on particular parts of the city where particular housing types are concentrated. Such an area is Glasgow is the postcode sector G45 9. Here we find the highest over-representation of *Mosaic* Group K: *Upper Floor Living* in the UK – 13.5 times more prevalent than in the country as a whole – the great majority of these living in that most distinctive of Glasgow housing types K46 *Tenement Living*. This would be where to come if one wanted to explore the sensibilities of the contemporary Glasgow tenement dweller. |
| Kirkcaldy – an example of L: *Elderly Needs* | Kirkcaldy, a town in Fife, on the east coast of Scotland, is located about 12 miles north of Edinburgh. It was one of the locations of a major ESRC funded study – the social change and economic life initiative (the SCELI as it was known) carried out in the 1980s. Two SCELI volumes within which the material from Kirkcaldy feature prominently are Anderson et al. (1994) and Gallie et al. (1994). Although the town has people living in neighbourhoods across the whole gamut of *Mosaic* Groups, it is the significant over-representation of people living in neighbourhoods classified as *Mosaic* Group L: *Elderly Needs*. Such people are almost four times as likely to be found in Kirkcaldy as they are in the country as a whole, with those living in *Mosaic* Type L50 *Pensioners in Blocks* being an especially large group. |
| Port Talbot – an example of M: *Industrial Heritage* | Port Talbot was the location of Ralph Fevre's 1988 study *Wales is Closed*, which investigated the impact of the privatization of British Steel on the local population. The steelworks, now owned by a private company, Tata Steel, still employs about one in ten of the local workforce, but its future continues to be uncertain. It is this history of steel making that, more than anything else, defines the dominant geodemographics of Port Talbot. |

*(Continued)*

**Table 11.3**  Field Sites and Study Narratives Field Sites and Study Narratives in 15 Emblematic Geodemographic Groups

| Field site | Study narrative |
|---|---|
|  | Here would be a good place to study people living in areas classified as M: *Industrial Heritage*, over 18 per cent of the population live in such neighbourhoods, well over twice the national average. Also important here are those classified as I: *Ex-Council Community*, those classified as I38 *Settled Ex-Tenants* in particular, make up over 22 per cent of the adult population. |
| Sparkbrook – an example of<br><br>N: *Terraced Melting Pot* | Sparkbrook in Birmingham was the location of the classic study of *Race, Community and Conflict* by Rex and Moore (1967), which did much to popularize the concept of 'housing classes', and it remains an enduring contribution to the sociology of race and ethnicity. Here we find a huge over-representation of those classified as living in the *Mosaic* Group N: *Terraced Melting Pot* – almost 11 times the prevalence compared to the country as a whole. In Sparkbrook and environs we discover that some 80 per cent of adults live in the *Mosaic* Type N58 *Asian Identities*. Sparkbrook continues to be an important location if we want to understand the social dynamics of provincial neighbourhoods in which a significant proportion of the population are Muslims, the majority with origins in Pakistan and Bangladesh, living alongside other minority ethnic groups. |
| London N1 – an example of<br><br>O: *Liberal Opinion* | London N1 covers the London borough of Islington; a key location in the history of urban studies. It was here that the concept of 'gentrification' was first developed by Ruth Glass (1964: xviii). It was here also a few years before the financial crash of 2008 that Butler and Lees (2006) claimed to be able to identify the emergence of what they termed 'super-gentrification' in Barnsbury, a specific part of Islington. Their data show that the 'traditional gentrifiers' of places such as Cloudesley Square, Lonsdale Square, Thornhill Square and Richmond Crescent (where Tony Blair and his family lived between 1986 and 1997), were slowly being replaced by far more affluent professionals working in the City of London. Examining the geodemographic data for London N1 as a whole, a population of some 67,787 adults reveals a complex population. Those living in O: *Liberal Opinion*, containing many 'classic gentrifiers' are almost five times more likely to be found here than elsewhere in the UK. However, there is also a significant concentration of those classified as A: *Alpha Territory*, which will contain people of the sort described by Butler and Lees. |

**Table 11.3** *(Continued)*

| Field site | Study narrative |
| --- | --- |
|  | What is also distinctive about Islington however is the huge over-representation of people living in K: *Upper Floor Living* – almost 11 times the national average; those living in *Mosaic* Type K48 *Multicultural Towers* in particular, who make up over a third of the adult population. This, then, is the classic territory of the 'liberal metropolitan elite', affluent and very affluent gentrifers and, now, super-gentrifers, living in close proximity to poorer multi-ethnic populations. |

*Money*, Britain's most popular soaps, *EastEnders* and *Coronation Street*, are set in neighbourhoods described by *Mosaic* as *Ties of Community*. So too is *The Last of the Summer Wine*. When the behaviours of *Serious Money* have been represented, as in *Footballers' Wives* and *Made in Chelsea*, it has been done with mockery. By contrast, higher ratings are achieved by accounts of country life as in *Emmerdale* and *The Archers*, a particularly faithful observation of the changes in the *Mosaic* Group *Rural Isolation* described in Chapter 9. *Doc Martin* and *Fawlty Towers* both find comedy among coastal communities, *Doc Martin's* Portwenn (Port Isaac) being situated in as classic an example of *Rural Retirement Mix* as it would be possible to find. Many other examples will likely suggest themselves to the reader.

## Notes

[1] See www.postcodes-uk.com/post-towns. Note that the boundary of the post town is somewhat more generous than that of the local authority district.

[2] This label turns out to be less pejorative than it initially sounds when one reads the detailed narrative accompanying the category; it essentially refers to neighbourhoods dominated by poor quality low rise social housing where older workers employed in low skilled work or who are unemployed live; many such neighbourhoods would have previously been classified as *Low Horizons* in the 2003 version of the classification, see Chapter 7.

[3] In some ways this idea of touchstone sites of sociological knowledge resonates with the aesthetics of filmmaker Patrick Keiller whose 'fictional documentaries' – *London* (1992), *Robinson in Space* (1997), *Dilapidated Dwelling* (2000) and *Robinson in Ruins* (2010) – all offer thought-provoking insights on the socio-economic and cultural landscape of the country (Hatherley, 2012). His work 'can be thought of as "travelogues" – each taking the form of an explorative journey across urban and rural locations' (Malpas and Jacobs, 2016: 1134). It is the

selection of the locations that are key to his films; the narrator and his companion journey to various interconnected sites as if on some unspoken quest to decipher the essential nature of the nation's history, politics and economics.

[4] A similar exercise was attempted by Ronnie Frankenberg (1966) in his classic account of *Communities in Britain*, which, interestingly, included an examination of an urban housing estate in Liverpool originally studied by Lupton and Mitchell (1951) (Frankenberg, 1966: 214–22).

[5] The process of creating the table also provides interesting evidence of differences in the preference of the research community for where to do their fieldwork. For some geodemographic Groups one is spoilt for choice as to the locations and studies one might select, whilst for others we have sometimes struggled to locate indicative studies (and thus locations).

# 12

# GEODEMOGRAPHICS IN THE FUTURE

## Geodemographics and the social life of methods

In the Preface to this book we argued that because no research method is value free, any account of the history and adoption of a new quantitative research technique such as geodemographics should be considered within the broader context of the 'social life of methods', however interesting in its own right it may be. The emergence of big data in particular has brought into clear relief the inter-relationship that exists between the topics which the social scientific community considers to constitute legitimate subjects of research, the metrics by which empirical evidence is organized and the theoretical constructs by which findings are operationalized. If data collection methods determine the metrics by which theoretical constructs are operationalized then it is inevitable that, just as a prism does, these constructs will reveal certain patterns of behaviour more clearly than they do others. What we see, know, understand and what we don't see, know or understand are therefore highly dependent on the prism through which we collect and then organize our data.

For example, Chapter 7 showed how access to administrative data collected via PLASC makes it possible to measure, research and comment in considerable detail on changes in the level of segregation in schools. Can such changes be assumed to reflect equivalent changes in levels of residential segregation? And among which minority groups are the patterns of segregation found in schools reflected in corresponding patterns of residential segregation? Public servants and academics are much less clear about the latter since it would involve access to data from a quite different source, such as *Origins*, but unless we are alert we can easily slide into the assumption that changes in the level of segregation in the classroom, which we can measure, is an adequate proxy for changes in the level of segregation in the community, which until recently we could not.

This is why, rather than restricting ourselves to a review of the features and merits of neighbourhood classification as a method in its own right, we have included the five chapters of Part II of this book. The purpose of these chapters has been to reveal the insights that tend not to have been visible through traditional prisms: empirical evidence from sources other than answers to questionnaire-based methods of data collection. These chapters focus on just five of a much larger number of possible Types of neighbourhood we could have examined and discussion restricted to just five issues of topical interest. The scope of these chapters is therefore limited to illustrating rather than providing an exhaustive account of the types of insight to which geodemographics lends itself. It is on the basis of the relevance, value and broadness of insights of this sort that a new methodological approach is likely to win adherents, not merely on its ability to validate or qualify existing theories.

Arguing that a method should be evaluated on the basis of its ability to generate fresh insights into established issues should not be taken as implying that there are no specific theoretical reasons why a method of analysis such as geodemographics is likely to contribute additional insights to policy debates. A number of these reasons have been put forward in Part I. Primary among them is the contention, based on observation and evidence, that by comparison with their recorded occupation, the place where people live has become an increasingly powerful predictor of their behaviour.

This contention is supported by a number of secondary theoretical propositions. These are: that constructs which combine multiple dimensions provide better representations of the complexity of individual circumstances than ones which are univariate; that the use of finer classifications, for example ones with 60 or more categories, necessarily captures nuances which are capable of advancing theories to a more detailed level; that for existing generalized explanations of behaviour these more nuanced distinctions make it possible to establish the specific contexts within which these explanations are likely to operate or fail to hold; that misalignment between the rankings of clusters on highly correlated variables should not be considered a result of 'error' but as an opportunity to identify more nuanced explanations; that a classification system where each category has a high degree of uniformity in different environments provides a more reliable basis for inferring local levels of service demand or operational performance; likewise that this uniformity provides opportunities for more accurate data fusion, the imputing of links between data from different databases pertaining to the same object; and the explicit link to geography via the postcode system makes it practical both to test and to apply theoretical understandings in specific operational situations.

Thus Neighbourhood Watch Schemes, promoted by the police, are more likely to be effective in *Mosaic* Types such as *Ties of Community* and *Rural Isolation*, where there are strong community ties, or in *Suburban Comfort*, where people have possessions worth stealing. Campaigns to improve levels of electoral registration or census response are likely to achieve most impact in *Mosaic* Groups such as *Welfare Borderline* and in *Mosaic* Types such as D25 *Town Centre Refuge*, D26 *South Asian Industry* and F36 *Metro Multiculture* due to a combination of population turnover, non-standard household arrangements, lack of familiarity with electoral registration and low standards of literacy.

## The outlook for geodemographic classification

Considered within the framework of the social life of methods, we believe that the future prospects for this particular method depend less on considerations of methodology, which is what tends to be the focus of most debate, than on the likely changes in the social world it is classifying and on the commercial pressures placed on its vendors by its users and by legislators.

Though there is little specific evidence from which we can adduce it, our sense is that over time the level of granularity at which neighbourhoods differentiate themselves is gradually becoming coarser. Thus, whilst it will continue to be appropriate to build neighbourhood classifications at the level of the unit postcode, the finest possible level of geographic detail, in future the algorithms that build them may need to assign a higher weight to data variables for coarser levels of geography. This does not present an operational problem but does run contrary to popular assumptions and to the commercial pressures currently being placed on vendors.

Geodemographic systems work best where there is a high level of social homogeneity of the neighbourhoods that they classify and are adversely affected by any trends that cause the social homogeneity of neighbourhoods to decline, an issue that is of obvious concern to their builders. Currently there are a number of aspects of the housing market in particular which are causing neighbourhoods to become more heterogeneous.

In London in particular, problems of affordability increasingly result in well-educated and higher income young households living in types of neighbourhoods whose low status would have rendered them socially inappropriate choices in their parents' generation. In a similar way the growth in the number of properties rented from private landlords is causing the demographics of many postcodes' owner-occupiers to diverge from those of its private renters. In theory the condition of planning approval imposed on developers that they should include a quota of 'affordable' accommodation within new developments is also likely to reduce the homogeneity of demographics at the neighbourhood level, assuming that this requirement is adhered to.

Another potential source of concern is regional divergences in house prices. This causes neighbourhoods which are otherwise similar in terms of demographics to become increasingly different in terms of attitudes and behaviours. This is reflected in younger people having a lower level of disposable income in highly priced regions than in neighbourhoods of similar demographics elsewhere. For older people this is reflected in terms of the increasing disparity between the proportion of their assets which are liquid and illiquid in otherwise demographically similar neighbourhoods in regions of high and low house values. An example of the likely impact of this disparity within a particular *Mosaic* Type is differences in the level of support for a person's property being treated differently from their financial assets when assessing liability for inheritance tax or charges for social care.

Another threat to the long-term use of geodemographic classification is the pressure placed on vendors of geodemographic classifications to construct classifications at the person level. Although current data protection regulations permit the use of person-level classifications, the General Data Protection Regulations, implemented in 2018, have provoked some anxiety on the part of users.

As we explained earlier, in Chapter 4, although personal-level classifications are more powerful predictors of personal behaviour, they are necessarily less effective in capturing social processes than when operating at a neighbourhood level. Their adoption strengthens the assumption, common in social media advertising, that the best way to predict differences in personal behaviour is by using information relating to a person's personal circumstances. The awareness that neighbourhood effects and peer group influences exercise a very real influence on how people behave, generated by the Café Royale seminar all those years ago, may be in danger of becoming lost.

Another source of uncertainty relates to the survival of the cross-disciplinary expertise needed for the design and interpretation of geodemographic systems. Consideration of the labels developed in the first generation of *PRIZM* and early versions of *Mosaic* attests to the fact that these systems were designed and built by people with a strong interest in and awareness of socio-spatial processes. As the ownership of these products increasingly falls within the control of complexly layered multinational corporations, there is a danger that over-stretched corporate managers will lose awareness of the importance of these skills. It is understandable that they should become wary of investing in products whose commercial returns may appear modest in relation to the level and breadth of social scientific and analytical expertise needed to create and support them.

As a result there are legitimate grounds for concern over the direction of their development by multinational information companies, especially by contrast with the specialist entities who now operate geodemographic systems in markets such as Canada and the Netherlands. It is not certain that those responsible for naming and visualizing future clusters, let alone creating them, will continue to have the inter-disciplinary expertise that has contributed to the success of previous classifications.

Sooner or later the construction of genuinely neighbourhood-based classifications will start to incorporate feeds from social media data. This will result in improved representations of cultural behaviour and in more regular and faster updating. It is also likely that systems will begin to incorporate information on the geographical movement of members of different clusters during the day as well as when they are at home (Smith, 2017) and use sentiment analysis to report on swings in popular mood in real time. The precise form in which these derivatives of geodemographic clusters systems will emerge is not easy to predict but the results are likely to be very exciting.

Chapter 9 presented some innovative material on how the demographics of rural populations have changed. A frequent criticism of geodemographic classification is the absence of systems for tracking temporal change in the demographic composition of different types of neighbourhood. Cohort studies make it possible to track the relationship between demographics and the development of individuals over time. Tracking demographic change at the level of local authority is made possible by the decennial publication of census statistics. Sadly it did not occur to vendors that future generations would want to retrieve records of the assignment of wards, census EDs or postcodes to the earliest versions of *Acorn* or *Mosaic*. So today it is difficult to identify changes in the demographic character of Types of geodemographic neighbourhoods such as those inhabited by *Affluent Workers* in Luton or of examples of *Coronation Street* in inner cities. One hopes that it will not be too long before it becomes possible to overcome this omission as attempts are made to locate and link the results of various historical classifications using a common geography.

# The adoption of geodemographic classifications

As has been implied from time to time in Part I of this book, the adoption of neighbourhood classification has been uneven. Analysts in teams which are given greater autonomy in deciding which technique will best improve their understanding of how public and private services can be best delivered have been relatively more willing and able to adopt innovative techniques such as geodemographic analysis.

Innovation has been less evident among analysts constrained by the requirements that the material or policy advice they deliver to superiors should conform to pre-existing mental constructs used by elites who lack the time, inclination or interest to re-evaluate established representations of social structure.

Among such groups it is common for people to avoid the intellectual effort to make an objective evaluation of a new mode of analysis by focusing on an essentially trivial aspect – such as that a particular *Mosaic* label used to describe a geodemographic cluster may not be to their liking or, as in the case of *Origins*, that an individual is entitled to assert the category by which they want to be classified – even though it is on the basis of their name rather than their self-identification that most members of minority ethnic groups find themselves being discriminated against.

Perhaps surprisingly for an account of the 'social life' of a quantitative method, the preceding chapters have made many references to the obstacles that exist in the communication of different concepts between different groups. In particular we have identified the way in which most lay people (and probably many professional people too when in a lay capacity) recognize neighbourhoods more readily in terms of visual images rather than through textual descriptions; how 'experts' distinguish themselves from lay people by using terms which are specific to their area of expertise when describing concepts which lay people are perfectly well equipped to understand, and how considerations of political correctness can sometimes take priority over intelligibility, as for example when what can be described as 'Asian Enterprise' is referred to as 'Comfortable middle-aged families with school-age and older children, predominantly from an Asian background'. Each of these considerations help to explain discrepancies between the relevance of geodemographic classification in particular professional fields and its level of adoption among practitioners.

Perhaps the most telling of these discrepancies occurs in the field of politics. In every general election over the last 20 years, each of the principal political parties has routinely added a geodemographic code to its national database of electors in order both to analyse canvass returns and to customize campaign activity to specific categories of elector. The parties themselves must have sanctioned this activity and have found it very useful so it would be surprising if at least some elected Members of Parliament were unaware of the relevance to the analysis of government-sourced data and to government communication of at least some of the tools that contributed to a victory for their party at the ballot box. *Origins* likewise will have been used in a similar manner.

The explanation for these patterns of differential adoption, so we have come to believe, is more likely to be found in terms of institutional factors than in terms of relevance (Webber and Phillips, 2016). Among the factors which are most predictive of the use of geodemographic is whether the application supports a long-term, routine and repeated process, of which parties' election campaigning is a good example, rather than a one-off research exercise, in which case the 'cost' of learning a new language is unlikely to justify the return. It is our opinion that a second key consideration is the degree to which the impact of the application is likely to be statistically monitored within the period of involvement of the people responsible for the project. A third is the extent to which decisions regarding choice of data or methods are delegated to data specialists or considered matters of sufficient political importance to be decided by non-specialist committees, most members of which will not have the time, inclination or expertise to make a properly informed judgement. A fourth is the extent to which the organization or the individual researcher is exposed to reputational risk, either in the form of public challenge in the case of organizations, or peer group challenge in the case of individual researchers. A fifth predictor of non-use of geodemographic is that the service is outsourced under the terms of a complex performance agreement.

Considerations of this sort suggest that in central government and the academic community, the scope for the adoption of geodemographics is relatively modest other than where persons or units benefit from a high level of job security and long-term independence. By contrast the method is more likely to be used by technical teams, whether in the commercial sector or in local government, responsible for the long-term operational effectiveness of decision support systems. Medicine is just one of a number of fields with long-established mechanisms for measuring the operational effectiveness of different targeting strategies. It is also more suited for adoption by organizations seeking to justify or explain their decisions to non-specialist audiences.

A further factor shaping adoption of course is ease of access, the policy over which is obviously a matter at the discretion of vendors. Though it is difficult to obtain clear information about vendors' policies, it can be presumed that where a geodemographic system is the intellectual property of a large organization, with its expensive overheads but economies of scale, pressure is continuously being exerted on sales forces to maximize revenues from a limited number of potential high-value clients. Occasional, small value users, however interesting and welcome their use of these systems may have been in the earlier days of geodemographics, are increasingly at risk of no longer being considered as profitable prospects. This situation provides opportunities for specialist third party organizations to negotiate distribution agreements enabling them to meet the needs of lower value users and or bundle distribution within other applications which require specialist advisory services for particular markets. The use of geodemographics within arts marketing is a good example of such practice.[1]

## The user experience

The presenters at the launch of *Acorn* at the Café Royale spoke with great enthusiasm. They had clearly enjoyed the opportunity to gain new and different forms of insight, often from data sets they were unaccustomed to treating as potential sources of research evidence. They were positive about the ease with which these insights could drive the application of segmentation to previously untargeted forms of communication. But the excitement applied equally to the nature of the method. Its multi-dimensional form and the use of visual imagery gave it a fresh, organic air, being derived directly from data themselves without the intermediation of established theoretical constructs. It conveyed a slight air of magic (Robbin, 1980). Users found it immediately accessible but its nested, modular structure and the supporting visualization tools gave users the freedom to explore at whatever level of depth and across whatever topics they chose. Compared with mechanical systems it seemed enjoyable to use and sufficiently open-ended in its scope to have no obvious constraints.

Through familiarity, some of this original excitement may have worn off during the 35 years since the Café Royale seminar. But provided they are equipped with the tools they need, most contemporary users continue to find the taxonomies both of great practical value and a stimulating and enjoyable source of new understanding of human behaviour. In conclusion, we hope that the reader has also found our account of geodemographic classifications an engaging and helpful one, and that they might be encouraged to critically draw upon the approach in their own work.

## Note

[1] See, for example, www.culturehive.co.uk/resources/using-geo-demographic-reports-and-customer-data-for-arts-marketing.

# REFERENCES

Abbott, A. (1999) *Department and Discipline. Chicago Sociology at One Hundred.* Chicago, IL: Chicago University Press.

Abbott, A. (2000) 'Reflections on the Future of Sociology', *Contemporary Sociology*, 29(2): 296–300.

Abler, R., Adams, S. and Gould, O. (1971) *Spatial Organization.* Englewood Cliffs, NJ: Prentice Hall.

Anderson, M., Bechhofer, F. and Gerhuny, J. (eds) (1994) *The Social and Political Economy of the Household.* Oxford: Oxford University Press.

Atkinson, R., Burrows, R., Glucksberg, L., Kei-Ho, H., Knowles, C. and Rhodes, D. (2016a) 'Minimum City? A Critical Assessment of Some of the Deeper Impacts of the "Super-Rich" on Urban Life', in R. Forrest, B. Wissink, and S. Yee Koh (eds) *Cities and the Super-Rich: Real Estate, Elite Practices, and Urban Political Economies.* London: Palgrave, pp. 253–72.

Atkinson, R., Burrows, R. and Rhodes, D. (2016b) 'Capital City? London's Housing Market and the "Super Rich"', in I. Hay and J. Beaverstock (eds) *International Handbook of Wealth and the Super Rich.* Cheltenham: Edward Elgar, pp. 225–43.

Back, L. (2016) 'Tape Recorder', in M. Bull and L. Back (eds) *The Auditory Culture Reader.* London: Bloomsbury, pp. 137–50.

Bacqué, M., Bridge, G., Benson, M., Butler, T., Charmes, E., Fijalkow, Y., Jackson, E., Launay, L. and Vermeersch, S. (2015) *The Middle Classes and the City: A Study of Paris and London.* Basingstoke: Palgrave.

Baker, K. (1991) 'Using Geodemographics in Market Research Surveys', *Journal of the Royal Statistical Society. Series D (The Statistician)*, 40(2): 203–7.

Bales, K. (1992) 'Charles Booth's *Survey of Life and Labour of the People in London 1889–1903*', in M. Bulmer, K. Bales and K. K. Sklar (eds) *The Social Survey in Historical Perspective.* Cambridge: Cambridge University Press, pp. 66–110.

Barker, F. and Aldous, T. (2009) *Guardians of the Heath.* London: Blackheath Society.

Batty, M. and Longley, P. (1994) *Fractal Cities.* London: Academic Press.

Bell, C. and Newby, H. (eds) (1977) *Doing Sociological Research.* London: Allen & Unwin.

Bell, C. and Roberts, H. (1984) *Social Researching.* London: Routledge & Kegan Paul.

Bermingham, J., Baker, K. and McDonald, C (1979) 'The Utility to Market Research of the Classification of Residential Neighbourhoods', *Proceedings of the Market Research Society Annual Conference*, Brighton, pp. 253–71.

Berry, B. and Kasarda, J. (1977) *Contemporary Urban Ecology*. New York: Macmillan.

Bishop, B. with Cushing, R. (2009) *The Big Sort*. Boston, MA: Houghton Mifflin.

Booth, C. (1902–3) *Life and Labour of the People in London* (3rd edn), 17 vols. London: Macmillan.

Botterill, J. (2013) 'Property Porn: An Analysis of Online Real Estate Advertising', in M. McAllister and E. West (eds) *The Routledge Companion to Advertising and Promotional Culture*. London: Routledge, pp. 326–37.

Bourdieu, P. (1984) *Distinction: A Social Critique of the Judgement of Taste*. Cambridge, MA: Harvard University Press.

Bowker, G. and Star, S. (1999) *Sorting Things Out: Classification and its Consequences*. Cambridge, MA: MIT Press.

Bradshaw, J. and Millar, J. (1991) *Lone Parent Families in the UK*. London: HM Stationery Office.

Bridge, G. (2006) 'It's not just a Question of Taste: Gentrification, the Neighbourhood and Cultural Capital', *Environment and Planning A*, 38(10): 1965–78.

Bulmer, M. (1984) *The Chicago School of Sociology: Institutionalization, Diversity, and the Rise of Sociological Research*. Chicago, IL: University of Chicago Press.

Burgess, E. (1964), 'Research in Urban Sociology: A Longer View', in E. Burgess and D. Bogue (eds) *Contributions to Urban Sociology*. Chicago, IL: University of Chicago Press.

Burnap, P., Gibson, R., Sloan, L., Southern, R. and Williams, M. (2016) '140 Characters to Victory?: Using Twitter to Predict the UK 2015 General Election', *Electoral Studies*, 41: 230–3.

Burrows, R. (1997) 'Virtual Culture, Urban Social Polarisation and Social Science Fiction', in B. Loader (ed.) *The Governance of Cyberspace*. London: Routledge, pp. 38–45.

Burrows, R. (1999) 'Residential Mobility and Residualisation in Social Housing in England', *Journal of Social Policy*, 28(1): 27–52.

Burrows, R. (2003) 'How the Other Half Lives: An Exploratory Analysis of the Relationship between Poverty and Home-Ownership in Britain', *Urban Studies*, 40(7): 1223–42.

Burrows, R. and Ellison, N. (2004) 'Sorting Places Out? Towards a Social Politics of Neighbourhood Informatization', *Information, Communication and Society*, 7(3): 321–36.

Burrows, R., Ellison, N. and Woods, B. (2005) *Neighbourhoods on the Net: Internet-Based Neighbourhood Information Systems and their Consequences*. Bristol: Policy.

Burrows, R. and Gane, N. (2006) 'Geodemographics, Software and Class', *Sociology*, 40(5): 793–812.

Burrows, R. and Rhodes, D. (1998) *Unpopular Places? Area Disadvantage and the Geography of Misery*. Bristol: Policy Press.

Burrows, R. and Savage, M. (2014) 'After the Crisis? Big Data and the Methodological Challenges of Empirical Sociology', *Big Data and Society*, 1(1) 10.1177/2053951714540280.

Burrows, R., Webber, R. and Atkinson, R. (2017) 'Welcome to "Pikettyville"? Mapping London's *Alpha Territories*', *Sociological Review*, 65(2): 184–201.

Butler, T and Lees, L (2006) 'Super-Gentrification in Barnsbury, London: Globalization and Gentrifying Global Elites at the Neighbourhood Level', *Transactions of the Institute of British Geographers*, 31(4): 467–87.

Butler, T. with Robson, G. (2003) *London Calling: The Middle Classes and the Remaking of Inner London.* London: Berg.

Camina, M. and Wood, M. (2009) 'Parallel Lives: Towards a Greater Understanding of What Mixed Communities Can Offer', *Urban Studies*, 46(2): 459–80.

Catney, G., (2016) 'Exploring a Decade of Small Area Ethnic (De-) Segregation in England and Wales', *Urban Studies*, 53(8): 1691–709.

Chaney, P. and Sherwood, K. (2000) 'The Resale of Right to Buy Dwellings: A Case Study of Migration and Social Change in Rural England', *Journal of Rural Studies*, 16(1): 79–94.

Cheshire, P. (2012) 'Why do Birds of a Feather Flock Together? Social Mix and Social Welfare: A Quantitative Appraisal', in G. Bridge, T. Butler and L. Lees (eds) *Mixed Communities: Gentrification by Stealth?* Bristol: Policy Press, pp. 17–24.

Christie, I. (1974) 'Covent Garden: Approaches to Urban Renewal', *The Town Planning Review*, 45(1): 30–62.

Clapson, M. (2004) *A Social History of Milton Keynes: Middle England/Edge City.* London: Routledge.

Crewe, I., Fox, A. and Day, N. (1995) *The British Electorate, 1963–1992: A Compendium of Data from the British Election Studies.* Cambridge: Cambridge University Press.

Crow, G. and Ellis, J. (eds) (2017) *Revisiting Divisions of Labour.* Manchester: Manchester University Press.

Curry, M. (1998) *Digital Places: Living with Geographic Information Technologies.* London: Routledge.

Dale, A., Gilbert, G.N. and Arber, S. (1985) 'Integrating Women into Class Theory', *Sociology*, 19(3): 384–408.

Dalton, C. and Thatcher, J. (2015) 'Inflated Granularity: Spatial "Big Data" and Geodemographics', *Big Data and Society*, 2(2): doi: 10.1177/2053951715601144.

Davis, M. (1998) *Ecology of Fear.* New York: Metropolitan Books.

Davies, W. (2016) 'The New Neoliberalism', *New Left Review*, 101: 121–34.

Davies, W. (2017) *The Limits of Neoliberalism: Authority, Sovereignty and the Logic of Competition* (2nd edn). London: Sage.

Davison, G., Dovey, K. and Woodcock, I. (2012) '"Keeping Dalston Different": Defending Place-Identity in East London', *Planning Theory and Practice*, 13(1): 47–69.

Dennis, N., Henriques, F. and Slaughter, C. (1956) *Coal is our Life: An Analysis of a Yorkshire Mining Community.* London: Eyre & Spottiswoode.

Devine, F. (1992) *Affluent Workers Revisited: Privatism and the Working Class.* Edinburgh: Edinburgh University Press.

Dunn, R., Forrest, R. and Murie, A. (1987) 'The Geography of Council House Sales in England – 1979–85', *Urban Studies*, 24(1): 47–59.

Ellison, N. and Burrows, R. (2007) 'New Spaces of (Dis-) Engagement? Social Politics, Urban Technologies and the Rezoning of the City', *Housing Studies*, 22(3): 295–312.

Eversley, D. (1973) *The Planner in Society: The Changing Role of a Profession.* London: Faber and Faber.

Featherstone, J. M. (1974) *Human Ecology and Sociology: The Development of Human Ecology in the Department of Sociology at the University of Chicago 1914–39*. Durham Theses, Durham University. Available at Durham E-Theses Online: http://etheses.dur.ac.uk/10049.

Fevre, R. (1988) *Wales is Closed*. Nottingham: Spokesman Books.

Filandri, M. and Bertolini, S. (2016) 'Young People and Home Ownership in Europe', *International Journal of Housing Policy*, 16(2): 144–64.

Forrest, R., Murie, A. and Williams, P. (1990) *Home Ownership*. London: Unwin Hyman.

Forrest, R. and Wissink, B. (2017) 'Whose City Now? Urban Managerialism Reconsidered (again)', *Sociological Review*, 65(2): 155–67.

Franklin, M. (1985) *The Decline of Class Voting in Britain*. Oxford: Clarendon Press.

Frankenberg, R. (1957) *Village on the Border: A Social Study of Religion, Politics and Football in a North Wales Community*. London: Cogen and West.

Frankenberg, R. (1966) *Communities in Britain: Social Life in Town and Country*. Harmondsworth: Pelican.

Fuller, M. and Harwood, G. (2016) 'Abstract Urbanism' in R. Kitchin and S. Y. Perng (eds) *Code and the City*. London: Routledge, pp. 61–71.

Gallie, D., Marsh, C. and Vogler, C. (1994) *Social Change and the Experience of Unemployment*. Oxford: Oxford University Press.

Galpin, C. J. (1915) *The Social Anatomy of an Agricultural Community*, Research Bulletin no. 34. Madison, WI: University of Wisconsin Agricultural Experiment Station.

Galpin, C. J. (1937) 'The Story of My Drift Into Rural Sociology', *Rural Sociology*, 2(3): 299–310.

Gane, N. (2005) 'Max Weber as Social Theorist: Class, Status, Party', *European Journal of Social Theory*, 8(2): 211–26.

Glass, R (1964) 'Aspects of Change', in R. Glass, E. Hobsbawm, H. Pollins et al. (eds) *London: Aspects of Change*. London: MacGibbon & Kee, pp. xiii–xlii.

Goldthorpe, J. H., Lockwood, D., Bechhofer, F. and Platt, J. (1968a) *The Affluent Worker: Industrial Attitudes and Behaviour*. Cambridge: Cambridge University Press.

Goldthorpe, J. H., Lockwood, D., Bechhofer, F. and Platt, J. (1968b) *The Affluent Worker: Political Attitudes and Behaviour*. Cambridge: Cambridge University Press.

Goldthorpe, J. H., Lockwood, D., Bechhofer, F. and Platt, J. (1969) *The Affluent Worker in the Class Structure*. Cambridge: Cambridge University Press.

Goodhart, D. (2017) *The Road to Somewhere: The Populist Revolt and the Future of Politics*. London: C. Hurst & Co.

Goss, J. (1995a) 'Marketing the New Marketing: The Strategic Discourses of GIS', in J. Pickles (ed.) *Ground Truth: The Social Implications of GIS*. New York: Guilford Press, pp. 130–70.

Goss, J. (1995b) 'We Know Who You Are and We Know Where You Live: The Instrumental Rationality of Geodemographic Systems', *Economic Geography*, 71(2): 171–98.

Graham, S. (2005) 'Software-Sorted Geographies', *Progress in Human Geography*, 29(5): 562–80.

Graham, S. (2016) *Vertical: The City from Satellites to Bunkers*. London: Verso.

Groth, P. (1994) *Living Downtown: The History of Residential Hotels in the United States*. Los Angeles, CA: University of California Press.

Hardy, T. (1974) *Tess of the d'Urbervilles: A Pure Woman*. London: Pan Macmillan.

Harris, R., Sleight, P. and Webber, R. (2005) *Geodemographics, GIS and Neighbourhood Targeting*. Hoboken, NJ: John Wiley & Sons, Inc.

Hatherley, O. (2012) 'How Patrick Keiller is mapping the 21st-century landscape', The *Guardian*, 30 March. Available at: www.theguardian.com/artanddesign/2012/mar/30/patrick-keiller-robinson-tate-exhibition.

Hawley, A. (1950) *Human Ecology: A Theory of Community Structure*. New York: Ronald Press.

Healey, E. (1978) *Lady Unknown, The Life of Angela Burdett-Coutts*. London: Sidgwick and Jackson.

Heath, O. (2015) 'Policy Representation, Social Representation and Class Voting in Britain', *British Journal of Political Science*, 45(1): 173–93.

Hurd, R. (1903) *Principles of City Land Values*. New York: The Record and Guide.

Jackson, B. and Marsden, D. (1962) *Education and the Working Class*. Harmondsworth: Pelican.

Jennings, W. and Stoker, G. (2016) 'The Bifurcation of Politics: Two Englands', *The Political Quarterly*, 87(3): 372–82.

Kandt, J. (2015) *The Social and Spatial Context of Urban Health Inequalities: Towards an Interpretive Geodemographic Framework*, PhD Thesis, University College London. Available at: http://discovery.ucl.ac.uk/1472789.

Karn, V. (1977) *Retiring to the Seaside*. London: Routledge & Kegan Paul.

Kitchin, R. (2014) *The Data Revolution: Big Data, Open Data, Data Infrastructures and their Consequences*. London: Sage.

Kennett, P. and Forrest, R. (2006) 'The Neighbourhood in a European Context', *Urban Studies*, 43 (4): 713–18.

Kemp, P. A. (2015) 'Private Renting after the Global Financial Crisis', *Housing Studies*, 30(4): 601–20.

Knowles, C. (1996) *Family Boundaries: The Invention of Normality and Dangerousness*. Toronto: University of Toronto Press.

Knowles, C. and Burrows, R. (2017) 'Reimagining Chinese London', in R. Burdett and S. Hall (eds) *The SAGE Handbook of the 21st Century City*. London: Sage, pp. 87–101.

Lees, L., Slater, T. and Wyly, E. (eds) (2010) *The Gentrification Reader*. London: Routledge.

Le Grand, J. (1989) *The Strategy of Equality*. London: Allen & Unwin.

Leventhal, B. (2016) *Geodemographics for Marketers: Using Location Analysis for Research and Marketing*. London: Kogan Page.

Lupton, T. and Mitchell, D. (1954) 'The Liverpool Estate', in D. Mitchell, T. Lupton, M. Hodges and C. Smith (eds) *Neighbourhood and Community*. Liverpool: Liverpool University Press.

Lyon, D. (2003) *Surveillance and Social Sorting; Privacy, Risk and Digital Discrimination*. London: Routledge.

Malpas, J. and Jacobs, K. (2016) 'Place, Space, and Capital: The Landscapes of Patrick Keiller', *Environment and Planning D: Society and Space*, 34(6): 1132–49.

Marsden, T., Murdoch, J., Lowe, P. and Ward, N. (2012) *The Differentiated Countryside*. London: Routledge.

McKenzie, L. (2015) *Getting By: Estates, Class and Culture in Austerity Britain*. Bristol: Policy Press.

McKie, L. and Ryan, L. (eds) (2016) *An End to the Crisis of Empirical Sociology? Trends and Challenges in Social Research*. London: Routledge.

McPherson, M., Smith-Lovin, L. and Cook, J. (2001) 'Birds of a Feather: Homophily in Social Networks', *Annual Review of Sociology*, 27: 415–44.

Miller, M. (2006) *Hampstead Garden Suburb, Arts and Crafts Utopia?* Chichester: Phillimore.

Mitchell, D., Lupton, T., Hodges, M. and Smith, C. (eds) (1954) *Neighbourhood and Community*. Liverpool: Liverpool University Press.

Mol, A. (2002) *The Body Multiple: Ontology in Medical Practice*. Durham, NC: Duke University Press.

Monmonier, M. (2002) *Spying with Maps: Surveillance Technologies and the Future of Privacy*. Chicago, IL: University of Chicago Press.

Mowrer, E. R. (1938) 'The Isometric Map as a Technique of Social Research', *The American Journal of Sociology*, 44(1): 86–96.

Mullan, J. (2012) *What Matters in Jane Austen?* London: Bloomsbury.

Munck, R. (ed.) (2003) *Reinventing the City?: Liverpool in Comparative Perspective*. Liverpool: Liverpool University Press.

Nicholson-Lord, D. (1987) *The Greening of the Cities*. London: Routledge.

Openshaw, S., Cullingford, D. and Gillard, A. (1980) 'A Critique of the National Classifications of OPCS/PRAG', *The Town Planning Review*, 51(4): 421–39.

Osborne, T. and Rose, N. (1999) 'Do the Social Sciences Create Phenomena? The Example of Public Opinion Research', *The British Journal of Sociology*, 50(3): 367–96.

Osborne, T. and Rose, N. (2008) 'Populating Sociology: Carr-Saunders and the Problem of Population', *The Sociological Review*, 56(4): 552–78.

Osborne T., Rose N. and Savage M. (2008) 'Reinscribing British Sociology: Some Critical Reflections', *The Sociological Review*, 56(4): 519–34.

Pahl, R. (1965) *Urbs in Rure*. London: London School of Economics and Political Science, Geographical Papers no. 2.

Pahl, R. (1970) *Whose City? And Other Essays on Sociology and Planning*. London: Longmans.

Pahl, R. (1984) *Divisions of Labour*. London: Blackwell.

Panayi, P. (2010) *An Immigration History of Britain: Multicultural Racism Since 1800*. London: Routledge.

Park, R. E. (1929) 'Urbanization as Measured by Newspaper Circulation', *The American Journal of Sociology*, 35(1): 60–79.

Park, R. E. (1952) [1929] 'The City as a Social Laboratory', in R. E. Park, *Human Communities: The City and Human Ecology – The Collected Papers of Robert Ezra Park* (Vol. 2). Glencoe, IL: Free Press, pp. 73–87.

Park, R. E. and Burgess, E. (1921) *Introduction to the Science of Sociology*. Chicago, IL: Chicago University Press.

Park, R. E., Burgess, E. and McKenzie, R. (1925) *The City: Suggestions for Investigation of Human Behaviour in the Urban Environment*. Chicago, IL: Chicago University Press.

Parker, S. (2015) *Urban Theory and the Urban Experience: Encountering the City* (2nd edn). London: Routledge.

Parker, S., Uprichard, E. and Burrows, R. (2007) 'Class Places and Place Classes: Geodemographics and the Spatialization of Class', *Information, Communication and Society*, 11(6): 901–20.

Patrick, J. (1973) *A Glasgow Gang Observed*. London: Eyre Methuen.

Pfautz, H. (ed.) (1967) *On the City: Physical Pattern and Social Structure (Selected Writings of Charles Booth)*. Chicago, IL: University of Chicago Press.

Phillips, D. and Curry, M. (2002) 'Privacy and the Phenetic Urge: Geodemographics and the Changing Spatiality of Local Practice', in D. Lyon (ed.) *Surveillance as Social Sorting: Privacy, Risk and Digital Discrimination*. London: Routledge, pp. 137–52.

Pickles, J. (1994) 'Representations in an Electronic Age: Geography, GIS and Democracy', in J. Pickles (ed.) *Ground Truth. The Social Implications of Geographic Information Systems*. New York: The Guildford Press, pp. 1–30.

Platt, J. (1998) *A History of Sociological Research Methods in America, 1920–1960*. Cambridge: Cambridge University Press.

Plummer, K. (1997) *The Chicago School: Critical Assessments* (4 vols). London: Routledge.

Porter, J. R. and Howell, F. M. (2012) *Geographical Sociology* (Geojournal 105). New York: Springer.

Quinn, J. (1940) 'Topical Summary of Current Literature on Human Ecology', *American Journal of Sociology*, 44(2): 191–226.

Rees, P. (1972) 'Problems of Classifying Subareas within Cities', in B. Berry and K. Smith (eds) *City Classification Handbook: Methods and Applications*. New York: Wiley, pp. 265–330.

Reibel, M. (2011) 'Classification Approaches in Neighbourhood Research: Introduction and Review', *Urban Geography*, 32(3): 305–16.

Rex, J. and Moore, R. (1967) *Race, Community and Conflict: A Study of Sparkbrook*. Oxford: Oxford University Press.

Richardson, R. (1992) *Town and Countryside in the English Revolution*. Manchester: Manchester University Press.

Rienzo, C. and Vargas-Silva, C. (2017) *Migrants in the UK: An Overview* (6th Version). Oxford: The Migration Observatory/COMPAS.

Robbin, J. (1980) 'Geodemographics: The New Magic', *Campaigns and Elections*, 1(1): 25–34.

Rugg, J. and Rhodes, D. (2008) *The Private Rented Sector*. York: Centre for Housing Policy.

Ruppert, E., Law, J. and Savage, M. (2013) 'Reassembling Social Science Methods: The Challenge of Digital Devices', *Theory, Culture & Society*, 30(4): 22–46.

Saetnan, A, Lomell, H. and Hammer, S. (eds) (2011) *The Mutual Construction of Statistics and Society*. London, Routledge.

Sage, J., Smith, D. and Hubbard, P. (2012) 'The Diverse Geographies of Studentification', *Housing Studies*, 27(8): 1057–78.

Sage, J., Smith, D. and Hubbard, P. (2013) 'New-Build Studentification: A Panacea for Balanced Communities?', *Urban Studies*, 50(13): 2623–41.

Saunders, P. (1989) 'The Meaning of "Home" in Contemporary English Culture', *Housing Studies*, 4(3): 177–92.

Savage, M. (2005) 'Working-Class Identities in the 1960s: Revisiting the Affluent Worker Study', *Sociology*, 39(5): 929–46.

Savage, M. (2008) 'Elizabeth Bott and the Formation of Modern British Sociology', *The Sociological Review*, 56(4): 579–605.

Savage, M. (2010) *Identities and Social Change in Britain since 1940: The Politics of Method.* Oxford: Oxford University Press.

Savage, M. (2011) 'The Lost Urban Sociology of Pierre Bourdieu', in G. Bridge and S. Watson (eds) *The New Blackwell Companion to the City*. London: Blackwell-Wiley, pp. 511–20.

Savage, M. (2013) 'The Social Life of Methods: A Critical Agenda', *Theory, Culture & Society*, 30(4): 3–21.

Savage, M. (2016) 'The Fall and Rise of Class Analysis in British Sociology, 1950–2016', *Tempo Social*, 28(2): 57–72.

Savage, M. and Burrows, R. (2007) 'The Coming Crisis of Empirical Sociology', *Sociology*, 41(5): 885–99.

Savage, M. and Burrows, R. (2009) 'Some Further Reflections on the Coming Crisis of Empirical Sociology', *Sociology*, 43(4): 762–72.

Savage, M., Bagnall, G. and Longhurst, B. (2005) *Globalization and Belonging.* London: Sage.

Savage, M., Cunningham, N., Devine, F., Friedman, S., Laurison, D., McKenzie, L., Snee, H. and Wakeling, P. (2015) *Social Class in the 21st Century*. London: Penguin.

Savage, M., Barlow, J., Dickens, P. and Fielding, T. (1995) *Property, Bureaucracy and Culture: Middle-Class Formation in Contemporary Britain.* London: Routledge.

Selvin, H. and Bernert, C. (1985) 'Durkheim, Booth and Yule: The Non-Diffusion of an Intellectual Innovation', in M. Bulmer (ed.) *Essays on the History of British Sociological Research*. Cambridge: Cambridge University Press, pp. 70–82.

Schelling, T. (1971) 'Dynamic Models of Segregation', *Journal of Mathematical Sociology*, 1: 143–86.

Shevky, E. and Bell, W. (1955) *Social Area Analysis*. Stanford, CA: Stanford University Press.

Shevky, E. and Williams. M. (1949) *The Social Areas of Los Angeles*. Berkeley, CA: University of California Press.

Shiels, C., Baker, D., Barrow, S., Wright, G., McLennan, D. and Plunkett, E. (2013) 'How Accurately does Regeneration Target Local Need? Targeting Deprived Communities in the UK', *International Journal of Public Sector Management*, 26(3): 203–15.

Shucksmith, M. (2012) 'Class, Power and Inequality in Rural Areas: Beyond Social Exclusion?' *Sociologia Ruralis*, 52(4): 377–97.

Shucksmith, M. and Brown, D. (eds) (2016) *The Routledge International Handbook of Rural Studies*. London: Routledge.

Shucksmith, M. and Henerson, M. with Raybould, S., Coombes, M. and Wong, C. (1995) *A Classification of Rural Housing Markets in England*. London: HMSO.

Singleton, A. (2016) 'Cities and Context: The Codification of Small Areas Through Geodemographic Classification', in R. Kitchin and S. Y. Perng (eds) *Code and the City*. London: Routledge, pp. 215–35.

Singleton, A. and Spielman, S. (2014) 'The Past, Present, and Future of Geodemographic Research in the United States and United Kingdom', *The Professional Geographer*, 66(4): 558–67.

Simon, P. (2012) 'Collecting Ethnic Statistics in Europe: A Review', *Ethnic and Racial Studies*, 35(8): 1366–91.

Sleight, P. (2004) 'An Introductory Review of Geodemographic Information Systems', *Journal of Targeting, Measurement and Analysis for Marketing*, 12(4): 379–88.

Smith, D. (1988) *The Chicago School: A Liberal Critique of Capitalism*. Basingstoke: Macmillan.

Smith, H. (2017) *The Mobile Distinction: Economies of Intimacy in the Field of Location Based Marketing*. PhD, Faculty of Information, University of Toronto.

Smith, H., Hardey, M., Hardey, M. and Burrows, R. (2016) 'Social Cartography and Knowing Capitalism: Critical Reflections on the Geo-Spatial Web and Social Research', in N. Fielding, R. M. Lee and G. Blank (eds) *The Sage Handbook of Online Research Methods* (2nd edn). London: Sage, pp. 596–610.

Smith, T., Noble, M., Noble, S. et al. (2015) *The English Indices of Deprivation 2015: Research Report*. London: Department for Communities and Local Government.

Stacey, M. (1960) *Tradition and Change: A Study of Banbury*. Oxford: Oxford University Press.

Stacey, M., Batstone, E., Bell, C. and Murcott, A. (1975) *Power, Persistance and Change: A Second Study of Banbury*. London: Routledge & Kegan Paul.

Sturzaker, J. and Shucksmith, M. (2011) 'Planning for Housing in Rural England: Discursive Power and Spatial Exclusion', *Town Planning Review*, 82(2): 169–94.

Swami, V. (2016) *Attraction Explained: The Science of How We Form Relationships*. London: Routledge.

Thrasher, F. M. (1927) *The Gang: A Study of 1,313 Gangs in Chicago*. Chicago, IL: Chicago University Press.

Thrift, N. (2005) *Knowing Capitalism*. London: Sage.

Timmins, N. (2001) *The Five Giants: A Biography of the Welfare State*. London: Harper Collins.

Timms, D. (1971) *The Urban Mosaic: Towards a Theory of Residential Differentiation*. Cambridge: Cambridge University Press.

Tinniswood, A. (2016) *The Long Weekend: Life in a Country House between the Wars*. London: Jonathan Cape.

Tufail, W. (2015) 'Rotherham, Rochdale, and the Racialised Threat of the "Muslim Grooming Gang"', *International Journal for Crime, Justice and Social Democracy*, 4(3): 30–43.

Uprichard, E., Burrows, R. and Byrne, D. (2008) 'SPSS as an "Inscription Device": from Causality to Description?', *Sociological Review*, 56(4): 606–22.

Uprichard, E., Burrows, R. and Parker, S. (2009) 'Geodemographic Code and the Production of Space', *Environment and Planning A*, 41(12): 2823–35.

van Ham, M., Manley, D., Bailey, N., Simpson, L. and MacLennan, D. (2012) (eds) *Neighbourhood Effects Research: New Perspectives*. New York: Springer.

Voas, D. and Williamson, P. (2001) 'The Diversity of Diversity: A Critique of Geodemographic Classification', *Area*, 33(1): 63–76.

Warrington, M. (2005) 'Mirage in the Desert? Access to Educational Opportunities in an Area of Social Exclusion', *Antipode*, 37(4): 796–816.

Watt, P. (2009) 'Social Housing and Regeneration in London', in R. Imrie, L. Lees and M. Raco (eds) *Regenerating London: Governance, Sustainability and Community in a Global City*. London: Routledge, pp. 212–35.

Watkins, M. (2011) *Henrietta Barnett: Social Worker and Community Planner*. London: Hampstead Garden Suburb Archive Trust.

Webber, M. (1964) 'The Urban Place and the Non-Place Urban Realm', in M. Webber, J. Dyckman, D. Foley et al. (eds) *Explorations in Urban Structure*. Philadelphia, PA: University of Pennsylvania Press, pp. 79–153.

Webber, R. (1975) *Liverpool Social Area Study 1971 Data: Final Report.* London: Centre for Environmental Studies.

Webber, R. (1977) *An Introduction to the National Classification of Wards and Parishes*. London: Centre for Environmental Studies.

Webber, R. (1978a) *Parliamentary Constituencies: A Socio-economic Classification* (OPCS Occasional Paper 13). London: Office of Population Censuses and Surveys.

Webber, R. (1978b) 'Making the most of the Census for Strategic Analysis', *The Town Planning Review*, 49(3): 274–84.

Webber, R. (1979) *Census Enumeration Districts: A Socio-Economic Classification*. Occasional Paper 14. London: OPCS.

Webber, R. (1980) 'A Response to the Critique of the OPCS/PRAG National Classifications', *The Town Planning Review*, 51(4): 440–50.

Webber, R. (2004) *The Relative Power of Geodemographics Vis a Vis Person and Household Level Demographic Variables as Discriminators of Consumer Behaviour* (CASA Working Paper Series 84). London: Centre for Advanced Spatial Analysis.

Webber, R. (2006) 'How Parties used Segmentation in the 2005 British General Election Campaign', *Journal of Direct, Data and Digital Marketing Practice*, 7(3): 239–52.

Webber, R. (2007) 'The Metropolitan Habitus: Its Manifestations, Locations, and Consumption Profiles', *Environment and Planning A*, 39(1): 182–207.

Webber R. and Burrows R. (2016) 'Life in an *Alpha Territory*: Discontinuity and Conflict in an Elite London "village"', *Urban Studies*, 53(15): 3139–54.

Webber, R. and Butler, T. (2007) 'Classifying Pupils by Where they Live: How Well does This Predict Variations in Their GCSE Results?', *Urban Studies*, 44(7): 1229–53.

Webber, R., Butler, T. and Phillips, T. (2015) 'Adoption of Geodemographic and Ethno-Cultural Taxonomies for Analysing Big Data', *Big Data and Society*, 2(1): doi: 10.1177/2053951715583914.

Webber, R. and Craig, J. (1976) 'Which Local Authorities Are Alike?', *Population Trends*, 5: 13–19.

Webber, R. and Craig, J. (1978) *A Socio-Economic Classification of Local Authorities in Great Britain*. London: HMSO.

Webber, R. and Phillips, T. (2016) 'Minority Communities in Britain: Pathways to Success as Revealed by Big Data', in L. McKie and L. Ryan (eds) *An End to the Crisis of Empirical Sociology? Trends and Challenges in Social Research*. London: Routledge, pp. 29–48.

Weiss, M. (1988) *The Clustering of America*. New York: Harper & Row.

Weiss, M. (2000) *The Clustered World.* Boston, MA: Little, Brown and Co.

Wilkins, R., (2013) 'A Study of the Dominance of the Super-Wealthy in London's West End during the Nineteenth Century', in I. Hay (ed.) *Geographies of the Super-Rich.* Cheltenham: Edward Elgar, pp. 110–22.

Williams, R. (1977) *Marxism and Literature.* Oxford: Oxford University Press.

Willis, I. S. (2016) *The Application of Multivariate Cluster Analysis in the Assessment of Volcanic Social Vulnerability.* PhD Thesis, Birkbeck, University of London.

Winlow, S., Hall, S. and Treadwell, J. (2016) *The Rise of the Right: English Nationalism and the Transformation of Working-Class Politics.* Bristol: Policy Press.

Wyly, E. (2015) 'Gentrification on the Planetary Urban Frontier: The Evolution of Turner's Noösphere', *Urban Studies*, 52(14): 2515–50.

Young, M. and Willmott, P. (1957) *Family and Kinship in East London.* Harmondsworth: Pelican Books.

Zelinsky, W. (1970) 'Beyond the Exponentials; the Role of Geography in the Great Transition', *Economic Geography*, 46(3): 498–535.

# Appendix

## CURRENT SOURCES OF GEODEMOGRAPHIC DATA

Below is a list of websites providing details of geodemographc classifications for the UK that were available in mid-2017.

- Acorn – http://acorn.caci.co.uk
- Cameo – www.cameodynamic.com/why-cameo/cameo-for-consumer
- Censation – www.afd.co.uk/data-sets/censation
- Mosaic – www.experian.co.uk/marketing-services/products/mosaic-uk.html
- OAC – www.opengeodemographics.com
- P2 People and Places – www.p2peopleandplaces.co.uk
- Sonar – www.data360.co.uk/SonarOverview.aspx

OAC is open and free for anyone to use. However, it is constructed just using census data. All other classifications are commercial and a fee will normally be charged in order to use full versions of them. However, academic staff and students are able to access versions of both *Acorn* and *Mosaic* via the UK Data Archive – www.data-archive.ac.uk – in order to carry out non-commercial research of the sort demonstrated in Chapters 6–10 of the current volume. Details of the *Origins* classification used in Chapter 8 can be found here: http://originsinfo.eu.

# INDEX